THE SOCIAL FABRIC

American Life from the Civil War to the Present

Volume II

SIXTH EDITION

Editors

JOHN H. CARY *Cleveland State University*

JULIUS WEINBERG *Late, Cleveland State University*

THOMAS L. HARTSHORNE *Cleveland State University*

 HarperCollins*Publishers*

To Merle Curti

T.L.H.

Sponsoring Editor: Bruce Borland
Project Editor: Shuli Traub
Design and Cover Coordinator: Heather A. Ziegler
Cover Design: Wanda Lubelska Design
Cover Illustration: "The East River," 1901, by Maurice
    Prendergast, watercolor, 13¾ × 19¾ inches.
    Collection, The Museum of Modern Art,
    New York. Gift of Abby Aldrich Rockefeller.
Photo Research: Nina Page
Production: Willie Lane/Sunaina Sehwani
Compositor: BookMasters, Inc.
Printer/Binder: R. R. Donnelley & Sons Company
Cover Printer: New England Book Components, Inc.

THE SOCIAL FABRIC: American Life from the Civil War to the Present, Vol. II
Sixth Edition

Library of Congress Cataloging-in-Publication Data

The Social fabric / editors, John H. Cary, Julius Weinberg, Thomas L.
    Hartshorne. — 6th ed.
        p. cm.
        Contents: — v. 2. American life from the Civil War to the
present.
    ISBN 0–673–52044–7 (v. 2)
    1. United States—Social conditions. I. Cary, John H. (John
Henry), 1926– . II. Weinberg, Julius, 1922– . III. Hartshorne,
Thomas L.
HN57.S623 1990
306'.0973—dc20   90–5058
                                                        CIP

90 91 92 93 9 8 7 6 5 4 3 2 1

Contents

Preface   vii

I   POSTBELLUM AMERICA   2

1   After Slavery   5

How patterns of social segregation were established
— in prisons, in the use of public facilities, and in
transportation — during the era of Reconstruction.
From Joel Williamson, *After Slavery.*

2   The Death of the Plains Indians   23

How, by force and guile, the United States deprived
the Plains Indians of their land and freedom.
From Ralph K. Andrist, *The Long Death.*

3   The Farmers' Frontier   39

How settlers on the Great Plains adapted to the
harsh environmental and psychological conditions
of life there.
From Robert V. Hine, *Community on the American
Frontier.*

II   INDUSTRIAL AMERICA   52

4   The City in the Gilded Age   55

Solving the many problems that large-scale immigration, urbanization, and industrialization created
for the cities of the nation.
From Arthur M. Schlesinger, Sr., *The Rise of the City,
1878–1898.*

5   Labor in the Gilded Age   71

The working conditions faced by those who toiled in the southern textile mills.

From Jacquelyn Dowd Hall, James Leloudis, Robert Korstad, Mary Murphy, Lu Ann Jones, and Christopher B. Daly, *Like a Family*.

6   Labor Violence in Industrial America   87

A confrontation between immigrant coal miners and the coal operators in a Pennsylvania mining town, and its tragic consequences.

From Michael Novak, *The Guns of Lattimer*.

III   PARADOXES OF PROGRESSIVISM   102

7   The Immigrant Ghetto   105

A portrait of the Jewish quarter on New York's Lower East Side at the turn of the century.

From Moses Rischin, *The Promised City*.

8   The Settlement House   119

The educational, cultural, and social programs provided the "new" immigrants by the idealistic social workers of the Progressive era.

From Allen F. Davis, *Spearheads for Reform*.

9   Black Migration   135

Why and how millions of black Americans abandoned the rural South for the urban centers of the North in the first two decades of the twentieth century.

From Florette Henri, *Black Migration*.

10   The Red Scare   151

The arrest and deportation of suspected radicals in a climate of hatred and violence following World War I.

From Robert K. Murray, *The Red Scare*.

IV   THE TENSIONS OF PROSPERITY   164

11   The Klan in Indiana   167

The bizarre and frightening aspects of a Ku Klux Klan convention.
From Robert Coughlan, "Konklave in Kokomo."

12   Heyday of the Bootlegger   185

How bootlegging flourished in upstate New York during the Prohibition era.
From Allan Everest, *Rum Across the Border.*

13   Women and Housework in the 1920s   199

How modern mass-production technology changed the American home.
From Ruth Schwartz Cowan, *More Work for Mother.*

V   DEPRESSION AND WAR   216

14   The Nation Confronts the Great Depression   219

Poverty, fear, and bewilderment changed the outlook and way of life of Americans in the Depression of the 1930s.
From Caroline Bird, *The Invisible Scar.*

15   Work Relief in the Great Depression   233

The variety of programs fashioned by Franklin Delano Roosevelt's New Deal to find work for the millions of Americans unemployed in the 1930s.
From Edward Robb Ellis, *A Nation in Torment.*

16   The Home Front During World War II   253

Employment, business, housing, mental health, marriage, and morals at home during the war.
From Richard R. Lingeman, *Don't You Know There's a War On?*

VI   AFFLUENCE AND ITS DISCONTENTS   270

17   The Baby Boom   273

How postwar affluence enabled Americans to search for the good life in suburbia.
From Landon Y. Jones, *Great Expectations.*

18   The Struggle for Civil Rights   285

What happened during the 1964 voter registration drive known as Mississippi Freedom Summer.
From Doug McAdam, *Freedom Summer.*

19   The Counterculture   309

How and why the hippies rebelled against the American cultural mainstream.
From Jay Stevens, *Storming Heaven.*

20   Vietnam — and After   329

What American soldiers experienced in Vietnam and what they encountered when they returned home.
From Loren Baritz, *Backfire.*

21   Sexuality in Contemporary America   343

How ideas and behavior are changing in regard to sex, marriage, and the family.
From John D'Emilio and Estelle B. Freedman, *Intimate Matters.*

Preface

I know histhry isn't thrue Hinnessy, because it ain't like what I see ivry day in Halsted Sthreet. If any wan comes along with a histhry iv Greece or Rome that'll show me th' people fightin', gettin' dhrunk, makin' love, gettin' married, owin' the grocery man an' bein' without hard-coal, I'll believe they was a Greece or Rome, but not befure.

The sentiment of Mr. Dooley, Finley Peter Dunne's comic Irish philosopher, expresses the attitude of many people toward history. Young Americans, especially, question the relevance of a history that deals only with politics, diplomacy, governments, and famous leaders, and ignores the daily life of average men and women. Two recent trends, however, are doing much to remedy this neglect. One is increased popular interest in the forgotten mass of men and women who tilled our fields, built our cities, and fought our wars, but who achieved no particular fame and left very little record of their lives and thought. The second development is the renewed concern of historians with social history.

This kind of history has more meaning for us, and touches our lives more directly, than any other aspect of our past. In an age seeking "relevance" nothing is more relevant than American social history. Each of us has direct experience, or an intimate awareness, of being part of a family, of falling in love and marrying, of poverty and pain, of suffering in war, of earning a living, of social oppression and reform. By understanding the social life of an earlier age, we can gain an understanding of ourselves and of others.

This is an anthology of American social history for college history courses. It began with our belief that college students would find more meaning in the kind of history described by Mr. Dooley than in political, diplomatic, or constitutional history. This and the companion volume of *The Social Fabric*, which covers the period from the earliest settlement of America to Reconstruction, touch upon marrying and making love, fighting and getting drunk, owing the grocer, and going without heat.

Covering the time from the end of the Civil War to the present, this volume contains descriptions of the segregation of southern blacks during Reconstruction, labor's efforts to organize in the coal mines of Pennsylvania, the Great Depression of the 1930s, and the protest movements of the 1960s and 1970s.

No single book can treat every aspect of our history, but these volumes examine American life in much of its diversity. There are essays on women as well as men, on Indians and blacks as well as whites, and on the poor and the oppressed as well as the rich and powerful. The sectional, class, racial, and religious differences among our heterogeneous people have created serious strains that at times threatened to tear the nation apart. But with all their diversity, the American people have also shared many common attitudes and traditions that provided a common social fabric to bind them together.

We have selected the readings from some of the most interesting writing on the American past. We have prefaced each reading with an introductory note, explaining the relation of the subject to broader developments in American history of the period. Each selection is also accompanied by an illustration, which provides a visual commentary on the topic under consideration. The study guide that follows the selection will help you review the special aspects of the reading, and may suggest issues for class discussion. The bibliographical note will help you find further material, should you wish to read more on the topic.

THE SIXTH EDITION

The sixth edition of Volume II of *The Social Fabric* retains many of the readings from previous editions. Five new selections have been added. One deals with working conditions in southern textile mills in the late 1800s, another with the transformation of housework and the American home resulting from the impact of mass-production technology in the 1920s. A third gives an intimate look at the civil rights movement. The fourth, on the counterculture of the 1960s, has been included in response to several suggestions from readers that it is an important and interesting subject that deserves attention. The last deals with recent changes in attitudes and behavior concerning such matters as sex, marriage, and the family. The second and fifth of the new selections directly address questions dealing with women and their roles in American society, subjects that we, and a great many readers, feel received insufficient attention in previous editions.

We have been extremely gratified by the response of both teachers and students to this anthology. Many have given us advice about how it could be improved and we have often taken it. We are grateful for their help and hope that the revisions will make these volumes even more useful.

We are also grateful to Sydney R. Bland, James Madison University; Siv Wheeler, West Valley College; M. Paul Hossinger, Illinois State University; Richard Aquila, Ball State University; David Moore, Loyola University; and Raymond Champagne, University of Scranton, for their helpful reviews.

John H. Cary
Thomas L. Hartshorne

The Social Fabric

I POSTBELLUM AMERICA

The Civil War surpasses all other wars in our history for the tragedy and destructiveness it brought to the American people. Earlier wars had not touched most people's lives; they consisted largely of military encounters between relatively small numbers of soldiers or sailors. While later wars, the two world wars in particular, engaged the mass of the American people, they were fought away from our continent. Not so the Civil War. For four years, the plantations and the cities of the Confederacy served as a battlefield, and by the war's end the toll in lives exceeded the total number of Americans killed in World War I and World War II.

The various regions of the nation responded differently to the aftermath of the war. For Southerners, the principal tasks were threefold: to repair the material and the economic damage caused by the war, to adjust to the social and psychological trauma of their defeat, and, finally, to work out a mode of relating to the millions of slaves freed by the war. With few exceptions, white Southerners sought to establish a social system that would retain the privileges of white supremacy under a structure of law, federal and state, that declared the races to be equal. The white Southerner's search for ways to segregate the races is the topic of our first selection.

In contrast to the South, the North and the West came out of the war stronger in many ways than they had been at its beginning. The North's cities and farms were untouched, its currency and economy intact, and its political leadership and institutions unharmed. Northerners turned to building an enterprising way of life for themselves both in the city and on the farm. In the West, particularly on the Great Plains, a transformation of culture and economy took place. It was first necessary to deal with the original inhabitants, the American Indians. The second essay, dealing with the fate of Chief Joseph and the Nez Percé, shows how they were pushed to one side. With the way thus cleared, first miners and then cattlemen came West, to be followed closely by farmers, whose lives on the Plains in the late 1800s is the subject of the third selection.

Southern blacks in the post–Civil War South soon learned that emancipation did not bring social equality.

1

JOEL WILLIAMSON

After Slavery

Few dreams in the history of the United States have been so cruelly unrealized as the hope that with the end of the Civil War and the destruction of the institution of slavery, black Americans would be accorded some measure of equality and opportunity in American life. With the end of the war in 1865, reform-minded Republicans, known as Radical Republicans, sought to make this dream a reality. Through their control of Congress they initiated Reconstruction, a program designed to restructure the social and political relations between whites and blacks in the defeated South. In 1865 and 1866, Congress funded the Freedmen's Bureau to feed, clothe, and protect the ex-slaves; civil rights legislation was passed in 1866 and reinforced by the Civil Rights Act of 1875, intended to outlaw varied forms of segregation; and three amendments were added to the Constitution. The Thirteenth Amendment (1865) outlawed slavery, the Fourteenth Amendment (1868) extended federal citizenship to blacks and made illegal many parts of the black codes, and the Fifteenth Amendment (1870) protected the black man's right to vote.

Despite this and other legislation, and despite the ascension to power of Reconstruction governments in the southern states — state governments in which political power was shared by a combination of southern scalawags, northern carpetbaggers, and emancipated blacks — the Radical Republican effort to reconstruct the relations between the races in the South ended in failure. The first stage of that failure, what one historian has so aptly called "darkness at noon," came with the end of Reconstruction. Reconstruction was ended by the disputed election of Republican Rutherford B. Hayes over Democrat Samuel J. Tilden in 1876 and by the Compromise of 1877, in which the rights of black Americans were made secondary to the economic opportunities and social privileges of white Americans, both Democrats and Republicans. The second stage in the disfranchisement and segregation of American blacks came between the end of Reconstruction and the American entry into World War I in 1914. The caste system created in these decades paralleled, to a degree, the relations between the races in parts of southern Africa today.

The selection that follows tells us about the origins of the southern caste system. In his book *After Slavery: The Negro in South Carolina during Reconstruction, 1861–1877*, Joel Williamson finds that patterns of segregation came to South Carolina in the Reconstruction period. Williamson thus refutes a cardinal assumption made by C. Vann Woodward, the dean of southern historians. Woodward contends that until the 1890s, southern whites still held open options in their treatment of southern blacks and that "Jim Crow," the disfranchisement and the segregation of blacks, was a product of decisions made by southern whites *after* Reconstruction, closer to the turn of the century. Williamson's essay, taken from his study of the Reconstruction in South Carolina, demonstrates that in South Carolina this was not so.

The physical separation of the races was the most revolutionary change in relations between whites and Negroes in South Carolina during Reconstruction.

Separation had, of course, marked the Negro in slavery; yet the very nature of slavery necessitated a constant, physical intimacy between the races. In the peculiar institution, the white man had constantly and closely to oversee the labor of the Negro, preserve order in domestic arrangements within the slave quarters, and minister to the physical, medical, and moral needs of his laborers. In brief, slavery enforced its own special brand of interracial associations; in a sense, it married the interests of white to black at birth and the union followed both to the grave. Slavery watched the great mass of Negroes in South Carolina, but those Negroes who lived outside of the slave system were not exempt from the scrutiny of the whites. Even in Charleston, the free Negro community was never large enough to establish its economic and racial independence. In the mid-nineteenth century, as the bonds of slavery tightened,

From *After Slavery: The Negro in South Carolina during Reconstruction, 1861–1877*, by Joel Williamson. Copyright 1965 The University of North Carolina Press. Reprinted by permission of the publisher.

the whites were forced to bring free Negroes under ever more stringent controls and to subject their lives to the closest surveillance.

During the spring and summer of 1865, as the centripetal force of slavery melted rapidly away, each race clearly tended to disassociate itself from the other. The trend was evident in every phase of human endeavor: agriculture, business, occupations, schools and churches, in every aspect of social intercourse and politics. As early as July of 1865, a Bostonian in Charleston reported that "the worst sign here . . . is the growth of a bitter and hostile spirit between blacks and whites — a gap opening between the races which, it would seem may at some time result seriously." Well before the end of Reconstruction, separation had crystallized into a comprehensive pattern which, in its essence, remained unaltered until the middle of the twentieth century.

There is no clear, concise answer to the question of why separation occurred. Certainly, it was not simply a response of Negroes to the prejudiced fiat of dominant whites; nor was it a totally rationalized reaction on the part of either race. Actually, articulate whites and Negroes seldom attempted to explain their behavior. Yet, the philosophies and attitudes each race adopted toward the other lend a certain rationality to separation, and, if we are always mindful that this analysis presumes a unity which they never expressed, can be applied to promote an understanding of the phenomenon.

For the native white community, separation was a means of avoiding or minimizing problems which, they felt, would inevitably arise from the inherent inferiority of the Negro, problems which the North, in eradicating slavery and disallowing the Black Code, would not allow them to control by overt political means. In this limited sense, segregation was a substitute for slavery.

Thus, first, total separation was essential to racial purity, and racial purity was necessary to the preservation of a superior civilization which the whites had labored so arduously to construct, and suffered a long and bloody war to defend. After the war, that civilization was embattled, but not necessarily lost. Unguarded association with an inferior caste would obviously endanger white culture. In this view, children were peculiarly susceptible to damage. "Don't imagine that I allow my children to be with negroes out of my presence," wrote the mistress of a lowcountry plantation in 1868, "on one occasion only have they been so with my knowledge." Even the Negro wet nurse, that quintessence of maternalism upon which the slave period paternalist so often turned his case, emerged as the incubus of Southern infancy. "We gave our infants to the black wenches to suckle," lamented an elderly white, "and thus poisoned the blood of our children, and made them *cowards* . . . the Character of the people of the state was ruined by slavery and it will take 500 years, if not longer, by the infusion of new blood to eradicate the hereditary vices imbibed with the blood (milk is blood) of black wet nurses." . . .

Separation also facilitated the subordination of the inferior race by constantly reminding the Negro that he lived in a world in which the white man was dominant, and in which the non-white was steadfastly denied access to the higher caste. Further, the impression of Negro inferiority would be constantly re-enforced by relegating the baser element, whenever possible, to the use of inferior facilities. The sheer totality of the display alone might well serve to convince members of the lower caste that such, indeed, was in the natural order of things.

Many whites had envisioned the early elimination of the freedman from the southern scene, and many had eagerly anticipated this event. In time, however, it became evident to all that the Negro would be neither dissolved nor transported to Africa. In a sense, separation was a means of securing the quasi elimination of Negroes at home. It was, perhaps, a more satisfactory solution than their demise or emigration, since it might produce many of the benefits of their disappearance without losing an advantageous, indeed, a necessary supply of labor.

Finally, separation was a logical solution to the problem posed by the widespread conviction that the races were inherently incompatible outside of the master–slave relationship. If the white man could not exist in contentment in the proximity of Negroes, then partial satisfaction might be achieved by withdrawal from associations with members of the inferior caste. This spirit was evident among some of the wealthier whites who voluntarily dispensed entirely with the services of Negro domestics. Elderly William Heyward, in 1868 still second to none in the ranks of the rice aristocracy, stopped taking his meals at the Charleston Hotel because, as he said, he found "the negro waiters so defiant and so familiar in their attentions." "A part of the satisfaction is," he explained to a friend, "that I am perfectly independent of having negroes about me; if I cannot have them as they used to be, I have no desire to see them except in the field." Planters were often manifesting precisely the same sentiment when they deserted their land and turned to grain culture, or to the use of immigrant labor. Separation was also a way of avoiding interracial violence. B. O. Duncan and James L. Orr, both native white Republicans, argued against mixing in the public schools because they were convinced that minor irritations between children would generate major altercations between parents of different races. Conceived as a means of avoiding violence, separation, ironically, was subsequently enforced by the use of violence. . . .

Contrary to common belief, the separation of the races was not entirely the work of the whites. Suspicious, resentful, and sometimes hateful toward the whites, chafed by white attitudes of superiority, and irritated by individual contacts with supercilious whites, Negroes, too, sought relief in withdrawal from association with the other race. In many instances, the disassociation was complete — that is, many Negroes left the state. During the war, Corporal Simon Crum of the First South Carolina declared his intention of leaving South Carolina after the capitulation because, as he phrased it, "dese yer Secesh [secessionists] will neber be cibilized in my time." For those who could not or would not leave, alternative forms of withdrawal were possible. A major facet in the new pattern of agriculture was the removal of Negro labor from the immediate supervision of white men. As the Negro agriculturalist moved his labor away from the eye of the white man, so also did he move his family and his home. Plantation villages became increasingly rare as Negro landowners and renters either built new houses on their plots or, in a rather graphic symbolic display, laboriously dragged their cabins away from the "Negro street." Negroes in the trades and in domestic service followed similar trends. Furthermore, Negroes chose to withdraw from white-dominated churches, though they were often urged to stay, and they attended racially separated schools in spite of the legal fact that all schools were open to all races. Negroes also tended to withdraw from political association with members of the white community.

Finally, on those few occasions when Negroes entered into polite social situations with whites, northern as well as southern, they were often ill at ease. For instance, while driving along a road near Columbia, a planter and his wife met William, "a fine looking light mulatto" who had been their stableboy as a slave. William was driving a buggy and seated beside him was a young white woman, elegantly attired. The woman was a "Yankee school marm," probably one of the new teachers in Columbia's Negro school. As he passed his late master and mistress, the Negro averted his gaze and did not speak. The following day, he approached the planter and apologized for having been escort to a "white woman." He had met the teacher at a celebration, he explained, and she had insisted on his taking her to see the countryside.

During Reconstruction, the Negro's withdrawal was never a categorical rejection of the white man and his society. In the early days of freedom, it was primarily a reaction against slavery, an attempt to escape the unpleasant associations of his previous condition and the derogatory implications of human bondage. However, as the memory of slavery faded, a more persistent reason for withdrawal emerged. Essentially, it was the Negro's answer to discrimination. Almost invariably, attempts by individual Negroes to establish satisfactory relations across the race line were unsuccessful, and, all too often, the pain of the experience was greater than the reward for having stood for principle. During Reconstruction and afterward, only a few were willing to undergo such pain without the certainty of success. It was much easier, after all, simply to withdraw.

Withdrawal as a solution to the race problem was by no means satisfactory to the Negro leadership. Implicit in the behavior of Negro leaders during Reconstruction was a yearning for complete and unreserved acceptance for members of their race by the white community. However, overtly, and rather politically, they carefully distinguished between "social equality" and what might be appropriately termed "public equality." For themselves, they claimed only the latter. "Our race do not demand social equality," declared W. J. Whipper, a member from Beaufort, on the floor of the house of representatives in Columbia. . . .

What the Negro leadership did insist upon was public equality, that is, absolute civil and political parity with whites and full and free access to most public facilities. These latter included restaurants, bars, saloons, railway and street cars, shipboard accommodations, the theater, and other such places of public amusement. Once they gained political power, Negro leaders hastened to embody this attitude in legislation. Within a week after the first sitting of the Constitutional Convention of 1868, a Negro delegate introduced a resolution which was eventually included in the state's bill of rights: "Distinction on account of race or color, in any case whatever, shall be prohibited, and all classes of citizens shall enjoy equally all common, public, legal and political privileges." Similarly, one of the first bills passed by the Republican legislature prohibited licensed businesses from discriminating "between persons, on account of race, color, or previous condition, who shall make lawful application for the benefit of such business, calling or pursuit." Convicted violators were liable to a fine of not less than $1,000 or imprisonment for not less than a year. During the debate on the measure in the house, not a single Negro member spoke against the bill, and only five of the twenty-four votes registered against it were cast by Negroes, while fifty-three of the sixty-one votes which secured its passage were those of Negro legislators.

Negro Congressmen were no less ardent in championing the same cause in Washington, particularly in 1874, when a federal civil rights bill was up for consideration. " . . . Is it pretended anywhere," asked Congressman R. B. Elliott, who had only recently been denied service in the restaurant of a railway station in North Carolina on his journey to the capital, "that the evils of which we complain, our exclusion from the public inn, from the saloon and the table of the steamboat, from the sleeping-coach on the railway, from the right of sepulture in the public burial-ground, are an exercise of the police power of the State? . . . Are the colored people to be assimilated to an unwholesome trade or to combustible materials, to be interdicted, to be shut up within prescribed limits?" Several days later, in the same place, Congressman R. H. Cain declared, "We do not want any discrimination to be made. I do not ask any legislation for the colored people of this country that is not applied to the white people of this country. All that we seek is equal laws, equal legislation, and equal rights throughout the length and breadth of this land."

It was upon this emotional, uneven ground that an essentially new color line was drawn. It was established in a kind of racial warfare, of assaults and withdrawals, of attacks and counterattacks. Nevertheless, well before the end of Reconstruction, both forces had been fully engaged and the line was unmistakably formed.

Even before the Radicals came into power in South Carolina in 1868, native whites had already defined a color line in government-supported institutions, on common carriers, in places of public accommodation and amusement, and, of course, in private social organizations. The degree of separation in each of these areas varied. In many instances, obviously, some compromise between expense and the desire for complete separation had to be made. Usually, the compromise involved the division of available facilities in some manner. If this was thought to be inconvenient, Negroes were totally excluded.

Typical was the treatment of Negro and white prisoners in the state penitentiary under the James L. Orr regime [1865–1868; South Carolina]. Criminals of both races were confined in the same institution but were quartered in separate cells. Ironically, the racial concepts of white prison officials sometimes redounded to the benefit of Negro inmates. Minor violations of prison rules were punished every Sunday by the offenders being tied closely together, blindfolded, and forced to work their way over a series of obstacles in the prison yard. The chief guard explained that the white offenders were placed in the most difficult middle positions of the "blind gang" because "they have more intelligence than the colored ones and are better able to understand the rules of the institution."

It is paradoxical that the Negro leadership, once in office, pressed vigorously for an end to separation in privately-owned facilities open to the public but they allowed a very distinct separation to prevail in every major governmental facility. The most obvious instance was the schools, but the distinction also stretched into the furthermost reaches of gubernatorial activity. For example, a visitor to the state insane asylum in Columbia in 1874 found that "The Negro female inmates occupy a separate part of the same building" in which the white women were housed.

On the other side, within a month after they had gained the vote, Negroes in South Carolina opened a frontal attack against racial discrimination on common carriers. Typical was their assault on the Charleston Street Car Company. At the time of its inauguration, the facilities of the company consisted of double tracks running the length of the peninsula with a spur branching off near the mid-point. Horse-drawn cars, each manned by a driver and a conductor, ran along the tracks at regular intervals. The cars contained seats in a compartment, and front and rear platforms. Before the cars began to run in December, 1866, the question of the accommodation of Negro passengers was thoroughly canvassed. "Proper arrangements will in due time be made to allow persons of color to avail themselves of the benefits of the railway," the management assured the Negro community, but it had not then decided between providing "special cars" for the Negroes as was done in New Orleans, "or assigning to them a portion of the ordinary cars as is more usual in other cities." Negro leaders rejected both alternatives. As a Northerner wrote from Charleston in January, 1867, "Every scheme that could be devised that did not contemplate the promiscuous use of the cars by whites and negroes alike, was scouted by the Negro paper here; and the result is that negroes are now debarred the use of the cars altogether, unless they choose to ride upon the platform." . . .

After the Negro gained political power, the battle against discrimination became more intense and assumed a wider front. The so-called anti-discrimination bill, passed in the summer of 1868, on paper was a most formidable weapon. In essence, it imposed severe penalties upon the owners of public accommodations who were convicted of discrimination. Burden of proof of innocence lay on the accused, and state solicitors (public prosecutors) who failed to prosecute suspected violators were themselves threatened with heavy punishments.

The effect of the new legislation on common carriers was immediate. A Northern teacher returning to Beaufort in the fall of 1868, after a few months' absence in the North, observed a portion of the results:

> We took a small steamer from Charleston for Beaufort. Here we found a decided change since we went North. Then no colored person was allowed on the upper deck, now there were no restrictions — there could be none, for a law had been passed in favor of the negroes. They were everywhere, choosing the best staterooms and best seats at the table. Two prominent colored members of the State Legislature were on board with their families. There were also several well-known Southerners, still uncompromising rebels. It was a curious scene and full of significance. An interesting study to watch the exultant faces of the negroes, and the scowling faces of the rebels. . . .

The same legislation applied to railway facilities; and, apparently, it was applied without a great amount of dissent. Adjustment was made easier, perhaps, by the acquisition of some of the railroad companies by Radical politicians within the state, or by Northern capitalists, and by the close understanding which usually prevailed between Republican officeholders and those Conservatives who managed to retain control of their railroads. While formal discrimination was not practiced by railway operators, unofficial racial separation did occur on a large scale. On all of the major lines first- and second-class cars were available. Most Negroes apparently deliberately chose to ride in the more economical second-class accommodations, and virtually all of the whites — particularly white women — took passage on the first-class cars. The separation thus achieved was so nearly complete that the first-class car was often referred to as the "ladies' car." It is highly relevant that the first Jim Crow legislation affecting railroads in South Carolina provided for the separation of the races only in the first-class cars, because, of course, this was the only place on the railroads where there was any possibility of a significant degree of mixing. . . .

In the winter of 1869–1870 and through the summer which followed, a concerted attempt was made by the Negro leadership to win the full acceptance of Negroes into all places of public amusement, eating, drinking, and sleeping. Special provisions for the accommodation of Negroes at public entertainments had been made in ante-bellum times, but physical separation of the races was invariably the rule. In December, 1868, Charles Minort, a mulatto restaurateur and lesser political figure, nearly provoked a riot in a Columbia theater by presuming to seat his wife and himself in the front row, a section traditionally reserved for tardy white ladies. Presumably, he should have chosen seats among the other Negroes present who "had taken their seats, as has always been the custom, in the rear." Minort yielded to the clamor of the whites in the audience, but, a year later, the Negroes of Charleston instituted judicial proceedings against the manager of the Academy of Music for refusing to mix the races in the boxes of the theater. The management barely succeeded in winning a postponement but was able to complete the season before the case came to trial.

In the spring of 1870, Negro leaders in Charleston launched an attack against discrimination in restaurants, bars, and saloons. On March 25, for instance, Louis Kenake, accused of violating the antidiscrimination act, was brought before Magistrate T. J. Mackey and put on a bond of one thousand dollars while awaiting trial. Other white restaurant keepers of Charleston united to oppose and test the validity of the act, but, in the week which followed, at least six additional charges were lodged against operators of such businesses. The assault was not confined to Charleston and demonstrations by Radical politicians were frequent during the campaign of 1870. In April, a Laurens woman wrote to her son in Missouri that "On Monday the yankees & some negroes went to Hayne Williams' and asked for drink, which 'Ward' refused them, that is, to drink at the gentlemans bar. They quietly marched him off to jail, & locked the doors, putting the keys in their pockets. The family are all at Spartanburg, we look for H. Williams to night, and I am afraid of a fuss, for he is a great bully." In the same month, during a Radical meeting in Lancaster, a Negro was refused service in a local bar with the comment that no "nigger" could buy a drink there. Lucius Wimbush, a Negro senator, hearing of the incident, went to the bar, ordered a drink, and was refused. He immediately had the barkeeper arrested and placed under bail. . . .

Negroes were also ambitious to open sleeping accommodations to their race. In the summer of 1868, as the first Negro legislators gathered in Columbia, native whites had been extremely apprehensive that they would attempt to occupy rooms in the city's hotels. Even *The Nation,* which had applauded the opening of common carriers to both races, declared that hotels were another and "delicate" matter, where separation was everywhere observed. The white community was vastly relieved to find that no such invasion was attempted, one upcountry newspaper having sent a special correspondent to Columbia to ascertain the fact. Nevertheless, when Negro legislators debated the antidiscrimination bill early in the session, they made it very clear that hotels were included. William E. Johnson, the African Methodist Minister then representing Sumter County in the statehouse, noting that the management of Nickerson's Hotel was concerned lest Negroes apply for rooms, declared that if he found private accommodations filled he would want to know that this resort was open to him. George Lee, a Negro member from Berkeley, observed that a group of junketing legislators had recently failed to find lodging in Greenville and that this law was desired to prevent that sort of occurrence. "Equal and exact justice to all," he demanded, " . . . it is what we must have." Negroes were subsequently allowed to attend meetings in Columbia hotels, but it is apparent that none were ever given lodging.

Negroes also decried the fact that places of permanent rest occupied by whites, as well as those of a more temporary variety, were denied to their race. For instance, S. G. W. Dill, the native white Radical who was assassinated in Kershaw in the summer of 1868, and Nestor Peavy, his Negro guard who was killed in the same assault, were buried in racially separated cemeteries.

Thus, from 1868 until 1889, when the antidiscrimination law was repealed, Negroes in South Carolina could legally use all public facilities which were open to whites. However, in actual practice, they seldom chose to do so. "The naturally docile negro makes no effort at unnecessary self-assertion," a Northern visitor in Charleston explained in 1870, "unless under the immediate instigation of some dangerous *friends* belonging to the other race, who undertake to manage his destiny." This particular reporter was certainly prejudiced against the race; but four years later another Northern observer congratulated the Negroes of South Carolina on the "moderation and good sense" which they exhibited in their "intercourse with the whites." He concluded, "They seldom intrude themselves into places frequented by the whites, and considering that in South Carolina they have a voting majority of some thirty thousand and control the entire State Government, it is somewhat remarkable that they conduct themselves with so much propriety." Indeed, after 1870, even the Negro leadership hardly seemed inclined to press further their political and legal advantage to end separation. Of the numerous charges lodged under the antidiscrimination law, not a single conviction was ever recorded.

Even when Negroes pressed themselves in upon the prejudice of whites, the latter adjusted by total or partial withdrawal, so that a high degree of separation was always and everywhere maintained.

Some whites responded to the pressure by total withdrawal, that is, by leaving the state entirely. Of course, many of those who left South Carolina did so primarily for economic reasons, but many also departed from purely racial motives. A Winnsboro lawyer and pre-war fire-eater revealed the thinking of many emigrants when he asked William Porcher Miles, in April, 1867, how he could live in a land where "Every 'mulatto' is your Equal & every 'Nigger' is your Superior." Pronouncing the Negro majority "revolting," he advised Miles to go to England. " . . . I have no doubt you could succeed & at any rate w[oul]d not have as many Negro Clients & negro witnesses to offend y[ou]r nostrils as in these USA. I can't conceive of any ones remaining here who can possibly get away — Suppose, it were certain, wh[ich] it is not, that no U S Congress will ever pass a Law requiring that your Daughter & mine shall either marry Negroes or die unmarried. Still the Negro is already superior to them politically & to their Fathers also, & must ever be so henceforth." . . .

After Negroes were firmly entrenched in official positions in government, native whites evinced a distinct tendency to refrain from associations which recognized the authority of Negro officers over white citizens. For instance, in the heavily Negro county of Abbeville, in 1870, a distressed guardian asked one of the magistrates, who happened to be a Democrat, to dispatch a constable to return an orphan girl stolen away from his house. "When you send for Laura," he begged, "please send a white man, as she is a white girl under my charge, and I would not like to subject her to the mortification of being brought back by a colored man. Besides that I would be censured by the community as they would know nothing of the circumstances of the case." . . .

Withdrawal was also the means by which native whites combatted attempts by Republican officials to end separation in institutions supported by the government. The withdrawal of native whites from the University and the State School for the Deaf and Blind at the prospect of Negro admissions are illustrations of white determination either to maintain separation or to dispense with the services afforded by related state institutions. If the Radicals had attempted to end separation in the common schools, it is virtually certain that the whites would have removed their children from these schools too. As one post-Redemption [post-Reconstruction] proponent of universal education argued, separation was essential to academic progress. Only by this means, he explained to Governor [Wade] Hampton, could it be achieved "without any danger of social equality — *and this is the great bug bear.*" Doubtless, it was the threat of withdrawal by the whites which dissuaded the Radical leadership from further attempts to end separation in institutions over which they had, by political means, absolute control.

Whites also refused to engage in normal civic activities in which the color line was not distinctly drawn. Thus, native whites chose not to join militia companies in which Negroes participated and were reported to be extremely apprehensive of being forced to undergo the "humiliation" of joining a mixed company. Too, whites were reluctant to sit with Negroes in the jury box. An elderly Spartanburg farmer verbalized his feelings on this point in the summer of 1869: "When I go to court & see negroes on the jury & on the stand for witnesses it makes me glad that I am so near the end of my race to sit on a jury with them I dont intend to do it we have a law that exempt a man at 65 & I take the advantage of it." This kind of withdrawal often reached odd extremes. In the spring of 1870, at the peak of the Negro leadership's drive for admission to privately owned public accommodations, the white Democrats of the Charleston Fire Department refused to decorate their engines and join in the annual parade because Negro fire companies were being allowed to march in the procession. . . .

Native whites also tended to withdraw from public places where the color line could not be firmly fixed and the Negro could easily assert his equality. "The whites have, to a great extent — greater than ever before — yielded the streets to the negroes," wrote a Columbian on Christmas Day, 1868. Similarly, in Charleston, in the late spring of 1866, a young aristocrat noted that the battery with its music and strollers had been yielded to the ladies and gentlemen of non-noble lineage on Saturdays, and by all whites to the Negroes on Sundays. On Saturdays, he declared, "the battery is quite full of gentlemen and ladies but it is not much patronized by the elite. . . . On Sunday afternoon the ethiops spread themselves on the Battery."

The same reaction was manifested by the whites wherever the Negro leadership succeeded by legal means in ending separation. For instance, when Negroes won admission to the street cars of Charleston, the whites simply withdrew. "On Sunday I counted five Cars successively near the Battery crowded [with] negroes, with but one white man, the Conductor," wrote a native white in May, 1867. "The ladies are practically excluded." When the Academy of Music was threatened with a discrimination suit in 1870, the white community replied with a counterthreat to withdraw its patronage and thus close the theater. Adjustment which fell short of complete separation remained unsatisfactory to whites. "Even the Theatre is an uncertain pleasure," complained a Charleston lady in 1873, "no mat-

ter how attractive the program, for you know that you may have a negro
next to you." Probably many of her contemporaries found the exposure
too damaging and stayed home.

The social lives of native whites were, of course, absolutely closed to
Negroes. Access to the homes of the whites was gained by Negroes only
when they clearly acquiesced in the superior-inferior relationship dictated by the owners, and even then entrance was often denied. "I told
him I would never allow negroes to go in it while I owned it," wrote a
Laurenville woman, incensed that a man who had bought her former
home had rented it to Negroes. In spite of the fact that some Negro domestics lived in quarters behind the houses of their employers, whites
were already rejecting Negroes as neighbors. A real estate agent in Aiken
in 1871 responded to this sentiment when he refused offers from Negroes for city lots at triple prices because, as he explained to the owner,
"purchasers among the whites will not settle among the Negroes, and I
am afraid to sell to only a few of the latter." Negroes were also not permitted to join any of the numerous social organizations in which native
whites participated. The Patrons of Husbandry (the Grange), waxing
strong in the state in the early 1870s, was not only exclusively white in
membership, but was accused of widening the racial gap by its attitudes
and actions toward Negroes. Of course, such separation had been practiced before, but the exclusion of the Negro in freedom from the social
organizations of the whites was not so much tradition as it was deliberate
decision. . . .

Separation is, of course, a relative term. It was obviously not possible
for Negroes and whites to withdraw entirely from association with each
other. If intimate contact led to irritation and violence, it also led to
warm personal friendships — often with the superior–inferior, paternal
bias, but no less real for all of that. Cordiality could and did breach the
barrier of race. Yet the fact remained that it was difficult to establish a
human bond across the color chasm and, once established, the tie had to
be assiduously maintained against the constant erosion induced by a
thousand and one external forces of social pressure.

That there was sometimes tenderness between individuals of different
races is abundantly evident. On the Elmore plantation near Columbia, in
the fall of 1865, the young white master was nightly importuned by the
Negro children to get out his fiddle and play. Frequently he did so, the
dozen or so Negro boys and girls dancing around the fire, begging for
more after the fiddler had exhausted himself in a two-hour concert. The
concern of many late masters for their ex-slaves was matched by the interest of individual Negroes in the welfare of their recent owners. A
freedman seeking relief for a white family from a Bureau officer explained his motivation: "I used to belong to one branch of that family,

and so I takes an interest in 'em." Occasionally, ex-slaveowners retained the friendship and assistance of their erstwhile bondsmen when all others had deserted them. . . .

Sometimes, intimacy became miscegenation. The census reports are uncertain witnesses and contemporaries are typically mute on the point; but scattered references suggest that racial interbreeding was markedly less common after emancipation than before. "Miscegenation between white men and negro women diminished under the new order of things," a Bureau officer later wrote. "Emancipation broke up the close family contact in which slavery held the two races, and, moreover young gentlemen did not want mulatto children sworn to them at a cost of three hundred dollars apiece. In short, the new relations of the two stocks tended to separation rather than to fusion." A Northern traveler visiting the state in 1870 concurred: "From all I could see and learn, there are far fewer half-breed children born now than before the Rebellion. There seems, indeed, a chance that the production of original half-breeds may be almost done away with. . . . "

Legal, moral, and social pressures exercised by the white community upon its members, as well as the physical separation of the races suggest that these were valid observations. The Black Code pointedly declared that "Marriage between a white person and a person of color shall be illegal and void," and when the code was revised in 1866 this portion emphatically remained in force. Children born of Negro mothers and white fathers, so recently especially prized for their pecuniary value, became simply illegitimate issue and a liability to the community. In addition, the laws of bastardy came to be applied against the fathers of mulatto children. Perhaps most important was the fact that, in the minds of the native whites, children of mixed blood personified the adulteration of the superior race and embodied in living form the failure of Southern civilization. Many whites, turned to soul-searching by their defeat, fixed upon miscegenation as their great sin. "It does seem strange that so lovely a climate, and country, with a people in every way superior to the Yankees, should be overrun and destroyed by them," wrote a rice aristocrat in 1868. "But I believe that God has ordered it all, and I am firmly of opinion with Ariel that it is the judgment of the Almighty because the human and brute blood have mingled to the degree it has in the slave states. Was it not so in the French and British Islands and see what has become of them."

Just as complete separation of the races was physically impossible, there was little possibility that miscegenation might entirely cease. One does not have to travel far into contemporary sources to discover instances in which white men had children by Negro women. In 1867, a lowcountry planter, accused of fathering the mulatto child of his Negro house servant, wrote plaintively to his mother: "This child was begotten during my absence in Charlotte & Charleston, from the middle of December until nearly the middle of January, & the Father of it was seen night after night in Emma's house, this I heard on my return, but as it was no concern of mine I did not give it a thought. She was *free*, the Mother of 5 Children & could have a dozen lovers if she liked. I had no control over her virtue." In 1874, a planter on the Cooper River in St. John's noted the existence of circumstances on his plantation which might have led to similar results. "Found a white man staying with one of the colored people on the place," ran the laconic note in his journal. "He being engaged in rebuilding Mayrents Bridge." Some of these liaisons were of prolonged duration. In 1870, Maria Middleton, a Negro woman, brought suit against a Pineville physician for failure to support her three children which he had allegedly fathered. Strangely, the defendant's lawyer did not deny the paternity, but sought dismissal on the plea that the plaintiff had no legal grounds for suit.

Once in power, the Radicals hastened to repeal the prohibition against interracial marriage. Thereafter, informal arrangements were sometimes legalized. In the spring of 1869, a reporter stated that three such marriages had occurred within the state — a Massachusetts man had married a Beaufort mulatto woman, and two white women had married Negro men. In 1872, the legislature explicitly recognized interracial unions by declaring that the "children of white fathers and negro mothers may inherit from the father if he did not marry another woman but continued to live with their mother."

There were a surprisingly large number of cases in which white women gave birth to children by Negro fathers. During his stay in Greenville, Bureau officer John De Forest heard of two such births and noted other instances in which white women were supported by Negro men. Such situations, he believed, were largely the result of the loss of husbands and fathers in the war and the destitution of the country generally. In 1866, in neighboring Pickens District, a case came into the courts in which Sally Calhoun, "a white woman of low birth," and a Negro man were brought to trial for the murder of their child. Ironically, the Negro was freed, though obviously implicated, and the woman was convicted and imprisoned. Apparently, some of these liaisons were far from casual as a Spartanburg farmer rather painfully suggested to his brother in Alabama: "My dear Brother as you have made several Enquiries of me and desiring me to answer them I will attempt and endeavor to do So to the best information that I have on the Various Subjects alluded to by you the first Interrogatory is Relative to John H. Lipscomb's daughter haveing Negro Children, I am forced to answer in the affirmative no doubt but she has had two; and no hopes of her Stopping. . . . "

By the end of Reconstruction, Negroes had won the legal right to enjoy, along with whites, accommodations in all public places. In reality, however, they seldom did so. On the opposite side of the racial frontier, the pattern of separation was fixed in the minds of the whites almost simultaneously with the emancipation of the Negro. By 1868, the physical color line had, for the most part, already crystallized. During the Republican regime, it was breached only in minor ways. Once the whites regained political power, there was little need to establish legally a separation which already existed in fact. Moreover, to have done so would have been contrary to federal civil rights legislation and would have given needless offense to influential elements in the North. Finally, retention of the act had a certain propaganda value for use against liberals in the North and against Republican politicians at home. Again and again, the dead letter of the law was held up as exhibit "A" in South Carolina's case that she was being fair to the Negro in the Hampton tradition [a reference to the relatively mild and paternalistic forms of racism practiced by upper-class whites, who, for many years, were led by Governor, and later senator, Wade Hampton]. After the federal statute was vitiated in the courts, after racial liberalism had become all but extinct in the North and as the Negro was totally disfranchised in South Carolina, the white community was ready and able to close the few gaps which did exist in the color line, and to codify a social order which custom had already decreed.

Ultimately, the physical separation of the races is the least important portion of the story. The real separation was not that duo-chromatic order that prevailed on streetcars and trains, or in restaurants, saloons, and cemeteries. The real color line lived in the minds of individuals of each race, and it had achieved full growth even before freedom for the Negro was born. Physical separation merely symbolized and reinforced mental separation. It is true that vigorous assaults by one side or the other forced the enemy to yield his forward trenches and to alter slightly the precise line of the color front. It is also true that material changes in post-Reconstruction Southern society pushed the trenches into areas which had not existed before. This often gave the illusion of basic change, of a breakthrough by the dominant whites in the war of races, whereas, actually, it merely represented the extension of the old attitudinal conflict onto new ground, only to bring with it the stalemate that marked the struggle elsewhere. Viewed in relation to the total geography of race relations, the frontier hardly changed; and the rigidity of the physical situation, set as it was like a mosaic in black and white, itself suggested the intransigence of spirit which lay behind it. Well before the end of Reconstruction, this mental pattern was fixed; the heartland of racial exclusiveness remained inviolate; and South Carolina had become, in reality, two communities — one white and the other Negro.

STUDY GUIDE

1. What motives, according to the author, led Southern whites to seek segregation from their ex-slaves? Does Williamson consider these motives to be entirely rational?

2. What were the basic demands of the black leadership?

3. List the various institutions of the South in which segregation took place, and explain how.

4. Williamson draws a distinction between separation by segregation and separation by withdrawal. When did Southern whites tend to practice one and when the other?

5. Intimacy between the races does not appear to have ceased after emancipation. What evidence does the author have for this, and how does he account for it?

6. Would you, on the basis of this selection, agree that segregation began in the immediate postwar years? If so, why; if not, why not?

BIBLIOGRAPHY

The Reconstruction experience is dealt with in a number of volumes. James G. Randall and David Donald, *The Civil War and Reconstruction* (1960) is basic. More specialized are the following: Kenneth M. Stampp, *The Era of Reconstruction* (1965); John Hope Franklin, *Reconstruction: After the Civil War* (1961); and Rembert W. Patrick, *The Reconstruction of the Nation* (1967). Studies of race relations in individual states will be found in Joel Williamson, *After Slavery: The Negro in South Carolina during Reconstruction, 1861–1877* (1965), from which the above selection was taken; Vernon C. Wharton, *The Negro in Mississippi* (1965); Herman Belz, *Emancipation and Equal Rights* (1978); and Howard Rabinowitz, *Race Relations in the Urban South* (1978). White resistance to black freedom and equality is dealt with in Allen W. Trelease, *White Terror: The Ku Klux Klan Conspiracy and Southern Reconstruction* (1971) and in Michael Perman, *Reunion without Compromise: The South and Reconstruction, 1865–1868* (1973). The institutionalization of white racism before the turn of the century is traced in the following: C. Vann Woodward, *The Strange Career of Jim Crow* (1974); Hortense Powdermaker, *After Freedom: A Cultural Study in the Deep South* (1930); John Dollard, *Caste and Class in a Southern Town* (1937); and Allison Davis, Burleigh B. Gardner, and Mary R. Gardner, *Deep South: A Social Anthropological Study of Caste and Class* (1941).

*Chief Joseph of the peaceful Nez Percé, who were driven from their
land and forced into a hopeless war with the American army.*

2

RALPH K. ANDRIST

The Death of the Plains Indians

In early 1973, a group of militant Indians occupied and laid siege to Wounded Knee, a historic Indian settlement located in South Dakota. The choice of Wounded Knee by the American Indian Movement (AIM) was no accident — for it was there, in 1890, that the Oglala Sioux, the tribe of Red Cloud and Crazy Horse, were finally subdued by the federal government. The massacre of two hundred Sioux by the United States Army proved to be the end of the Plains Indians' resistance to the white man's culture and economy.

The history of the treatment of the Indian by the white man is not a happy one — nor, from the point of view of the American Indian, an equitable or a merciful one. In the early 1830s, President Andrew Jackson felt that the Indian problem could be dealt with best by removing the Five Civilized Tribes — whose lands were coveted by southern planters and farmers — to territory west of the Mississippi River. By the end of the Civil War it became clear that the Great Plains, too, had to be cleared of Indians if the white ranchers and farmers were to flourish in the region. And so, for more than a quarter of a century, the federal government employed a variety of techniques to remove the Indian as an obstacle in the path of the white settler.

The coming of the cattle kingdom and the farmer to the trans-Mississippi brought an end to the plains culture created by the Indians. Having created a way of life and an economy based upon the use of the horse, land in common, and free-roaming buffalo, the Plains Indians proved no match for the white man's civilization. Within two decades after the end of the Civil War, the Plains Indians suffered a loss of food, clothing, shelter, household utensils, and military equipment as hunters exterminated what had been estimated in 1866 to be a total of 40 million buffalo. Forced onto reservations, the Indians had to contend with contagious diseases, alcoholism, and incompetent or corrupt federal agents. In 1887, through the Dawes Severalty Act, the Indian lost much fertile and productive land and gained only the right to vote if he chose to become a farmer.

The combination of guile and force that was employed by the federal government in order to deprive these Indians of their land and freedom is graphically described by Ralph K. Andrist in *The Long Death: The Last Days of the Plains Indians*. From his book, we have selected the tragic narrative concerning the fate of Chief Joseph and the Nez Percé, a peaceful tribe that settled, with the blessings and the consent of the United States Government, in the Wallowa country in the northeastern corner of Oregon prior to the Civil War. The nobility of Chief Joseph and the justice of his cause will be found in the last sentence of Andrist's narrative — Charles Erskine Wood's eloquent statement on the occasion of Chief Joseph's death in 1904. "I think that, in his long career, Joseph cannot accuse the Government of the United States of one single act of justice."

The company guidons still snapped in the wind when cavalry patrols passed on the plains just as they had for years, but there was a difference. The patrols no longer really expected trouble. There would be no ambush ahead; there was no chance that they would come on the burned wagons and the scalped bodies of a party of emigrants. Their main call to action was likely to be a request from an Indian agent to round up and escort back a few tribesmen who had wandered off the reservation. The Army on the plains had changed from fighting force into jail warden.

Custody of the Sioux had been returned to the Indian Bureau again, now that the war was over, and the Army had relinquished control. But the military was always close at hand. There were Army posts on almost all the reservations, most of them nearly within shouting distance of the

Reprinted with permission of Macmillan Publishing Company from *The Long Death* by Ralph K. Andrist. Copyright © 1964 by Ralph K. Andrist.

agency and ready for any trouble. The chances of further trouble would appear remote, but while most tribes now settled down to empty and frequently hungry existences, a few last flickering fires of resistance born of desperation were to break out during the next several years. Then, and only then, would it all be over, and the white man would at last have conquered and caged every Indian, from sea to shining sea.

The year after the Little Bighorn, it was the turn of the Nez Percés — or rather, a band of nontreaty Nez Percés — to face the United States Army. The Army never fought a more unjust war, nor did it ever oppose so superior a type of Indian foe. If any people deserved well of the United States, they did, and in the end they got less than nothing.

The Nez Percés are a people of the Pacific Northwest, who originally lived in the region where Washington, Oregon, and Idaho meet, in the valley of the Clearwater River and in part of the valleys of the Salmon and Snake. It was — and is — a magnificent country of deep canyons, ridges, evergreen forests, and grassy meadows carpeted in season with flowers of many colors and kinds. They had lived here for hundreds of years, hunters of deer, bear, mountain sheep, and lesser game, eaters of salmon which the rivers supplied bountifully, dwellers in semipermanent lodges. Then about 1760 they acquired the horse, and it worked the same revolution in their lives as it had with so many other tribes. They became superb horsemen and were deeply influenced by the horse-and-buffalo culture of the Plains, to the extent that they actually became buffalo Indians to a degree, crossing the Continental Divide and traveling three or four hundred miles to the nearest buffalo ranges in Montana on hunting trips. They adopted the tepee and a seminomadic way of life, and many other attributes of the Plains people, although in other ways retaining their old culture.

Lewis and Clark came through Nez Percé lands in 1805 on their famous trip to the Pacific, and again on their return when they stopped with the tribe for several weeks while waiting for the snow to melt in the mountain passes. The Nez Percés were hospitable hosts, and it continued to be their claim through succeeding decades and increasing provocations that they had never killed a white man.

At the Council of Walla Walla in 1855, when treaties were made restricting the tribes of the region to reservations, the Nez Percés managed to retain about half the country they claimed, partly because no one was yet interested in such wild and remote country, partly because the government wanted the backing of the powerful Nez Percés in negotiating with other tribes. White indifference to the country disappeared when prospectors came looking for gold, and the Indians, after turning them back for a time, were at last persuaded to let the gold-hunters in — under proper restrictions, of course.

There is no point in detailing the betrayal of the Nez Percés once the whites had an entering wedge. The prospectors spread beyond the limits set for them; settlers followed although it had been a clearly stated part of the agreement that no farmers should enter the Nez Percé lands; Indian fences were torn down, their pastures taken over and they were driven off lands they were farming. When the Nez Percés demanded that the government enforce the 1855 treaty, there was a cry of outrage at such impertinence. The government did at last intervene in 1863 to set things right — which it accomplished by a new treaty taking away three-quarters of the Nez Percé lands. The remaining reservation lay entirely in Idaho on the Clearwater River; the lands in Washington and Oregon were outside the reduced reserve. Despite gaining so much land, however, whites only increased their depredations against what remained.

Two-thirds of the chiefs present at the council had refused to sign the treaty, saying there was no point in a new agreement when the government had not honored or enforced the old one. One of the nontreaty chiefs was known as Joseph, a name he had taken long ago when he had become a Christian. A good and long-time friend of the whites, he now tore up his New Testament and swore to have nothing more to do with white men in whom no trust could be placed. Joseph and his band were more fortunate than many of the nontreaty Nez Percés who were living on land where they were now being pushed around by settlers, because Joseph's home was in the country of the Wallowa River in the northeastern corner of Oregon, a region no white man had yet become interested in. The band was still living there in peace in 1871 when Joseph, very old, died, leaving two sons: Ollikut, a great athlete and warrior, and Hinmatonyalatkit (Thunder-Rolling-in-the-Mountains), better known as Young Joseph. Young Joseph, the elder son, became Chief Joseph on his father's death. "I buried him in that beautiful valley of the winding waters," Joseph later said. "I love that land more than all the rest of the world."

Love it he might, but keep it he could not. The time came, as inevitably it would, when settlers began moving into the area. They and state officials set up the familiar anguished cries for soldiers to come and take Joseph's band away to the reservation. For a time the Federal government resisted the pressure and set aside part of the Wallowa country as a reserve for "roaming Nez Percés" by presidential order in 1873, but minds were changed two years later and the entire region thrown open to homesteaders.

Chief Joseph, however, continued to maintain that the land belonged to him and his people. His father had not given it up, neither had he parted with it. Old Joseph, in his last days, had told him never to sell the land. "This country holds your father's body," he told his son. "Never sell the bones of your father and mother."

A five-man commission was sent to talk to Chief Joseph. Two members were Army officers, three civilians. One of the officers, whom the Nez Percés were to have considerable to do with very soon, was Major General Oliver O. Howard, who had lost his right arm at Fair Oaks in the early part of the war, and had commanded a wing of Sherman's army during the March to the Sea during the last part. Howard was a man of pinch-nosed religiousness. . . . He was much interested in helping the recently freed Negroes (he was instrumental in founding Howard University for Negroes) but his heart did not go out in like manner to the Indian in his time of trouble.

Joseph made the commissioners uneasy. He was a man of quiet dignity and commanding presence. He was confident, calm, intelligent, capable of expressing himself with a logic the five white men found difficult to answer. Moreover, he nettled them because there was no trace of obsequiousness in his manner. He acted with the quiet assurance that he was the equal of the white men to whom he was talking — and as every Indian ought to be taught, no red man was the equal of any white. He denied the commissioners' contention that the Wallowa country had been signed away by the Nez Percés in the Lapwai Treaty in 1863. His father had not signed the treaty, said Joseph, and the Wallowa belonged to his father. "If we ever owned the land we own it still, for we have never sold it," Chief Joseph said. . . .

But in spite of Joseph's logic, . . . the five whites decided that Joseph's band should be removed to the Lapwai reservation, by force if necessary, and there receive about sixty plots of twenty acres each (they had about a million acres in the Wallowa country). Just about six months earlier, the other officer on the commission, Major H. C. Wood, had made another investigation of the Wallowa question and had decided that the right was all on Joseph's side, and General Howard had rendered a similar opinion. The truth and right could vary from month to month where Indian policy was involved.

Joseph bowed to the inevitable. He selected land on the reservation on May 15, 1877, and then was given one month by General Howard to bring his band in. Joseph asked for more time. The stock was foaling and calving at that season; the animals were still scattered in dozens of secret valleys and it would take time to round them up. Even more serious, the Snake River, which the band would have to cross — women, infants, aged — was half a mile wide and raging with melt waters. One month, Howard repeated. If the band delayed one day beyond that time — only one day — the troops would be there to drive them in.

The band was in no position to resist — it had only 55 men of fighting age — and the thing was somehow accomplished. Stock was rounded up, although hundreds of head were missed in the haste, and the crossing of the Snake was made without loss of human life, with the very young and the very old of the band towed on rafts through the swift, wide current. More livestock was lost when several hundred head were swept away in the river, and white settlers hanging around the edge of the band like jackals were able to cut out and stampede a large number of horses.

After the crossing, the band stopped to camp for the ten days or so still remaining before they had to come on the reservation. Other nontreaty bands, likewise ordered to settle down, joined them, and the encampment became a lively and cheerful place, considering the circumstances. But some tempers were thin. During a parade two days before the deadline date, someone became irritated by the antics of a young man named Wahlitits who was clowning on a horse and made a waspish comment to the effect that he had not been such a big man when it had come to avenging his father's murder two years before.

Wahlitits's father had died at the hands of a white man who had squatted on his land while he had been away; when the Nez Percé had returned and protested, the white man shot him. The dying man made his son promise not to take revenge, but now, burning from the taunt made at the parade, Wahlitits set out the next day with a cousin and another youth to take belated vengeance. They were unable to find the guilty man but they killed four others, at least two of whom well deserved it. They returned to camp, recruited another fifteen or twenty firebrands, and set out on a carnival of raiding and murder. With the help of liquor which they found and dipped into heavily, they killed fifteen more white men, plundered homes, and assaulted women.

The Nez Percés had always claimed they had never killed a white man, but now they had done in a good number of them, and rather messily, in a few hours. The encampment was shocked at the news, and broke up rapidly as families left to disassociate themselves from the murderers. Many went south, to the canyon of White Bird Creek, a stream emptying into the Salmon River. Joseph had been away from the encampment when the raids had taken place, but he knew that neither that circumstance, nor that none of the murderers were members of his band, was likely to be taken into consideration when retribution was dealt out. He stayed for two days with his wife who had just given birth to a daughter, then the three joined the others at White Bird Canyon.

General Howard, at Lapwai on the reservation, got the news on June 15, and at once sent Captain David Perry with two companies of the 1st Cavalry after the Indians. . . . As the force neared the Indian camp at White Bird Canyon, the Nez Percés sent several men with a flag of truce to meet it, but they were fired on. The Indians were outnumbered; they had only about sixty to sixty-five men, some of them old, some still in sorry condition from too much stolen whiskey the night before, about a third armed with bows and arrows, many of the rest with old muzzle-loaders. But fighting a battle which they improvised as they proceeded, they routed the troops, cut them into sections, pinned one group of nineteen men against a rocky wall and wiped them out, and killed thirty-four and wounded four, while suffering only two wounded themselves. . . .

General Howard moved more cautiously now. He called in more men from posts throughout the entire Pacific Northwest while reserves were brought in from as far as Atlanta, Georgia, to stand by in case the war spread. The Nez Percés picked up some strength, too. Two competent warriors, Five Wounds, and Rainbow, returning from a buffalo hunt in Montana, met the fugitives and joined them with their small bands. General Howard, through a stupid act, gave them more recruits. A prominent chief named Looking Glass was camped on the reservation with his band, completely divorced from all the violence that had been occurring. Nevertheless, when wild-eyed settlers brought stories that Looking Glass was preparing to join the hostiles, Howard, without investigating, sent a Captain Whipple with two companies of cavalry against Looking Glass's village. Nor did he direct Whipple to investigate before he took action, so Whipple did not hesitate to launch an attack when he found a peaceful camp. Only three or four Indians were killed in what was a completely treacherous attack, but the village was destroyed. The infuriated Indians thereupon left the reservation and set out to join the hostile force.

While Captain Whipple was making his ill-advised raid on Looking Glass's camp, General Howard had been decoyed across the swollen Salmon River and led on a chase through the rugged, almost trackless country south of that river. Then the Indians doubled back, leaving Howard to flounder about in the wilderness. The Nez Percés headed north to a new camping place on the Clearwater River. . . . At the Clearwater camp, they were joined by Looking Glass and his still-angry band, giving them just under 200 men, and about 450 women and children.

By July 11, General Howard, with his army reinforced and increased to 400 soldiers and 180 scouts, teamsters, and packers, had caught up with the hostile band, who were still camped on the Clearwater, and took them completely by surprise by opening fire from the bluff across the river with a howitzer and two Gatling guns. However, before Howard could get his attack underway, Toohoolhoolzote, chief of one of the non-treaty bands, an elderly man but a noted warrior, dashed across the river and up the bluffs with only twenty-four men to hold the soldiers off until reinforcements could follow and swing around Howard's flanks and rear.

In spite of a numerical advantage of six to one, and despite his possession of artillery, the chagrined General Howard soon found himself completely surrounded and besieged, with his forces drawn up in a hollow square. For more than a day, the Indians kept up the close siege, sometimes coming near enough for hand-to-hand fighting. Then, tiring of the battle, they broke it off, after first giving the camp plenty of time to move on. They had lost four killed and six wounded, the Army thirteen killed and twenty-three wounded.

After traveling a safe distance to the east, the Nez Percés camped to take stock of their situation and decide their future course. They had fought their battle on the Clearwater as five separate bands, each under its own chief (Ollikut, Joseph's brother, had led the Wallowa band) and with no clear idea of what they were fighting for except to defend themselves. Now it was decided that the only course open to them was to leave Idaho Territory and go east across the mountains. There they could join their friends, the Crows, on the buffalo plains in Montana. Chief Joseph objected; he wanted to continue to fight for his beautiful land, to the death if need be, but he was overruled. . . .

The band passed over the high point of the Bitterroots and were moving down its eastern slope into Montana when they found their way blocked by hastily built fortifications manned by about thirty-five regular Army infantrymen and some two hundred volunteers, under the command of Captain Charles C. Rawn. Chief Joseph, Looking Glass, and old Chief White Bird rode forward to parley. They explained that they had no quarrel with anyone but General Howard and would harm no one if permitted to pass. The volunteers knew the Nez Percés well and favorably from their buffalo-hunting trips. They decided that, since they were there only to defend their homes from Indians, and since their homes needed no defending from these Indians, they might as well go home. Most of them did; only thirty volunteers remained with Rawn and his regulars. . . .

The band moved on to Stevensville where supplies were replenished, not by looting and pillage, but by decorous purchase in the town's stores. These strange Indians, who could easily have taken anything they wanted, quietly paid with gold and currency for their sugar, coffee, and tobacco, and at prices which the merchants had raised sky-high for the occasion. There was, however, no buying of liquor because the chiefs had told the town fathers to have all supplies locked up till the band had moved on.

Now they turned south, following the Bitterroot River to its head, then crossed the Continental Divide and passed into the Big Hole Valley just south of it, where at last they set up their tepees for a long rest and to repair some of the ravages of the hard trip. They were sure they were in friendly country now, with nothing to fear. But Colonel John Gibbon had come by forced marches from Fort Shaw on the Sun River, gathering men from other posts as he came, and at dawn on August 9, he attacked the sleeping camp with approximately two hundred men. There was no warning. The shot that killed a solitary horse herder came almost at the same instant as the crash of rifle fire into the lodges and the whoops of charging soldiers. Women were shot without hesitation; children were gunned down; even babies had their head crushed with a kick or a clubbed rifle. Such, at least, is the testimony of an officer who took part in the campaign.

But despite the overwhelming surprise of the attack, some of the Indians recovered and began to fight back, rallied by doughty old White Bird. One sharp stroke of luck fell their way; the lieutenant commanding Gibbon's left wing was killed, and as the leaderless troops lost purpose, the Indians opposing them organized a counterattack that continued until it had rolled up Gibbon's entire force, which was now giving too much of its attention to plundering. The marksmanship of the Nez Percés was taking a heavy toll (their accurate shooting, unusual among Indians, was remarked in every engagement). Gibbon was soon on the defensive and besieged; Chief Joseph had taken charge of getting the camp packed up and moving, and the weary, never-ending flight was on again.

When a detachment of soldiers attempted to set up a howitzer, a handful of Indians drove them off, seized the cannon, and, since they did not know how to use the weapon, wrecked it. Gibbon, running out of food, water, and ammunition, was saved only by the arrival of General Howard. He had lost thirty-three dead and thirty-eight wounded, including himself. He claimed the Indians lost eight-nine, and this appears to be correct, or very nearly so, but most of those dead were women, children, and aged. The Nez Percés later said that only twelve warriors died, but they included some of the best, among them Rainbow and Five Wounds.

The Nez Percés buried their dead before withdrawing; Howard permitted his Bannock Indian scouts to dig up the bodies to scalp and mutilate them. This barbarism, coming on top of the savage slaughter of noncombatants, shocked the Nez Percés, who had been fighting by all the rules of so-called civilized warfare. Howard became the most despised man in the world as far as they were concerned, not completely logically, for it was Colonel Gibbon who had been guilty of killing the women and children.

Looking Glass was displaced as war leader because he had let the camp be taken by surprise, his place taken by a chief named Lean Elk who had recently joined the band; he had been buffalo hunting and was camped in the Bitterroot valley with half a dozen lodges when the fugitives came by shortly after the affair of Fort Fizzle. But the stories going out to the country — and the public was by now intensely interested in what was occurring — all credited Chief Joseph with the military leadership of the band. General Howard, recalling Joseph's astuteness in council and his leadership in peace, assumed that he was continuing to guide the Nez Percés in battle. So the legend arose of a rude military genius in the northern mountains, a red-skinned Napoleon, maneuvering his outnumbered warriors so skilfully as to confound, confuse, and defeat, time and again, the trained troops of the United States.

The truth is somewhat less exciting. Joseph was not a war chief, and although he took part in the fighting once or twice, he usually took charge of the camp to see that it was struck, packed for traveling, and on its way, with women and children taken care of. It was an important and necessary function and not to be denigrated — most tribes had peace chiefs and war chiefs — but it lays to rest the myth of the master tactician in moccasins. The Nez Percé victories were due, not to any unusual brilliance in battle, but to a combination of bravery, determination, and the rare ability to stand fast when caught off-balance and then recover and take the initiative. That, along with overconfidence and some fortuitous (for the Nez Percés) mistakes on the part of their white foes.

The fleeing band paralleled the general line of the Continental Divide, which swung in a great arc toward the east. General Howard was pushing them hard. . . .

The fugitives passed on into Yellowstone Park, then only five years old but already attracting a considerable number of hardy tourists. They barely missed one party containing General William Tecumseh Sherman, but swept up another, shooting and almost fatally wounding one man. . . .

The flight continued, through Yellowstone Park and the northwestern corner of Wyoming; then the Indians swung northward where more trouble awaited. Part of the 7th Cavalry, commanded by Colonel Samuel Sturgis . . . tried to head them off, but the Nez Percé band found its way through mountainous country which had been considered impassable for men with horses and came out behind Sturgis on Clarks Fork of the Yellowstone River.

The decision was made to continue the weary journey on to Canada. . . .

. . . Their course took them north across Montana, as far as a low range called the Bear Paw Mountains which rose from the plains in the northern part of the Territory. There, only thirty miles from the Canadian border, the fugitive band made camp to rest and to hunt and lay in a supply of dried meat and buffalo skins against the coming winter.

Once again they had reckoned without the telegraph. Colonel Nelson E. Miles was hurrying up from Fort Keogh on the Yellowstone with six hundred men. . . . Another day and the Nez Percés would probably have made it to Canada, for most of the pack animals already had their burdens lashed on and the band was making ready to move again when Miles's scouts sighted their lodges on the morning of the last day of September.

Colonel Miles ordered an immediate attack, hoping to smash the Nez Percés with a single charge. But he had begun the charge a good four miles away, and the Indians had that much warning; old White Bird quickly posted his men in front of the camp, and as the onrushing battle line of troops came within range, it met a withering fire which killed two officers and twenty-two men, and injured another four officers and thirty-eight men. The charge stopped as though it had been poleaxed, and the men took shelter behind rocks and in gullies. But they did not retreat; the camp remained under fire.

White Bird had only 120 men against Miles's six hundred. . . . When the soldiers gave up the pursuit, many of the warriors turned back, too, and slipped into camp.

Two brave leaders, Chief Toohoolhoolzote and Ollikut, were among the good men who died in the first confused fighting. Chief Joseph and his twelve-year-old daughter had been with the horse herd when the attack came. He told the girl to catch a horse and join those who were cut off from the camp. Then he galloped his horse through the line of soldiers, unharmed, though his horse was wounded and his clothes pierced many times. His wife met him at the entrance of his lodge and handed him his rifle. "Here is your gun. Fight." . . .

On October 4, General Howard arrived with more troops, making the situation of the Nez Percés hopeless. Negotiations were begun through two treaty Nez Percés who had come with Howard as interpreters. The few remaining chiefs were told that Howard would treat the band with honor if they surrendered and would send them back to the Lapwai reservation in the spring, when the mountains were clear of snow again. Looking Glass and White Bird wanted to fight on, but Chief Joseph insisted that they must make their decision for the freezing women and children crouching in the pits that had been dug for shelter from Miles's howitzer.

Just as the council broke up, brave Looking Glass fell dead, struck in the head by a chance bullet. For four months, and over a trail 1,300 miles long, the Nez Percés band had fought and fled, to be caught only thirty miles from freedom. A short distance still remained for Chief Joseph to travel, the ride from the camp to the hill where General Howard and Colonel Miles were waiting, but for him it would be the longest part of the journey. He had already sent his message of surrender ahead with Captain John, one of the Nez Percés interpreters, who had carried it to General Howard and repeated it with tears in his eyes.

> . . . I am tired of fighting. Our chiefs are killed. Looking Glass is dead. Toohoolhoolzote is dead. The old men are all dead. It is the young men who say yes and no. He who led the young men [Ollikut] is dead. It is cold and we have no blankets. The little children are freezing to death. My people, some of them, have run away to the hills, and have no blankets, no food; no one knows where they are — perhaps freezing to death. I want to

have time to look for my children and see how many I can find. Maybe I shall find them among the dead. Hear me, my chiefs, I am tired; my heart is sick and sad. From where the sun now stands, I will fight no more forever.

About two hours later, Joseph rode over, with several of his men walking beside him. He dismounted and handed his rifle to Howard, who motioned that he should give it to Colonel Miles. Thereafter, he was treated as a prisoner of war.

Chief White Bird escaped to Canada that night with a handful of followers.... A few more than 400 were captured of about 650 who had started on the long trip; probably close to 200 died during the flight or on the plains. But Joseph's fears that his own children might be dead were groundless; of his six children, only the baby born on the eve of the long journey remained with him at the time of the surrender, but all were later found safe.

The captives were taken to Fort Keogh, a logical place to hold them until they could be returned to Idaho in the spring. But soon an order came from General Sheridan to send them to Fort Abraham Lincoln. It would be too expensive, he said, to maintain them at Fort Keogh through the winter. Colonel Miles, after making a futile protest, put most of his prisoners on flatboats to make the long trip down the Yellowstone and Missouri without military guard or escort except for one enlisted man on each boat. The able-bodied men and some of the women marched overland with Miles and his troops. All arrived safely.

When Miles arrived in Bismarck with the overland contingent of Nez Percés, a remarkable thing occurred. Bismarck, it will be remembered, was still a frontier community, and most of its people were convinced of the basic rightness of Sheridan's dictum, "The only good Indian is a dead Indian." Not only that, it was at Fort Abraham Lincoln, near Bismarck, that the 7th Cavalry had been stationed. Many of the townspeople had had friends who had died only a year before with Custer.

Bismarck would, in short, seem an unwise place to bring a group of Indians who had lately been at war with the Army. But as the column rode through the main street, with Chief Joseph on horseback beside Colonel Miles and the rest of the Nez Percé following, enclosed by a protecting square of soldiers, crowds of townspeople surged out into the street and against the cordon of troops. However, there was no hate and no violence intended; they carried food, and broke through the square of troops to give it to the Indians. Only when the people had exhausted all their gifts was the column able to proceed on to Fort Lincoln.

Two days later an even more remarkable event occurred. The good ladies of Bismarck were hostesses at a dinner at which Chief Joseph and the other chiefs were guests of honor. But these were the only two bright spots in their treatment by white people since their war began and would be just about the last. Two days after the dinner, they were on a train, headed for Fort Leavenworth, with Indian Territory as their eventual destination. Colonel Miles and General Howard protested this betrayal of the promises made by Howard to the Nez Percés at the time of the surrender, but the higher powers in Washington felt under no kind of obligation to honor the promises. General Sherman, while refraining from talking about extermination in this case, announced that the Nez Percés must be suitably punished to discourage other tribes who might feel moved to defend their rights.

The Nez Percés were settled in a low, malarial part of Indian Territory, especially deadly to these highland people whose resistance to disease had been lowered by their recent hardships and suffering. Within a few months, more than a quarter of them were dead. They got along fairly well after they became somewhat acclimated to their new surroundings and even prospered in a small way through their skill at stock raising, but they remained hopelessly homesick for their mountains. Strong public sentiment had been aroused by their magnificent retreat and by the way they conducted themselves during it, and the public was not permitted to forget their story. Colonel Miles (brigadier general after 1880), a firm friend of Joseph since the end of the war, regularly recommended that the Nez Percés be permitted to return.

A few widows and orphans were allowed to go to the Lapwai reservation in 1882, and the rest were sent north three years later. Slightly more than half went to Lapwai; the rest, among them Joseph, were for some reason sent to the Colville reservation in northern Washington to live among the several small tribes there. None of Joseph's six children returned north with him; he had buried them, one by one, in alien soil, victims of the climate and disease of the south.

Chief Joseph, during the rest of his life, asked to be permitted to return to the Wallowa country, of which he had said, "I love that land more than all the rest of the world." But where the rest of the country had come to admire Joseph, the ranchers in his former home opposed his return, and the government supinely gave in to their wishes. Joseph died, still grieving for his lost country, in 1904. Charles Erskine Wood, aide to General Howard during the Nez Percé War, wrote what might be Joseph's epitaph: "I think that, in his long career, Joseph cannot accuse the Government of the United States of one single act of justice."

STUDY GUIDE

1. Trace the stages in Chief Joseph's relationship with the white man, explaining the occasion for each encounter, the agreements made, and the

course of action taken by the federal government following each of these meetings.

2. What were the attitudes of the whites toward the Indians? Fear? Hatred? Admiration? Contempt? Can you generalize for all whites and at all points in the narrative? If not, why not?

3. What role did the federal government play in subduing the Indian? What instruments were employed, and how?

4. Placing the Plains Indians on reservations appears to have been unjust and even cruel. Were there any alternatives? If not, how could reservation life have been made more tolerable than it was for Chief Joseph?

5. Can you explain why the United States Army pursued the Nez Percé to the Canadian border? Why were the Indians not permitted to cross into Canada and to freedom?

6. Considering the entire question of Indian-white relations, was there anything in our historical experience that would have prepared white Americans for dealing sympathetically or equitably with the Plains Indians? Did Americans deal with one another more humanely? If so, how would you explain the brutality of the Civil War or the violence of the Pullman and Homestead strikes in the late nineteenth century?

BIBLIOGRAPHY

A number of books provide further reading on the Indian and the impact of the white man's civilization on Indian life. A brief introduction to the subject is William T. Hagan, *American Indians* (1961). An informed survey of the culture of the American Indian, incorporating historical material as well, is Ruth M. Underhill, *Red Man's America* (1953). A widely read and classic indictment of the white man's treatment of the Indian is Helen Hunt Jackson, *Century of Dishonor* (1885); more recent volumes include the following: Gary E. Moulton, *John Ross, Cherokee Chief* (1974) and H. Craig Miner and William E. Unrau, *The End of Indian Kansas* (1978). The treatment of Indians by the United States Army is covered in Robert M. Utley, *Frontier Regulars: The United States Army and the Indian* (1973), while interpretations of the impact of Protestant reformers on Indian life and education are contained in several volumes: Henry E. Fritz, *The Movement for Indian Assimilation, 1860–1890* (1963); Francis Paul Prucha, *American Indian Policy in Crisis: Christian Reformers and the Indian 1865–1890* (1975); and Robert W. Mardock, *The Reformers and the American Indian* (1971). Several volumes by Mari Sandoz — *These Were the Sioux* (1961), *Crazy Horse: Strange Man of the Oglalas* (1961), and *Cheyenne Autumn* (1962) — offer a sympathetic view of the Indian's plight in the face of the cruelty and the superior technology of the white man. In a similar vein is Dee Brown's popular, but controversial, volume, *Bury My Heart at Wounded Knee* (1971). Should you want to know more about the Nez Percé, you can consult Merrill D. Beal, *I Will Fight No More* (1963), and Mark H. Brown, *The Flight of the Nez Percé* (1967), as well as the book from which the preceding selection was taken, Ralph K. Andrist, *The Long Death: The Last Days of the Plains Indians* (1964).

Farmers on the Great Plains often resorted to cooperation to cope with the harsh environment, but creating settled conditions was also the result of individual drive and determination and a source of individual pride.

3

ROBERT V. HINE

The Farmers' Frontier

The quarter-century after the Civil War was a period of very rapid growth for the United States. A significant part of that growth was geographical. At the end of the war, the area west of the Mississippi River was sparsely populated except for the first tier of states on the west bank, Texas, and a line of settlement on the Pacific Coast. But by 1890, according to the official census of that year, this hitherto largely empty territory had been settled. It was no longer possible to draw a line on a map of the United States marking the boundary between settled and unsettled areas. The frontier, which according to Frederick Jackson Turner's theory of 1893 had been the chief determining element in forming the United States, had come to an end.

The process of settlement was filled with danger and excitement and has continued to exercise a firm hold on Americans' imaginations. We still entertain ourselves with stories of battles with Indians, of prospectors searching for the elusive big strike that would make them wealthy overnight, of cattle barons and cowboys in conflict with the elements or each other in their efforts to raise beef to feed the growing cities of the East. But while fur trappers before the Civil War, and miners and cattlemen afterwards, played vital roles in opening up the trans-Mississippi West and awakening people to its enormous possibilities, its actual settlement was accomplished by less glamorous figures in less exciting ways. It was farmers who were primarily responsible for establishing a settled society in the area from the Mississippi to the Pacific, and their story, while not having the same aura of glamour as surrounds the mountain man or the prospector or the Indian fighter or the cowboy, has its own share of human drama.

In the first place, farmers on the Great Plains had to learn to adapt to an unfamiliar and harsh environment. Bitter cold in winter, burning hot in summer, lacking timber and stone for building materials, and subject to periodic droughts, windstorms, and insect plagues, the Plains were a mighty challenge to those who chose to try their fortunes there. Further, as they learned the techniques enabling them to deal with nature, they found themselves confronted with other problems, particularly steadily falling prices for the crops they grew and large fixed debts for the land, tools, and machines they needed to grow them. Caught in this economic squeeze, farmers began to band together to seek solutions to their problems, first through the Patrons of Husbandry, or Grange, in the 1870s and then through the Populist Movement in the 1880s and 1890s. These attempts at political action enjoyed only partial success, but did pave the way for some of the reforms of the Progressive Movement of the twentieth century.

In the meantime, however, farmers on the Plains still had to learn to deal with the everyday problems created by the stringent conditions under which they had to live. The following selection from Robert V. Hine's *Community on the American Frontier: Separate But Not Alone* talks about some of the problems, including the psychological ones, they endured and the methods they devised for trying to cope with them.

"I was alone all the daylight hours with the cattle, and all around me the prairie was dying. The sound of death was in the wind that never stopped blowing across the whitening grass, or rustling the dead weeds at the edges of the fields. There was a forlorn, lonely note in the bawl of a calf for its mother and in the honking of wild geese down the pale sky." Grace Snyder's thoughts were the aftermath of death, the obliteration of a distant neighbor boy who had died while hurrying through his noon dinner. She and her family had walked the half mile to the funeral, where the glass-topped coffin exposed the bloated face of John, as lonely in death as the prairies were in life. Grace had known solitude playing among the bleached bones in the buffalo wallow, she and her sister alone because the Snyder farm was so far from neighbors. Grace's father had migrated with his proud wife and three daughters from Missouri to the Platte River Valley in Custer County, Nebraska. That was 1885, and

Grace was three. Their father had preceded them and prepared housing, but Grace later remembered her first sight of "two naked little soddies" on a bare, wind-swept ridge. Nothing else. The flatness of the prairies threatened her with a child's unconscious fear of abandonment, perhaps of lost identity, perhaps even of oblivion beneath that unbroken sky. . . .

Seth Humphrey became a mortgage collector, traveling across the Great Plains in the early 1890s. Everywhere he found abandoned claims, shacks pulled apart and used by others, the winds and the horizon taking their toll. Guy Divet, an Irishman who had come to Dakota with his family in the 1870s and prospered, told the story of another couple who had not. Ned and his young, pregnant wife moved into the neighborhood, and in their first winter Margie was "sick and out of her mind with loneliness and fear." So the warm, caring Divets took them in for the winter, putting up a bed in their living room.

That spring Mrs. Divet helped with the birth, but the young mother remained half-crazed, and the young father grew more and more depressed. So they left with Margie still ill. The neighbors raised thirty-six dollars to help them. The baby died on the journey, and the mother shortly after. Ned sold the wagon and team to pay for the burials. "Grist for the prairie mill," the Divets said. Ned's claim was jumped, but before that the Divets rode over to see his cabin. There were unwashed dishes and a homemade crib. The Divets piled dry weeds, lit them, and watched reverently as the cabin burned to the ground. It did not take long.

But the fire could not erase the memory, and the prairie continued to stare. Mrs. Divet herself developed a goiter, and when her husband offered a visit to her family in Wisconsin, she refused, sadly pointing to her straggly hair and sagging body and "this hideous bag that hangs at my throat." "No," she cried, "its too late now. I don't want to go." The Divet manuscripts are memorials to "the frayed ends" of these lives, "the heartstrings broken in the process of uprooting never to be brought together again."

The lives of the Snyders, the Humphreys, and the Divets were in many respects full and rewarding. Nevertheless, as with all settlers on the Great Plains between the Civil War and the close of the century, the fact of isolation underlay all other facts, social, economic, and political. Isolation was the environment in which the structure of the community must grow. Shortly after the turn of the century, when the President's Commission on Country Life asked over 100,000 rural inhabitants what could improve their lives, an overwhelming response was better roads, or, in other words, a way of overcoming isolation.

Eugene Virgil Smalley spelled out the central problem in similar terms. A newsman, he had lived and worked from Ohio to Minnesota, served in the government, and traveled abroad. "In no civilized country," he wrote, "have the cultivators of the soil adapted their homelife so badly to the

conditions of nature." He saw only one solution: to draw farmers together into village communities. He knew that it would be difficult because of land laws and, even more important, American ways of thinking.
There is an old western saying, he quoted, that the prairies would not
produce until the Indian was beaten out of them, something savage
wrested from the land by individual struggle. Smalley told of four farm
families who, like many others, had decided to work more closely by
building their houses and barns on the adjacent corners of their claims.
But in a few years they had all moved to the far corners because, they
explained lamely, when they were together their chickens had gotten
mixed up. Such was the "crusty individuality" that Smalley felt had produced the inheritance of isolated lives. . . .

Some cultural identities, however, did stem from the use of, if not love
of, the land. Sometimes one part of the ecology, one feature of the natural
environment, can become the center of the culture, the heart of the community, like corn for the Latin-American natives or the buffalo for the
Sioux. Thus on the plains cultural differences arose between wheat and
corn farming. Corn cultivation spread into the plains following the water-
courses, and carrying a certain life-style. The cornhusker reflected his
"corn-belt mentality" when he spoke of huskings, cribs, and fodder, topics
irrelevant to the wheat grower. And, more basically, he and the wheat
farmer would argue over proper use of the upland plains. Each wave of
newcomers to Nebraska between the 1850s and 1880s brought new and
conflicting concepts of land use. In time attitudes would change, but before the late 1870s two potential cultural communities existed.

Separate crop cultures, however, did not really develop on the plains,
partly because the environment was a common hazard, a common hardship, and it dictated fast, cooperative action from cornhusker, wheat
grower, or cattle grazer alike. Prairie fires, for example, were a threat to
all. And wolves, jackrabbits, and rattlesnakes, like fires, were more effectively controlled by cooperative drives. Cooperative coyote hunting in pioneer Nebraska was probably the only occasion when farmers, cattlemen,
and sheepmen worked in concert — although afterward, eating cold pies
with their wives in the nearest barn mow, in their conversations they
dwelled on only safe topics like past hunts. Natural disasters such as
floods could be better withstood by groups. The common threat of the
environment is suggested in the tall tales and weather jokes. Why did the
western farmer so love to tell of the drought when the fish in the river
kicked up such a dust that the volunteer fire department had to sprinkle
them down? Or why did he like to repeat the details of the well that ran
so dry that a tornado lifted it from one county to another? Perhaps because the common experience welded them in a psychic community. That
same drought of the tall tales, for example, brought the farmers of Roten

Valley, Nebraska, to act in concert regarding their suffering livestock. Thus the environment bred cooperative action.

Prairie farmers followed a long tradition of frontier cooperation. In colonial New England all nonfarming artisans and laborers were required by law to help with the mowing and reaping. In western Pennsylvania in the eighteenth century neighbors would donate three days to build a newcomer's house, including furniture. In Kentucky about 1810 an observer described a cooperative "bond of amity." "In no other part of the world," he wrote, "is good neighborship found in greater perfection." Everywhere the tradition was built on the problem of getting big jobs done, tasks too large for the individual — clearing acres of land, house and barn raising, road building, threshing before the rains. These were situations in which men were grappling most desperately with the environment.

On the plains cooperative house raising retained its full vigor. Howard Ruede, a thin young Pennsylvania Moravian who went to Kansas in 1877, explained that neighbors would gather from miles around to construct a settler's house, and they would finish in a day. Eleven men had helped a neighbor shortly before, though Ruede was sure six could have done the job. Houses were raised frequently enough that men fell in accustomed roles based on their skills. Such raisings were not always signs of stability, for many a house soon needed moving, sometimes for long distances, as to a new homestead. More often, though, the move for which the neighbors would gather would be short, like putting Percy Ebbutt's cabin on rollers to relocate on a hilltop or dragging Faye Lewis's house on skids to a site nearer the well.

Hospitality itself was largely an exchange of goods and services. A farmer, for example, would sometimes have to ride for days to round up stray cattle, but he would never want for lodging or provender. Some distant, lonely neighbor could be found for roof, a meal, and hay. "You'll do the same for me," he would hear, "when I'm in your parts." It was an outright exchange, the neighbor expecting reciprocity. When the farmer moved on main-traveled roads, he would more likely pay for his lodging. In such a situation the Snyders were once amazed to be charged a whopping eight dollars.

The height of cooperative work came at harvest time. In those autumn days of thronging threshers and aching backs, the traditions of cooperation prospered. Crews made the rounds from farm to farm, and men sweated together over one another's fields. The men talked at dinner, cooked by women whose backs also ached. Later there was talk in the barn as the men waited for a squall to pass. One Iowa farmer described these moments as "inner neighborhood." Such was the conversational stuff of community, and it grew from simple but universal topics like the weather — the breeze from the east, the nervousness of the horses, the "sun dogs" in the west that portended storm. Or it could be the state of the crops or the advantages of this country over another region or another land.

The threshing crew was a mixed lot. In addition to the local neighbors exchanging work, there could be a few leftover hired hands, some unemployed seasonal workers like timbermen in Minnesota, perhaps a hobo, and a schoolboy or two. The nonneighbors were paid. A band cutter got $1.50 a day in Minnesota in the early 1880s. These men slept in haymows and were fed plenty of chicken and pumpkin pie. Ebbutt thought they "lived off the fat of the land."

The cooperative element in threshing should be placed in the context of a rather large, extensive operation that was partly local cooperation and barter, partly capitalistic investment, and partly involvement in wider economic markets. The threshing machine itself, for example, was usually owned by one or two of the neighbors, who would assemble the crew, arrange the schedule, and bring the rig around for a cash fee or a portion of the crop. If the machine was owned by a Swede and you were the only non-Swede in the area, your turn might well come last. But you probably had little choice, for the cost of a thresher in 1851 was $175. Few farmers could afford that, since most had already invested a minimum of $400 just to begin farming. . . .

. . . Threshing was typical of other mixes of cooperation, barter, and cash. If you exchanged work and brought along a team for a day, you got three days' work from a man without a team. In exchange for sporadic labor over many months as a hired hand, Howard Ruede received help in breaking three acres of his own land, 11½ bushels of wheat, a few bushels of rye, and five dollars.

Reciprocal labor resulted far more often from an absence of capital than from a desire to cooperate. Anyone could offer labor, but few could offer cash. . . .

. . . Howard Ruede's Kansas neighborhood in the 1870s circulated a paper seeking help in building the school, either work or money. Eighty-one hours were pledged, but only eighteen dollars in cash. Pockets then were empty because of hard times following 1873; but in depression or not, reciprocal work expanded the cash supply. The neighbors were a reservoir of cooperative labor that assumed the nature of capital. . . .

So the plains environment and an immature economy spawned cooperative activities that could become community. Irrespective of economic forces, however, the isolation of farms called up a strong psychic yearning for companionship. Starved emotions cried for nourishment. Certainly the community was small enough in numbers, but the distances reduced practical contacts to the level of acquaintances in a large city. Neighborhoods in Kansas are measured in miles, not blocks, wrote Charley

O'Kieffe, adding sadly if not typically that there was little social intermingling, and only two dances a year.

Edgar Watson Howe had an explanation for the kind of gloomy picture O'Kieffe drew. Howe thought his neighbors in Missouri in the 1850s were so habituated to isolation that they could socialize for only a short time, as in church, and then they would immediately head for their farms to resume their lives of misery. It was an immature or arrested social life. Richard Weston had earlier described a frontier party in which forty couples engaged in "puerile and frivolous sport," like kissing games, and usually in silence because the art of conversation was so little known. Of course, the preponderance of accounts of social life on the plains frontier is of vital, engaging, lively times, but the more grim commentators would say that the happier descriptions were reflections of the infrequency of the contacts, etching them in memory and exaggerating them in reminiscence.

Still there is abundant evidence of pleasurable social life among prairie farmers. In North Dakota in the 1870s a ring of eight families rotated their dances every Friday night. Even Grace Fairchild, a big woman whose strong face reflected her hard life, recalled that the dances were so popular around her house that in rapid succession they outgrew the parlor, the machine shed, and the barn. These parties were usually open, nonselective affairs. At least Percy Ebbutt always assumed that if anyone had a party everyone else was invited.

There were quilting bees, husking bees, apple bees, and "fulling bees" (for the fulling or thickening of cloth). To be sure, all these had practical ends, but they skillfully blended play with cooperative work, "a means of enlivening the spirits of old and young." As in any other true community, these occasions sparked tension. Hamlin Garland remembered Mrs. Whitwell's ostracism from the quiltings because she was too loud and told vulgar stories. There were limits to which loneliness would compel acceptance, but Garland understood as well as anyone else the gratifying cohesive force in this cooperative socialization — the vigor, the laughter, the rejoicing. Imagine what it meant even to children playing together under the frame with adults chattering and stitching on the quilt above.

At least two holidays embraced the whole community. Decoration Day combined spring with a communal memorial. Everyone picked flowers, decorated the graves, and remained for the picnic. But no community event pulled together the straggling farms as did the Fourth of July. At some nearby fort or crossroad there were flags and speeches and cold chicken, and the day was full of horse races, foot races, sack races, and baseball. There were greased pigs, greased poles, and gallons of cold drinks. At Fort Scott, Kansas, in 1859 it took four horsedrawn wagons to draw ice for the lemonade alone. Faye Lewis, a shy adolescent in South Dakota, was taken to the celebration her first year on the plains. She feared that, for families like hers, farmers who could not afford the expense or time, it would be an "irresponsible and reckless binge," but she later understood the "immeasurable benefits" from the three days, from the four-hour wagon ride, the parade, the singing, the merry-go-round, the popcorn, the fireworks. For similar reasons Friday night "literaries," often sedate enough, occasionally reverted to nonsense: Resolved that pigs are smarter than sheep; or, Resolved that it is better to be kicked by a mule than bitten by a rattler.

Between special occasions and formal gatherings, there was always visiting. In Oklahoma in the 1890s, Allie Wallace thought that her house enjoyed so many visitors because her mother owned a sewing machine; but the need being met was deeper than practicality. Grace Snyder observed an increase in visiting during a period of extended drought. The relief of tensions through social intercourse was well expressed by Grace's father, who, even when weary, wished to go visiting. He took his family, weather permitting, as often as once a week, jolting over the miles, bearing a few gifts of flowers or fresh eggs, hoping for a sip of wine and a face. For a time isolation would thaw in the warmth of human contact.

Worship services, prayer meetings, evening sings, and especially camp meetings were social events too. Small groups of neighbors could always pray together in farmhouses, but the outdoor revivals, lasting from three days to a week, provided the most highly charged release of emotion. Families came from dozens or hundreds of miles. Religion in wagons, Charles Reed called it, and like most other farmers he happily welcomed any preacher who stopped at his sod-house door. The word flew. Soon there would be "tenting tonight" in the old grove at the forks of Clear Creek. Preachings and bonfires and a few true conversions there were, but the serious reclamation of souls was overlaid with the spirit of the Fourth of July. Everyone came — Baptists, Mennonites, Catholics. The circuit rider preached to a heterogeneous congregation. Most people went, even when they had to sit under clumps of hay on poles for shade. At least, Allie Wallace said, it "broke the monotony." Whatever their backgrounds, they joined or witnessed members of their community publicly confessing sin or publicly accepting the Lord. . . .

The place as an ecological system demanded economic cooperation, and the size of the group, small but scattered, shaped the need for social gatherings; but neither would bring community without the values of sharing and caring. Such values were once held aloft by Fred Shannon as a distinctive culture revolving around cooperative rural life. Such a cooperative culture based on values might indeed be a community, but, on the other hand, group cooperation does not necessarily mean community. Was it evidence of cooperative culture when, during a measles epidemic, neighbors fed stricken families and took in their healthy children to stem the spread of the disease? Or when neighbors banded together to help the surviving families of two murdered men? Or when settlers shared the cost of a school teacher by rotating her residence among them? Or when, after a disastrous fire, the farmers near Torkel Fugelstad threshed his crop while he was away?

Was, for example, Mrs. Lockhart living the cooperative life when, unpaid, she brought her "little kit and some tools" either to deliver babies or to prepare bodies for burial? Or the "angel of mercy," who came to the smallpox house to nurse the sick while others whipped their horses to get by faster? Or Mollie Sanford, who was always feeding wanderers? Or the bachelor nursing a neighbor through a long illness? Or the neighbors in North Dakota who walked to one another's farms after severe storms to make sure everyone could get out? Or the boy in Iowa who hunted daily to feed an entire area stricken by a grasshopper plague? Or Mrs. King, who, after caring for her own twelve children, nursed the neighborhood sick, carrying their chamber pots and wet-nursing their babies?

Like exchange work, altruistic acts embodied the techniques of survival. Mollie Sanford once said that she took care of others but also expected others to care for her when she needed help. In this sense charity is individualistic, and its arena may more realistically be called the neighborhood than the community. A neighborhood is a loose collection of people, informal, unofficial, with no binding force over its members. It is reflected in many simple acts like the willingness to stop and talk over the fence. The altruism of the plains farmer, the aesthetics of the cooperative life, may have stopped at the level of neighborhood.

Of course, if there was a community on the plains, individual tensions would rise within it. There is no paucity of evidence for individualism. When John McConnell, for example, distilled from his lifetime on the Illinois prairie a composite pioneer settler, his figure was not cooperative but proud and solitary. This farmer might welcome a stranger, but he would not want him to stay long. "It was but little assistance that he ever required from his neighbors, though no man was ever more willing to render it to others in the hour of need." These were types like Jules Sandoz in Nebraska, egotistical and even antisocial. They were not likely to keep memoirs. But their figures emerge in the accounts of others. They were smudges on the record of community building. When the Wares, dirty but proud, were kindly offered some potatoes to help them over a hard time, they went to the cellar and took a bushel of the biggest and best. The Cogills, when offered chicken feed, took fine seed corn. The Fairchilds once failed to tell a neighbor that he had eaten carbolic acid in their house because they were afraid they would be blamed if he died.

A strong competitive spirit was a boon to individualism and a bane to the furthering of community. "They were always racing in those days," Garland said. Holiday rivalries were perpetuated in the shooting matches and tugs-of-war. At log rollings men struggled to build the largest piles. Harvest crews raced to the ends of the rows. And those who did not win could still tell a tall tale, for the language was peculiarly braced with competitive exaggeration. Behind the bragging was often severe privatization. Some subjects were retained for the individual or family alone, topics into which the community had no entry. Curiously, for example, bedbugs, known to be legion and battled by all, could not be discussed.

The vigorous individualism of the plains farmer has been overemphasized in the annals of the West. But it should not be dismissed. . . . Among pioneers there was a common bond, so ingrained that conformity to it was assumed, and nonconformists were instinctively ostracized. The essence of the bond was endurance, the triumph over a hostile wilderness. Although the end might be a common tie, the beginning was not in the ethics of the group but in the supreme value of the individual.

Walter Prescott Webb claimed that the 100th meridian, symbol of the passage to the Great Plains, shook to the foundation the culture of those who crossed it. In one respect Webb was wrong — the plains did not change the institution of the family. . . . The pattern of frontier family life was remarkably nuclear and similar to patterns elsewhere in the nation. James Davis, for example, in a study of ten thousand pioneer households between 1800 and 1840, found practically no one living alone. Even the few hired hands resided in the households. On the northern plains families were small — at any given time the largest number of children was only one or two, owing to birth control (abstinence), the young age of the couples, and the absence of economic incentives for large families. The pioneer farm family was nuclear in the sense that it was isolated from the community, a separate unit not subject to community controls. Of course, there were exceptions where the family appeared to be intimately linked with the community. In the Dakotas in the earliest days baptisms, weddings, shivarees, and funerals were often community affairs. Weddings in Kansas dugouts often brought so many neighbors that they had to move outside for the feasting and dancing. At Bell's Lake, Iowa, worship was held in homes before the public services, reminiscent of Puritan family prayers, but Bell's Lake was an unusual community with a religious base. Elsewhere most cases of community-oriented families came from the earliest dugout times. In the great thrust of the plains experience "the hearth of the lonely farm" was the center, with otherwise only kin and a few neighborly connections binding people together.

In fact, the family persisted through desperate circumstances. Children sometimes retained the family unit long after parents had died. A seventeen-year-old girl in early Texas, for example, maintained a house of seven brothers and sisters. A sixteen-year-old boy alone supervised two siblings. The community did not intervene in these situations unless the arrangement proved absolutely impossible.

Although often enough denied, social and economic class lines were always evident on the frontier. Some people lived in dugouts, and some in houses of pine boards. There was never any doubt in the mind of Allie Wallace that the Stewarts, who had built the biggest house in the area, were in a "different" category from the Germans and Russians in the neighborhood. She drew her "class" lines by means of the shawls of the immigrant women, their unshapely bodies from bearing babies, and the strict discipline their children received. These were hardly satisfactory guides to class distinctions, but they existed. Class consciousness was blurred, of course, by the proud equality stemming from shared hard-ships.

Still the community of endurance could not last indefinitely. For one thing, it was subject to invasions from outside. Think of land agents, "the wool hat people" as Grace Fairchild called them, filtering into a commu-nity's space. Mrs. Fairchild would give them a bed, meat, potatoes, and "spud varnish" for twenty-five cents, but the presence of these specula-tors did not please her, as if they embodied a vaguely threatening force. Seth Humphrey was playing a similarly invasive role when he came into Nebraska as a mortgage agent. He lodged with farm families but always left fifty cents on the table, symbol of the gulf between them. He noted too that as soon as a house was identified as a foreclosure the settlers quickly stole the movables. The same property was safe for months if the owner was only temporarily away. Humphrey told of a man named George who had combined with a fellow homesteader to build one house squarely across their common section line. Inside the house they dutifully slept and lived each over his own land. But the friend gave up and let the mortgage company foreclose. When Humphrey arrived, George was hitching a team to the house to pull it entirely on his own land. Hum-phrey protested. The man firmly explained, "I'm not touching yours; I'm pulling mine and yours is following." Knowing the climate of opinion, the mortgage man did not interfere. . . .

The environment, the place, inspired a community of hardship, but it also injected a constant dilution of community caused by separation. Even the cooperation of exchanging work and the emotionally warming social events and revivals seemed to be measures of separation rather than cornerstones in community. Altruism, heroic and soul-stirring as it was, remained individualistic, not group-oriented. The family, dominant, vital, clung to itself. Growing class distinctions, especially after the community of hardship was suspended and national economic forces pushed in, worked against unity. Thus the total experience was of limited associations, not genuine community. Grace Snyder's brooding thoughts of death as a child on the Nebraska prairie had foreshadowed the unusual difficulties faced by community on the plains.

STUDY GUIDE

1. According to Frederick Jackson Turner's influential essay, "The Significance of the Frontier in American History," frontier conditions created a strong sense of individualism in the people who lived there. Does Hine's account of the lives of the settlers on the Plains tend to confirm or deny that judgment?

2. What forces bred a spirit of cooperation among settlers on the Plains? Would city-dwellers of the time have more or less reason than these farmers to enter into cooperative arrangements with their neighbors?

3. Hine makes a distinction between cooperation and a true sense of community. What seems to be the essence of the distinction?

4. What did the settlers do for amusement? Which of their amusements were distinctively rural in nature and which would they have shared with people who lived in cities or small towns?

5. According to Hine, there was a conflict between the values of individualism and community on the Plains. Which predominated? Why? How, if at all, would such a conflict have been manifested in an urban setting at the time? How, if at all, is it manifested in American society today?

BIBLIOGRAPHY

Walter Prescott Webb's *The Great Plains* (1931) is still the best general account of the problems the environment created for the early settlers there and how they went about solving them. It can be supplemented by W. Eugene Hollon's more recent *The Great American Desert: Then and Now* (1966). Everett Dick deals with the social history of Plains settlement in *The Sod-House Frontier, 1854–1890* (1947). Fred A. Shannon's *The Farmer's Last Frontier: Agriculture, 1860–1897* (1945) deals with the problems of all American farmers during the period, not just those on the Plains, and provides a good introduction to the farmers' turn to politics, a subject Lawrence Goodwyn takes somewhat further in *Democratic Promise: The Populist Movement in America* (1976).

Other aspects of the westward movement in the postbellum period are discussed in Rodman Wilson Paul, *Mining Frontiers of the Far West, 1848–1880* (1963); Ernest Staples Osgood, *The Day of the Cattlemen* (1929); and Robert R. Dykstra, *The Cattle Towns* (1968). Mark Twain's account of life in western mining camps in *Roughing It* (1903) is very much worth reading not only because of the vivid and accurate picture he paints, but because it remains genuinely funny. Hamlin Garland's stories in *Main-Travelled Roads* (1891) give insights into the inner lives of the Plains settlers that cannot be found in conventional history books. In *Main Street on the Middle Border* (1954), Lewis E. Atherton deals with the social life of American small towns during the period after the Civil War.

II INDUSTRIAL AMERICA

For the American people, the industrialization of our economy was the most significant development of the closing decades of the nineteenth century. The factors that enabled the United States to become the world's leading industrial power were many: a Yankee tradition of trade and commerce that provided both the skill and the capital required for industrial expansion; a commitment to private property and the profit system that gave the Rockefellers, the Morgans, and the Carnegies the incentive to build corporate empires; an abundant and skilled labor supply; political institutions and a constitution that fostered the growth of business and prohibited tariffs within the boundaries of the United States; immense and easily accessible raw materials; excellent transportation facilities; and expanding markets at home and abroad.

The statistics on the growth of industry in the late nineteenth century are awesome — some industries recording a tenfold increase in production within a period of two or three decades. But production figures provide only a small segment of the total picture of a nation being transformed from one of wood and stone to one of steel and concrete.

More interesting, perhaps, is the impact of this process on the social aspects of American life — where Americans lived, how they earned their livelihood, and how they related to one another. In these years, homemade or custom-made clothing gave way to ready-to-wear suits and dresses; horse-drawn transportation gave way to the railroad and later to the automobile; and improved transportation combined with developments in communications to provide enterprising businesspeople with a nationwide market for their products and services.

This section touches upon a number of facets of the Gilded Age, Mark Twain's name for this period of excessive ornamentation and ostentation. The first essay describes life in the growing cities of the United States. The second details the working conditions that existed in one industry. The third examines a specific example of the labor violence that was widespread during the period.

By 1895, New York's Seventh Avenue had street lights and convenient public transportation facilities.

4

ARTHUR M. SCHLESINGER, Sr.

The City in the Gilded Age

In contrast to European cities such as London, Paris, and Rome, which are looked upon as possessing historical and aesthetic worth, American cities have found little favor with intellectuals and have traditionally been considered a source of social problems. Thomas Jefferson warned the nation not to abandon the farm for the town; Henry David Thoreau sought peace and creativity at Walden Pond; and Frederick Jackson Turner, the historian of the American West, located the origins of political democracy and social equalitarianism on the frontier — not in the city. Despite these typically negative assessments of life in the city, Americans have been moving to the city in greater and greater numbers since the eighteenth century. Indeed, as one historian has noted, America was born on the farm and moved to the city.

The movement from the farm to the city was especially great in the closing decades of the nineteenth century. Although the spread of urbanism could be found in all regions of the country, the cities of the East and the Middle West surpassed all others in their rate of growth. New York's population, a million in 1880, burgeoned to a million and a half within ten years. Chicago's population leaped from a half-million in 1880 to more than a million in 1890. Minneapolis and St. Paul, the twin cities, trebled in size in the same period, and other cities in the Middle West — Detroit, Milwaukee, and Cleveland — were not far behind in their rate of growth. Much of this urban growth was a result of two developments: the mechanization of farming and the growth of industry. The first freed many from the time-consuming work on the farm and, at the same time, produced a high volume of farm products to feed the growing multitudes in the city; the second — industrialism — brought job opportunities and wealth to those who were venturesome enough to abandon the countryside for the new metropolitan centers. In addition to the native-born Americans who were rapidly migrating from the farm to the cities of the nation, a tide of "new immigrants" — from southern and eastern Europe — flocked to the cities of America during this period. In 1890, there were as many immigrants as native-born Americans living in Chicago. In that same year, a quarter of the people of Philadelphia were foreign born and a third of the population of Boston were immigrants. In the city of New York, four out of five residents were either of foreign birth or of foreign parentage.

In *The Rise of the City, 1878–1898,* Arthur Meier Schlesinger, Sr., traces the growth of urbanism in American life in the late nineteenth century and the many social, religious, and cultural implications of this phenomenon. The chapter we selected from the Schlesinger volume focuses on the cities' early attempts to provide such essential services as lighting, hygiene, transportation, sanitation, and sewerage for their rapidly increasing populations. The record of the nation in making the city a habitable environment, Schlesinger points out, was by no means a negative one. "No other people," this distinguished historian concludes, "had ever met such an emergency so promptly or, on the whole, so successfully."

In America in the eighties urbanization for the first time became a controlling factor in national life. Just as the plantation was the typical product of the *antebellum* Southern system and the small farm of the Northern agricultural order, so the city was the supreme achievement of the new industrialism. In its confines were focused all the new economic forces: the vast accumulations of capital, the business and financial institutions, the spreading railway yards, the gaunt smoky mills, the white-collar middle classes, the motley wage-earning population. By the same token the city inevitably became the generating center for social and intellectual progress. To dwell in the midst of great affairs is stimulating and broadening; it is the source of a discontent which, if not divine, is at least energizing. In a populous urban community like could find like; the person of ability, starved in his rural isolation, might by going there to find sympathy, encouragement and that criticism which often refines talent into genius.

Moreover the new social needs created by crowded living stimulated inventors to devise mechanical remedies — appliances for better lighting,

From *The Rise of the City, 1878–1898* by Arthur M. Schlesinger, Sr. Reprinted by permission.

for faster communication and transit, for higher buildings — which reacted in a thousand ways on the life of urban folk. Density of population plus wealth concentration also facilitated organized effort for cultivating the life of mind and spirit. In the city were to be found the best schools, the best churches, the best newspapers, and virtually all the bookstores, libraries, art galleries, museums, theaters and opera houses. It is not surprising that the great cultural advances of the time came out of the city, or that its influence should ramify to the farthest countryside. . . .

But the heirs of the older American tradition did not yield the field without a struggle. To them, as to [Thomas] Jefferson, cities were "ulcers on the body politic." In their eyes the city spiritual was offset by the city sinister, civic splendor by civic squalor, urban virtues by urban vices, the city of light by the city of darkness. In politics they sought to preserve or restore their birthright of equality by stoutly belaboring their capitalistic foe embattled in his city fortress; but against the pervasive lure of metropolitan life, felt by their sons and daughters, they could do no better than invent sensational variations of the nursery tale of the country mouse and the city mouse. Urban growth evoked a voluminous literature of bucolic fear, typified by such titles as *The Spider and the Fly; or, Tricks, Traps, and Pitfalls of City Life by One Who Knows* (N.Y., 1873) and J. W. Buel's *Metropolitan Life Unveiled; or the Mysteries and Miseries of America's Great Cities* (St. Louis, 1882). It may be questioned, however, whether such exciting accounts with their smudgy but realistic pictures did more to repel than entice their breathless readers to partake of the life they depicted.

To traveled persons familiar with the distinctive personalities of European centers American cities presented a monotonous sameness. Apart from New York, Boston, Washington, New Orleans and a few other places [James] Bryce believed that "American cities differ from one another only herein, that some of them are built more with brick than with wood, and others more with wood than brick." Most places possessed the same checkerboard arrangement of streets lined with shade trees, the same shops grouped in much the same way, the same middle-class folk hurrying about their business, the same succession of unsightly telegraph poles, the same hotels with seedy men lounging in the dreary lobbies. Few foreign visitors stopped to think, however, that American cities were the handiwork not of many national states but of a fairly uniform continent-wide culture. If they lacked the colorful variety of ancient European foundations, they also lacked the physical inconveniences and discomforts which picturesqueness was apt to entail. But it could not be gainsaid that a tendency toward standardization, as well as toward higher standards, was one of the fruits of American urban development.

While in the European sense there was no single dominant city in America — no city both metropolis and capital — yet all agreed in according the foremost position to New York. Nowhere else were there such fine buildings, such imposing financial houses, such unusual opportunities for business and recreation. No other place had such an air of rush and bustle, the streets constantly being torn up, dug up or blown up. To New York an unending stream of visitors discovered some pretext to go each year; in it many foreign travelers, going no further, found material for pithy, if ill-informed, comments on the whole American scene. "The streets are narrow," wrote on observer in 1883, "and overshadowed as they are by edifices six or more stories in height, seem to be dwarfed into mere alley-ways." At that time the well-populated district did not extend much beyond Fifty-ninth Street; and Madison Square at the intersection of Broadway and Fifth Avenue had recently supplanted Union Square as the nerve center of New York life. But the period of growth and expansion was at hand. The corporate limits, which before 1874 had not reached beyond Manhattan Island, spread rapidly until in 1898, as Greater New York, they embraced Bronx County, Kings County (Brooklyn), Richmond County (Staten Island), and a portion of Queens County (on Long Island).

As earlier, Broadway was the main artery of New York life, lending itself successively to wholesale trade, newspaper and magazine publishing, retail shopping, hotels and theaters, as it wended its way northward from the Battery. Manhattan's other famous thoroughfare, Fifth Avenue, offered a continuous pageant of "palatial hotels, gorgeous club-houses, brownstone mansions and magnificent churches." Different from most American cities, the finest residences stood side by side without relief of lawn or shrubbery; only on the striking but as yet unfinished Riverside Drive, with its noble view of the Hudson, was architecture assisted by nature. Merchant princes and Wall Street millionaires vied with one another to sustain Fifth Avenue's reputation of being the most splendid thoroughfare in America, "a very alderman among streets." During the 1880's a dark brown tide swept up the avenue. The late A. T. Stewart's marble palace at the corner of Thirty-fourth Street, long a magnet for sightseers, was eclipsed by the newer brownstone mansions of the Vanderbilts and others farther up the avenue, inclosed by forbidding iron fences. In the late afternoon Fifth Avenue churned with "a torrent of equipages, returning from the races or the park: broughams, landaus, clarences, phaetons . . . equestrians in boots and corduroys, slim-waisted equestriennes with blue veils floating from tall silk hats.". . .

The New Yorker was already famed for his provincialism: his proud ignorance of the rest of the nation and lofty condescension toward cities of lesser note. Yet foreign tourists found much to interest and detain them in these other centers, and at least one felt a native New Yorker to be "less American than many Westerners born on the banks of the Oder or on the shores of some Scandinavian *fjord*." Boston charmed with the quiet tenor of her life, her atmosphere of intellectuality, her generally

English appearance. With the reclamation of the Back Bay, a great engineering project completed in 1881, the city acquired over a hundred acres of filled land which made possible its expansion southward and the development of straight, wide thoroughfares to Copley Square and beyond.

Even more than Boston, Philadelphia impressed her visitors as a city of homes, with row upon row of prim brick houses with white wooden shutters, owned by their occupants. "If there are few notable buildings, there are few slums." In Washington the traveler found America's most beautiful city, "one of the most singularly handsome cities on the globe." Its parks and wide shaded avenues, its spacious vistas, the dazzling white of its public edifices, were reminiscent of great European capitals. In the absence of an army of factory workers the general tone was one of dignified ease in pleasing contrast to the feverish anxiety typical of other cities. "The inhabitants do not rush onward as though they were late for the train . . . or as though the dinner-hour being past they were anxious to appease an irritable wife. . . . "

Farther to the west lay Chicago, "the most American of American cities, and yet the most mongrel," a miracle city risen Phoenix-like from its great fire of 1871. Its business and shopping district, rivaling New York's in high buildings, noise and impressiveness, was fringed by three residential areas: the north side, its broad streets lined with handsome abodes, churches and club houses overlooking the lake; the south side, a newer and hardly less aristocratic section, studded with stately mansions and spacious parks; and the vast west side, more populous than the other two combined, where dwelt the immigrants and laboring folk. Like every other great city, Chicago offered a study in contrasts: squalor matching splendor, municipal boodle contending with civic spirit; the very air now reeking with the foul stench of the stockyards, now fresh-blown from prairie or lake. A "splendid chaos" indeed, causing the roving [Rudyard] Kipling to exclaim, "Having seen it, I urgently desire never to see it again." . . .

Certain problems growing out of crowded living conditions vexed all municipalities, differing among them in degree rather than in kind. None was more important in 1878 than that of adequate traffic facilities. Even in the major cities streets were ill paved, if paved at all, and in the business sections were apt to be choked with rushing, jostling humanity. "The visitor is kept dodging, halting and shuffling to avoid the passing throng. . . ," asserted one timid contemporary. "The confusing rattle of 'busses and wagons over the granite pavement in Broadway almost drowns his own thoughts, and if he should desire to cross the street a thousand misgivings will assail him . . . although he sees scores of men and women constantly passing through the moving line of vehicles. . . . " Cobblestones and granite blocks were the favorite paving materials in the

East because of their local availability, just as wood blocks were in the Middle West. . . .

In . . . twenty years the streets of America were greatly improved, though the civic conscience did not regard it essential that good streets should be kept clean. By the end of the century Washington and Buffalo had become the best-paved cities in the world while Boston and the borough of Manhattan in New York were not far behind. Chicago remained the Cinderella of great American municipalities, closely rivaled by Baltimore. In 1890 only 629 of Chicago's 2048 miles of streets were paved at all, about half with wood block, the rest with macadam, gravel, stone block, asphalt, cinders or cobblestones. Despite the civic lift given by the World's Fair of 1893 the situation was but little better at the close of the decade.

Since most large cities were intersected by waterways, the needs of rapidly growing municipalities required an adequate system of bridges. The problem appeared in its most acute form in New York where hordes of people must cross over each day to their places of work on Manhattan Island. . . .

When finished, Brooklyn Bridge was the longest suspension bridge in the world. The formal opening on May 24 [1883] was attended by President [Chester A.] Arthur and his cabinet, the governors of nearby states and many other distinguished persons. The only discordant note in the chorus of rejoicing came from Hibernian New Yorkers who denounced the choice of Queen Victoria's birthday for the grand occasion. Majestic in the sweep of its great cables from tower to tower, the completed structure was over a mile long, with a central river span of nearly sixteen hundred feet and a passageway wide enough for two rail lines, two double carriage lanes and a footpath.

Though the traffic relief was considerable it was not sufficient. Between 1886 and 1889 Washington Bridge was built over the Harlem River, its two great steel arches each over five hundred feet in span, and in 1896 a second bridge, the Williamsburg, was begun to link Brooklyn and New York. Other cities wrestled with the same problem. Thus Pittsburgh built the Seventh Street suspension bridge over the Allegheny River in 1884, Philadelphia completed a cantilever bridge carrying Market Street over the Schuylkill two years later, and Richmond, Indiana, spanned the Whitewater River with a suspension bridge in 1889.

Horse cars, omnibuses, cabs and other similar vehicles had suited the needs of simpler days, but the age of the great city called for swifter conveyance. The old "bobtail" cars, modeled on the stagecoach and pulled by horses or mules, did not suffice for moving an enormous mass of people to and from their places of work at about the same hours of the day. Already New York had shown the utility of an overhead railway, four-car trains being drawn by diminutive steam locomotives which scattered oil and live ashes on the heads of unwary pedestrians. . . . Kansas City also elevated some of her tracks in the mid-eighties, and Brooklyn built an extensive system the same decade. But Chicago did not open her first line until 1892, and Boston, which meantime had begun to burrow underground, not until 1901.

The slow adoption of the overhead system was due partly to its ugliness and noise, but even more to the initial cost of construction. Of greater popularity in the eighties was the cable car, first contrived by a Scotch immigrant, Andrew S. Hallidie, in 1873 to solve the problem of transit over the hilly streets of San Francisco. The car moved by means of a grappling device which descended from the floor to an endless steel cable moving in a slotted trench between the tracks. After a few years the system was taken over by cities which lacked San Francisco's peculiar need. In 1882 Charles T. Yerkes laid a cable road in Chicago, achieving not only a success for the city but a fortune for himself. Philadelphia followed the next year and New York in 1886. By the mid-nineties Eastern cities had one hundred and fifty-seven miles in operation, the Middle West two hundred and fifty-two, the Far West two hundred and seventeen and the South six.

While the cable system was yet in its heyday, this generation made its most substantial contribution toward solving the problem of urban transit. For many years — at least since 1835 — inventors in America and abroad had been working on the idea of an electrical railway. Until the development of a practicable dynamo in the 1870s, however, they had been baffled by the lack of an adequate supply of cheap current. The 1880s saw the launching of trial lines at points as far removed as Boston and Denver, but the credit for the first American electric railway successfully operated for profit over city streets belongs to Lieutenant Frank J. Sprague. In 1887–1888 he installed two and half miles of track in Richmond, Virginia, the cars securing their current from an overhead trolley wire fed from a central power house.

Its instant success started a veritable revolution in urban transit. Not only were electric-propelled cars fast and comfortable but they were relatively cheap to construct and maintain. Fifty-one cities installed the new system by 1890, and five years later eight hundred and fifty lines were in operation, mostly in the East and Middle West, with a total mileage of ten thousand. Though horse and cable cars lingered on many streets, their doom was sealed. European cities lagged far behind those of America in adopting electric transit. At the close of the century Germany, with a trackage as great as all other European countries combined, possessed only one ninth the mileage of the United States.

Traffic congestion, however, kept even pace with the new facilities for dealing with it. The tangled situation in down-town Boston, whose narrow crooked streets exemplified the old adage that one good turn deserves another, led to the final effort of this generation. Taking a leaf from the experience of London and Budapest, Boston between 1895 and 1897 constructed a subway line a mile and a half long under Tremont Street. It was a notable engineering feat costing the city four and a quarter million dollars. Plans were at once made for extensions, and New York, as was fitting, projected a much more ambitious tunnel system which, however, did not open to the public until 1904. Except for the last two instances, the varied and heroic endeavors made during these twenty years to clear the city streets were all carried out under private auspices.

Hardly less urgent than the need for better transit was the need for readier communication. In 1878 the recently invented telephone was hardly more than a scientific toy. To use it a person, after briskly turning a crank, screamed into a crude mouthpiece and then, if the satanic screechings and groanings of static permitted, faintly heard the return message. There was no central exchange station, telephone users being directly connected with one another by separate wires. Besides these disadvantages the sheer novelty of Bell's miracle made it unpopular. People felt "a sense of oddity, almost of foolishness," in using the instrument. "The dignity of talking consists in having a listener and there seems a kind of absurdity in addressing a piece of iron. . . . " For a number of years [Alexander Graham] Bell traveled about the country exhibiting his invention. On one such trip he offered Mark Twain stock in the enterprise at twenty-five, but that usually gullible humorist "didn't want it at any price," though before the year was out he put up the first telephone wire in Hartford, Connecticut, connecting his home with the *Courant* office. . . .

In 1880 eighty-five towns had telephone exchanges with nearly fifty thousand subscribers and about thirty-five thousand miles of wire. Ten years later the number of subscribers had grown fivefold and the wire mileage sevenfold. From the first intercity line joining Boston and Lowell in 1879, the reach of the telephone grew constantly greater until by 1892 Boston and New York were talking with Washington, Pittsburgh, Chicago and Milwaukee and a few years later with Omaha. And presidential candidate [William] McKinley sat in his home at Canton, Ohio, and talked with his campaign managers in thirty-eight states. When in 1893 the patents owned by the Bell Company expired, many independent companies sprang up, especially in the smaller towns of the Middle West where the Bell system had not found it worthwhile to extend its service.

Nearly eight hundred thousand phones were in use by 1900, one for every ninety-five persons as compared with one for every nine hundred and twenty-three twenty years before; the United States had twice as many telephones as all Europe. In two decades Bell's invention had, from a mechanical curiosity, become a necessity of American life. That it added to the speed of living and the breaking down of personal privacy cannot be doubted. That it helped make the American people the most talkative nation in the world is likewise clear. On the credit side of the ledger, however, must be put the enormous gains resulting from the facilitation of social and business intercourse and from the extension of urban influences into areas of rural isolation.

Largely because of the greater utility of the telephone the telegraph expanded slowly during these years. In 1874 [Thomas Alva] Edison had doubled the carrying capacity of the wires by his invention of quadruplex telegraphy, which allowed two messages to be sent simultaneously from opposite ends of the same line. Actual wire mileage, however, grew but fourfold between 1878 and 1898. By the mid-nineties only one telegram per person per year was being sent in the United States while the people were using the telephone ten times as much. The telephone far outstripped its elder sister even for long-distance use; only in submarine communication did the telegraph continue to reign unchallenged. In the closing years of the decade, however, new vistas opened for it in a field in which it was thought the telephone could never compete. This was wireless telegraphy, the invention in 1896 of Guglielmo Marconi, an Italian engineer. Still in the experimental stage, the chief use of "wireless" before the coming of the new century was for ocean vessels. . . .

Improved lighting was almost as great a necessity as improved communication, for the new conditions of city life required something better than the dim rays shed from gas lamp-posts on the streets and the yellow glow of kerosene lamps or open-flame gas jets indoors. For years inventors in many countries had been seeking to harness electricity to the service of illumination, but success, as in the case of the trolley car had to await the development of the modern dynamo. Though the Russian engineer, Paul Jablochkoff, in 1876 devised an arc lamp which was used with some success to light the boulevards of Paris, his achievement was quickly eclipsed by the ingenuity of Charles F. Brush, a young Ohio engineer, who in 1879 illuminated the public squares of Cleveland, Ohio, by means of a system which could maintain sixteen arc lamps on a single wire. The superiority of the new device won immediate public favor. Soon the hissing, sputtering noise of the carbons and the brilliant glare of the lamp were familiar sights on American city streets, San Francisco leading the way by setting up a central power plant the same year as the Cleveland trial. The Brush system quickly spread across the Atlantic and presently, too, to the cities of Japan and China.

Satisfactory as was the arc lamp for outdoors it proved of little use for interior illumination. For this purpose some method had to be found of minutely subdividing the electric current so as to produce lights corresponding to gas jets in size and cheapness. Inventors on both sides of the Atlantic labored at the problem; but success came first to Thomas A. Edison, whose wizardry in the domain of electricity was already presaged by his improvements on the telegraph and the telephone. Edison was at this time thirty-two years old, "a pleasant looking man of average size . . . with dark hair slightly silvered, and wonderfully piercing gray eyes," who was apt to be found "with acid-stained garments, dusty eyebrows, discolored hands and dishevelled hair." Since 1876 he had been conducting his experiments in a great laboratory at Menlo Park, New Jersey; but this establishment had been acquired only after years as a tramp telegrapher and mechanical tinker had led him by devious paths from his native town of Milan, Ohio, to Boston and New York, where his inventions won generous financial backing.

The problem of incandescent lighting quickly reduced itself, in Edison's mind, to finding a suitable filament which, when sealed in a vacuum bulb, would burn more than a few hours. . . . His incandescent lamp was patented in January 27, 1880. It not only gave a steadier, cooler and brighter light than gas, but he had also solved the problem of switching lamps off without affecting others on the same circuit.

The public gazed with wonder at the new illuminant in Edison's show-room at 65 Fifth Avenue. In 1882 central lighting stations were erected in London and New York. Perhaps no mechanical invention ever spread so swiftly over the world. The new light first entered American homes at the residence of J. Hood Wright in New York; it began to burn in American hotels at the Blue Mountain House in the Adirondacks; it first appeared in a theater when six hundred and fifty bulbs lighted up a performance of Gilbert and Sullivan's opera "Iolanthe" at the Bijou in Boston on December 12, 1882. The number of central electric stations for all purposes — incandescent and arc lighting, traction power, etc. — rose from thirty-eight in 1882 to nearly six hundred in 1888 and to approximately three thousand in 1898. . . .

Improved lighting not only dispelled much of the darkness of urban night life but also many of its dangers. By helping erase the difference between day and night it lengthened the working hours for the intellectual toilers, made possible continuous operation of factories and, at the same time, gave an enormous stimulus to after-dark amusements and the theater. Better illumination also meant less eye strain, though this advantage may have been offset by the constant temptation to overwork on the part of the studious. The vastly increased productivity of mind and mill in this period owes more than has ever been recognized to the services of Brush, Edison and [Carl Auer von] Welsbach.

Municipalities were less successful in coping with the problem of waste elimination. Since the middle of the century and earlier, places like New York, Boston and Chicago had had public underground conduits for discharging sewage into near-by bodies of water. But their facilities lagged behind the growth of population and most other cities employed village methods of surface-draining their streets and of using private vaults and cesspools for family wastes. In 1877 Philadelphia had eighty-two thousand such vaults and cesspools, Washington fifty-six thousand and Chicago, despite its sewerage system, thirty thousand. Two years later a noted sanitary engineer called proper sewage disposal "the great unanswered question of the day." Its solution involved grave problems of community health, for dense populations made private uncleanliness increasingly a public concern.

In the two decades following, however, sewerage facilities were greatly extended, while important improvements were effected in sewer construction and in methods of ultimate disposal. This last problem was an especially difficult one. Cities with water fronts usually discharged their sewage into sea or river with always a danger of water pollution, especially where there was a tidal backwash; elsewhere filter beds and farm irrigation systems were commonly used. Progress was very uneven. While Boston and Washington spent millions in improving their sewerage works during these years, Philadelphia and St. Louis had at the close of the period little more than half as great a mileage of sewers as of streets, and Baltimore, New Orleans and Mobile continued to rely for drainage mainly on open gutters. The allied problem of garbage disposal was taken care of hardly better. In New York, Boston and other ports such matter was carried in scows and barges several miles out to sea and discharged upon an outgoing tide. A common practice in inland towns was to contract for its collection by farmers who fed it to swine. Since animals so fed were subject to trichinae, with a consequent danger to meat eaters, after 1885 furnaces began to be introduced, especially in Middle Western cities, for the reduction of garbage by fire.

The growing volume of urban wastes complicated the problem of a potable water system. This generation, however, gave less heed to the quality of the water than to its quantity. Only about six hundred cities had public waterworks in 1878, but in the next two decades their number grew nearly sixfold. At the same time some of the greater cities enlarged their existing facilities. Thus between 1885 and 1892 New York, at a cost of twenty-four million dollars, constructed the New Croton Aqueduct with a carrying capacity of nearly three hundred million gallons a day.

Gradually, however, as a result of European example and the advance of the germ theory of disease, attention was also given to the purity of the water. The Massachusetts board of health in 1886 was granted by law general oversight of all inland waters of the state with power to advise municipal authorities in regard to water supply, sewage disposal and methods of preventing pollution. Within the next few years careful investigations were also made by the state health boards of Connecticut, Minnesota, New Jersey, New York, Ohio and Rhode Island. Cities differed greatly as to the purity of their water supplies, and public-health guardians were not slow in pointing out corresponding differences as to mortality from typhoid fever. Between 1880 and 1890 about half as many people proportionately died of typhoid fever in New York and Boston, where the water was comparatively pure, as in Philadelphia and Chicago, where the supply was contaminated. Pollution by sewage and manufacturers' wastes was especially serious in the case of cities drawing their water from rivers or other natural sources.

The activity in developing municipal water plants was in part caused by the greatly increased fire risks which resulted from the crowding together of buildings and the extensive use of electric wiring. This generation was resolved to have no such conflagrations as those of Chicago and Boston in the early seventies. Though they succeeded in this aim, scarcely a year passed without one or more million-dollar fires and the waste of thousands of lives. The estimated total fire losses in 1878 were over sixty-four million dollars. In 1883 they passed permanently beyond the hundred-million-dollar mark and in 1892 and 1893 rose above one hundred and fifty million.

That the situation was no worse was due to the new methods devised for combating the danger. While small towns and the more backward cities still clung to the volunteer system of fire fighting, with sometimes a nucleus of professional firemen, the large places possessed full-time paid departments, though Philadelphia's dated only from 1871 and St. Paul did not have one until ten years later. With more efficient organization appeared improved apparatus and equipment. Swinging harness for hitching the horses to the fire wagons came into use in the seventies, as did also the fire boat, the fire-alarm signal box and the water tower. In the next decade chemical engines were introduced in Chicago, Milwaukee, Springfield, Ohio, and elsewhere. The invention of the Grinnell automatic fire sprinkler in 1877, added to the widening use of fire-resistant building materials — concrete, terra cotta, brick, steel, asbestos — helped further to reduce fire hazards, particularly in factories and office buildings. Though wide differences continued to exist among cities, the fire departments in general compared favorably with those of any other country. Chicago, for example, had twice as many men and horses and half again as many steam fire engines as London, a city three times as populous.

Conditions of lodging varied as widely as types of people and differences in income. For well-to-do transients the great cities offered hotels constantly increasing in number, size and sumptuousness. . . .

Such hotels, gorgeously decorated and furnished, with a steadily diminishing emphasis on the "steamboat style," made a special appeal with their private baths, electric elevators, electric-call service and other up-to-the-minute conveniences. Though the incessant "tinkle, tinkle, tinkle, of the ice-pitcher" proved "positively nauseous" to the British compiler of *Baedeker,* he otherwise thought well of the American institution and had even a word of praise and commiseration for that "mannerless despot," the hotel clerk. Every large city also had hotels of second and third class or no class at all, falling as low in New York as lodging places in Chatham Street (now Park Row) and the Bowery where one could secure sleeping space for a few pennies a night. In general, hotels in the South were apt to be poorer than in any other section, while in the West, even in the newer towns, they were unexpectedly good. . . .

In contrast to this agreeable picture must be placed another, that of the living conditions of the less prosperous classes and particularly of the immigrants. Of the great cities of the land Philadelphia and Chicago were least scarred by slums. Boston, Cincinnati, Jersey City and Hartford had badly diseased spots, but the evil was most deeply rooted in New York City, where land rentals were highest and the pressure of immigrants strongest. In all Europe only one city district, in Prague, was half as congested as certain parts of Manhattan. Bad as conditions had been earlier in New York, they became worse in 1879 with the advent of a new type of slum, the "dumbbell" tenement, so called because of the outline of the floor plan. This became virtually the only kind erected there in the next two decades.

Five or six stories high, the bleak narrow structure ran ninety feet back from the street, being pierced through the center by a stygian hallway less than three feet wide. Each floor was honeycombed with rooms, many without direct light or air and most of them sheltering one or more families. Almost at once such barracks became foul and grimy, infested with vermin and lacking privacy and proper sanitary conveniences. The sunless, ill-smelling air shafts at the sides of the building proved a positive menace during fires by insuring the rapid spread of flames. In rooms and hallways, on stairs and fire escapes, in the narrow streets, dirty half-clad children roamed at will, imbibing soiled thoughts from their soiled surroundings. The dense slum district bounded by Cherry, Catherine, Hamilton and Market streets was known as "lung block" because of the many deaths from tuberculosis. No wonder such rookeries were nurseries of immorality, drunkenness, disease and crime. The real surprise is, as the state tenement-house commission pointed out in 1900, that so many of the children grew up to be decent, self-respecting citizens. . . .

Remedial legislation, following the first tenement-house statute of 1867, was passed in 1879, 1887 and 1895. But in spite of the reformers the laws contained loopholes and enforcement was sporadic. The tenement-house commission of 1900 felt that, on the whole, conditions were worse than they had been fifty years before. Yet one year later a comprehensive statute was adopted which showed that the humanitarian energies of this generation had not been spent in vain. The act of 1901 not only insured real housing reform in New York, but prompted other states and municipalities to a fundamental attack on the evil. . . .

Criminologists and publicists pointed with alarm to the portentous increase of lawlessness in the United States. A census inquiry disclosed a fifty-percent rise in the number of prison inmates from 1880 to 1890. . . .

Yet it seemed to an acute observer like James Bryce that the Americans were at bottom a law-abiding people. Indeed, in the absence of adequate data for earlier periods, it is possible that crime, being mainly concentrated in the cities, had become merely more conspicuous rather than greater in volume. However this may be, all agreed that the evil was accentuated by lax law enforcement. The official guardians of society only too often were in league with the antisocial elements, passively or actively. In most large centers a crook could secure police "protection" provided he agreed to hunt his prey elsewhere or, if operating locally, to share his profits with the authorities. It was the opinion of the widely experienced Josiah Flynt that, from Maine to California, the aim of police departments was merely "to keep a city superficially clean, and to keep everything quiet that is likely to arouse the public to an investigation." Beyond that point they felt no genuine concern. . . .

If we consider only the sordid aspects of urban life the American city of the period seems a cancerous growth. But the record as a whole was distinctly creditable to a generation which found itself confronted with the phenomenon of a great population everywhere clotting into towns. No other people had ever met such an emergency so promptly or, on the whole, so successfully. The basic facilities of urban living — transit, lighting and communication — were well taken care of by an outburst of native mechanical genius which helped make these years the Golden Age of Invention. Some places moved forward faster than others, of course, and all lagged in some respects while advancing in others. If the rural spirit of neighborliness was submerged in the anonymity of city life, there developed in its place a spirit of impersonal social responsibility which devoted itself, with varying earnestness and success, to questions of pure water, sewage disposal and decent housing for the poor, sometimes taking the extreme form of municipal ownership. Moreover, what the great cities felt obliged to do under the whip of necessity, smaller towns undertook in a spirit of imitation, so that the new standards affected urban life everywhere. What most impresses the historical student is the lack of unity, balance, planfulness, in the advances that were made. Urban progress was experimental, uneven, often accidental: the people were, as yet, groping in the dark. A later generation, taking stock of the past and profiting by its mistakes, would explore the possibilities of ordered city planning, not only in the interests of material welfare and community health but also with an eye to beautification.

STUDY GUIDE

1. Do you agree with the author that there is an "agrarian bias" — a prejudice in favor of the country over the city — in American thought? Does

this bias show itself in our contemporary culture? What is your evidence one way or the other?

2. How do you account for the differences that Schlesinger appears to have found among various cities? To what degree are these variations a result of: (a) historical factors; (b) economic conditions; (c) geography; and (d) ethnic factors?

3. Schlesinger appears to feel that the cities, on the whole, made good progress in finding solutions to a number of the problems that confronted them. Consider the following problems and rank them from 1 to 6 according to how successfully each was dealt with in the cities: (a) housing; (b) transportation; (c) lighting; (d) communication; (e) sanitation; and (f) crime. Would you agree that problems that lent themselves to material solutions were more easily solved than those requiring alterations in human behavior?

4. How many of the problems (a) to (f) just listed have been completely solved today? Is it possible to find final solutions to these problems? How would you grade our recent performance in comparison to accomplishments of the American people in the period described by Schlesinger?

BIBLIOGRAPHY

The urbanization of the United States and American attitudes toward the city are the subjects of a large number of books on American history. Morton and Lucia White, *The Intellectual Versus the City* (1962) is an excellent survey of antiurbanism, or the "agrarian bias," in American thought. A very scholarly and detailed study of the city in late-nineteenth-century America is Blake McKelvey, *The Urbanization of America, 1860–1915* (1963). *Streetcar Suburbs: The Process of Growth in Boston, 1870–1900* (1969), by Sam Bass Warner, Jr., is a pathbreaking analysis of an important development in this period — the emergence of the suburb as a response to the new forms of urban and interurban transportation. For those interested in the impact of the city on the religious life of the nation, the introductory chapter in *The Church and the City* (1967), edited by Robert Cross, is well worth reading. The impact of the city on our nation's political life is the subject of Carl Degler, "American Political Parties and the Rise of the City: An Interpretation" in *The Journal of American History*, Vol. LI (June 1964), pp. 41–59. Two other general books on urbanism may be of interest: Charles N. Glaab and A. Theodore Brown, *A History of Urban America* (1967), which includes a bibliography on the subject, and Zane L. Miller, *The Urbanization of Modern America* (1973), which is similar to Glaab and Brown's book but restricted to recent times.

Women and children were a large part of the labor force in Southern textile mills.

5

JACQUELYN DOWD HALL, JAMES LELOUDIS,
ROBERT KORSTAD, MARY MURPHY, LU ANN
JONES, AND CHRISTOPHER B. DALY

Labor in the Gilded Age

There can be no doubt that the industrialization of the United States established the foundations for economic expansion, prosperity, and a standard of living higher than Americans had enjoyed in the past and higher, too, than the inhabitants of practically any other country in the world. But there was a price to be paid for these advances. Many of the fruits of industrialization took some time to become fully ripe and could only be enjoyed in the long run. In the short run, the process often led to social dislocation, confusion, conflict, and a great deal of misery.

The growing industrial labor force, or substantial portions of it, was one group that paid the price of industrialization. Largely without the protection that unions and labor legislation would later provide, industrial workers in the late nineteenth century were overworked, underpaid, routinely subjected to dangerous or unhealthy working conditions, frequently laid off without warning, and compensated little or not at all for such layoffs or for any accidents they suffered or diseases they contracted as a result of the conditions under which they worked. All of this helped to keep labor costs low and profits high. It can reasonably be suggested that America's industrial might was built not only upon the labor of its workers, but also upon their suffering.

Despite this, America's industries continued to attract workers. Beginning in the late nineteenth century, many of them came from Europe. An even larger reservoir of industrial labor, however, was made up of native-born Americans pushed off farms by the declining economic rewards to be found in agriculture and attracted by the prospect of the more or less steady pay to be had in industry. This was particularly true in the South, where the textile industry began to grow in the late nineteenth century. There were almost no immigrants to draw on to supply the mills' needs for workers, but there was a ready supply of rural folk willing to give up farming for "public work," as the early mill workers termed it. As the following selection by Jacquelyn Dowd Hall, et al. indicates, after a while, many began to doubt the wisdom of their choice, but by that time, it was too late to return to the agricultural way of life they had left. More important, it may well have been that they had had no real choice in the first place, having been driven into the mills by sheer economic necessity.

First-generation workers in southern mills had more to learn than just the mechanics of a new job. On the farm they had chosen and ordered their tasks according to their needs and the demands of their crops. Now they drove themselves to the continuous pace of a machine. Whereas most men, women, and children had once worked together and enjoyed the fruits of their own labor, now they were "hands," working under a boss's orders and for someone else's profit. Farm work, to be sure, had been hard, but mill work took a different toll. Millhands rose early in the morning, still tired from the day before. For ten, eleven, or twelve hours they walked, stretched, leaned, and pulled at their machines. Noise, heat, and humidity engulfed them. The lint that settled on their hair and skin marked them as mill workers, and the cotton dust that silently entered their lungs could eventually cripple or kill them. At best, mill work was a wrenching change.

Chester Copeland came from a long line of farmers and carpenters in rural Orange County, North Carolina, and he remained a devoted farmer except for brief, and unhappy, sojourns in the mills. To him, mill work was "nothing but a robot life. Robot-ing is my word for it — in the mill you do the same thing over and over again — just like on a treadmill. There's no challenge to it — just drudgery. The more you do, the more they want done. But in farming you do work real close to nature. There's

From *Like a Family: The Making of a Southern Cotton Mill World*, by Jacquelyn Dowd Hall, James Leloudis, Robert Korstad, Mary Murphy, Lu Ann Jones, and Christopher B. Daly. Copyright © 1987 by The University of North Carolina Press. Reprinted by permission. References have been omitted.

always something exciting and changing in nature. It's never a boring job. There's some dirty jobs in farming, but there's nothing you get more pleasure out of than planting, growing, and then harvesting. In other words, you get the four seasons just like there are in a person's life — the fall and winter and spring and summer."

Despite this loss of control, most workers stayed with the factory because it provided a steady income and the work seemed easier than farming, at least to some. Forrest Lacock found farming "a very satisfactory job — you've got no boss man." "But," he continued, "the trouble with what we call one-horse farming, you can't have an income sufficient to take care of all your bills. A public job is more interesting because you can meet your bills." Dewey Helms's father had another reason for coming to the mill. "He wasn't worried about the income he made on the farm; he made as much as he cared about. He wanted to get rid of the harder work. Working in the cotton mill was not as hard work as running one of them mountain farms." Mill work was not for everybody, but the majority of those who came to the factories "never did want to live on the farm no more. They learned how to work in the mill."

Reliance on the family labor system meant that the southern textile industry's growth was based to a large extent on the labor of children. Between 1880 and 1910 manufacturers reported that about one-quarter of their work force was under sixteen years of age, and many more child workers went unreported. Indeed, in the industry's early years, youngsters of seven or eight commonly doffed, spun, and did all sorts of casual labor. Originally the official definition of "children" applied to youngsters up to age eight but later rose to age twelve, then fourteen, and finally sixteen; nevertheless, young people remained crucial, both to the industry's profit margins and to their own families' survival.

Child labor was by no means unique to the South. The textile industry, wherever established, tended to rely on the labor of women and children. But the technical breakthroughs that enabled the South to enter and eventually capture the market in cotton goods also encouraged a particularly intense exploitation of the young. Women and children led the first wave of migrants to the region's mills, and manufacturers matched them with the low-skill jobs created by the advent of ring spinning. A study of women and children laborers conducted by the U.S. Bureau of Labor in 1907–8 found that half the spinners were under fourteen and 90 percent were under twenty-one. As Naomi Trammel put it, "That's where they put the children. You could run a frame where you couldn't run anything else."

Technology made child labor practical, but not necessary. The practice spread primarily as a solution to problems of labor recruitment and as a system of socializing and controlling a prospective labor force. South

Carolina industrialist William Gregg, founder of Graniteville, the Old South's premier cotton mill, had hoped to attract the daughters of impoverished farmers. Young single women failed to show up in large numbers, but Gregg continued to believe that the "large class of miserable poor white people among us . . . might be induced to place their children in a situation in which they would be educated and reared in industrious habits." His words captured the industry rationale: children made up a large portion of the surplus labor in the countryside; the lure of wages for everyone in the family could induce hard-pressed farmers to cast their lot with the mills; and children who went to work at an early age would eventually grow into efficient, tractable, long-term workers.

Critics of child labor were not hard to find. In the 1880s and 1890s the opposition was led by the Knights of Labor and the National Union of Textile Workers (NUTW), who complained that the low wages paid to children held down the earnings of adults. But after the turn of the century a new group of middle-class social reformers took up the banner of the child labor crusade. Educational and religious leaders such as Alabama's Edgar Gardner Murphy and North Carolina's Alexander J. McKelway organized opposition at the state level and then helped form the National Child Labor Committee (NCLC). These reformers worried that the mills' unlettered children would one day become a blight on the body politic. "In a democracy," McKelway argued, "the people all rule. Also, the people are ruled. And when it comes to the people's ruling us by their votes, electing our governors and presidents, initiating and vetoing legislation, taxing our incomes, we grow mightily concerned over the intelligence and independence of the electorate. We do not like to trust our interests now and the lives and fortunes of our children to a mass of voters who have been deprived of all opportunity for an education . . . who have been embittered by the robbery of their childhood, who are the material for the agitator, and the prey of the demagogue."

Mill men themselves were divided on the issue of child labor. Some firmly believed that hard work, commencing at a young age, was the best education available. Others championed the practice as a necessary evil in the natural progress of society. Daniel Augustus Tompkins traced the problem to the poverty caused by the Civil War, particularly to the resultant lack of educational opportunities. "In the absence of schools, the discipline of the mill and its training down to twelve years of age is much better for children than idleness and no discipline or training. . . . It would be far better to have ample school facilities and compel all children to go to school ten months in the year, and give them the other two months for vacations and recreation. But in the absence of such facilities, the discipline and training of the mill is best for the children of working people." Whatever the personal feelings of mill men, their duties to their stockholders demanded that they oppose restrictions on the employment of children. The fact of the matter, as the president of the American Cotton Manufacturers Association admitted to McKelway, was that without the labor of boys and girls under the age of fourteen, Piedmont mills simply could not operate.

Bit by bit, reformers chipped away at the opposition. By 1913 North Carolina, South Carolina, Alabama, and Georgia had laws that prohibited the employment of children under twelve and restricted the hours of labor for those below fourteen. Exemptions and lack of enforcement, however, enfeebled state regulations. The 1907–8 Bureau of Labor study found that an astounding 92 percent of the mills in South Carolina and 75 percent of those in North Carolina ignored child labor regulations. Flora McKinney's boss was one of those who paid little attention to the law. Her family moved to Lando, South Carolina, when she was nine or ten, and she soon followed her father into the mill. "When I got old enough, well, I really weren't old enough, but they'd take children to work then. We were supposed to be twelve years old before we could go to work, but I've hid from inspectors a lots of times. They'd come through and the section in front of us would send word to hide the kids, and we'd run to the water house. Then we'd all cram in there 'til they left."

Given the inadequacy of state legislation, members of the NCLC felt the need for federal action. To mobilize public opinion against child labor, the NCLC devised a highly effective propaganda campaign. Key to this effort were the photographs of Lewis Hine, which poignantly revealed the youthfulness of southern workers. Hine's images — of little girls dressed in long skirts and aprons and little boys wearing their workingmen's caps and suspenders, all swallowed up in rows of towering machines — became the crusade's symbols of the worst evils of industrialization. The NCLC convinced the public and members of Congress that the employment of children had to be stopped. In 1916 President Woodrow Wilson signed the Keating-Owen Child Labor bill to achieve that end.

Adamantly opposed to federal intervention, which might open the way to other protective laws and undermine their competitive advantage over the North, southern industrialists fought back. When federal child labor legislation was first suggested, David Clark, editor of the *Southern Textile Bulletin,* organized mill owner opposition. The son of Walter Clark, who was chief justice of the North Carolina Supreme Court and one of the South's most liberal jurists, David Clark seemed an unlikely opponent of progressive reform. But as a young man, Clark embarked on a course quite different from his father's. After earning degrees in civil and mechanical engineering from the North Carolina College of Agriculture and Mechanic Arts and Cornell University in the late 1890s, David entered the textile business, first as a mill designer and later as an investor. When his own mill failed in 1907, he turned to textile journalism. As founder and editor of the *Southern Textile Bulletin*, Clark gained a reputation as "a volunteer spokesman for an ultra-conservative philosophy in business and education matters" and "a stirrer-upper of no mean proportions." Shortly after passage of the Keating-Owen bill, he arranged to test the constitutionality of the law. At Clark's behest, a Charlotte mill worker — perhaps fearful of losing his job, his children's earnings, or a combination of the two — petitioned the courts to restrain a local mill from discharging his two underage sons. A federal judge agreed that the law violated the rights of the worker, and a year later the Supreme Court concurred. The child labor law was dead.

Despite this setback, child labor gradually did decline, largely in response to changes in the industry and the growing supply of adult workers. The trend toward finer yarns, the integration of yarn spinning with cloth-weaving operations that required more strength and skill, and the technological advances of the 1920s all worked against the practice. By World War I the number of children under sixteen employed in the Carolinas had decreased to 6 percent of the total work force, almost the level in the leading New England textile states. Yet until 1938, when the federal Fair Labor Standards Act outlawed employment of children under sixteen, many southern industrialists skirted the law so as to make use of the mill village's young, and captive, work force.

Child labor involved more, however, than the exploitation of youth. There were stories behind the expressions captured on film by Lewis Hine, stories that fit neither the rationalizations of mill owners nor the fears of reformers. Mill work was a source of pride as well as pain, of fun as much as suffering; and children made choices, however hedged about by their parents' authority and their bosses' power.

For mill children, life was paced from the outset by the ringing of the factory bell. Working women, who often had to return to their jobs within a few weeks of childbirth, adapted their nursing schedule to breaks in the workday. "People used to go out," recalled Ada Mae Wilson. "They didn't have bottle babies like they do now. They nursed the breast. A lot healthier children. You'd come out at nine o'clock, and then at twelve you'd come home for lunch. And then at three they'd let you come back, and then you'd be off at six." If labor was scarce, a woman who had neither relatives nor older children at home might take her baby to the mill. Jessie Lee Carter had a neighbor with a nursing baby who would "take a quilt and lay that baby in her roping box while she worked. And she'd bring her baby down and keep it in the mill all day long."

As children got older, the mill was like a magnet, attracting their youthful curiosity and, all too soon, their labor. Until the 1920s no barbed wire fences, locked gates, or bricked-in windows separated the factory from the village. Children could easily wander in and out of the mill, and their first "work" might be indistinguishable from play. After school and in the summers, Emma Williams accompanied her mother to the mill. "I'm sure I didn't work for the money. I just wanted to work, I reckon. Oodles of kids. All of us used to do it together. [We] didn't do much, and it was real fun. I guess maybe one reason that it was fun was because that was the only time we got with other children. When we stayed home, well, we stayed home."

Most children first learned about factory labor when they tagged along with a parent or sibling, carried hot meals to the mill at dinnertime, or stopped by after school. But this casual contact had serious consequences, for on such visits relatives began teaching children the skills they would need when they were old enough for jobs of their own. Ethel Faucette carried lunch to her sister. "While she was eating," Faucette explained, "I learned how to work her job. I was already learned when I went to work." Geddes Dodson's father gave him specific chores during his daily visits. "When I was a little fellow, my daddy was a-working in the Poinsett Mill. He was a loom fixer. He'd run the weavers' looms through the dinner hour so they could go eat their dinner. We lived about a mile and a quarter from the mill, and I'd carry his lunch every day. He'd tell me to come on in the mill, and he made me fill his batteries while he run the weavers' looms — and I was just a little fellow. See, I knew a whole lot about the mill before I ever went in one."

"Helping," then, was a family affair, a form of apprenticeship by which basic skills and habits were transmitted to each new generation. But helping was also a vital part of the family economy and the mill labor system. A child's help could increase a parent's or older sibling's piecework earnings or simply relieve the strain of keeping up production. An Englishman who reported on the American textile industry visited a mill in South Carolina where weavers who had their sons or little brothers helping could take on two additional looms. Besides, with parents working twelve-hour days in the mills, children often had no place else to go. Owners profited from such family needs. Early child labor legislation in the Carolinas only prohibited "employing" children under certain ages, so owners could stay within the letter of the law by "permitting" or "suffering" underage children to "help." A story related by a federal investigator in Georgia illustrated the system's coercive potential. "A woman reported that her little daughter ten years old worked every day helping her sisters. The child quit for a while, but the overseer said to the mother, 'Bring her in; the two girls cannot tend those machines without her.' The mother asked that the child be given work by herself, but the overseer replied that the law would not permit it."

Given the laxity of enforcement, mill owners could essentially set their own policies according to individual conscience or the bottom line of profit and loss. Allie Smith provided a child's-eye view of the confusion that often resulted. Shortly after Allie's birth, her family moved to Saxapahaw, a community in Alamance County on the Haw River. By the time they left for Carrboro, in neighboring Orange County, when Allie was eleven, she knew how to spin from having helped an older sister. But Julian Shakespeare Carr, owner of the Carrboro mill, believed that mill men should voluntarily avoid child labor in order to stave off government interference. "When we moved to Carrboro," Allie recalled, "I thought I could go in and help her, and I did. But Mr. Carr owned this cotton mill, and I hadn't been over here long when he came over and said I couldn't come in and help. I would have to be on the payroll, so they put me on the payroll. And I worked there, I don't know how long — several months — and they said I couldn't work unless my father signed me up for being twelve years old. Well, he wouldn't do it. He said he didn't want me to work. They put me out and wouldn't let me work. And then when I got to be twelve, I went in and went to work."

Playing and helping could thus shade into full-time work. But getting that first official, full-time job was a major turning point. Managers, parents, and children themselves influenced the decision. Occasionally, mills openly dictated the age at which a child had to begin work. In 1904 the owners of a South Carolina mill mandated that "all children, members of a family about twelve years of age, shall work in the mill and shall not be excused from service therein without the consent of the superintendent for good cause." More often, pressure came from supervisors, who were personally responsible for keeping a quota of workers on hand. Jessie Lee Carter was four in 1905 when her family left their Tennessee farm for the Brandon Mill in Greenville. Six of her older brothers and sisters went to work right away; eight years later Jessie joined them. "When I got twelve years old, my uncle [who was a second hand in the spinning room] come to my daddy, and daddy let me quit school and go to work." During slack times children like Jessie Lee could be sent back to school, then called in again when the need arose.

For a large family with many mouths to feed, outside pressure was often unnecessary. Lela Ranier's parents took her out of school when she was twelve and sent her to the mill. "Ma thought it was time. They thought maybe it would help 'em out, you know. They was making such a little bit. And they thought the little bit I made would help." Lacy Wright's father asked him to quit school when he reached twelve because his two oldest sisters had married and Lacy's father could not support the family on $1.25 a day. Other children realized the importance of their labor to the family's well-being and took it upon themselves to get a job. This was particularly true in families where the father was dead or disabled. Grover Hardin, for example, dropped out of school after the second grade. "I started out in the mill — the main reason — to help my mother. She wanted me to go to school until I got in the fifth grade. I told her, 'You need the help worse than I need the education, because I can get it later on, or I can do without it.' And so I went to work as quick as I possibly could. I started in as a sweeper."

Many parents wanted their children to stay in school, but youngsters often had their own plans. Ila Dodson insisted on quitting school when she was fourteen. "I wanted to make my own money. I done had two sisters go to work, and I seen how they was having money, and so I couldn't stand it no longer. My parents wanted me to go on to school, but I couldn't see that. Back then, didn't too many children go on to high school. It was just a common thing that when they'd get old enough, let them go to work. I like to worried them to death." Finally, Ila's parents relented and agreed to sign her worker's permit, required at that time in South Carolina for children under sixteen. But, she recalled, "Mama wouldn't even take me to town to get it, and my daddy wouldn't go with me. I said, 'Well, give me the Bible and give me a dime and I'll go get it.' A nickel streetcar fare up there and a nickel back, and I [took] the Bible because I had to prove my age."

Alice Evitt and Curtis Enlow also preferred mill work to schoolwork. "They'd let you go in there seven, eight years old," Alice recalled. "I'd go in there and mess around with my sisters; they'd be spinning. I liked to put up the ends and spin a little bit, so when I got twelve years old, I wanted to quit school. So I just quit and went to work, and I was twelve years old!" Both of Curtis's parents and two of his sisters worked in the card room at a Greenville mill. During summer vacation Curtis joined them there. "I was about thirteen years old, and I decided I would go to work. Well, I went to work, and my dad says if I quit when school started, he'd let me work. I went back to school, but I wasn't learning nothing — I didn't think I was. So I went and told him, and he says, 'All right, you ain't learning nothing. Well, you can go back to the mill.' "

Mamie Shue's parents had better luck keeping her in school. Although North Carolina's compulsory education law at the time required attendance only until age fourteen, Mamie's folks used it to frighten her into staying in school until she was sixteen. "I hated school all my life. But my parents told me if I didn't go to school, they'd put my daddy in jail. And I loved my daddy to death. So I went to school 'til I was sixteen." She did, however, start working after school in the spooling room. "I was fifteen when I started doing that. So when I was sixteen years old, they just give me a job, 'cause I could spool as good as the rest of them."

Learning to "spool as good as the rest of them" was often a by-product of helping in the mills, but for those who had not started out as

timer or whether they should just send a committee. Some said everyone should go, or else the company might blacklist the men on the committee. This idea was generally approved.

The men recalled John Fahy's instructions of the night before about the sheriff and his armed men. Fahy had warned them not even to take marching sticks, like the garden fence poles that walkers in these parts usually carried. He instructed them about the rights of free assembly, but also about the sheriff's use of the riot act. Yesterday, he told them, the sheriff's men had fired warning shots and were reported to be more and more hostile; great caution was necessary. Fahy did not plan to accompany the marchers to Lattimer. He said he would be posting signs in nearby Milnesville; he would come over to Lattimer later. He never took part in marches.

John Eagler, who was to lead the march, was excited. He had sent a message to Alex McMullen inviting the McAdoo men to come along. McMullen said no. Echoing Fahy, he warned Eagler again not to march without an American flag. So Eagler told the men to hold off until he could find a flag to carry. With three companions, Andro Sivar, Joseph Michalko, and August Kosko, he hiked over to Humboldt.

Those who waited behind decided that the youngest boys would not be permitted to march. It would be twelve miles or more, round trip, under a broiling sun. Only boys over fifteen would be allowed to accompany the men; these were sent inside to put on shoes and decent dress. Some of the men may have fortified themselves with a little whiskey; in any case, the sheriff was later to allege so. Meanwhile, unknown to the marchers, someone from Harwood — possibly an employee at the company store — telephoned Sheriff Martin about the plan to march, its route, and destination.

In the days just before the march, visible signs of conflict frightened some of the American women of Harwood, who nervously embroidered on them at the trial. Thus, for example, Mrs. Catherine Weisenborn heard one foreigner threaten another: "If you don't come, we'll kill you." She also testified she heard some strikers threaten people like her: "We'll show the *white people* what we'll do when we come back!" . . .

By the time John Eagler got back, the men had had time for an early lunch. A cheer went up when they saw Eagler and Sivar return with not one, but two flags. Stragglers poured out of the houses. Steve Jurich kissed his pretty bride, and the others teased them both. The older men waved good-bye to their families. At almost every doorway and out in the street women and children waved and shouted as the men moved into position. Eagler and Joseph Michalko walked down the line, telling individuals to discard their walking sticks and suggesting that they start out four abreast. There were between 250 and 300 men. They started from two separate locations and met at the picnic grounds. Joseph Michalko and Steve Jurich walked out in front with the American flags snapping in the breeze. A crowd of breaker boys fell in behind the flags, but their elders sent them unhappily away. As this unarmed band got themselves organized to answer the request of their Italian brothers at the Lattimer Mines, many were taking part in the first civic act of their lives. Most had not been in the previous marches; Eagler hadn't; Cheslak hadn't. Most had never laid eyes on Sheriff Martin; none, perhaps, had seen the guns of the deputies. It was just after one when the command "Forward march!" was shouted by Michalko.

As they walked along, they picked up new recruits. They did not aim to create a big crowd, and they did not plan to have a large rally. Frequently, they called out to friends lined up to watch them on their route. . . . The men were relaxed and festive. For the past year, most had worked only one day out of every two, and the activities of the strike — giving promise of some small but basic changes in their lives — seemed far preferable to being out of work.

The night before, the strikers had formulated three grievances and taken them to the superintendent at Harwood. They demanded a pay raise of 10¢ a day, a reduction in the price of powder from $2.75 a keg to $1.50, and an end to the company store and the company doctor. They particularly resented the prices at the company store: a dozen eggs that cost 13¢ at an independent store cost 23¢ from the company; butter at 8¢ a pound elsewhere cost 26¢; and the powder they needed for their work came from the manufacturer at 90¢ to $1.00 a keg. On the average, excess charges to miners in the Hazleton region worked out to $217.50 per capita per annum.

Their ranks swollen by recruits from Crystal Ridge and Cranberry, four hundred men were now raising a cloud of dust on their way toward Hazleton, jackets over their arms, their handkerchiefs often in use to wipe their necks and brows. No effort was made on this day, as there had been on others, to close down other breakers as they passed. They passed the Cranberry breaker, calling to their friends, shouting threats to scab workers. The marchers were unarmed and determined to be peaceful, in order to avoid trouble with the sheriff.

The strikers felt patriotic under the flag. They also felt protected. Marching down into the valley and up the opposite hill, the thin yellow dust rising in the still air behind them, many felt a surge of purpose and accomplishment. John Eagler, at nineteen, although walking at their head, was not really in charge; neither was Michalko. Older leaders like Anthony Novotny, Mike Cheslak, Andrej Sivar, and others quite naturally talked things through and decisions emerged among them by common consent. Each had been carefully reared not to be boastful, assertive, or proud. No one should be in the position of attracting criticism.

The traditions of serfdom and peasant life operated like censors upon anyone who might stand out too far above the group. Oppression from above had been internalized. The community cut would-be leaders down to size.

Harwood lay two miles southwest of Hazleton. The plan was to proceed by the road at the bottom of Buck Mountain and on up through the city of Hazleton. This would be the shortest route to Lattimer Mines on the far northeast side of town. Even so, the march would be about six miles.

It was almost two when the marchers in the front line caught sight of armed men hurrying toward them in West Hazleton. . . .

Deputy Ario Pardee Platt boasted of ancestors who had fought in the Revolutionary War, in the War of 1812, and in the Civil War. (During 1861–65, little Hazleton had supplied almost two thousand men to the Union cause.) Platt was the chief bookkeeper of the Pardee company, and the general manager of its company stores in Hazleton, Harwood, and Lattimer Mines. It made his blood boil to see all these foreigners carrying the flag his ancestors had championed. Platt was looking for action, he had wanted action all along and was not happy with the overcareful way the sheriff had been handling things.

Thomas Hall, another deputy, was a leader in the Coal and Iron Police. He was a man who had organized the posse for the sheriff and who directed it in the sheriff's absence. Before the strike had even begun, as far back as August 12, the owners of the mine companies had called a meeting in Hazleton to discuss their dissatisfaction with the performance of the Coal and Iron Police. Even without a strike looming up before them, they were complaining that they were paying for one hundred policemen, paying well, too, and not getting the protection they needed. The police were spending too much time at Hungarian weddings, they said, and not enough time protecting property. They were paying for protection and they intended to have it. The tenor of the meeting was then leaked to the newspapers. So now, only one month later, Thomas Hall was not of a mind to occasion any further dissatisfaction from his employers. It would be his task to teach Sheriff Martin the way things were done in the lower end of the county and to keep the pressure on him to do them. His own neck was at stake.

Deputy Alonzo Dodson was a miner who lived in Hazleton. He was heard to say, "We ought to get so much a head for shooting down these strikers. I would do it for a cent a head to make money at it."

Deputies George and James Ferry — the latter known to everyone as Pinky — were also heard to say at McKenna's Corner that they would blow the strikers' brains out. Perhaps it was the power of suggestion that was working on the consciousness of the deputies, for one of them, Harry Diehl, even threatened to blow out the brains of Herman Pottunger, if he did not get off the road. Pottunger himself heard Deputy Wesley Hall say of the marchers: "I'd like to get a pop at them." . . .

Also among the deputies were Robert Tinner, the superintendent of the Central Pennsylvania Telephone and Supply Company, Willard Young, a lumber merchant and contractor, and Samuel B. Price, who held the contract to build a new breaker in Harwood, work on which was being held up by the strike. All in all about forty deputies had accompanied Sheriff Martin to West Hazleton. Nearly all these men owed their livelihood, or a portion of it, to the mining companies. Other deputies were waiting for the marchers at Lattimer.

Sheriff Martin's fondest hope seems clearly to have been to put an end to the march right at West Hazleton. But he was in something of a spot. He knew he didn't have jurisdiction inside the city, at least not without consultation, and the marchers had already reached McKenna's Corner. He was being pressured to "teach the strikers a lesson" that would get them off the roads. His own inclination still seemed to be to keep matters peaceable and under his control.

The sheriff walked directly toward the two men carrying flags, Andro Sivar and Joseph Michalko. He had his pistol in one hand. He took the nearest man, John Yurchekowicz, by the coat, brandishing the revolver in his face, and announced vigorously: "I'm the sheriff of Luzerne County, and you cannot go to Lattimer."

Steve Juszko pushed past Yurchekowicz, saying defiantly, "Me no stop. Me go to Lattimer."

The sheriff again said: "If you go to Lattimer, you must kill me first."

John Eagler, who had been fifty paces back in the line when it stopped, walked forward and now spoke up in a reedy voice. "We ain't goin' to. We are going to Lattimer. We harm no one. We are within the law."

Before the words were fully out of Eagler's mouth, Anthony Kislewicz [variants: Kascavage, etc.] bent over for a flat rock (he later said) to strike a match for his pipe during the halt. One of the deputies brought the butt of his rifle down viciously on Kislewicz's arm. Then Deputy Hall moved toward Steve Juszko, who had stepped forward, and swung through the air twice with his rifle butt, crunching across the two arms the boy raised to protect himself and hitting his head. Blood flowed. Both arms hung limp.

The sheriff pointed his pistol right and left as though holding off a legion.

Ario Pardee Platt, fired up by the bloodshed, ripped the flag from Joseph Michalko's hands, broke the stick across his knee, and stood there shredding the flag with contempt. He dropped the torn rags in the dust.

John Eagler, watching Deputy Cook raise his gun, stopped to pick up a stone. The sheriff waved his pistol and Eagler dropped the stone. Other deputies mixed it up briskly with the marchers.

Deputy Cook fired a shot into the air and the hillside reverberated. The marchers did not move. They were baffled.

John Eagler stepped forward to obtain the name of the deputy he had seen hit Juszko. Sheriff Martin held Eagler with a gesture and pulled a paper from his pocket. The sheriff had seen disorder and now had his opportunity. "This is my proclamation and you can't go any farther. It's against the law."

Then Chief of Police Jones walked forward shouting to John Eagler and the sheriff, and Sheriff Martin put his paper back in his pocket. Jones told the sheriff the strikers had a right to march peacefully, and he, the sheriff, knew it. To Novotny the chief said he had confidence in the way the marchers were conducting themselves; he would let them march around the edges of West Hazleton but not go through the city. He was willing to show them how they could go, so as to continue on to Lattimer in peace. . . .

Murderous joking, meanwhile, seems to have gripped the deputies. They had talked all morning about shooting and killing. Herman Pottunger heard a deputy say quietly to a friend: "I bet I drop six of them when I get over there." August Katski and Martin Lochar stood near the trolley car as the departing deputies were boarding. Two deputies went after them and hit them, but one said: "Let them go until we get to Lattimer and then we'll shoot them." It may have been a form of macabre humor, intended only to frighten.

William A. Evans, the reporter, arrived just after the confrontation, while the men were still standing on opposite sides of the road. He saw one of the strikers picking up a stone as Ario Pardee Platt tore the flag. No stone was actually thrown.

Doctor John Koons of Hazleton was called by the chief of police to treat the two wounded men in the jail. One of the men — Juszko — had to be examined by force. His scalp wounds required nine stitches. Juszko appears to have been listed the next day as among the wounded in the hospital. Six months later, he was still unable to use his arms.

Chief Jones did, as he offered, point the way for the marchers to cut through West Hazleton, adding another mile or so to the trip. It was after 2:30 when the marchers returned to their original plan. Now only one American flag waved in the sun, but the men were feeling vindicated and safe under the law. Mike Krupa from Crystal Ridge had joined them in West Hazleton with several of his friends, and the marchers made Krupa and his friends throw away their walking sticks. George Yamshak also joined them and was told to throw away the small stick he was carrying. The marchers had learned that their best protection was lack of arms. . . .

Later, the editorialists were not to overlook the symbolism of the day and the hour. It was almost three o'clock and the detachment of deputies assigned to wait at Lattimer was restless. A mile away, at Harleigh, Sheriff Martin and the deputies who had seen action at West Hazleton sat in the trolley and waited. Some removed plug hats to wipe away the sweat under their hatbands. Others fingered their Winchesters. A few of them were later to claim that they believed then that the miners had guns in their pockets; some even may have believed it. . . .

For the deputies sitting on that trolley in front of Farley's Hotel in Harleigh, the waiting was almost over. In a cloud of dust, the marchers were beginning to appear around the bend, the lone American flag still at their head. The deputies watched the strikers pause while eight men or so from the first two lines huddled. The other marchers broke ranks to drink water from a pump. The question for the huddled leaders, posed by John Eagler, was whether to march first to breaker Number One in Lattimer Mines or to breaker Number Three. Finally the strikers started walking again. John Laudmesser, the hotel-keeper, counted the marchers as they passed, there were 424. . . .

In the past, strikers had often changed plans in unexpected ways, and the sheriff was taking no chances. He ordered the trolley to stay right alongside the marchers. For almost a mile, deputies and strikers went along eyeing one another. A few insults may have been exchanged. At the last fork in the road, when it was plain that the strikers could be taking no other road except into Lattimer, the sheriff ordered the trolley to speed up and race ahead to the village.

In Lattimer there was by now considerable commotion. The colliery whistle sounded a warning. Those deputies and private police who had already been waiting in Lattimer had made their preparations. One of them told Mrs. Craig, "Go inside, as there may be some shooting today." Trolley cars shuttled in from Milnesville, Drifton, and points north. Doors slammed. Some mothers hurried to the school to bring their children home. Fear of the foreigners had been intense ever since the Tuesday before, when a band of noisy strikers had marched through the village.

On his arrival by trolley, Sheriff Martin took command of the assembling deputies. His force, bolstered by some of the new deputies from Drifton, now numbered almost one hundred and fifty. Some of them stood guard at the breakers and the superintendent's office. He divided the others into three companies, under Samuel Price, A. E. Hess, and Thomas Hall. He called the men down off the trolley bank and stationed them across the single road leading into Lattimer, just before it forked into Main Street and Quality Row, with the schoolhouse lane above. Dissatisfied, he then ordered all of them off the road to take up positions in an enfilading crescent on the lower, north side of the road. In this way, they would be able to cover the entire length of the march as it filed in front of them. The Craig house on the end of Main Street was surrounded by a white picket fence. Inside, Mrs. Craig fretted nervously. Outside, across the street, stood a tall gumberry tree, later to become known as "the massacre tree." Almost in its shade, Sheriff Martin stood near the house with the white fence and looked up the empty road toward Harleigh. As he did so, A. E. Hess was showing his men one last time how to fire their guns.

From where the sheriff stood, the road swept gently upward over the brow of a distant hill. Not far from where it came over the hill, the trolley track crossed over it and continued to parallel it on the south but on a raised embankment. The marchers would come over the hill and then be caught between the embankment and the line of Winchesters. In addition, the road then gradually curved closer and closer to the deputies down toward the house where the sheriff was now standing. Thus, if the marchers kept coming, their first rank would be no farther than fifteen yards from the line of deputies, and those in the last ranks would be no farther than thirty or forty yards. The sheriff was satisfied and strode up the line a little, nearer to the center of his deputies. . . .

At last the marchers came over the hill. Next door to the Craig house, John Airy watched from his home as the unarmed marchers walked in rank toward him. As at West Hazleton, so at Lattimer the marchers felt secure under the law. In the first two rows were Steve Jurich, carrying the flag, John Eagler, John Pustag, Michael Malody, Mike Cheslak, wearing an odd pointed cap, Andro Novotny, and George Jancso. All were from the two counties of Sariš and Zemplin in Slovakia.

After dismissing their students when anxious mothers came to gather their youngsters, Charles Guscott and Grace Coyle, the teachers, stood at the doorway of the schoolhouse, and watched the slow-motion drama unfold. They stood about one hundred yards from the gumberry tree. About sixty of the ninety men in the deputies' line, they later recalled, had their rifles raised in firing position as the strikers, led by the flag, began to file past them.

Sheriff Martin told Hess and Price to keep an eye on him. He said he would find out the marchers' intentions. "If they say they are not going to do anything I may let them go on and we will go along with them." When the flag had come about two-thirds of the way past the far flank, Sheriff Martin strode forward as he had now done on four previous occasions to see if he could handle the situation alone. He had his revolver drawn. He held up one hand. The men kept coming as he advanced and he had his hand almost in their faces when he announced in official manner: "You must stop marching and disperse." Those a few ranks back could not hear him at all, and the others behind them could not see him. "This is contrary to the law and you are creating a disturbance. You must go back. I won't let you go to the colliery."

The front ranks stumbled, trying to halt. Someone from behind called out in English, "Go ahead!" The marchers behind kept coming. The front row was pushed forward.

Angered, the sheriff reached first for the flag. But Steve Jurich pulled it erect. Then the sheriff reached into the second row and grabbed Michael Malody by the coat, thinking that he was the one who had said, "Go ahead!" The sheriff didn't know which man was the leader. Frightened, Malody insisted he hadn't said a word. Andro Novotny, who was next to Malody, intervened in his defense. The sheriff then grabbed Novotny with one hand and pulled his revolver up, aiming it at Novotny's chest. By now, the sheriff had pulled four or more men to the deputies' side of the road. The other marchers continued on. Eagler was among those pushed partially forward down the road. Those near the sheriff — including, now, men from the rear like John Terri and Martin Shefronik (Šefronik) — were afraid and puzzled.

"Where are you going?" the sheriff asked, pulling on Novotny and beginning to panic. The front of the column was getting farther and farther past him. Novotny said in English, "Let me alone!" He swept his arms up and pushed the barrel of the sheriff's revolver away from his own chest.

George Jancso reached in and pulled the sheriff's other hand free from Novotny. The sheriff then grabbed Jancso's coat and pointed his pistol at Jancso's forehead; Jancso and Eagler heard the pistol snap — Sheriff Martin also felt it snap — but it did not fire.

In that instant, the sheriff's second in command, Samuel Price, left the line of deputies and stepped forward to come to the surrounded sheriff's assistance. Other deputies frantically called him back, since he was now in the line of fire. He stepped back.

Mrs. Kate Case from her third-floor window heard someone shout "Fire." She thought the deputies were firing over the marchers' heads. Then she saw some marchers fall. She screamed.

Novotny heard the sheriff command, "Fire," and Jancso heard him shout "Give two or three shots!" Some witnesses thought that in the struggle the sheriff had fallen briefly to his knees; others said he remained standing. His body was directly between the deputies and Jancso when a shot rang out, then three or four in unison. The sheriff raised both arms as though to stop the action. But a full volley rang out again and again.

Watching from the schoolhouse, Charles Guscott saw the first puff of smoke come from the fourth or fifth man from the farthest end of the deputies' line, Hess's men. It seemed to those closer that the whole line erupted with fire.

Steve Jurich had held the flag and was the first to fall. *"O Joj! Joj! Joj!"* he cried in the ancient Slovak cry to God. "Enough! Enough!" Bullets shattered his head and he died as he bled.

John Eagler saw Cheslak drop, his peculiar peaked hat falling from his head, so he, too, dropped to the ground. Eagler saw trickles of blood flowing in the dust toward him from Cheslak's head. He realized then that the deputies were not using blanks.

John Terri threw himself on the ground. Another striker fell on him, dead. Terri saw Cheslak beside him and tried to speak to him. Cheslak's eyes were open but he did not speak. Then Terri got up and ran.

Andro Sivar, in the fourth row, turned his back at the first shot. When the man beside him caught a bullet in the back, Sivar fell with him. Michael Kuchar, nineteen, was about ten yards from the sheriff and could neither hear nor see what was happening in front; at the loud shouting, he threw himself down. George Jancso tore himself from the hands of the sheriff and ran to throw himself in a ditch as flat and close to mother earth as he could press himself.

Martin Shefronik stood close to Jurich, and saw blood spurt out the back of Jurich's head and also from his mouth. As he dropped, Jurich was completely drenched with blood. Shefronik ran toward the schoolhouse, until he was thrown forward by the impact of a bullet in his shoulder. John Putski of Harwood also ran toward the school-house until a bullet in his right arm and another in his leg spun him to the ground. Andrew Jurechek ran toward the schoolhouse and almost reached safety before a bullet struck his back and exploded through his stomach.

Watching from the schoolhouse, teachers Charles Guscott and Grace Coyle had looked on in horror as dust and acrid gunsmoke filled the air. "They're firing blanks," Miss Coyle said. "No, see them dropping," Guscott said. The firing went on for two or three minutes. Some deputies turned, wheeled, and followed running men, shooting some down at a distance of 300 yards. Many men ran toward the schoolhouse; one was hit, spinning, just before he reached the terrified teachers. Other shots crashed into the schoolhouse sending showers of splinters. Running toward the teachers, Clement Platek clutched his side; he too was crying: *"O Joj! Joj! Joj!"* The teachers saw, in addition to those mentioned: the brains of one man splattered forward; still another hapless man shot through the neck so that his head was almost severed. Grace Coyle ran forward to help Andrew Jurechek, who was clutching at the entrails slipping from his stomach and who cried out to her: "No! Me want to see wife. Before die." He died before her eyes. His wife was heavy with child.

Mathias Czaja had been standing ten or twelve feet from the sheriff. He had seen the sheriff pull his revolver and point it at the man with the flag. He had heard him say, "If you go any farther, I will shoot you." He had been frightened. He did not hear the order to fire. His back was blown open by a bullet.

Michael Srokach (Srokač) saw eight deputies run forward thirty yards or so to gain better shots. From the public road, the miners fled backward toward the trolley line and up over its bank, either up the hill west toward Harleigh or east toward the schoolhouse.

One man fled as far as a telephone pole on the trolley line when he was hit. He pulled himself up, holding to the pole. As other shots poured into him, his body buckled two or three times. He slid to the earth.

William Raught and another deputy, according to several witnesses, broke from the line of deputies in order to pursue the fleeing strikers. In order to get a line of fire, Raught and the other man climbed up on the trolley tracks, still firing. Srokach heard some deputies answer pleas from the wounded with the shout: "We'll give you hell, not water, hunkies!" Others heard: "Shoot the sons of bitches!"

The smoke from the first volley was thick. Dust was raised by men running. For a while it was difficult to see. From his home, John Airy saw deputies take careful aim and pick men off as they were running to get in the shelter of the hillside. "They shot man after man in the back," he reported. "The slaughter was awful." He estimated that the deputies fired "at least 150" shots. "They kept firing for some time. Men fell on the ground and screamed in agony and tried to drag themselves from the murderous guns. At last it was all over."

Cries of pain, groans, and shrieks remained. Andro Sivar got up from a circle of dead and wounded. Andrew Meyer — seventeen-year-old breaker boy — pleaded for help for his shattered knees. John Slobodnik, wounded in the back of the head just above the neck cried out for water. Slobodnik and John Banko, also shot in the head, were carried by friends to Farley's Hotel in Harleigh, looking for medical attention of some kind. John Eagler ran, bent over, for 150 yards before he turned. He saw one of the men from Crystal Ridge bleeding from his arm and back. The man asked him: "Butty, loosen me suspenders and collar, they hurt me much." Eagler pulled down the man's shirt and saw a big hole in the back of his neck spouting thick blood. He pushed a handkerchief in the hole. Then he bent to help Frank Tages. He pulled off his own coat, put it around his friend, led him to a trolley car for a ride to the hospital. Sick and afraid, Eagler saw some of the deputies begin to offer water to the wounded. Then he started on the long walk back to Harwood. In shock, he could not comprehend what had just happened.

Cornelius Burke was eleven years old and lived in Lattimer II, the next settlement up from Lattimer. During recess from school, he was overcome by curiosity about the commotion in town and ran down to Lattimer to see the excitement. He was part way up Main Street when he heard the terrific crack of rifles. When he got up to the site, he recalls, " . . . Oh, my God, the poor fellows were lying across the trolley tracks on the hillside, some had died and some were dying. Some were crying out for water." Connie picked up a little can and carried water to one of the dying miners. "It was a terrible sight and so much confusion existed. Everyone was running in all directions. They searched the men who were shot and found they carried no weapons."

One of the deputies, George Treible, was wounded by a bullet that creased both his arms. The Wilkes-Barre *Times* reported that he believed he was shot by one of his own men, who had wheeled to fire after the dispersing strikers. Bullets flew, Treible said, in every direction. Some of the deputies at the right end of the crescent (farthest from Lattimer), who seem to have fired most of the shots, were shooting back toward Lattimer at the strikers fleeing toward the schoolhouse. "The deputies," said the paper, "were not under control. The odor of smoke inflamed them."

The fury of some was not yet spent. Some of the deputies walked among the fallen, kicking them and cursing them. A. E. Hess told one bystander who was crying shame, "Shut up or you will get the same dose." John Terri, who had fallen beside Cheslak, went through the smoke of battle to find water for his wounded uncle and cousin. Asked for water, a deputy named Clark said, "Give them hell," grabbed Terri, kicked him, and held him prisoner for an hour. Joseph Costello, a Hazleton butcher, saw Hess kick a prostrate victim (who was in fact Andrew Meyer) and denounced Hess for the butchery. Hess told him, too, to shut up. Grace Coyle, the schoolteacher, upbraided Hess for his manner among the fallen, with his cigar in his mouth. Hess did not defend himself.

John Welsh saw Sheriff Martin after the shooting and asked him how he was.

"I am not well," Sheriff Martin said.

The sheriff was pale and shaken. He turned his revolver over to a detective. Many of his deputies had fled and some went into hiding. Some of the others were lifting the wounded into conveyances. But John Airy witnessed the most saddening scene of all: "The trolley car in which the sheriff and his deputies came was right in front of my house and the officers got in it. They were laughing and telling each other how many men they killed." Another bystander also heard them: "Yes, and one of them said he took down a dozen 'Hunks,' and knew what he was shooting at every time. He was boasting of what a fine shooter he was. They sat there for some time, joking and laughing about it, and then they rode back to the city."

STUDY GUIDE

1. What impression do you get of the relationships in this mining town — between the workers and their employers, the workers and the law enforcement officers, and among the workers?

2. Is there any nativistic (anti-immigrant) sentiment in the community? If so, what evidence is there for it; if not, how do you account for its absence? Also, do the nativistic tendencies appear to be universal in the community?

3. What is the attitude of the workers toward their adopted country — the United States? Document your answer.

4. What impression do you get of the degree of professionalism of the deputies?

5. Do you feel, on the basis of the narrative, that the verdict of the jury (see the Introduction to the selection) was a fair one? If so, why; if not, why not?

6. Turn to the author of the narrative. (a) Is he dispassionate in his account, or do you sense that he has some strong feelings about what happened? Document your answer — either way. (b) Does it surprise you to learn that he is a spokesman for ethnicity in our country, the founder of a movement to promote ethnic pride among immigrant groups and their descendants? (c) What evidence is there in this essay of ethnic pride on Novak's part? Is it, in your opinion, justified, or to put the question another way: did the miners, in your opinion, act in a legal and patriotic manner? If so, on what evidence; if not, on what evidence?

BIBLIOGRAPHY

The conditions of American workers described by Michael Novak did not go unchallenged by labor or labor leaders in the late nineteenth and early twentieth centuries. Should you want to learn more about labor organizations as well as the opposition to them, begin by reading the entirety of *The Guns of Lattimer* (1978), by Michael Novak. Other books that focus on specific strikes are equally informative, especially in their conclusions about the attitude of the courts and government toward labor's effort to organize and bargain collectively: Robert V. Bruce, *1877: Year of Violence* (1957), the story of the nationwide railroad strikes of that year; Henry David, *The History of the Haymarket Affair* (1936); Almont Lindsey, *The Pullman Strike* (1942);

Wayne G. Broehl, Jr., *The Molly Maguires* (1964); and Leon Wolff, *Lockout: The Story of the Homestead Strike of 1892* (1965). For an account of an important strike of the early twentieth century, see David Brody, *Labor in Crisis: The Steel Strike of 1919* (1965). General histories of the efforts of labor to organize include Foster Rhea Dulles, *Labor in America: A History* (1949); Henry Pelling, *American Labor* (1960); and Joseph Rayback, *A History of American Labor* (1959).

III PARADOXES OF PROGRESSIVISM

The two decades between the opening of the twentieth century and the end of World War I were dominated by strenuous efforts on the part of a large number of Americans to improve the quality of life at home and abroad. Progressive reformers assumed that behavior could be altered and the performance of institutions improved. As Eric F. Goldman wrote in *Rendezvous with Destiny*, Progressives believed that "an environment . . . made by human beings . . . could be changed by human beings."

Until 1914, Americans concentrated largely on domestic reforms. At the grass-roots level, there were numerous programs to improve municipal government and administration. Some reform mayors — Tom L. Johnson in Cleveland and Samuel M. "Golden Rule" Jones in Toledo — sought to reduce trolley-car fares and inaugurate municipally owned utilities to compete with those that were privately owned. Seth Low in New York and James D. Phelan in San Francisco were more concerned with efficiency than equality, and consequently set about modernizing the collection of taxes and the budgetary procedures of their municipal administrations. Still other Progressives sought to enact legislation for urban zoning, the inspection of the milk supply, or the improvement of public education. Reforms on the state and national level followed and paralleled these early local efforts. And while the ultimate worth of these efforts is being reassessed by historians, many of the instrumentalities through which our public utilities are regulated and our bank system is coordinated originated in the legislation of the Progressive era.

Activism dominated our foreign policy as well in the Progressive period. Following the end of the Spanish-American War in 1898, the American people turned their attention outward. The student of American history can draw a line from the assertiveness of Theodore Roosevelt's acquisition of the Panama Canal in 1903 to Woodrow Wilson's intervention in Mexico and our entry, in 1917, into World War I. The ebullient confidence with which we entered the Great War — in Wilson's words, "to make the world safe for democracy" — is closely related to the profound disillusionment that set in after the war. The failure of Wilson to achieve at Versailles the realization of his Fourteen Points, in many ways a Progressive program for international affairs, led the nation to reject the treaty and the League of Nations written into it.

The selections that follow illustrate the realities and the paradoxes of the Progressive era. A typical immigrant enclave is the subject of the first essay. The second essay describes the settlement house — one of the principal institutions through which Progressive reformers sought to acculturate the immigrant. Far less attention was paid by the Progressive reformers to the blacks in the South or, as the third selection makes amply clear, to those making their way North. The final selection offers a glimpse of another negative aspect of the Progressive era — the violations of the constitutional rights of native- and foreign-born Americans in the witch-hunt called the Red Scare of 1919.

Hester Street on New York City's Lower East Side.

7

MOSES RISCHIN

The Immigrant Ghetto

The United States is a nation of immigrants. Some, like the English and the Scotch-Irish, came in large numbers prior to the Revolution of 1776; others, like the Germans and the Scandinavians, came in the nineteenth century; still others — the Italians, the Slavs, the Poles, and the Russo-Polish Jews — came at the very end of the nineteenth century and in the first three decades of the twentieth. Some thirty million immigrants came to the United States in the nineteenth and twentieth centuries — five million from 1815 to 1860, ten million from 1860 to 1890, and fifteen million from 1890 to 1924.

After the turn of the century, social scientists and historians divided the immigrants into two principal categories: the "old" and the "new." The first group included those born in northern and western Europe, while the "new" immigration had its sources in southern and eastern Europe. Unfortunately, a number of native-born Americans favoring immigration restriction made unfair comparisons between these two immigrant groups. With little justification, they described the "old" immigrants as having come to America out of idealistic motives and as having an inborn instinct for freedom and liberty; while the "new" immigrants, they charged, came to the United States for material gain and would make little contribution to the democratic ideals and institutions of our country. Those who opposed America's policy of unrestricted immigration won their fight with the passage of the Immigration Restriction Act of 1924. This legislation limited immigration from Europe to a maximum of 150,000 a year and provided that the overwhelming majority of these immigrants come from the British Isles and northern Europe. The gates were shut in 1924, but not before many immigrants from

Europe established ghettoes for themselves in the nation's urban centers. These ethnic enclaves provided a measure of security in an alien, and sometimes hostile, environment.

The ghetto experience, the institutions, and the old-world values described by Moses Rischin in the following selection can easily be translated into the cultural context of other ghettoes — those enclaves established in the same decades and often in the same neighborhoods by the Italians, the Poles, the Slavs, and the Greeks. Those groups, like the Russo-Polish Jews described in this essay, were trying to fuse the old and the new, to preserve aspects of their European past in order to ease the process of their inevitable Americanization.

By the first decade of the twentieth century, the Lower East Side had become an immigrant Jewish cosmopolis. Five major varieties of Jews lived there, "a seething human sea, fed by streams, streamlets, and rills of immigration flowing from all the Yiddish-speaking centers of Europe." Clustered in their separate Jewries, they were set side by side in a pattern suggesting the cultural, if not the physical, geography of the Old World. Hungarians were settled in the northernmost portion above Houston Street, along the numbered streets between Avenue B and the East River, once indisputably *Kleindeutschland*. Galicians lived to the south, between Houston and Broome, east of Clinton, on Attorney, Ridge, Pitt, Willett, and the cross streets. To the west lay the most congested Rumanian quarter, "in the very thick of the battle for breath," on Chrystie, Forsyth, Eldridge, and Allen streets, flanked by Houston Street to the north and Grand Street to the south, with the Bowery gridironed by the overhead elevated to the west. After 1907 Levantines, last on the scene and even stranger than the rest, for they were alien to Yiddish, settled between Allen and Chrystie streets among the Rumanians with whom they seemed to have the closest affinity. The remainder of the great Jewish quarter, from Grand Street reaching south to Monroe, was the preserve of the Russians — those from Russian Poland, Lithuania, Byelorussia, and the Ukraine — the most numerous and heterogeneous of the Jewries of Eastern Europe.

The leading streets of the Lower East Side reflected this immigrant transformation. Its most fashionable thoroughfare, East Broadway, bisected the district. To the north lay crammed tenements, business, and

From *The Promised City* by Moses Rischin, Cambridge, Mass.: Harvard University Press. Copyright © 1962, 1977 by the President and Fellows of Harvard College. Reprinted by permission of the publishers. Footnotes have been omitted.

industry. To the south lay less crowded quarters where private dwellings, front courtyards, and a scattering of shade trees recalled a time when Henry, Madison, Rutgers, and Jefferson street addresses were stylish.

The Russian intelligentsia, for whom the Lower East Side was New York, fancied East Broadway as New York's Nevsky Prospect, St. Petersburg's grand boulevard. In addition to the physicians and dentists who occupied the comfortable brownstone fronts that lined its shaded curbs, an evergrowing number of public and communal buildings came to endow it with a magisterial air. By the second decade of the twentieth century, the ten-story edifice of the *Jewish Daily Forward*, set off by Seward Park on Yiddish Newspaper Row, loomed commandingly over the two Carnegie-built libraries, the Educational Alliance, the Home for the Aged, the Jewish Maternity Hospital, the Machzike Talmud Torah, the Hebrew Sheltering House, the Young Men's Benevolent Association, and a host of lesser institutions.

Only second to East Broadway was Grand Street. Long a leading traffic artery and a major retail shopping center of lower New York, Grand Street fell into eclipse after the turn of the century with the widening of the Delancey Street approach to the Williamsburg Bridge and the comparative decline in ferry traffic. Grand Street's popular department stores, Lord and Taylor's, Lichtenstein's, and O'Neill's, moved uptown, and Ridley's closed, leaving the way open for conquest by the newcomers. Bustling Delancey Street, lined with naphtha-lit stalls crammed with tubs of fish; Hester Street, with its agents on their way to becoming bankers after the example of Jarmulowsky's passage and exchange office; and the Bowery, with the largest savings bank in the world, symbolized the district's new retail character.

Only after 1870 did the Lower East Side begin to acquire an immigrant Jewish cast. In the early years of the century a small colony of Jewish immigrants had lived there. Dutch, German, and Polish Jews had settled on Bayard, Baxter, Mott, and Chatham streets in the 1830's and 1840's. Shortly thereafter, German and Bohemian Jews took up quarters in the Grand Street area to the northeast and subsequently Jews of the great German migration augmented their numbers. Except for highly visible store fronts, Jews made little impress on the dominantly German and Irish neighborhood. But practically all East European immigrants arriving after 1870 initially found their way to the Lower East Side. Virtually penniless upon their arrival in the city, they were directed to the Jewish districts by representatives of the immigrant aid societies, or came at the behest of friends, relatives, or employers. . . .

Once the immigrants had come to rest on the Lower East Side, there was little incentive to venture further. Knowing no English and with few resources, they were dependent upon the apparel industries, the tobacco and cigar trades, and other light industrial employments that sprang up in the area or that were located in the adjacent factory district. Long hours, small wages, seasonal employment, and the complexity of their religious and social needs rooted them to the spot. It was essential to husband energies, earnings, and time. Lodgings of a sort, coffee morning and evening, and laundry service were available to single men for three dollars a month. Bread at two and three cents a pound, milk at four cents a quart, a herring for a penny or two, and apples at from one to five for a cent, depending on quality, were to be had. Accustomed to a slim diet, an immigrant could save much even with meager earnings and still treat himself to a bracing three-course Sabbath dinner (for fifteen cents). Thrift and hard work would, he hoped, enable him in time to search out more congenial and independent employment. Until new sections of the city were developed at the turn of the century only country peddlers were to stray permanently beyond the familiar immigrant quarters.

There was a compelling purpose to the pinched living. Virtually all immigrants saved to purchase steamship tickets for loved ones and many regularly mailed clothing and food parcels to dependent parents, wives, and children overseas. The power of home ties buoyed up the spirits of immigrants wedded to the sweatshop and peddler's pack, whose precious pennies mounted to sums that would unite divided families. Among the early comers women were relatively few, but the imbalance between the sexes soon was remedied. . . . Among the major ethnic groups of New York, only the Irish, 58 per cent female, exceeded the Jewish ratio. . . .

The Tenement Boom

Ever since the 1830's New York's housing problem had been acute. Manhattan's space limitations exacerbated all the evils inherent in overcrowding, and refinements in the use of precious ground only emphasized the triumph of material necessities over human considerations. New York's division of city lots into standard rectangular plots, 25 feet wide by 100 feet deep, made decent human accommodations impossible. In order to secure proper light and ventilation for tenement dwellers twice the space was needed, a prohibitive sacrifice considering real estate values. No opportunity was overlooked to facilitate the most economical and compact housing of the immigrant population. To the improvised tenements that had been carved out of private dwellings were added the front and rear tenements and, finally, the dumbbell-style tenement of 1879.

With the heavy Jewish migration of the early 1890's, the Lower East Side, still relatively undeveloped compared to the Lower West Side, became the special domain of the new dumbbell tenements, so called because of their shape. The six- to seven-story dumbbell usually included four apartments to the floor, two on either side of the separating corridor. The front apartments generally contained four rooms each, the rear apartments three. Only one room in each apartment received direct light and air from the street or from the ten feet of required yard space in the rear. On the ground floor two stores generally were to be found; the living quarters behind each had windows only on the air shaft. The air shaft, less than five feet in width and from fifty to sixty feet in length, separated the tenement buildings. In the narrow hallways were located that special improvement, common water closets. In 1888 a leading magazine described typical dumbbell tenements on Ridge, Eldridge, and Allen streets.

> They are great prison-like structures of brick, with narrow doors and windows, cramped passages and steep rickety stairs. They are built through from one street to the other with a somewhat narrower building connecting them. . . . The narrow court-yard . . . in the middle is a damp foul-smelling place, supposed to do duty as an airshaft; had the foul fiend designed these great barracks they could not have been more villainously arranged to avoid any chance of ventilation. . . . In case of fire they would be perfect death-traps, for it would be impossible for the occupants of the crowded rooms to escape by the narrow stairways, and the flimsy fire-escapes which the owners of the tenements were compelled to put up a few years ago are so laden with broken furniture, bales and boxes that they would be worse than useless. In the hot summer months . . . these fire-escape balconies are used as sleeping-rooms by the poor wretches who are fortunate enough to have windows opening upon them. The drainage is horrible, and even the Croton as it flows from the tap in the noisome courtyard, seemed to be contaminated by its surroundings and have a fetid smell.

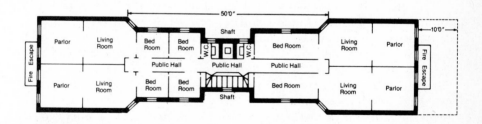

As if the tenement abuses were not degrading enough, the absence of public toilet facilities in so crowded a district added to the wretched sanitation. It was reported that "in the evening every dray or wagon becomes a private and public lavatory, and the odor and stench . . . is perfectly horrible."

Conditions became almost unendurable in the summer months. Bred in colder and dryer climates, tenement inhabitants writhed in the dull heat. Added to the relentless sun were the emanations from coal stoves, the flat flame gas jets in lamps, and the power-producing steam boilers.

Inevitably, roofs, fire escapes, and sidewalks were converted into sleeping quarters, while the grassed enclosure dividing Delancey Street and Seward Park supplied additional dormitory space. Late July and early August of 1896 were especially savage. . . .

Fire and the possibilities of fire brought added terror to the inhabitants of overcrowded tenements. "Remember that you live in a tenement house," warned insurance agents. In 1903, 15 percent of the tenements in the district still were without fire escapes. Of 257 fatalities in Manhattan fires between 1902 and 1909, 99 or 38 percent were on the Lower East Side, all victims of old-law tenements.

Few families could afford the privacy of a three- or four-room flat. Only with the aid of lodgers or boarders could the $10 to $20 monthly rental be sustained. The extent of overcrowding in the tenements, reported a witness before the United States Immigration Commission, was never fully known.

> At the hour of retiring, cots or folded beds and in many instances simply mattresses are spread about the floor, resembling very much a lot of bunks in the steerage of an ocean steamer. . . . The only way to properly determine the census of one of these tenements, would be by a midnight visit, and should this take place between the months of June and September, the roof of the building should not be omitted.

However trying tenement living proved to be for adults, for children it was stultifying, concluded a settlement worker. "The earlier years of the child are spent in an atmosphere which . . . is best described by a little girl, 'a place so dark it seemed as if there weren't no sky.' "

Evictions for nonpayment of rent and rent strikes were perennial. Uncertainty of employment, nonpayment of wages, unexpected obligations, dependents, and adversities contributed to the high incidence of evictions. In the year 1891–1892 alone, in two judicial districts of the Lower East Side, 11,550 dispossess warrants were issued by the presiding magistrates. In 1900 the absence of mass evictions was regarded as a mark of unexampled well-being.

Earlier residents of the Lower East Side and hereditary property owners profited from the overcrowding.The rise in real estate values, exorbitant rents, and the low upkeep provided tenement owners with ample returns upon their investments. Even allowing for losses due to nonpayment of rent and an average occupancy of ten months in the year, landlords earned ten percent. By more studied neglect, a resourceful agent might reap even higher returns. The Lower East Side tenements soon came to be recognized as the most lucrative investment in the city. Nowhere else did the speculator's market in tenement properties flourish as luxuriantly as it did here, where earlier immigrants had learned to exploit the misery of later comers.

In 1901 the further construction of dumbbell tenements was prohibited. The Tenement House Law of that year set new standards for future housing and attempted to correct the worst abuses in the existing buildings. All new tenements were to have windows that opened at least twelve feet away from those opposite. Toilets and running water in each apartment, unobstructed fire escapes, and solid staircases were required. In the old buildings modern water closets were to be installed in place of the outside privies. Finally, a Tenement House Department was established to supervise and enforce the provisions of the law. While the law never was effectively enforced, its initial achievements proved encouraging.

Many new tenements were quickly built according to the new specifications. In the fiscal year ending July 1, 1903, 43 percent of New York's new tenements were located on the Lower East Side. Its inhabitants eagerly welcomed the brightly lighted rooms, bathtubs, and other improvements. At first, landlords on the Lower East Side were more prompt to make alterations in old-law tenements than landlords elsewhere in the city, for the heavy pressure of population made even remodeled properties attractive. . . .

While new housing was on the rise, the fast developing clothing trades also were relocating and building. As the heavy settlement of East Europeans decisively affected the housing of the city's earlier residents, so the new growth of the apparel industry, manned by Lower East Side Jews, helped to transform the city's business districts. Once legislation and the advent of electric power combined to reduce Lower East Side sweatshops, thousands of garment shops and factories pushed up the axial thoroughfares of Lower Manhattan. By 1910 the continued march uptown found the garment industry intruding upon once fashionable Madison Square, the site of New York's tallest skyscrapers. Brownstones and brick residences were razed to be displaced by 16- to 20-story steel-girdered loft buildings trimmed with granite and marble and housing scores of clothing shops. In the course of this displacement, the city's central retailing district and its theater and hotel district were forced northward. . . .

Disease and Crime

Superficially, East European Jews seemed ill-prepared to contend with the demands that tenement living thrust upon them. "Their average stature is from five feet one inch to five feet three inches, which means that they are the most stunted of the Europeans, with the exception of the Hungarian Magyars." Shortest were the Galicians, tallest and sturdiest, the Rumanians. Undersized and narrow-chested, a high proportion were described as "physical wrecks." Centuries of confinement, habituation to mental occupations, chronic undernourishment, and a deprecation of the physical virtues ill-fitted them for heavy labor. Between 1887 and 1890 nearly five thousand immigrants were returned to Europe labeled physically "unfit for work." Seemingly helpless and emaciated, they were to exhibit exceptional capacity for regeneration; traditional moral and religious disciplines were to serve them in good stead.

Despite the trying conditions under which the immigrants lived, they showed a remarkable resistance to disease. With the highest average density of tenants per house in the city, the tenth ward had one of the lowest death rates. Indeed only a business ward and a suburban ward surpassed it in healthfulness. Dr. Annie Daniel, a pioneer in public health, volunteered her interpretation of this before the Tenement House Committee:

> The rules of life which orthodox Hebrews so unflinchingly obey as laid down in the Mosaic code . . . are designed to maintain health. These rules are applied to the daily life of the individuals as no other sanitary laws can be. . . . Food must be cooked properly, and hence the avenues through which the germs of disease may enter are destroyed. Meat must be "kosher," and this means that it must be perfectly healthy. Personal cleanliness is at times strictly compelled, and at least one day in the week the habitation must be thoroughly cleaned.

True, only some 8 percent of Russian Jewish families had baths, according to a study of 1902, and these often without hot water. Yet the proliferation of privately owned bathhouses in the city was attributable largely to the Jewish tenement population. "I cannot get along without a 'sweat' (Russian bath) at least once a week," insisted a newcomer. In 1880, one or two of New York's twenty-two bathhouses were Jewish; by 1897, over half of the city's sixty-two bathhouses (including Russian, Turkish, swimming, vapor, and medicated bathhouses) were Jewish. If standards of cleanliness were not as faithfully maintained as precept required, the strict regimen of orthodoxy, even when weakened, contributed to the immigrant's general well-being.

Nevertheless, close crowding and unsanitary conditions made all communicable diseases potentially contagious. Despite great apprehension between 1892 and 1894, Jewish immigrants did not carry to New York the cholera and typhus epidemics raging at the European ports of embarkation. But in 1899 the United Hebrew Charities became alarmed by the Board of Health's report on the mounting incidence of tuberculosis in the city. That Jewish immigrants might become easy victims of the "White Plague" was hardly to be doubted. "As many as 119 Jewish families have lived in one tenement house on Lewis Street within the past five years." Hundreds of flats had been occupied by fifteen successive families within a brief period. "Many of these houses are known to be hotbeds of the disease, the very walls reeking with it." Increasingly, the dread disease with its cough and crimson spittle took its toll. . . .

Alcoholism, a prime contributor to poverty, ill-health, and mortality among other national groups, was unusual among Jewish immigrants. As Jews replaced the earlier inhabitants, the many saloons of the Lower East Side, trimmed with shields that proclaimed them "the workman's friend," declined. Those that survived drew few clients from a neighborhood addicted to soda water, "the life-giving drink"; they depended on the throng of transients that passed through the district. Jews did not abstain from drink. Yet only upon religious festivals and during the Sabbath ritual . . . did alcohol appear in the diet of most immigrants. In 1908, $1.50 a year for holiday and ritual wine seemed adequate for a family of six. "The Day of Rejoicing of the Law and the Day of Purim are the only two days in the year when an orthodox Jew may be intoxicated. It is virtuous on these days to drink too much, but the sobriety of the Jew is so great that he sometimes cheats his friends and himself by shamming drunkenness," Hutchins Hapgood noted. Jews habitually imbibed milder beverages. Russians were notorious tea drinkers. Hungarians were addicted to coffee. The less austere Galicians and Rumanians tippled mead and wine respectively. But in the New World all fell victim to the craze for seltzer or soda water with its purported health-giving powers. In his long experience, reported the president of the United Hebrew Charities in 1892, he had known only three chronic Jewish drunkards.

Neurasthenia and hysteria, however, took a heavy toll of victims. Their sickness was the result of a history of continual persecution and insecurity, intensified by the strains of settlement in unfamiliar surroundings. Diabetes, associated with perpetual nervous strain, was common. Suicide, rarely recorded among the small-town Jews of Eastern Europe, also found its victims in the tenements of New York. Despair, poverty, and the fears generated in the imagination led some immigrants to take their own lives. "Genumen di gez" (took gas) was not an uncommon headline in the Yiddish press. . . .

However desperate the straits in which Jewish immigrants found themselves, confirmed paupers among them were few. The rarity of alcoholism, the pervasiveness of the charitable impulse, the strength of ties to family . . . , and a deep current of optimism preserved the individual from such degradation. . . .

The major crime and violence in the area did not stem from the immigrants. They were its victims. The Lower East Side had always attracted much of the city's criminal element to its margins. By the last decades of the nineteenth century, it had shed the ferocity of earlier years when the "Bowery B'hoys" and the "Dead Rabbits" terrorized the area. But Mayor Hewitt's reform drive in 1887 inadvertently reinforced the district's frailties by forcing criminals and prostitutes from their accustomed uptown resorts into the less conspicuous tenements of the tenth ward, where they remained, undisturbed even by the Parkhurst crusade. . . .

Crime was endemic to the Lower East Side. The close collaboration between police officers, politicians, and criminals, revealed in detail in the Lexow and Mazet investigations of the 1890's, had turned the district into a Klondike that replaced the uptown Tenderloin as a center of graft and illicit business. Invariably the culprits in these activities were not immigrants, but Americanized Jews learned in street-corner ways and shorn of the restraints of the immigrant generation. "It is not until they have become Americanized, have adapted themselves to the environment of the district and adopted its ways and vices, that they become full-fledged wretches," commented Dr. I. L. Nascher. In the early years of the twentieth century the effect of such conditions upon the young deeply disturbed those anxious for the public weal. In 1909 some 3000 Jewish children were brought before Juvenile Court and in the next few years Jewish criminals regularly made newspaper headlines. The appearance of an ungovernable youth after the turn of the century was undeniable and excited apprehension.

The violations of the law that characterized the immigrant community differed from the crimes of the sons of the immigrants. The former were an outgrowth of occupational overcrowding, poverty, and religious habits. Straitened circumstances contributed to the large number of cases of family desertion and nonsupport. Concentrated in marginal commerce and industry, Jews were prone to transgress the codes of commercial law. "The prevalence of a spirit of enterprise out of proportion to the capital of the community" gave rise to a high incidence of felonious larceny, forgery, and failure to pay wages. Peddlers and petty shopkeepers were especially vulnerable to police oppression for evading informal levies as well as formal licensing requirements. Legislation controlling business on Sunday found Jewish immigrants natural victims. In so congested a district, the breaking of corporation ordinances was unavoidable and the slaughtering of chickens in tenements in violation of the sanitary code proved to be a distinctly Jewish infraction.

The Bowery, way-station of derelicts, transients, and unsuspecting immigrants, attracted the less stable and wary of the immigrant girls. The dancing academies that sprang to popularity in the first decade of the twentieth century snared impetuous, friendless young women. Lured by promises of marriage, they soon were trapped by procurers for the notorious Max Hochstim Association and other white slavers who preyed upon the innocent and the unsuspecting. The appearance of prostitution, previously rare among Jewesses, alarmed the East Side.

The Lower East Side, girded by the Bowery with its unsavory establishments and Water Street with its resorts of ill-fame that catered to the seafaring trade, was surrounded by violence. Bearded Jews often were viciously assaulted by young hoodlums, both non-Jews and Jews, the area adjacent to the waterfront being especially dangerous. In 1898 and 1899, the newly organized American Hebrew League of Brooklyn protested a rash of outrages in the wake of the Dreyfus affair. Nevertheless there was only one instance of mass violence: the riot of July 30, 1902 at the funeral of Rabbi Jacob Joseph. This incident, the only one of its kind, can be attributed to the stored-up resentment of the Irish who were being forced out of the area by the incursion of Jews.

Signs of Change

Gradually the miseries and trials of adjustment were left behind. For those who had inhabited the hungry villages of Eastern Europe, the hovels of Berditchev, and the crammed purlieus of Vilna and Kovno, the factories and sweatshops of New York provided a livelihood and possible stepping-stone. Despite unsteady and underpaid employment, tenement overcrowding and filth, immigrants felt themselves ineluctably being transformed. The Lower East Side, with its purposeful vitality, found no analogue in the "leprous-looking ghetto familiar in Europe," commented the visiting Abbé Félix Klein. Physical surroundings, however sordid, could be transcended. Optimism and hope engulfed every aspect of immigrant life. For a people who had risen superior to the oppressions of medieval proscriptions, the New York slums acted as a new-found challenge. Each passing year brought improvements that could be measured and appraised. Cramped quarters did not constrict aspirations. "In a large proportion of the tenements of the East Side . . . pianos are to be seen in the dingy rooms." And soon the phonograph was everywhere. "Excepting among the recent arrivals, most of the Jewish tenement dwellers have fair and even good furniture in their homes."

The East Europeans began to venture beyond the boundaries of the Lower East Side into other areas where employment was available on terms compatible with religious habits. Brooklyn's German Williamsburg district, directly across the East River, where Central European Jews had been established for some decades, was settled early. In the late 1880s a few clothing contractors set up sweatshops in the languid Scottish settlement of Brownsville, south and east of Williamsburg. The depression delayed further expansion for a decade despite the extension of the Fulton Street El in 1889. Then the tide could not be stemmed. Between 1899 and 1904 Brownsville's population rose from ten thousand to sixty thousand. Land values soared as immigrants came at the rate of one thousand per week. Lots selling for two hundred dollars in 1899 brought five to ten thousand dollars five years later. As the real estate boom revolutionized land values, many a former tailor was suddenly transformed into a substantial landlord or realtor who disdained all contact with shears and needles of bitter memory.

The mass dispersion of Jews from the Lower East Side to other parts of the city was in full swing in the early 1890's, as the more prosperous pioneers hastened to settle among their German coreligionists in Yorkville between 72nd and 100th streets, east of Lexington Avenue. For many a rising immigrant family in this period of swift change, it was judged to be a ten-year trek from Hester Street to Lexington Avenue.

The unprecedented flow of immigrants into the old central quarter, exorbitant rents, and the demolition of old tenements incidental to the building of parks, schools, and bridge approaches drastically reduced the area's absorptive capacity and spurred the search for new quarters. The construction of the Delancey Street approach to the Williamsburg Bridge in 1903 displaced 10,000 persons alone. The consolidation of the city and the growth and extension of rapid transit facilities connected what were once remote districts with the central downtown business quarters. In the new developments, cheaper land made possible lower rents that compensated for the time and expense of commuting. On Manhattan Island, the construction of underground transit opened to mass settlement the Dyckman tract in Washington Heights and the Harlem flats. The new subway also opened the East Bronx to extensive housing development. In Brooklyn, in addition to the heavy concentrations in Brownsville, Williamsburg, and South Brooklyn, Boro Park with "tropical gardens" and "parks" became increasingly accessible. Even distant Coney Island was brought into range by improved transit facilities.

With 542,061 inhabitants in 1910, the Lower East Side reached peak congestion. Thereafter, a decline set in. By 1916 only 23 percent of the city's Jews lived in the once primary area of Jewish settlement, compared to 50 percent in 1903 and 75 percent in 1892. By the close of the first decade of the twentieth century the Lower East Side had lost much of its picturesqueness. In tone and color, the ghetto was perceptibly merging with the surrounding city. East European Jews had scattered to many sections of the city and were swiftly becoming an integral, if not as yet a fully accepted, element in the life of the community. . . .

STUDY GUIDE

1. What impression do you get of the Lower East Side of New York from the author's opening paragraphs regarding the following: (a) the demography of the area; and (b) the subethnic divisions *within* the Jewish immigrant community?

2. What were the advantages of ghetto life that drew large numbers of immigrants to the Lower East Side? Were there any disadvantages? Enumerate.

3. What is meant by a dumbbell tenement? When were they erected, and why? Describe the structure of the dumbbell tenement and its impact on immigrant families — their living quarters, sanitary facilities, and adaptability to the seasons of the year. Given the negative features of the dumbbell tenements, why did they flourish until 1901? Conversely, why were they banned after that date, and by whom?

4. What appears to have been the impact of the ghetto on the following aspects of immigrant life: health and disease, alcoholism, mental health, crime, and intergroup relations? Summarize.

5. By the turn of the century, there were "signs of change," as Rischin notes. What were they, and why did they occur?

6. In retrospect, what parallels can you find between the social conditions of the turn-of-the-century ghetto described by Rischin and contemporary ghetto life? Are there any major differences? Elaborate.

BIBLIOGRAPHY

The topic of immigration has received a great deal of attention from American historians in recent years. Among the older volumes still worth reading are the following: Carl F. Wittke, *We Who Built America* (1939) and Marcus Lee Hansen, *The Immigrant in American History* (1940). More recent surveys include Maldwyn A. Jones, *American Immigration* (1960) and *Destination America* (1976) and Philip A. M. Taylor, *The Distant Magnet: European Emigration to the U.S.A.* (1971). An important contribution to the literature on immigration has been made in the following books by Oscar Handlin: *The Uprooted: The Epic Story of the Great Migrations That Made the American People* (1951); *Children of the Uprooted* (1966); and *Immigration as a Factor in American History* (1959). Scholarly yet highly readable portraits of particular immigrant groups will be found in Humbert S. Nelli, *Italians in Chicago: 1880–1930* (1970); Theodore Saloutos, *The Greeks in the United States* (1964); and Moses Rischin, *The Promised City: New York's Jews, 1870–1914* (1962), from which the preceding selection was taken.

Jane Addams and student, 1931. Settlement workers tried to teach art as well as practical skills to the "new" immigrants.

8

ALLEN F. DAVIS

The Settlement House

Although there is much controversy among historians concerning the precise character of Progressivism — that broadly based movement for social reform that flourished in the first decade and a half of the twentieth century — we can, in retrospect, divide the accomplishments of the Progressive movement into three broad categories: a greater measure of regulation of our economy, the democratization of politics, and what one historian has called a "quest for social justice." From the waning years of the nineteenth century until World War I, numerous programs were launched in order to solve a number of the social problems created by the unbridled industrial and urban growth in the late nineteenth century. Whatever may have been the motives of the Progressives — and here, too, historians disagree — it is clear that a large measure of idealism motivated the men and women who participated in the social-justice movements of this era.

One of the most idealistic and interesting institutions of the Progressive era was the settlement house, established among the immigrants in the nation's urban centers. These settlement houses — devoted to the cultural, artistic, vocational, and psychological uplifting of the immigrants and their families — clearly reflected the humanitarian strain that in part propelled the Progressive movement. The "settlement idea," as it is called by the movement's chronicler, Allen F. Davis, originated in London with the establishment of Toynbee Hall by two Oxford students who hoped, through this kind of institution, to bring culture to the workers of that city. Within a few years, the programs offered by settlement houses were broadened and the number of such institutions, in both England and the United States, increased. Under the leadership of idealistic, yet highly competent and pragmatic pioneers — Jane Addams in Chicago, Robert A. Woods in Boston, and Lillian Wald in New York — settlement houses began to dot the ghettos of American cities in the East and in the Middle West. In 1891, there were more than a hundred, and by the end of the decade, more than four hundred. As Professor Davis's history of the movement in the United States, *Spearheads for Reform*, makes amply clear, the settlement houses touched upon many aspects of the lives of those they served: in addition to providing programs of a vocational, educational, and artistic character, the settlement house leaders agitated for more honest politics, better housing, more parks, schools and playgrounds, improved working conditions for adults, and a ban on child labor. In many instances, the settlement houses were the first institutions to recognize the plight of the urban black in the North, and a number of leaders in the movement actively participated in the organization of the National Association for the Advancement of Colored People.

The influence of this idealistic movement went beyond the Progressive era. In the concluding chapter of his book, Professor Davis demonstrates how the ideas and values of the settlement house movement lived on to influence the thought and the programs of the New Deal of the 1930s. Here are his closing words on the subject: "All those who today join the war on poverty or try to rehabilitate the nation's cities are influenced, whether they know it or not, by a generation of settlement workers who dared to dream that American cities could be safe and stimulating for all citizens, and who worked from their bases in urban neighborhoods to make a part of that dream come true."

Many early settlement residents were teachers by training or inclination. Some of them even had classroom experience, but rejected a career in high school or college teaching as too routine and narrow, and too far removed from the pressing problems of an urban, industrialized country. They came to the settlement as educational innovators, ready to cut down the barriers that separated learning from reality. "A settlement is a protest against a restricted view of education," Jane Addams once remarked, and like most settlement workers, she considered education a method of social reform.

Jane Addams and the other settlement pioneers drew heavily on the English settlements and university extension movements. They planned to extend the advantages of a college education to workingmen in order to narrow the gulf between factory worker and college graduate through classes, lectures, and discussions. Stanton Coit patterned his Neighborhood Guild in part on Frederick Denison Maurice's Working Men's College in London, and in 1890 Morrison Swift planned a settlement in Philadelphia that would be a social university. Jane Addams and Ellen Starr began to teach and to lecture as soon as they unpacked at Hull House. Miss Starr organized a reading group to discuss George Eliot's *Romola*, which broadened to include Dante, Browning, and Shakespeare. Julia Lathrop started a Sunday afternoon Plato Club for the discussion of philosophical questions. Vida Scudder and Helena Dudley organized a Social Science Club at Denison House in Boston in 1893, and for a time forty or fifty businessmen, professionals, workingmen, and students gathered weekly to hear lectures and discussions on such topics as "The Ethics of Trade Unions" or "German Socialism." But attendance dwindled after a few months, and the club collapsed after the third year.

Almost every settlement had its lecture series and its educational conferences, and a few like Hull House had university extension classes for college credit. John Dewey and Frank Lloyd Wright were among those who spoke at Hull House. George Santayana once gave a lecture on St. Francis and the beauty of poverty at Prospect Union in Cambridge that left most of the hearers aghast. Some of the lectures and discussions were exciting at least to the residents and students if not to the workingmen in the neighborhood. And although Sinclair Lewis exaggerated in *Ann Vickers* when he described the educational fare in his fictional settlement as composed mostly of "lectures delivered gratis by earnest advocates of the single tax, troutfishing, exploring Tibet, pacifism, sea shell collecting, the eating of bran, and the geography of Charlemagne's Empire," there was an element of the unreal and the esoteric about the early settlement workers' attempts to dispense the culture of the universities to workingmen.

There was also something unrealistic about the attempt to turn settlements into art galleries. . . . Ellen Starr and Jane Addams collected reproductions of great art in Europe before they founded Hull House and took pride in hanging the pictures in the settlement. Miss Starr was the leader in the "attempt of Hull House to make the aesthetic and artistic a vital influence in the lives of its neighbors." She taught classes in the history of art, patiently explaining the meaning of each picture. She also organized exhibitions gathered from the homes of wealthy Chicagoans with the hope of limiting the pictures to those which combined "an elevated tone with technical excellence." Edward Burchard, the first male resident of the settlement, was elected to guard the pictures at night and to carry placards up and down the streets and into the saloons to advertise the exhibitions. . . .

University Settlement in New York also held art exhibitions, but the men in the neighborhood were openly hostile. Edward King reported that many of his friends thought they were "a cleverly disguised trick on the part of the eminent mugwumps in the University Settlement Society to get a grip on the district in the ante-election months." The women were less suspicious. A young immigrant girl hung a reproduction of a Fra Angelico angel on the wall of her tenement. Many workingmen and their families were genuinely interested in art, but they found nothing in the public schools to satisfy this interest; the schools did not even have pictures on their walls.

The first building especially constructed for Hull House contained a gallery, and the settlement continued its art exhibits until the opening of the Chicago Art Institute made them unnecessary. Ellen Starr also led the movement to put art in the schools. She donated a series of reproductions to the school nearest Hull House and helped the Chicago Women's Club form a committee to exhibit pictures in all other schools in the city. Thus began the Chicago Public School Art Society. It was a small beginning that did not revolutionize public education in the city, but it was significant as the first of many experiments tried first in the settlements and then adopted by the public schools.

Art exhibitions, lectures, and university extension classes were fine; they satisfied the desire of many settlement residents to make use of their college training. Moreover they provided intellectual stimulation for "the transfigured few" in the neighborhood capable of abstract thought. Men like Philip Davis, Meyer Bloomfield, Henry Moskowitz, and Francis Hackett found the programs stimulating and were thus inspired to continue their education. In addition, settlement lectures and classes served to bring the real world to a number of university professors (or at least they liked to think so). But it soon became obvious that the great majority of the people in the settlement neighborhood were not interested in extension classes. Although thousands attended art exhibitions they took little away that would vitally influence their lives.

What most people in a working-class neighborhood needed was something useful and concrete, something closely related to their daily lives.

This might mean courses in manual training, or homemaking; it might simply mean instruction in English or basic American government and history. Large groups of immigrants made both English-type university extension courses and American public schools inadequate in the urban setting, thus forcing settlement workers, whether they liked it or not, to experiment with new methods and techniques.

They quickly learned that among the most useful things were child care and kindergarten classes for young children whose mothers worked all day. Stanton Coit opened a kindergarten at Neighborhood Guild only a few months after the settlement was organized, and Hull House, New York College Settlement, Chicago Commons, and most other pioneer settlements, established them soon after opening their doors. . . .

The goals of the settlements and the kindergartens seemed so similar that one kindergarten teacher labeled the social settlement "the kindergarten for adults." Most settlements were more than that, but many had actually developed from kindergartens. In Boston a number of neighborhood kindergartens and day nurseries established by Mrs. Quincy A. Shaw in the late 1870s and early 1880s became settlements in the nineties. Also in Boston, a group of men and women who sought consciously to combine the principles of the kindergarten and the settlement established the Elizabeth Peabody House. Neighborhood House in Chicago, Kingsley House in New Orleans, and others scattered around the country, developed this same way. Mary McDowell was trained as a kindergarten teacher and directed classes at Hull House before becoming the head resident of the University of Chicago Settlement. Eleanor McMain, who had taught preschool children, became head resident of Kingsley House in New Orleans. Still others brought some of the kindergarten ideals to the settlement and introduced a large number of college-trained men and women to [Friedrich] Froebel and the possibilities of creative play. Many settlements trained kindergarten teachers in a more formal way. Amalie Hofer, the editor of *Kindergarten Magazine,* and her sister, Mrs. Bertha Hofer Hegner, directed the Pestalozzi-Froebel Kindergarten Training School at Chicago Commons. The Chicago Kindergarten Institute met for several years at the University of Chicago Settlement. Mrs. Alice H. Putnam's Kindergarten Training School used Hull House, and South End House had a kindergarten normal school after 1897.

While the settlements did not originate the kindergarten idea, they played a significant part in popularizing it, especially since they often pressured the public schools to take over their work. Teaching little children could be a thankless occupation, but the idea of developing the whole child through art and music and creative play provided a challenge also to revise the whole educational system. It led to attempts to apply the same principles to adult education; for grown men and women could also learn by "playing." It led to a search for playgrounds, parks, and gymnasiums, and to campaigns against child labor. The kindergarten ideas of Froebel, taken seriously, could lead to reform. In the case of the settlement workers they often did.

The kindergarten classes brought mothers and sisters as well as little boys and girls to the settlement and led naturally to attempts to provide them with something useful and meaningful. Usually this meant classes in homemaking, cooking, sewing, and shopping. Some courses taught useless skills, such as the art of serving tea from a silver service or accepting a calling card on a tray. Many of the women settlement workers were appalled at the way their immigrant neighbors kept house. Their wastefulness and disorderliness bothered those brought up in neat middle-class American homes. Some settlement workers could never quite overcome their feeling of superiority, and these homemaking classes only made the immigrant woman more conscious of differences and deficiencies. But many newcomers, baffled by unfamiliar urban ways of household management, acquired helpful suggestions and new confidence at the settlement. Of course, the immigrants did not always listen; and, indeed, sometimes they knew more than the settlement workers. . . . Settlement workers soon discovered that they could get the attention of neighborhood women by setting up model flats and housekeeping centers similar to tenement apartments. There they taught cooking, cleaning, caring for children, and other household tasks, in a more realistic setting. In this way they tried to relate their teaching to the real problems that their neighbors faced. Eventually the public schools borrowed many of their techniques.

The practical needs of the people in the neighborhood usually dictated the types of classes offered. Many settlements were located near textile factories where women and children could take out work. Skill and speed in making buttonholes or operating a sewing machine was vitally important and meant increased family income. Most settlements attempting to satisfy the real needs of their neighborhoods soon found themselves very much involved in manual training and industrial education. Hartley House in New York maintained a carpentry shop; Boston's South End House had a lace-making shop and, after 1903, a separate building equipped with a stage for plays; carpentry and clay-modeling rooms; and kitchen and kindergarten equipment. Hull House held classes in pottery, metalwork, enameling, wood carving, weaving, dressmaking, sewing, millinery, and cooking. Greenwich House in New York began a handicrafts school and shop in 1907 to teach young women how to make lace, pottery, and other articles, and also to employ the many immigrant women in the neighborhood who already had special skills. Settlement workers combined lectures and visits to museums with the teaching of practical skills in order that the newcomers might see that they were engaged in artistic work that had a long history and real importance. Greenwich House started the shop and school primarily to aid the people in the neighborhood, but after three years it was self-supporting and was taken over as a private enterprise by two young women.

Most settlement workers wanted to do more than just teach practical skills to their neighbors. Borrowing from Ruskin and Morris, they also tried to preserve handicraft skills in an industrial age. Moreover, they were concerned with the wider implications of the teaching and learning process in an urban setting. They saw immigrant women who felt useless and out of place in a strange land. They observed sons and daughters employed in meaningless jobs and rebelling against their parents and the language and customs of the old country. When Jane Addams and Ellen Starr decided to establish the Hull House Labor Museum in 1900 they were anxious to preserve the spinning and weaving art of the Italian women. But they also saw a chance to help the younger generation appreciate this talent, and by teaching the girls something of the history of the textile industry, something of the relationship between raw material and the finished product, they hoped to transform their lives from drudgery to more meaningful activity. . . .

Not all settlement workers were realistic in their educational experiments, and there was something romantic and nostalgic about their attempt to revive handicrafts in the face of increasing industrialism. But they were usually concerned with real problems and tried to satisfy important needs. The early residents who provided art exhibitions and musical concerts for people in the area were aware of a craving for beautiful things on the part of many who lived in those dreary surroundings. But they realized only gradually that this need could be better satisfied and utilized by letting the people themselves create things rather than by having them merely look and listen. A few settlements, therefore, began to hold exhibitions, not of reproductions of great art, but of painting actually done by the neighborhood people, and they asked those skilled in painting or sculpture to teach others. Hull House, Greenwich House, and several other settlements supported successful amateur theaters which provided an artistic outlet for some and helped a great many immigrants learn English. "The number of those who like to read has been greatly overestimated," Jane Addams decided, and the theater gave these knowledge of the language, and an education in the broadest sense. . . .

Many settlements also utilized and encouraged the musical talent of those in their neighborhood; a few offered musical instruction as well. The Hull House Music School was begun in 1893 under the direction of Eleanor Smith, and the following year Emilie Wagner began giving piano and violin lessons in College Settlement in New York. After 1899 the project was sponsored jointly by University and College settlements and in 1903 a separate organization, the Music School Settlement, was begun. There was no attempt to turn every student into a professional musician, but rather to allow those who loved music to find a way to express themselves through it. Some critics charged that by teaching the children of the poor to enjoy music and the finer things of life the settlement workers would only make them more unhappy and dissatisfied. Thomas Tapper, director of the New York Music School Settlement, admitted that this was occasionally true; he wished it would happen more often for he believed unhappiness was the first step on the road out of the slums.

Most of the immigrants had to struggle desperately to survive and to learn something about their new country. Language was a difficult barrier, and the public schools did little to teach immigrants English: a few conducted evening classes in English or Civics, but these usually treated immigrant adults as American children just learning to read. Grown men read, "I am a yellow bird. I can sing. I can fly. I can sing to you," or "Oh Baby, dear baby, / Whatever you do, / You are the king of the home, / And we all bend to you." Philip Davis remarked that an English primer placed in the hands of the immigrant "should emphasize less the words 'cat,' 'rat,' and 'mat' and dwell more on the words 'city,' 'citizen,' and 'state.' " The settlements often tried to combine the teaching of English with the teaching of citizenship. Because they understood some of the immigrants' needs, settlement workers treated them like adults and tried to relate the problems of language and of government to their experiences.

Kindergarten classes, classes in English for adults, in music, art, handicrafts, and homemaking — all these areas of education settlement workers experimented with before most public schools considered adding them to their curricula. They were important to the individual experiences and needs of the local population. In a sense they were practical courses, although few could earn a living in music or art.

The settlement workers, interested in relating education more closely to life, could not long ignore the pressing problems of training young men and women in their neighborhoods for worthwhile jobs. They knew that they could inspire the few with exceptional ability to go to college, but that the majority could never go. What would happen to them? Would they merely drift into unskilled jobs, or could the settlements do something to prepare them for a meaningful role in the industrial world?

Robert Woods of South End House was perhaps more concerned with this problem than any other settlement worker. . . . We have been "training too much the consumer citizen and too little the producer citizen," he remarked, "and concentrating too much on the two percent who get to college and the eight or ten percent who get to high school." Like Ellen Starr, he was disturbed that industrialism had brought about a separation of cultural and vocational interests. The skilled workman, he believed, "must be helped to gain the position he had in the Middle Ages, when the artisans were poets and artists also." He advocated some manual training of everyone, so that even the lucky ones who went on to college would have an appreciation of the dignity and the difficulties of working with their hands or operating machines. . . .

Woods argued for state-supported vocational training in speeches before the National Education Association and at a meeting of the Harvard Teacher's Association. As early as 1901 he spoke out in favor of public vocational education in an article in the *Boston Globe*. Woods in 1904 investigated the existing facilities for vocational training in Massachusetts and in 1906 served for three months as temporary secretary of a state commission on industrial education which had the authority to set up industrial schools. There was opposition, of course. Labor leaders feared that trade schools would threaten their control of the skilled labor force, and educators were horrified by any attempt to change the curriculum of the public schools. However, other settlement workers joined Woods — Jane Addams, Ellen Starr, and Graham Taylor in Chicago, and Lillian Wald and Mary Flexner in New York — and they were especially insistent to point out the need for training hands as well as minds. When the National Society for the Promotion of Industrial Education was formed in 1906 Robert Woods and Jane Addams served on the board of managers. At the local and the national level settlement workers played a significant part in forcing public schools to take over the industrial and vocational training begun in the settlements.

The settlement workers' interest went beyond vocational education to concern for the school drop-outs. Vocational training, they decided, meant little without vocational guidance, so almost every settlement worker at one time or another advised about jobs and training programs. Some settlements operated an informal employment bureau, but Civic Service House in Boston even went beyond that.

Mrs. Quincy Agassiz Shaw established Civic Service House in the North End of Boston in 1901 to promote civic and educational work among the immigrant population of that area, with Meyer Bloomfield, a young, brilliant, and energetic reformer then fresh out of Harvard, as the guiding force behind the venture. Bloomfield, who had grown up on New York's Lower East Side and had attended clubs and classes at University Settlement, felt he owed something to the recent immigrants still caught, as he had once been, in the slums. He explained his plans for a new settlement to Mrs. Shaw, and she financed the experiment in reform.

Bloomfield was soon joined by Philip Davis, another who had risen from the ghetto. They organized clubs and classes, helped immigrants learn English, and encouraged them to join trade unions. They also began to attract an impressive group of intellectuals and reformers. Students from Harvard and Boston University came in the evening to teach classes in American government, history, and English. Ralph Albertson, an itinerant reformer who had organized the ill-fated Christian Commonwealth in Georgia, drifted to Boston and Civic Service House. One of Albertson's closest friends was Frank Parsons, law professor, municipal expert, prolific scholar, and impassioned reformer. Through Albertson and Bloomfield (who had studied under him at Boston University Law School), Parsons became interested in the new settlement venture. He was especially impressed with Philip Davis's idea for beginning a workingmen's institute at Civic Service House. Having followed the work of Toynbee Halls' Workingmen's Institute in London for some time, Parsons devoted himself to the task of creating a similar institution at Civic Service House.

The Breadwinner's College, as its founders named it, opened in 1905 with courses in history, civics, economics, psychology, and philosophy. Parsons and Albertson were the backbone of the faculty, aided by Philip Davis, Meyer Bloomfield, and Morris Cohen, a philosopher who had experience with a similar school in New York. There was also an occasional lecture by Josiah Royce and Lincoln Steffens, among others. . . .

Some of the students at Breadwinner's College were out of work; others were unhappily toiling at jobs that held no interest, no meaning, and no future. When Parsons invited groups of high school boys to the settlement he discovered that most had no vocational plans or else had plans that were completely unrealistic. Since there was no organization to help them choose the right job and none to help them utilize their latent and about-to-be-wasted talent, Parsons created one. In 1908 he asked Mrs. Shaw for more money to support another experiment, a vocational bureau. The bureau began operation on April 23, 1908. Parsons talked with scores of young men eager for help in choosing a career. He emphasized the need for guidance by a counselor carefully trained and armed with industrial statistics and information about job openings. And he wrote down his ideas about an orderly and scientific way to guide young people in their choice of job or profession in his book *Choosing a Vocation*, published in 1909. But Parsons did not live to see the book; he had died from the strain of overwork in the fall of 1908.

Frank Parsons was the founder of the modern vocational guidance movement which might never have been started if Bloomfield had not been ready to step in and take over as director. He expanded the activities, advertised in books like the *Vocational Guidance of Youth,* and *Youth, School and Vocation,* and in lectures at Harvard and elsewhere. Bloomfield helped "sell" the idea of vocational counseling to the school committee of Boston, which became the first city in the country to have such organized, systematic job counseling. Bloomfield also called the first National Conference on Vocational Guidance, which met in Boston in 1910 and led to the organization of the National Vocational Guidance Association in 1913. The experiment begun by a few dedicated men in a Boston social settlement thus stimulated a national vocational guidance movement, with far-reaching and significant results.

Vocational training and vocational guidance were later adopted by the public schools. This was somewhat unexpected because in the beginning, most settlement workers had no desire to alter or reform the public educational system; they saw their function only as supplementing schools. However, as soon as they became aware of the inadequacy of education, especially in the poorer districts of the great cities, the attempt to supplement became an attempt to change.

Some reforms were practical, such as the introduction of school nurses and school lunchrooms. Lillian Wald and her fellow workers at Henry Street Settlement simply demonstrated the need and proposed them as effective solutions to some chronic problems. Miss Wald had been troubled by the number of children she met who were kept out of school because of disease or sickness. Eczema or hookworm could prevent a child from receiving any education at all. Doctors had been inspecting school children since 1897, sending home those with diseases, but no one had made an attempt to treat these children. Ironically, the coming to power of Seth Low's reform administration in 1901 complicated rather than solved the problem, for the inspection of school children was made more efficient and more rigorous. Still, nothing was done in the way of treatment. At this point, Lillian Wald, well acquainted with the Health Commissioner and other officials of the Low administration, offered to show how school nurses could solve the problem by treating the diseases diagnosed by the doctors. First, however, she made the city officials promise that if the experiment proved successful they would use their influence to have the nurses put on a permanent basis with salaries paid out of public funds. The settlement nurses found that by making regular visits to the schools, working with the doctors, and in some cases visiting the families, all but the most seriously ill could be treated and kept in school. After only one month's trial, the Board of Estimate appropriated money to hire school nurses. Soon the experiment was being copied in other cities.

Hot lunches for a penny began in much the same way. In 1905 a number of people in New York were aroused by a widely misquoted statement from Robert Hunter's book, *Poverty,* claiming that 70,000 school children went to school in the city without breakfast (he had said, underfed). Lillian Wald and other settlement workers had tried to get the city to subsidize school lunches as early as 1901. They continued to argue in favor of cheap or inexpensive lunches: "The needs of the body are as imperative as those of the mind, and the successful training of the latter depends upon the adequate nourishment of the former," Miss Wald announced. But for a time the settlement workers' suggestions were ignored. Then the Salvation Army and several restaurants attempted to provide lunches for the children. However, the settlement workers realized that private charity was not the answer; they sought to have the school authorities take over the responsibility of serving hot lunches. Eventually they were successful, and the "homemaking centers" inaugurated by the settlements demonstrated that the idea was practical.

Another pioneer educational project at Henry Street Settlement involved mentally retarded and handicapped children. Settlement workers encouraged the work of Elizabeth Farrell, a neighborhood teacher interested in helping the retarded, and they persuaded the Board of Education to permit her to teach an ungraded class of handicapped children. They furthermore got special equipment for her and convinced the Board of the importance of her work. In 1908 the Board voted a separate department for teaching the retarded. . . .

A settlement worker's concern with local education often led him into broad reform movements, as the example of Florence Kelley illustrates. She taught at night in a nearby public school during her first year at Hull House. Although she had been concerned about child labor even before this, what she saw as a teacher played an important part in her decision to concentrate on winning better child labor laws. The frustration experienced by Jane Addams and others in trying to convince the City Council that the public school in the Hull House district needed enlarging led them to a futile attempt to unseat the local ward boss. They soon discovered that educational reform was closely related to economic and political reform.

While the settlement workers were most influenced by the concrete needs they saw about them, for improved school buildings, practical courses, and school nurses, they were concerned with educational theory, too, and with the implications of their experiments. Indeed, they made important contributions to the development of progressive education. They did not invent progressive education, but often borrowed from the advanced thinking of experts in many fields, frequently adopting the latest theories. They provided the practical testing ground for others' ideas. In their experiments with vocational training and their attempt to relate the work of the school to the reality of the world, through kindergartens, work with immigrants, and by their efforts to tailor the school to the needs of the student, the settlement workers tried to make the student the center of the school and the school the center of the community. Although they were never quite sure whether they sought to adjust the child and the immigrant to society, or whether they meant to transform society to meet the needs of their pupils, they used education as a method of social reform.

The settlement movement and progressive education intertwined at many points, and both drew support from a broad area. The mutual influence of the two movements is most obvious with John Dewey. He was a member of the first board of trustees at Hull House and a frequent visitor at the settlement. He lectured and on several occasions led the discussion at Julia Lathrop's Plato Club. He gave a formal address now and then and sometimes just dropped in to talk, to meet the interesting people who found their way to Hull House, to argue with the socialists, the anarchists, and the single-taxers, and to learn. . . . When he moved to New York and to Columbia University he became associated with Lillian Wald at Henry Street Settlement and became chairman of the educational committee at Mary Simkhovitch's Greenwich House. When he went to Boston or another city he often sought out a settlement house.

Dewey learned a great deal from his contacts with settlement workers. He sympathized with their attempts to broaden the scope of education and widen the impact of the school. Most of all, he learned from watching and participating in educational experiments and from taking part in the give-and-take of discussions.

The settlement workers also learned from Dewey. Possibly his greatest contribution was making them see the meaning and the consequences or implications of their day-by-day educational experiments. "I have always thought that we were trying to live up to your philosophy," Lillian Wald wrote him on one occasion. Jane Addams also saw the implications for social work of Dewey's ideas. "His insistence upon an atmosphere of freedom and confidence between the teacher and pupil . . . ," she wrote, "profoundly affected all similar relationships, certainly those between the social worker and his client." Dewey's writings had a large impact on the settlement movement; in turn, the settlement movement had an important influence on him. In one of his books, *Schools of Tomorrow,* there is a chapter entitled "The School as a Social Settlement." That sums up what

Dewey and the settlement workers were trying to accomplish in the city. They were trying to make the schools more like social settlements, and to a large extent they succeeded.

STUDY GUIDE

1. What rationale was developed by the settlement house founders to justify their general cultural and educational programs for immigrants and their art classes and exhibits in particular?

2. What role did the settlement house play in developing the kindergarten, and on what theoretical grounds were kindergartens established?

3. Explain how the settlement house helped the immigrant in the following areas: home economics, arts and crafts, music, vocational instruction, language, health instruction and treatment, hot lunches, and assistance to the unskilled and retarded children. Why do you think what was initially a cultural organization chose to become involved in the more practical problems of day-to-day urban life?

4. One of the nation's leading philosophers during the Progressive era was John Dewey. What was his relationship to the settlements, and what did the settlements contribute to his thinking?

5. Would you say that altruism, rather than self-interest, characterized the motives of the men and women who established the settlement houses? Or do you feel that this kind of social reform was in reality a means of social control — an effort to encourage the immigrants to conform to an accepted Anglo-Saxon pattern of behavior? During and after World War I, many Progressive programs turned into deliberate attempts to force conformity on immigrants. Why do you think such a change took place?

BIBLIOGRAPHY

In addition to *Spearheads for Reform: The Social Settlements and the Progressive Movement, 1890–1914* (1967), from which the preceding selection was taken, Allen F. Davis published a biography of Jane Addams entitled *American Heroine: The Life and Legend of Jane Addams* (1973). Additional material on the settlement house movement will be found in Josephine C. Goldmark, *Impatient Crusader: Florence Kelley's Life Story* (1953); in two autobiographical volumes by Jane Addams, *Twenty Years at Hull-House* (1910) and *The Second Twenty Years at Hull-House* (1970); in Lillian D. Wald, *The House on Henry Street* (1915); and in Robert A. Woods and Albert J. Kennedy, *The Settlement Horizon: A National Estimate* (1922). Other aspects of the social-justice movement are presented in Robert Bremner's factual *From the Depths: The Discovery of Poverty in the United States* (1956) and Clarke Chambers, *Seedtime of*

Reform: American Social Service and Social Action (1963). Another important book — tracing the evolution of social work from an idealistic activity of laymen to a full-time professional occupation — is Roy Lubove, *The Professional Altruist: The Emergence of Social Work as a Career, 1880–1930* (1965).

Black migrants making their way north.

9

FLORETTE HENRI

Black Migration

Throughout much of the twentieth century, American blacks abandoned the cotton fields and small towns of the South for the industrial cities of the North. In the last decade of the nineteenth century and in the first of the twentieth, 200,000 blacks came North. Between 1910 and 1920, a half-million more came, and larger and larger numbers migrated North in succeeding decades. They came, as Florette Henri makes clear in the essay that follows, for a number of reasons: some came to sightsee and never returned South; some came to escape the violently racist attitudes of the South; and some came to enjoy the economic opportunities the North afforded. Blacks who came to the North were motivated by the same search for opportunity that drew rural and small-town whites as well as the "new" immigrants to the cities — the millions of jobs for able-bodied men and women made available by a vibrant and ever expanding industrial economy. For many, a job even at the lowest of ranks in the factory provided an income higher than they could earn as sharecroppers or tenant farmers.

Many parallels can be found between the migration of American blacks from the South to the cities of the North and the "new" immigration to the United States by southern and eastern Europeans between 1880 and 1924. Both groups were abandoning a system of landholding where they were at once tied to the land and landless — blacks as sharecroppers in a system of tenant farming and sharecropping, the Europeans as peasants in a feudal land system. There are other parallels as well: both groups settled, for the most part, in the big cities, not in the rural areas of the country; both were relegated to the unskilled levels of the industrial work force; and both created

135

urban ghettoes as a shield from a strange, and even hostile, environment. But one important difference between these two groups of migrants remained: no white ethnic group had to overcome the barriers of color that confronted the black American.

[The] story of movement in the black population says clearly that many blacks did not sit quietly in one place waiting for things to change under them; that, in fact, they shared in the general American pattern of mobility. But early migrations were dwarfed by the surge of black people northward after 1900, and especially after 1910. According to various contemporaneous estimates, between 1890 and 1910 around 200,000 black Southerners fled to the North; and between 1910 and 1920 another 300,000 to 1,000,000 followed. . . .

What precipitated the mass migration of that period is succinctly expressed in this verse:

> Boll-weevil in de cotton
> Cut worm in de cotton,
> Debil in de white man,
> Wah's goin' on.

Drought, then heavy rains, and the boll weevils that flourish under wet conditions had ruined cotton crops in 1915 and 1916. Tenant farmers and croppers were desperate. Too, injustice, disfranchisement, and Jim Crow — "debil in de white man" — grew more severe and galling each year, until life in the South was intolerable for a black man. And at the same time, finally, there was a reasonable hope of escape from this suffering because of the Great War, as it approached and while it was going on. At precisely the time war production needed all the labor it could get, immigration was sharply curtailed, dropping from 1,218,480 in 1914 to 326,700 in 1915, to under 300,000 in 1916 and 1917, and finally to 110,618 in 1918 — less than 10 percent of the 1914 figure. If immigration had continued at the 1914 rate, almost 5,000,000 more immigrants would have entered the United States by the end of the war, and war production could probably have employed almost all the workers among them. It seems reasonable to believe, therefore, that even if one accepts the top figure of 1,000,000 black migrants during that period, they and the immigrants who did manage to enter the country during the peak production years could not have filled the void. Such friction, then, as developed between black and white workers was probably not based on economic competition so much as on racism.

Woodson claims that even before the unskilled and semiskilled black laborers went North, there was a substantial movement in that direction by educated and professional-level black people — the group that DuBois named the Talented Tenth — who could no longer bear the violence, intimidation, and suppression that were part of everyday life in the South. The increasing callousness of the Republican administrations of Roosevelt and Taft badly shook their faith in the party of liberation. The Brownsville incident of 1906, when President Roosevelt and Secretary of War Taft arbitrarily punished 167 black soldiers, may have been final proof that blacks were deserted by the federal government and must look after themselves. These political facts may have motivated some of the poor, uneducated blacks also to leave the South, although by and large they clung to their faith in the party of emancipation. When Ray Stannard Baker asked a black man why he was leaving Atlanta (after a riot there in 1908) for Washington, D.C., the answer was: "Well, you see, I want to be as near the flag as I can."

According to several contemporaneous studies of the motives of migrants, most blacks left the South simply to be able to feed themselves and their families. George Edmund Haynes, one of the Urban League founders, reported in 1912 that of southern black migrants in New York City, 47.1 percent had come for better jobs. In a 1917 study made for the Secretary of Labor, again the economic motive came first. In the light of what has been said in previous pages about the condition of southern blacks, a rundown of all the reasons given in that study is interesting:

1. low wages: "The Negro . . . appears to be interested in having some experience with from four to six times as much pay as he has ever had before" even if, in buying power, 50¢ to $1 a day in the South should equal $2 to $4 a day in the North;
2. bad treatment by whites — all classes of Negroes are dissatisfied with their condition;
3. injustice and evils of tenant farming — difficulty of getting a planter to settle accounts, about which his word cannot be questioned; also, the high prices charged by planters and merchants for necessary supplies;
4. more dissatisfaction than formerly with these conditions, in the light of the world movement for democracy.

Poor pay was the leading reason for migration in a survey of 1917 in the *Crisis,* followed by bad treatment, bad schools, discrimination, and oppression. Abram L. Harris, an economist and informed student of Negro migrations, concluded that all the movements away from the rural South, from the Civil War on, were "fundamentally the result of the growth of machine industry, and of the lack of economic freedom and the non-assurance of a margin of subsistence under the one-crop share system of the agricultural South."

There were undoubtedly some migrants who moved about simply for adventure or to see new places. Out of the 400 interviewed by Epstein, 85 said they were just traveling to see the country. Gilbert Osofsky in his Harlem study speaks of some who were just wanderers, criminals, hoodlums, or adventurers. But most evidence shows, as Louise Venable Kennedy wrote in her study of Negro urbanization, that blacks move about for the same reasons as other American groups — for jobs, education, better conditions — and not because of a racial trait of rootlessness, as many believed. John Daniels in his 1914 book on black people of Boston spoke of the "excessive migratoriness which is inherent in the Negro character." He added, "Obstacles in the environment are not opposed by a quality of rootedness," explaining why almost 2,000 blacks left Boston between 1900 and 1910. But such an attack on character was hardly necessary to explain why numbers of blacks left Boston. Daniels himself mentions a notable decrease of interest and tolerance on the part of white Bostonians. Even more important was the scarcity of any but menial jobs in nonindustrial Boston. Howard Odum, also, spoke of migratoriness as a race characteristic of blacks, claiming that they have little attachment to home, siblings, or parents. Dillard, however, said that migration was motivated by an effort to improve their condition of living, and as such deserved "commendation not condemnation." And the Atlanta *Constitution* stated bluntly: "The Negro does not move North because he is of a restless disposition. He would prefer to stay in his old home if he could do so on a wage basis more equitable to his race."

The industrial cities were magnets. To farm workers in the South who made perhaps $.75 a day, to urban female domestics who might earn from $1.50 to $3.00 a week, the North during the war years beckoned with factory wages as high as $3.00 or $4.00 a day, and domestic pay of $2.50 a day. As the Dillard report pointed out, blacks longed to get more money into their hands, even if more went out of them; and though living was higher in the North, it was generally not 400 percent higher, as wages might be. A migrant who had gone to Cleveland wrote that he regularly earned $3.60 a day, and sometimes double that, and with the pay of his wife, son, and two oldest daughters, the family took in $103.60 every ten days; the only thing that cost them more than at home, he said, was the rent, $12 a month.

In Pittsburgh in 1918, black migrants were earning between $3.00 and $3.60 a day; only 4 percent of them had earned that much in the South. A 1919 study showed that only 5 percent of migrants in Pittsburgh earned less than $2.00 a day; 56 percent of them had earned less than $2.00 a day in the South. A migrant working in a Newark, New Jersey, dye plant made $2.75 a day plus a rent-free room, and the company had paid his fare North; back home he would have earned less than $1.00 for a long day's work on a farm. Tenant farmers in the Deep South often made less than $15 a month; in 1920, the average annual income of a rural Negro family in Georgia was $290. Even where there was some industry, as in the foundries around Birmingham, unskilled workers got a top of $2.50 for a nine-hour day, while the same sort of worker could make $4.50 a day in Illinois. In Haynes's survey of Negro migrants in New York City, the great majority reported earning from 50 to 100 percent more than they had in the South.

In the complex of motives active upon most migrants it is hard to assess the weight of better educational opportunities for their children. Letters of potential migrants to Emmett Scott and others often speak of this motive. One such letter, written by a representative of a group of 200 men in Mobile, said the men didn't care where they went "just so they cross the Mason and Dixie line" to "where a negro man can appreshate beaing a man" and give his children a good education. Southern politicians of the Vardaman stamp were constantly trying to reduce the little schooling black children got. As governor of Mississippi, Vardaman told the legislature in 1906: "It is your function to put a stop to the worse than wasting of half a million dollars annually" — the cost of black schools — "to the vain purpose of trying to make something of the negro which the Great Architect . . . failed to provide for in the original plan of creation." The black man had no vote, and without a vote he was not likely to enlist any politician in the cause of black education. When Powdermaker's study of Mississippi was made in the 1930s, black schooling was still brief and inadequate; she found fifth-grade children, in that grade because of automatic promotions, who could not read; and she found black parents, especially mothers, with a burning desire to give their children an education at whatever sacrifice to themselves.

Also, it is hard to assay a motive like wishing to appreciate being a man, or wanting to go "where a man's a man" or any place "where a man will Be anything Except a Ker . . . I don't care where so long as I go where a man is a man." The theme is repeated over and over again, and it is a difficult thing to say, a hurtful thing, much harder than simply saying one wants better pay. But it was possibly the overriding reason for leaving the South. W. T. B. Williams, the writer of the report of the Dillard team and its only black member, pointed out that although better pay was most frequently named as a reason for migrating, "the Negro really cares very little for money as such. Cupidity is hardly a Negro vice." He quoted a Florida woman as saying: "Negroes are not so greatly disturbed about wages. They are tired of being treated as children; they want to be men."

Southern blacks were tired of "bene dog as [if] I was a beast"; of never, never being addressed, as they must always address the white man, with a title of respect. Powdermaker says that in Mississippi whites will address a black grade school teacher as "doctor" or "professor" to avoid the Mr., Mrs., or Miss; the consistent withholding of those titles endowed what is a mere polite form with such symbolic force that blacks felt the values of the whole system were concentrated in that Mr. or Mrs. or Miss, and not to be called so meant to be outcast by the system. The sense of being outside the society was reinforced by the equally consistent practice of better-class whites of addressing even the meanest, most illiterate white laborer or loafer as Mr., a cheap way of flattering him into docility by giving him, through the magic of the title, assurance that he was a white man and that as such he shared the superiority of other white men to blacks. This was most damaging to the black man's sense of who he was; because if he, a respectable black, perhaps well educated and fairly prosperous, was not treated like even the dregs of white society, then perhaps he was a different species, not a man at all.

In the many bitter complaints of blacks that they were never Mr. in the South although the white man always was, and in the boast of a migrant writing home that in the North you didn't have to "sir" the white men you worked with — in these there is the cry of the dispossessed and disinherited, a summing up of all the reasons for the black migration. A black minister in Philadelphia put it this way to Ray Stannard Baker: "Well, they're treated more like men up here in the North, that's the secret of it. There's prejudice here, too, but the color line isn't drawn in their faces at every turn as it is in the South. It all gets back to a question of manhood."

Scott said that fear of mob violence and lynching were frequently alleged reasons for migrating, and Booker T. Washington had said that "for every lynching that takes place . . . a score of colored people leave . . . for the city." In the statements of migrants themselves, however, these reasons are not mentioned nearly so often as jobs, pay, justice, better living, and education. Charles Johnson came to the conclusion that persecution, and its ultimate expression in lynching, were not nearly such dominant stimuli to migration as the hope of economic betterment. He claimed that many black migrants — almost 43 percent of them — had gone not North but Southwest, mostly to Arkansas, Oklahoma, and Texas — where economic opportunities might be better but where mob violence was far from uncommon; and that Jasper County in Georgia, and Jefferson County in Alabama, both with fearsome lynching records, had increases rather than declines of black population during the migration period. Kennedy's findings indicated that insecurity of property and life was more likely a supporting cause of migration than a fundamental one, underlying the frequently named reasons of social and educational inequities, humiliations, and insults. In Dutcher's analysis of changes during the 1910–20 decade is the statement that "social grievances appear never to have been sufficient of themselves to produce any considerable movement of the Negro population," and that economic betterment had much greater force. It is amazing, if true, that fear of lynching should not have been a chief reason for flight, considering that ninety-three blacks were lynched in 1908, and fifty, sixty, seventy, or more each year (except 1917) from then until 1920; but the fear may have been too terrible to be given expression in so many words.

Also, there appears to have been a generation gap that made for different motives among older and younger blacks. Many of the older generation, although desperately in need of financial succor, were not so rebellious against "keeping their place." But their sons, who had some schooling, who could read, did not take kindly to the old customs. They were not going to endure being knocked about and beaten on the job "to an extent hardly believable," as the Labor Department reported, and hit with anything that came to the white man's hand, a tool or a piece of lumber. Particularly they resented abuse when their women were with them, and black women were so terrified of what their men might do and what might happen to them as a result, that often the women defended themselves rather than expose their husbands or male friends to danger. A young black said to his father, who was trying to persuade him not to migrate to Chicago: "When a young white man talks rough to me, I can't talk rough to him. You can stand that; I can't. I have some education, and inside I has the feelin's of a white man. I'm goin'." . . .

Those who had left early wrote home about freedom and jobs in the North. Labor agents came South recruiting for the big industrial companies, especially the railroads. The Chicago *Defender* carried northern help-wanted ads and detailed accounts of southern lynchings in its "national edition," widely read in the South, thus both pulling and pushing black people. The idea of "exodus" became surrounded with religious fervor. Many believed that God had opened a way for them to escape oppression. Scott described a group of 147 Mississippi blacks who, when they crossed the Ohio River to freedom, knelt, prayed, and sang hymns; they stopped their watches to symbolize the end of their old life. "Exodus" was a matter of excited secret discussion among southern blacks. Anyone who advised against going was suspected of being in the pay of whites. If a black businessman opposed migration, his customers began to vanish; a minister who preached against it from the pulpit was stabbed the next day. Rumors of jobs and of transportation to them increased unrest. Incautiously, many blacks sold or gave away their belongings and followed any crowd of migrants without an idea of their destination. Some rural areas emptied out so thoroughly that one old woman complained she hadn't enough friends left to give her a decent funeral.

"I should have been here twenty years ago," a man wrote back from the North. "I just begin to feel like a man. . . . My children are going to the same school with the whites and I don't have to humble to no one. I have registered. Will vote in the next election and there isn't any yes Sir and no Sir. It's all yes and no, Sam and Bill." A man wrote from Philadelphia telling of good pay, $75 a month, enough so he could carry insurance in case of illness, and added that there you "don't have to mister every little white boy comes along" and that he hadn't heard "a white man call a colored a nigger" since he'd been North; what was more, he could sit where he chose on the streetcars — not that he craved to sit with whites "but if I have to pay the same fare I have learn to want the same acomidation"; still, this far from rootless wanderer would always "love the good old South," he said. A Columbia, South Carolina, Negro paper reported that a migrant brother had come home for a visit with "more than one hundred dollars and plenty of nice clothes." All this was hallelujah news to the home folks. They could easily ignore the occasional cautionary letter, like one from a Cleveland migrant who warned of loafers, gamblers, and pickpockets and said the city streets weren't safe at night. An unnamed but allegedly widely respected black educator is reported to have said: "Uncle Sam is the most effective [labor] agent at this time. All who are away are writing for others to come on in, the water's fine."

Stimulating the urge to "vote with their feet," as the migration was sometimes called, were the solicitations of northern labor agents. In 1916, the first year of large-scale movement, most agents were representing railroads or the mines. Baker reported: "Trains were backed into several Southern cities and hundreds of Negroes were gathered up in a day, loaded into the cars, and whirled away to the North." For example, in February 1917 a special train was sent to carry 191 black migrants from Bessemer, Alabama, to Pittsburgh at a cost to a coal company of $3,391.95. So great was the excitement, Baker said, that Negroes "deserted their jobs and went to the trains without notifying their employers or even going home." Between 75,000 and 100,000 got to Pennsylvania that way, Baker said, many of them to work for the Pennsylvania and Erie railroads, and still more for the steel mills, munitions plants, and other heavy industries. As might be expected, men so hastily and haphazardly gathered up included a good share of shiftless characters, and in addition, the companies had not prepared for their sudden arrival the necessary housing or facilities; because of this combination of circumstances, many of the labor recruits drifted off the job before they had worked out the railroad fare the companies had advanced.

Some of the labor agents were salaried employees of large industrial companies, and these included some blacks. Others were independent employment agents who charged the migrants from $1.00 to $3.00 for placing them in jobs, and collected from the companies as well if they could get anything. Often the labor recruiters gained access to Negro quarters in the cities where they worked by disguising themselves as salesmen or insurance agents. There were probably some honest men among them, but others were flagrantly unscrupulous in their promises. An agency soliciting workers in the Birmingham and Bessemer areas advertised in such phrases as: "Let's go back north where there are no labor troubles, no strikes, no lockouts; Large coal, good wages, fair treatment; Two weeks pay; Good houses; We ship you and your household goods; All colored ministers can go free; Will advance you money if necessary; Scores of men have written us thanking us for sending them; Go now while you have the chance." Some of the "agents" were downright crooks who collected fees from men wanting to migrate and then failed to be at the depot where they were supposed to rendezvous with their clients. Such was the fate of 1,800 Louisiana blacks who paid $2.00 each to an agent who promised them jobs in Chicago but never made good on the promise. The hardship was greatest when men had quit their jobs in the expectation of leaving the South. Micheaux described one agent who, after collecting $3.00 from a man, sent him to several places in search of imaginary jobs; in the end, the agent refused to refund more than $1.00, although he had done nothing for his client. Another racket was to induce ignorant black girls to sign contracts they could not read that obligated them for the cost of their journey plus a placement fee; in many cases the agents were recruiting for brothels, although what they promised the girls was domestic service.

Alarm spread throughout the white South as farm laborers and city menial and domestic help drifted off in twos, twenties, and two hundreds. State laws and city ordinances were passed to oust or curb the agents who were taking most of the workers. In the light of complaints against the agents by a number of migrants, it seems believable that licensing laws for agents were meant at first to protect black workers as well as their white employers. In South Carolina, for example, an 1891 law requiring all labor agents to pay $500 for a license might simply have been aimed at assuring the reliability of the man promising work out of the state; but when in 1907 the fee was raised to $2,000 it was due simply to panic on the part of whites who saw their cheap labor force dwindling. According to Scott, a license cost $1,000 in Jacksonville, under penalty of a $600 fine and 60 days in jail; in Alabama the state, city, and county fees totaled from $1,000 to $1,250; in Macon, a license cost $25,000, and the applicant had to be vouched for by 10 local ministers and 35 local businessmen, which seems not so much regulatory as prohibitive, as the Atlanta *Constitution* called such licensing. In Montgomery, recruiting labor for out-of-state jobs was punishable by a $100 fine and 6 months at hard labor on a convict gang. Force was not infrequently used to prevent the taking of blacks North, Scott says. Labor agents were arrested. Trains carrying migrants were stopped, the blacks forced to return, and the agents beaten. Blacks might be terrorized or lynched on suspicion of trying to leave the state. "But they might as well have tried to stop by ordinance the migration of the boll-weevil," Baker said; by ordinance, or by hitting them on the head, one by one.

Robert Abbott, editor and publisher of the Chicago *Defender* and himself a migrant from the "Negro town" of Yamacraw, was the loudest single voice calling for the northward flow of black labor, but not the only one. Many other Negro papers also encouraged migration, Baker reported. The Richmond *Reformer* spoke out against Jim Crow, segregation, and living conditions "like cattle, hogs or sheep, penned in" as evils that black people in the South must continue to endure "until they rise up in mass and oppose it openly"; self-respecting Negroes, said the Timmonsville (South Carolina) *Watchman,* should take a hint from a recent lynching and "get away at the earliest possible moment." But it was Abbott who fleshed out the vision of escape, who gave it a definite and dramatic form — even a birthday: the Great Northern Drive of May 15, 1917. Carl Sandburg wrote in the Chicago *Daily News:* "The Defender more than any other one agency was the big cause of the 'Northern fever' and the big exodus from the South." A Georgia paper called the *Defender* "the greatest disturbing element that has yet entered Georgia." The U.S. Department of Labor said that in some sections the *Defender* was probably more effective in carrying off labor than all the agents put together: "It sums up the Negro's troubles and keeps them constantly before him, and it points out in terms he can understand the way of escape." . . .

Abbott put out a "national edition" of his weekly, aimed at southern blacks. It carried in red ink such headlines as: 100 NEGROES MURDERED WEEKLY IN UNITED STATES BY WHITE AMERICANS; LYNCHING — A NATIONAL DISGRACE; and WHITE GENTLEMAN RAPES COLORED GIRL. Accompanying a lynching story was a picture of the lynch victim's severed head, with the caption: NOT BELGIUM — AMERICA. Poems entitled *Land of Hope* and *Bound for the Promised Land* urged blacks to go North, and editorials boosted Chicago as the best place for them to go. Want ads offered jobs at attractive wages in and around Chicago. In news items, anecdotes, cartoons, and photos, the *Defender* crystallized the underlying economic and social causes of black suffering into immediate motives for flight. Repeated stories of those who were leaving the South or who were already in the North conveyed the excitement of a mass movement under way and created an atmosphere of religious hysteria; the *Defender* called the migration the "Flight out of Egypt" and the migrants sang "Going into Canaan." The more people who left, inspired by *Defender* propaganda, the more wanted to go, so the migration fed on itself until in some places it turned into a wild stampede. Even illiterate people bought the paper, as a status symbol. A black leader in Louisiana was quoted as saying, "My people grab it [the *Defender*] like a mule grabs a mouthful of fine fodder." Sandburg wrote that there was in Chicago "a publicity or propaganda machine that directs its appeals or carries on an agitation that every week reaches hundreds of thousands of people of the colored race in the southern states." . . .

Abbott enlisted the aid of two very mobile groups of black people, the railroad men and the entertainers. Chicago was the end of the North – South railroad lines, and a great junction. Hundreds of Pullman porters, dining-car waiters, and traveling stage people passed through it, some of them on their way to remote whistle-stops in the South. The *Defender* paid many of them to pick up bundles of the newspaper in Chicago and drop them along their routes at points where local distributors would meet the trains, get the bundles, and circulate them. In a town where the *Defender* was unknown, the porters would give copies away to any black person they saw. Stage people took bundles of papers and distributed them free in the theaters. The well-known concert singer Sissieretta Jones, who was called the "black Patti" in the patronizing style of the day, asked the ushers in theaters where she performed to give out free copies to all comers.

By such devices the circulation of the *Defender* soared to 283,571 by 1920, with about two thirds of its readers outside of Chicago. This was by far the largest circulation any black newspaper had ever achieved. If each copy reached five readers, a reasonable guess, about 1,500,000 blacks saw it.

Abbott's master stroke in materializing a migration that in 1916 was more rumored than real was the setting of a date, a specific month and day in 1917, for what the *Defender* called "the Great Northern Drive." The incendiary message spread that on May 15 railroad cars would back into the stations of southern towns prepared to carry North any who wanted to go, at a very low fare. The word struck southern blacks with messianic force. There was to be a second coming of freedom on May 15, and it behooved everyone to be ready. . . .

They went with whatever possessions they could carry, "wearing overalls and housedresses, a few walking barefoot." . . . Although it is hard to see how they took their goats, pigs, chickens, dogs, and cats along, as he claims, they certainly must have carried provisions for their long, long journeys, a thousand miles or more for many of them, days and nights of travel with no prospect of any creature comforts along the way. To Chicago from Savannah was 1,027 railroad miles; to New York from San Antonio, 1,916 miles; to Cincinnati from Jacksonville, 822 miles; to Newark from Vicksburg, 1,273 miles; to Detroit from New Orleans, 1,096 miles; to Cleveland from Mobile, 1,046 miles. Some stopped at Chicago for a time before going to their destinations, but most went straight through: from Florida and Georgia to Pennsylvania and New York; from Alabama, Mississippi, Tennessee, and Louisiana to Illinois and Michigan. Most of these people had probably never been more than twenty miles from their homes. . . .

One cheap way to travel was in a group. The *Defender* encouraged the formation of "clubs" of ten to fifty persons and arranged special fares and travel dates with the railroad companies. Many people wrote to the newspaper that they could bring "about 8 or 10 men" or "a family of (11) eleven more or less" or "15 or 20 good men" or "25 women and men," and so on up to "300 or 500 men and women" and finally "as many men as you want." Some of these correspondents sent stamped return envelopes and asked the paper not to publish their letters — "whatever you do, don't publish my name in your paper" — or asked that, if an answer was sent by wire, there should be no mention of the number of people because "if you say 15 or 20 mans they will put me in jail." "This is among us collerd," says one letter offering to bring 20 men and their families.

With so many concerned for secrecy, many must have been too frightened to write at all. They never revealed the presence among them of labor agents. Migrants described how they had to slip away from their homes at night, walk to some railroad station where they were not known, and there board a train for the North. If they were found to have tickets, the police confiscated them. If three or four blacks were discovered together it was assumed that they were "conspiring to go North" and they would be arrested on some trumped-up charge.

For migrants to New York from a coastal city in the South — and most of those who went to New York were from the South Atlantic States — the cheapest and most direct passage was by boat. Steerage fare from Virginia, from which most New York migrants came, was $5.50 or $6.00, including meals. The Old Dominion Line ran boats twice a week from Virginia to New York, and the Baltimore, Chesapeake & Atlantic Railway ran steamers from Baltimore, Washington, and as far south as Florida. By train it would have cost at least $7.50 from Norfolk to New York City, without meals. So the boat was a good buy, although blacks might find themselves in a separate section of the vessel with the household pets of white travelers.

Toward the end of the peak migration period another category of southern blacks settled in northern cities: soldiers returning from France. Rudolph Fisher, a writer of the period, spoke in a short story of a family of Waxhaw, North Carolina, whose son "had gone to France in the draft and, returning, had never got any nearer home than Harlem." There were many such men whose fare, in a roundabout way, had been paid by Uncle Sam. "How're you gonna keep 'em down on the farm, / After they've seen Paree?" a popular song asked.

The rapid flow northward of black people, especially from 1916 when war production went into high gear, aroused much concern and discussion among whites and blacks, North and South. The word "exodus" was apparently so current that Octavus Roy Cohen used it as both noun and verb in his spurious Negro stories of the early twenties: "the merrymakers exodusted" from a party, he wrote; and, there was a "complete exodus from Decatur." Census figures show that in 1900 only 15.6 percent of black people (1,373,996) lived in a state other than that of their birth, whereas in 1910 the percentage born elsewhere had increased to 16.6 (1,616,608), and in 1920 to 19.9 (2,054,242). Of the 300,000 to 1,000,000 blacks estimated by contemporaries to have gone North, almost all went to urban centers. In 1900, 22.7 percent of Negroes lived in cities, North and South; in 1910 this had increased to 24.4 percent, and in 1920 to 34 percent, in numbers totaling more than 3,500,000. By 1920, almost 40 percent of the black population in the North was concentrated in the eight cities of Chicago, Detroit, New York, Cleveland, Cincinnati, Columbus, Philadelphia, and Pittsburgh, although those cities contained only 20 percent of the total northern population. The city with the most dramatic percentage increase in black population between 1910 and 1920 was Detroit, by an astounding 611.3 percent; Cleveland came next with a 307.8 percent increase; then Chicago, 148.2 percent; New York, 66.3 percent; Indianapolis, 59 percent; Cincinnati, 53.2 percent; and Pittsburgh, 47.2 percent. In numbers Chicago gained nearly 65,500 black residents, New York 61,400, and Detroit 36,240.

A question that immediately comes to mind is: what did these southern people know how to do that would earn them a living in the North? Since so much of the South was rural, it is amazing the number of occupations represented by the migrants whose letters are in the Scott collection. But indications are that about half the migrants came from towns, a Labor Department survey found. The largest number said they wanted work as laborers at unspecified common labor, with some longshoremen, stevedores, freight handlers, stokers, miners, packers, and warehousemen; many of these men had experience in southern industries such as lumbering, railroading, iron and steel foundries, sawmills, and turpentine stills. The next largest category was the semiskilled or skilled craftsman: plumbers and roofers, painters and plasterers, cleaners and pressers, hotel waiters, brickmakers and bricklayers, machinists and machinists' helpers, caulkers, carpenters, woodworkers, cabinetmakers, mailmen, auto workers, engineers, blacksmiths, glaziers, lumber graders and inspectors, foundry workers, and a large number of molders. The majority of women who wanted to migrate, and some of the men, sought menial or domestic jobs: cooks, laundresses, baby nurses, housemaids, butler-chauffeurs, janitors. Among the businesses represented by migrants were insurance man, barber, hairdresser, laundry owner, merchant, and packer and mover — memorably, the moving company owner who called himself "the

Daddy of the Transfer business" of Rome, Georgia. In the much smaller class of professionals and white-collar workers the majority were teachers, including the Alcorn College graduate who was four feet, six inches tall and weighed 105 pounds — a woman, presumably, as were many of the teachers who wanted to leave the South. There were also a sixty-three-year-old graduate of Howard University Law School, an eighteen-year-old artist and actor, and a fifteen-year-old cartoonist; also printers, a college-educated bookkeeper, and a stenographer-typist. Many of the educated class expressed their willingness to do any kind of work, even common labor, if only they could get jobs in the North. Only a few who wrote of their wish to migrate described themselves as farmers, and two of these wanted to go to Nebraska and Dakota to farm. But probably many of those who were looking for laborers' jobs were tenant farmers, sharecroppers, and farm workers; and probably also many other rural people could not write or were afraid to, so we do not know about them — they simply disappeared off the farms and took their chances of finding work in northern cities. Baker says that whole tenant-farming areas of Georgia and Alabama were emptied of prime-age workers. A small number wound up in the tobacco fields of Connecticut, but the great majority must have gone to industrial cities. The black rural population of the South dropped by almost 250,000 between 1910 and 1920.

As the trains and boats pulled out week after week and month after month, the South began to hurt from a loss of the black labor force, especially the Deep South. For the first time in their history, Mississippi and Louisiana showed a decrease in Negro population between 1900 and 1910; and between 1910 and 1920 Mississippi suffered a loss of 129,600 blacks, Louisiana a loss of 180,800. In that decade the black population of the East North Central states increased by 71 percent, and that of the Middle Atlantic states by over 43 percent, although the national increase was only 6.5 percent.

Contemporary estimates by observers such as Baker and Epstein of a million or so migrants seem wildly out of line with the 500,000 figure to be calculated from 1920 census figures, which were not available to them, but it may be that their estimates were more nearly correct than figures arrived at from census returns. For one thing, it has been and remains a fact, substantiated by recent studies by the Census Bureau of its own operation, that black males are significantly undercounted. . . .

If there was finally a black Joshua it was Robert Abbott, blowing the trumpet call of jobs through a rolled-up *Defender;* his troops were the Pullman porters and road shows, with labor agents as mercenaries. Half a million blacks followed behind. Where the metaphor breaks down is that their Jericho was a dirty, crowded, sickly, dangerous city ghetto, which must often have seemed scarcely worth the trouble of getting to.

But the getting there was a tremendous feat of initiative, planning, courage, and perseverance — qualities never appearing in any catalogue of Negro traits drawn up by white people, yet here demonstrated incontestibly not by one or two "exceptional individuals," as blacks were called who did not fit the stereotype, but by at least five hundred thousand perfectly average southern Negroes. They were not passive reactors, waiting for something to happen to them; they made it happen.

STUDY GUIDE

1. What blacks, according to the author, tended to come North first — and why?

2. Outline the motives that brought about this mass migration and then find similarities and differences (from your text) between these motives and those of the immigrants from Europe.

3. Were there migratory patterns in the movement from the South to the North and, if so, what were they?

4. Offer a generalization about the following: (a) the attitudes of the blacks toward the South and to the North once they arrived; (b) the means through which the blacks earned their livelihood in the South and in the North; and (c) the temperament of those who came North.

5. And finally: What role did Robert Abbott play in the Great Migration — and with what motives?

BIBLIOGRAPHY

A number of studies are available on the black experience in America. A scholarly introduction to the entire subject of black history, which includes a well-chosen bibliography, is John Hope Franklin, *From Slavery to Freedom: A History of Negro Americans* (1978). Another important work is the classic sociological study of the black in the United States by Gunnar Myrdal, *An American Dilemma: The Negro Problem and Modern Democracy* (1944), condensed in Arnold M. Rose, *The Negro in America* (1960). An influential, although in parts controversial, analysis of the relationship between blacks and whites in the United States is C. Vann Woodward, *The Strange Career of Jim Crow* (1974). For a comparison of the conditions of the blacks in the cities of the North, see Allan H. Spear, *Black Chicago: The Making of a Negro Ghetto, 1890–1920* (1967); Constance McLaughlin Green, *The Secret City: A History of Race Relations in the Nation's Capital* (1967), a study of black–white relations in Washington, D.C.; and Gilbert Osofsky, *Harlem: The Making of a Ghetto* (1966).

Federal agents raid the offices of Laisve, *a Lithuanian newspaper suspected of being radical and subversive, 1920.*

10

ROBERT K. MURRAY

The Red Scare

Chauvinism — excessive adulation of one's own country, its inhabitants, and its culture — was often the consequence of nineteenth- and twentieth-century nationalism. Among Europeans, this tendency to exalt native ways and institutions went hand in hand with the "white man's burden" of British imperialism and, in more extreme and vicious form, with the racist doctrines of the Nazis in Germany. The American people have not been immune to nativistic doctrines, and throughout our history there have been intermittent crusades by overly zealous and ultrapatriotic citizens to preserve the alleged purity of our institutions and national purpose. Although nativism in the United States never attained the genocidal proportions reached in some other nations, xenophobic manifestations have from time to time brought injustice — and even violence — to those who, for one reason or another, failed to conform totally to the so-called American way.

In his definitive study of American nativism from the end of the Civil War to the mid-1920s, historian John Higham isolates three varieties of American xenophobia: anti-Catholicism, racism (the belief in the superiority of Anglo-Saxons generally and American Anglo-Saxons in particular), and antiradicalism. Each of these nativistic movements crested at one time or another in the last century of American life. The last — a violent fear of radical subversion — climaxed twice: first in the "Red Scare" led by Attorney General A. Mitchell Palmer after World War I and more recently in the witch-hunts led by Senator Joseph P. McCarthy in the decade after World War II. The following selection, taken from Robert K. Murray's *Red Scare: A Study in National Hysteria, 1919–1920,* graphically describes the earlier antiradical crusade and its consequences for the American people.

The brief, yet hysterical, post–World War I Red Scare derived from a number of sources: the frenzied drive for conformity and 100 percent Americanism demanded by the administration of Woodrow Wilson to gain national support for participation in World War I; the success of the Bolsheviks in overthrowing the Czarist regime in Russia in 1917; the presence in the United States of native- and foreign-born Communists and assorted other radicals; and disillusionment with Wilson's campaign "to make the world safe for democracy." Although the Red Scare had come to an end by the time Woodrow Wilson left office in March 1921, it left a legacy for the decade that followed. The execution of the Italian anarchists Nicola Sacco and Bartolomeo Vanzetti, the passage of the Immigration Act of 1924 that discriminated against southern and eastern Europeans, the rise of the Ku Klux Klan, and the anti-Catholic campaign against Alfred E. Smith when he ran for the presidency in 1928 are clear indications that the hatred and violence stirred up by the Red Scare did not disappear in 1921.

Prior to the late fall of 1919, the federal government had moved rather slowly against the domestic Bolshevik menace. Because of the press of other postwar problems and a preoccupation with the League [of Nations] question, most officials in Washington had not been able to concentrate their thinking on the radical danger. To be sure, politicians talked now and again about the evidences of radicalism in the country and the newspapers played up such statements with zeal. But only a few politicians had yet become really demagogical. In fact, there was every indication that most officials in Washington were less concerned about the radical menace than were their constituents. They had not lost their heads, nor for the most part had they espoused hasty or ill-advised action to attack a nebulous Red threat. . . .

The person most responsible for the subsequent action of the federal government was Attorney General A. Mitchell Palmer. Under his direction the federal police power was set in motion so zealously against domestic radicalism that the months of November 1919 to January 1920 have sometimes been labeled "Government by Hysteria" or "Palmer's Reign of Terror." . . .

It has often been charged that Attorney General Palmer undertook his subsequent one-man crusade against the Reds to further his own per-

From Robert K. Murray, *The Red Scare: A Study in National Hysteria, 1919–1920.* University of Minnesota Press, Minneapolis. Copyright © 1955 by the University of Minnesota. Reprinted by permission.

sonal political ambitions. The Quaker from Pennsylvania did, without a doubt, have his eye on the White House and along with many other followers of the New Freedom hoped to be the heir apparent. His qualifications were certainly better than average. He was an ardent Wilsonian, he was a strong supporter of the League, and, for the moment at least, he had the confidence of the President. Moreover, he was an able administrator, a diligent worker, and a proof-tested reformer, having consistently opposed the infamous Penrose machine in Pennsylvania.

There is every indication that by the spring of 1920 Palmer played the Red Scare for all it was worth, hoping to use his aggressive stand against the Reds as the primary means by which he could project himself into the presidency. But in the fall of 1919 it appeared that the attorney general began his attack on radicalism partially to satisfy mounting clamor for the government to act and partially to soothe his own very real fear that the Reds were about to take over the United States. As alien property custodian, he had already gained a wide knowledge of anti-American and antidemocratic propaganda, and hence was much more sensitive to radical outbursts than he otherwise might have been. Moreover, in that capacity he had been made acutely aware of the problem of sabotage and fifth-column activity, and therefore was more suspicious than normal. Then, too, as a Quaker, Palmer was especially opposed to both the godlessness and the violence of the Bolshevik program and thus easily developed an abnormal attitude toward it. It would be difficult to estimate accurately the tremendous effect which the bombing of his own home had on his thinking. The June 2 incident unquestionably heightened Palmer's proclivity for exaggerating the radical menace anyway, and it is understandable how he came to scent "a Bolshevist plot in every item of the day's news."

Shortly after the bombing of his home, Palmer asked for and received an appropriation of $500,000 from Congress to facilitate the Justice Department's apprehension of those who sought to destroy law and order. Palmer now began his crusade in earnest. On August 1, he established within the Department's Bureau of Investigation the so-called General Intelligence, or antiradical, Division. As its head he appointed young J. Edgar Hoover, charging him with the responsibility of gathering and coordinating all information concerning domestic radical activities. Under the general guidance of bureau chief Flynn and through the unstinting zeal of Hoover, this unit rapidly became the nerve center of the entire Justice Department and by January 1920 made its war on radicalism the department's primary occupation. In fact, there are some indications that both Flynn and Hoover purposely played on the attorney general's fears and exploited the whole issue of radicalism in order to enhance the Bureau of Investigation's power and prestige. Certainly, the hunt for radicals during the 1919–20 period "made" the Bureau of Investigation and started it on the road to becoming the famous FBI of the present day.

In any event, shortly after the creation of the GID, an elaborate card index system was established; over 200,000 cards contained detailed information concerning all known radical organizations, societies, associations, and publications. Set up by Mr. Hoover on the basis of his earlier experience as an employee of the Library of Congress, this index was so constructed that a card for a particular city not only showed the various radical organizations in that area but also their membership rolls, names of officers, and time and place of meetings. By the late fall of 1919, according to Attorney General Palmer, this index also contained the complete case histories of over 60,000 dangerous radicals and housed "a greater mass of data upon this subject than is anywhere else available."

Under the direction of Hoover, the GID became the Justice Department's personal antiradical propaganda bureau as well as a vast repository of radical information. This was particularly true after the formation of the Communist parties in September. In the ensuing months, the division sent to all major newspapers and periodicals letters signed by the attorney general which began with the statement, "My one desire is to acquaint people like you with the real menace of evil-thinking, which is the foundation of the Red Movement," and ended with exaggerated accounts of domestic Communist activity. The division also distributed copies of the manifestoes of the Third International, the Communist party, and the Communist Labor party and warned Americans against falling for this Bolshevik claptrap. At the same time, the division, with the attorney general's full acquiescence, circulated much propaganda connecting the major fall strikes and the summer race riots with the Communists. It need hardly be added that such propaganda was widely circulated by the general press and that under the circumstances the United States Department of Justice was, itself, one of the major agents fostering Red Scare hysteria in the fall of 1919. . . .

. . . The pressure of ensuing events in the summer and fall of 1919 . . . tipped the scales in favor of more aggressive action, and agitation for the deportation of radical aliens became more vociferous while the failure of the government to deport caused increasing comment. Petitions from state legislatures, business organizations, and patriotic societies flooded Congress demanding that the government do something and that the Justice Department, in particular, be shaken out of its lethargy. Such sentiment became sufficiently strong by early October that Senator [Miles] Poindexter rose in the Senate and publicly denounced the Justice Department for not creating new "Red Specials" and securing the immediate deportation of all radical agitators. Such assaults on the Justice Department reached a climax when, on October 19, the Senate unanimously adopted a resolution which requested the attorney general " . . . to advise and inform the Senate whether or not the Department of Justice has taken legal proceedings, and if not, why not, and if so, to what extent, for the arrest and punishment [or deportation] . . . of the various persons within the United States who . . . have attempted to bring about the forcible overthrow of the Government. . . . "

This resolution, together with mounting public clamor, served as the immediate reason for Palmer's turning from less talk to more action. Realizing that in view of the cessation of hostilities with Germany it would be extremely difficult to proceed against radical citizens on grounds of either espionage or sedition, he centered his efforts on the apprehension of radical aliens who would be subject to the deportation provisions of the Alien Law of 1918. This procedure seemed at the moment to be most expedient anyway since the General Intelligence Division estimated that about 90 percent of all domestic radicals were aliens, and it was believed that the native-born element, if left alone, would never prove really dangerous. On this basis, orders were sent to Bureau of Investigation agents and confidential informants that their major activities "should be particularly directed to persons, not citizens of the United States, with a view of obtaining deportation cases."

On November 7 . . . Attorney General Palmer gave the public and Congress the action they had been waiting for by unloosing a nationwide raid against the Union of Russian Workers. Founded in 1907, this organization had its headquarters in the Russian People's House, 133 East 15th Street, New York City, and, according to its own statements, was composed of "atheists, communists and anarchists." It believed in the complete overthrow of all institutions of government and the confiscation of all wealth through the violence of social revolution. The estimated membership of the organization was 4000.

Although 250 officers and members of the URW were seized in simultaneous raids in eleven other cities, the main blow fell on the New York headquarters. The People's House raid was conducted with mathematical precision, bureau agents remaining outside the building in parked cars until the signal was given. At that moment, they closed in rapidly and took the establishment by surprise. Several huge truck-loads of radical propaganda were confiscated, and about 200 men and women were violently assisted out of the building by a special riot squad and driven away to Justice Department headquarters at 13 Park Row for questioning. The New York *Times* reported that some of the occupants had been "badly beaten by the police . . . their heads wrapped in bandages testifying to the rough manner in which they had been handled."

As a result of the questioning, only thirty-nine of those seized were finally held. Of the others, a few were found to be American citizens and were immediately released; the rest were simple workingmen of Russian nationality who spoke little or no English and who belonged to the organization for almost every conceivable reason except to promote revolution. Nevertheless, despite their obvious ignorance concerning the real aims of the URW, certain of these prisoners were held for excessively long periods of time before they were given their freedom. This was particularly true at Hartford, Connecticut, where some arrested members were kept in jail five months before even receiving a hearing. . . .

In spite of the obvious injustices involved and the small catch of truly revolutionary characters, the nation seemed delighted with the raids. To the government, and especially to Attorney General Palmer, went unstinting praise for having acted "In the Nick of Time" and having nipped "a gigantic plot" in the bud. Suddenly, the attorney general became the most popular figure in the nation and found himself enthroned as the third in a triumvirate of great saviors of the country — first Hanson, then Coolidge, now Palmer. His prestige was perhaps all the more enhanced since the government was temporarily leaderless; Woodrow Wilson lay stricken in the White House while the ship of state floundered helplessly in the rough seas of fear and reaction. To the man on the street, Palmer was "running the administration," "a lion-hearted man [who] has brought order out of chaos," and "A Strong Man of Peace." Newspapers excitedly described him as "a tower of strength to his countrymen" and declared that his actions brought "thrills of joy to every American." . . .

The federal raid of November 7 had proved an excellent laboratory experiment. It had shown that if any raid was to be followed by deportations, close cooperation with the Department of Labor was absolutely essential because of its jurisdiction over deportation matters. Therefore, in laying plans for his new move, the attorney general attempted to bring Labor Department officials into closer harmony with his own views. In this attempt, he was aided by the fact that, at the moment, Secretary of Labor [William B.] Wilson was ill and Assistant Secretary Post was otherwise occupied. This left John W. Abercrombie, solicitor of the Department of Labor, but in reality a member of the Justice Department, to function as acting labor secretary. Naturally, he proved most cooperative. Moreover, the Labor Department's top official on deportation affairs, Commissioner General of Immigration Anthony J. Caminetti, was currently evidencing as much hysteria over the Red menace as was the attorney general. Therefore he also fell easily into line.

After consultation with these men, it was unanimously decided that alien members of both the Communist party and the Communist Labor party were subject to deportation under the 1918 Alien Act. On this basis, Acting Secretary of Labor Abercrombie signed on December 27 more that 3000 warrants for the arrest of known alien adherents to the two Communist organizations and gave such warrants to the Justice Department for execution. Four days later, on the advice of Commissioner Caminetti (who in turn was acting upon a suggestion made to him by one of Palmer's emissaries from the Justice Department), Abercrombie also made an important change in the rule governing the procedure of deportation arrest hearings. Prior to December 31 the rule had read: "At the beginning of the hearing under the warrant of arrest, the alien shall be allowed to inspect the warrant . . . and shall be apprised that he may be represented by counsel." The rule, as changed, read as follows: "Preferably at the beginning of the hearing . . . or at any rate as soon as such hearing has proceeded sufficiently in the development of the facts to protect the Government's interests, the alien shall be allowed to inspect the warrant . . . and shall be apprised that thereafter he may be represented by counsel."

It should be noted at this point that deportation involved no criminal proceeding since it was not regarded as punishment. There was no judge or jury and the case was handled administratively through the secretary of labor by immigration officials who heard the case and rendered the decision. The government was perfectly within its rights in changing the grounds and procedures for deportation hearings at any time, for deportable aliens obviously did not have the protection of the ex post facto clause in the Constitution.

But even though no criminal trial was involved and the whole matter was merely an administrative process, it was generally understood that the alien did have certain safeguards — namely those in the Sixth Amendment such as the "right to a . . . public trial . . . to be confronted with witnesses against him; to have compulsory process for obtaining witnesses in his favor and to have the Assistance of Counsel for his defense." The alien also had two possibilities for relief from an adverse administrative decision. The secretary of labor might personally review the record and reverse any deportation decision, or the alien might obtain a writ of habeas corpus which would bring his case before a federal judge, but only if it could be shown that the deportation proceedings had been manifestly unfair.

For these reasons it becomes obvious why Attorney General Palmer did not try to detect and prosecute actual crimes of radicals against the United States. This would have required an indictment and a trial by jury, whether such crimes were committed by citizens or aliens. Rather, he relied on the administrative process for the apprehension and deportation of radical aliens and therefore circumvented most normal legal procedures. Moreover, by Abercrombie's change in the hearing rule, even under the administrative process the alien's opportunity for an able defense of his position was considerably weakened. Hence, through shrewd collusion with certain Labor Department and immigration officials, Palmer assured himself greater success in his drive on radicalism than if he had elected to arrest radical aliens as criminals and thus subject his whole anti-Red program to the vagaries of the courts of law.

Confident now that all was in readiness and that large-scale deportations offered the best solution to the domestic radical problem, the attorney general set the night of January 2, 1920, as the time for his all-out drive on the two Communist parties. Seven days before, on December 27,

Palmer sent specific orders to Bureau of Investigation district chiefs instructing them on exactly what to do. They were told to arrange with their undercover agents, some of whom had quietly slipped into radical ranks and had assumed the role of agitators of the wildest type, to have meetings of the two Communist organizations called for the night set if possible because such action would facilitate the making of arrests. Field agents were instructed to "obtain all documentary evidence possible," to secure "charters, meeting minutes, membership books, dues books, membership correspondence, etc.," and to allow no person arrested to communicate with any outside person until permission was specifically granted. Such permission could only come from Flynn, Hoover, or Palmer. Further orders specified that if an individual claimed American citizenship "he must produce documentary evidence of same" and that upon arrest "aliens should be searched thoroughly; if found in groups in meeting rooms, line them up against the wall and there search them."

Resultant action could not have been more stunning or more spectacular. On January 2, more than 4000 suspected radicals were rounded up in thirty-three major cities, covering twenty-three states. Virtually every local Communist organization in the nation was affected; practically every leader of the movement, national or local, was put under arrest. Often such arrests were made without the formality of warrants as bureau agents entered bowling alleys, pool halls, cafés, club rooms, and even homes, and seized everyone in sight. Families were separated; prisoners were held incommunicado and deprived of their right to legal counsel. According to the plan, those suspected radicals who were American citizens were not detained by federal agents, but were turned over to state officials for prosecution under state syndicalist laws. All aliens, of course, were incarcerated by the federal authorities and reserved for deportation hearings.

In the New England area, raids were conducted in such towns as Boston, Chelsea, Brockton, Nashua, Manchester, and Portsmouth. In all, about 800 persons were seized of whom approximately half were taken to the immigrant station in Boston and then shipped to Deer Island in Boston Harbor. In this shifting process, the prisoners were forced to march in chains from the immigrant station to the dock — a fact which newspapers played up as attesting to their dangerous, violent character. Upon arriving at Deer Island the prisoners found conditions deplorable; heat was lacking, sanitation was poor, and restrictions holding them incommunicado were rigidly enforced. One captive plunged five stories to this death, another went insane, and two others died of pneumonia.

The remaining half of the 800 who were not sent to Deer Island were released after two or three days when it was determined they were in no way connected with the radical movement. For example, thirty-nine bakers in Lynn, Massachusetts, arrested on suspicion of holding a revolutionary caucus, were released when it was learned that they had come together on the evening of January 2 for the inoffensive purpose of establishing a cooperative bakery. In Boston, a woman named Minnie Federman, who was mistakenly arrested in her bedroom at 6 A.M. on January 3, was released without even an apology when it was discovered belatedly that she was an American citizen and had no interest whatsoever in revolution.

In New York and Pennsylvania the pattern was the same. In New York City more than 400 individuals were arrested as the Communist party headquarters and the Rand School bore the brunt of the federal raid. Prisoners were rounded up and taken to 13 Park Row where they were questioned by GID agents before being sent on to Ellis Island or released. In these New York arrests it seems that brutality was practiced to an excessive degree. Prisoners in sworn affidavits later testified to the violent treatment they had received. One claimed he had been beaten by a Justice Department operative without any explanation; another maintained he was struck repeatedly on the head with a blackjack. Another alien asserted that his glasses had been knocked off by an agent, who then without the slightest provocation struck him in the face. Still another testified: "I was struck on my head, and . . . was attacked by one detective, who knocked me down again, sat on my back, pressing me down to the floor with his knee and bending my body back until blood flowed out of my mouth and nose . . . after which . . . I was questioned and released."

Meanwhile, in Philadelphia, more than 100 were arrested and the "third degree" was as shamefully practiced as in New York. In the Pittsburgh area, 115 individuals were seized although warrants had been issued for only twenty. Indeed, one Pittsburgh man was missed by his friends for almost a month before they discovered he was in jail, having been arrested without warrant and then held without explanation or bail.

In New Jersey, such towns as Jersey City, Passaic, Newark, Hoboken, Paterson, and Trenton experienced similar Red roundups. Altogether, about 500 arrests were made, but the majority were finally released for insufficient evidence. Again many arrests were made without warrant. For instance, one man was arrested about 10 P.M. while walking along Newark's Charlton Street simply because he "looked like a radical." Another, much to his surprise, was seized when he stopped to inquire what all the commotion was about. This zeal to ferret out dangerous radicals caused government agents not only to make many unjust arrests such as these but also to jump to ridiculous conclusions. In New Brunswick, while a Socialist Club was being raided, the drawings of a phonograph invention were found and were immediately forwarded to demolition experts because the raiders thought they represented "the internal mechanism of various types of bombs."

In the Midwest, the raids at Chicago and Detroit were particularly severe. In the Detroit raid about 800 persons were arrested and imprisoned from three to six days in a dark, windowless, narrow corridor in the city's antiquated Federal Building. The prisoners were forced to sleep on the bare floor and stand in long lines for access to the solitary toilet. Some, unable to wait, were forced to urinate in the corridor itself, and, as the custodian later testified, "Before many days . . . the stench was quite unbearable." It was later discovered that the prisoners were denied all food for the first twenty-four hours and thereafter were fed largely on what their families brought to them. Including among their number "citizens and aliens, college graduates and laborers, skilled mechanics making $15 a day and boys not yet out of short trousers," these 800 prisoners were closely questioned by bureau agents who finally released 300 by the end of the sixth day when it was proved that they had not even a cursory interest in the domestic radical movement.

Meanwhile, about 140 of those remaining were transferred from the Federal Building to the Detroit Municipal Building. En route these individuals, who had been unable to shave or bathe for almost a week, served as excellent subjects for press photographers, and local Detroit newspapers ran their pictures as examples of the unkempt, dirty, filthy Bolshevik terrorists the government had netted in its raids. Upon their arrival at the Municipal Building, the prisoners were placed in a room twenty-four feet by thirty feet which originally had been designed to hold offenders no longer than three to four hours. This "bull pen," as it was called, had only one window, a stone floor, and several wooden benches; yet the men remained here a whole week and were fed almost solely on food sent to them by their relatives. Indeed, conditions under which these prisoners lived were actually so wretched that even the Detroit press finally displayed some sympathy for them, and a citizens' committee was created to investigate their situation. This committee subsequently discovered that most of these "dangerous radicals" were but plain, ignorant foreigners who were completely unaware of why they were being so treated.

In Chicago, a most peculiar set of circumstances arose. For five months, state and city officials had laid careful plans for their own drive on radicalism in the Chicago area, and had finally decided on January 1 as the date for such a move. Much to their dismay they then learned that the Justice Department had planned its foray for January 2. Cook County officials persisted in their desire to conduct a raid of their own, and, as a result, raids were held a day apart on radicals in that area.

The state raid of January 1 involved some seventy or more radical clubs or gatherings and netted between 150 and 200 prisoners. As a result of these incursions, some eighty-five Communists, among them "Big Bill" Haywood and Rose Pastor Stokes, were arraigned in Chicago on criminal anarchy charges.

The federal raid which followed on January 2 was therefore somewhat anticlimactic. However, federal officials did nab 225 additional suspected radicals and after questioning held about 80 for deportation. One interesting sidelight on the Chicago raids was a riot which broke out in the municipal jail shortly after the various arrests were made. It seems that the jail's "patriotic" prisoners took violent exception to the fact that Reds were being thrown in the same cells with them. Remarked the Seattle *Times*, "There are some things at which even a Chicago crook draws the line."

In the West and Far West, while raids were conducted, they were not especially significant. Most radicals of any importance, particularly in the Far West, had already been apprehended in the various state raids following the Centralia massacre. Hence, the present forays were carried out only in a cursory manner and arrests were few in number. In Los Angeles, one was arrested; in Portland, twenty; Denver, eight; and Des Moines, sixteen. Only in Kansas City was there much activity, and there 100 were taken and 35 held.

The January raids dazzled the public. The mass of Americans cheered the hunters from the sidelines while Attorney General Palmer once again was hailed as the savior of the nation. In view of the obvious abridgement of civil liberties which the raids entailed, such support can only be explained on the basis that the public mind was under the influence of a tremendous social delirium — a colossal fear which condoned monstrous procedures and acts. Against a background of the three major fall strikes, the Centralia murders, and exaggerated press and official claims, that fear seemed so real it was positively overpowering. Said the Washington *Evening Star*, "This is no mere scare, no phantom of heated imagination — it is a cold, hard, plain fact." As far as the deleterious effect on civil liberties was concerned, the Washington *Post* exclaimed, "There is no time to waste on hairsplitting over infringement of liberty. . . . "

Agreeing therefore that the raids were a cause for satisfaction and willing to overlook the many dangers and injustices involved, most journals were now quick to counsel a rapid follow-through. The immediate deportation of the prisoners, variously described as "the kind of cranks that murder Presidents" or "send bombs through the mails to statesmen," was forcefully demanded. In fact, such action was regarded "as necessary as cauterizing a wound to prevent gangrene." Under such headlines as "ALL ABOARD FOR THE NEXT SOVIET ARK," the press advocated that "ships be made ready quickly and the passengers put aboard."

As to the success of the raids, Palmer and the Bureau of Investigation spoke in glowing terms. The attorney general claimed the raids "halted the advance of 'red radicalism' in the United States," while Flynn maintained they marked the beginning of the end of organized revolutionaries in this country.

As a matter of fact, the raids did have a devastating effect on the domestic radical movement. James Cannon later maintained that the movement disintegrated for the time being. Benjamin Gitlow testified the raids struck terror into the hearts of alien members of the two Communist parties and hurt membership tremendously. It was true that for many weeks after the government action the radical press ceased its activities and meetings of the Communist organizations were suspended. Perhaps the best indication of the effect of the raids can be seen in a report made in February 1920 by the American delegate to the Amsterdam meeting of the Bureau of Propaganda of the Third International. He claimed at that time that the January raids had so wrecked the Communist movement in the United States that it could not be counted on to exert any influence whatsoever.

While satisfied up to this point with the success of his antiradical program, Attorney General Palmer now allowed no lag to develop. With the aid of Flynn and Hoover, he intensified the department's propaganda campaign until it reached its height in late January 1920. Large numbers of antiradical articles and cartoons were sent to the nation's newspapers and magazines without charge, the postage being prepaid by the Department of Justice itself. A sample cartoon, secured by the Justice Department from the New York *Tribune* and used with its permission, depicted Uncle Sam as a farmer weeding up thistles, each one of which had a Bolshevik head, while in the background a woman named "America" was replacing the thistles with pure "American" grass seed. "Give the American Bluegrass a Show," it said.

At the same time, Palmer vigorously continued his drive to secure some kind of peacetime sedition legislation in order to give the federal government the power necessary to deal with citizen radicals effectively. Shortly after the January raids, he appealed to Congress for such legislation, underlining the potential danger which such citizens presented to the country.

Palmer also promised the nation more action to rid the country of all alien agitators. He declared there would be more raids and that on the basis of what already had been done there would be at least 2720 deportations. Like a barker in charge of a colossal sideshow, the attorney general promised New Yorkers, in particular, the exhilarating spectacle of "a second, third, and fourth Soviet Ark sailing down their beautiful harbor in the near future."

STUDY GUIDE

1. On the basis of this essay, offer an assessment of the magnitude of the threat the so-called radicals represented to American institutions.

2. Can you explain why Attorney General A. Mitchell Palmer, a reform-minded Progressive prior to 1919, launched a reactionary campaign to

persecute and prosecute men and women whose only crime, in some cases, was being born overseas?

3. What were the precise roles of the following in promoting the Red Scare: (a) President Wilson; (b) A. Mitchell Palmer; (c) J. Edgar Hoover; (d) the Congress; (e) the press; and (f) public opinion?

4. What impression do you have of the legality or the fairness of the government's actions? Can you think of parallels from more recent history? Consider, for example, the role played by the state authorities and the federal government in the relocation of the Japanese-Americans during World War II. From information you can find in your text, list some similarities or differences between the relocation of the Japanese in 1942 and the antiradical campaign of Palmer.

5. Consider the following question: Is it possible to conduct a war abroad (or a civil war) without a curtailment of the liberty of the individual at home? Consult your text or other sources for information regarding the repression of individual freedom during: (a) the Civil War; (b) the two world wars; (c) the Korean War; and (d) the protracted war in Vietnam in the 1960s and 1970s.

6. Can you see a relationship between the actions of the government during the Red Scare and the activities of the White House "plumbers" who broke into the office of Daniel Ellsberg's psychiatrist during the administration of Richard M. Nixon? What are the similarities? Are there any differences?

BIBLIOGRAPHY

The most comprehensive study of American nativism since the end of the Civil War is John Higham, *Strangers in the Land: Patterns of American Nativism, 1860–1925* (1955). Segments of the overall nativistic theme are treated in *Red Scare: A Study in National Hysteria, 1919–1920* (1955), from which the preceding selection was taken; Julian F. Jaffe, *Crusade against Radicalism* (1972); and Murray B. Levin, *Political Hysteria in America* (1972). See, too, Paul L. Murphy's article on "The Source and Nature of Intolerance in the 1920s" in the *Mississippi Valley Historical Review*, Vol. LI (1964), pp. 60–76. The action taken by the federal government over the years in the suppression of radicalism is described well in William Preston, Jr., *Aliens and Dissenters: Federal Suppression of Radicals, 1903–1933* (1963). The McCarthy witchhunt of the early 1950s — often called the "Second Red Scare" — is passionately dealt with by Elmer Davis, a newspaperman deeply dedicated to the cause of civil liberty, in *But We Were Born Free* (1954) and in the following more recently published texts: Earl Latham, *The Meaning of McCarthyism* (1965); Robert Griffith, *The Politics of Fear* (1971); and Fred Cook, *The Nightmare Decade* (1971).

IV THE TENSIONS
OF PROSPERITY

As the Republican candidate for the presidency in 1920, Warren Gamaliel Harding promised the American people "not nostrums but normalcy." Harding proposed that the idealism of the Progressive era and the moralistic fervor evoked by Woodrow Wilson give way to a more prosaic and less exalted vision of American life.

But, in retrospect, the 1920s were neither prosaic nor exalted. The maturing of the American economy of mass production and mass consumption produced social changes and social divisions. Many of those committed to the values, social practices, and institutions of native, rural, nineteenth-century Protestant America began to wonder whether "progress" was a virtue or a vice. Others — largely the "new" immigrants and middle-class city-dwellers — saw no value in maintaining the older, agrarian, and puritanical way of life, enjoyed the changes taking place, and looked forward to more.

The issues that polarized the nation were many and bitterly fought. In addition to the "Red Scare" of 1919 and the controversy that surrounded the Sacco and Vanzetti case, the nation debated immigration policy. Nativists wanted an end to unrestricted immigration and to make certain that most future immigrants to the United States would be Anglo-Saxons rather than southern and eastern Europeans. The Immigration Act of 1924 made both these demands law. Other controversies concerned the teaching of evolution in the public schools and the fitness of a Catholic for the office of President of the United States. John T. Scopes was sentenced to jail for teaching evolution to his students in Tennessee in 1925; and the defeat of Alfred E. Smith in the presidential campaign of 1928 can, in part, be attributed to the nation's distrust of Catholics.

The following selections offer a sense of the American experience of the 1920s. The first, on the activities of the Ku Klux Klan, deals with one of the nativist movements that divided the nation. The second examines Prohibition and the illegal activities that it spawned. The last shows how the floods of consumer goods pouring out of American factories changed American homes and the lives of the housewives who worked in them.

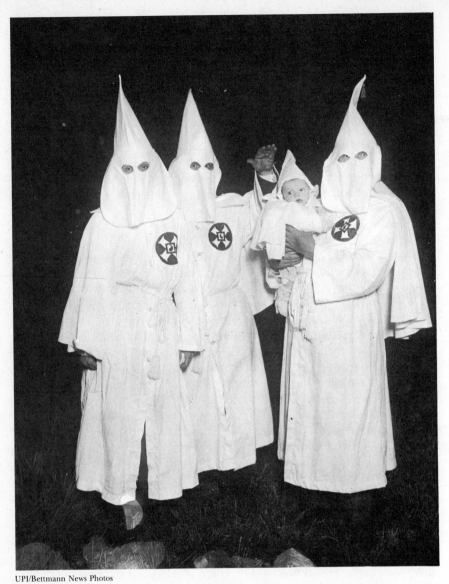

A legacy of bigotry and violence — for today and tomorrow.

11

ROBERT COUGHLAN

The Klan in Indiana

The 1920s were marked by strong social divisions and ideological differences between various segments of the American nation: between native-born Americans and immigrant Americans, between rural-born Americans and those raised in the city, between blacks and whites, between fundamentalists and modernists, and between Protestants, on the one hand, and Catholics and Jews, on the other. These divisions manifested themselves in many regions of the country and brought a number of social movements into being. One of the most frightening developments was the reappearance of the Ku Klux Klan — a reincarnation of the lily-white organization that had played a part in overthrowing the Radical Republican rule of the southern states and in terrorizing the ex-slaves during the Reconstruction era after the Civil War.

A number of similarities between the Ku Klux Klan of the Reconstruction period and the Klan of the 1920s should be noted: both were anti-black, both used violence and intimidation to achieve their ends, and both were composed of white, native-born Americans. There were important differences, however: unlike the nineteenth-century Klan, the Klan of the 1920s served as a source of profit to its leadership (through the sale of insurance along with memberships); it flourished in the Middle West, the Southwest, and on the Pacific Coast in addition to the South; and it broadened the focus of its hatred to include Catholics and Jews as well as blacks. The first Klan constituted a response to the defeat of the South in the Civil War and the threat of integration and equality between blacks and whites after the war. The Klan of the 1920s grew out of a fear that forces of change would destroy the values and way of life created by native-born Protestant, Anglo-Saxon Americans in the nation between the end of the Civil War and the outbreak of World War I.

The next selection by Robert Coughlan on the Ku Klux Klan in Indiana is a recollection by a Roman Catholic youngster of a Klan revival meeting in the summer of 1923 in rural Indiana. While the author, a journalist by profession, provides the reader with a history of the Klan — including its rise and fall in the 1920s — the real strength of his narrative lies in his vivid characterization of the Klan membership and leadership and the emotional tone of the Klan gathering in crossroads Indiana in the mid-1920s. The world view of the Klansmen, as portrayed by Coughlan, represented an effort to hold back the forces of change — the influence on American culture of the city, of science, of Catholics, Jews, and blacks.

On a hot July day in central Indiana — the kind of day when the heat shimmers off the tall green corn and even the bobwhites seek shade in the brush — a great crowd of oddly dressed people clustered around an open meadow. They were waiting for something; their faces, framed in white hoods, were expectant, and their eyes searched the bright blue sky. Suddenly they began to cheer. They had seen it: a speck that came from the south and grew into an airplane. As it came closer it glistened in the sunlight, and they could see that it was gilded all over. It circled the field slowly and seesawed in for a bumpy landing. A bulky man in a robe and hood of purple silk hoisted himself up from the rear cockpit. As he climbed to the ground, a new surge of applause filled the country air. White-robed figures bobbed up and down; parents hoisted their children up for a view. A small delegation of dignitaries filed out toward the airplane, stopping at a respectful distance.

The man in purple stepped forward.

"Kigy," he said.

"Itsub," they replied solemnly.

With the newcomer in the lead the column recrossed the field, proceeded along a lane carved through the multitude, and reached a platform decked out with flags and bunting. The man in purple mounted the steps, walked forward to the rostrum, and held up his right hand to hush the excited crowd.

"Konklave in Kokomo" by Robert Coughlan from Isabel Leighton, ed., *The Aspirin Age*. Copyright © 1949, 1976 by Simon & Schuster, Inc. Reprinted by permission of Simon & Schuster, Inc.

"My worthy subjects, citizens of the Invisible Empire, Klansmen all, greetings!

"It grieves me to be late. The President of the United States kept me unduly long counseling upon vital matters of state. Only my plea that this is the time and place of my coronation obtained for me surcease from his prayers for guidance." The crowd buzzed.

"Here in this uplifted hand, where all can see, I bear an official document addressed to the Grand Dragon, Hydras, Great Titans, Furies, Giants, Kleagles, King Kleagles, Exalted Cyclops, Terrors, and All Citizens of the Invisible Empire of the Realm of Indiana. . . .

"It is signed by His Lordship, Hiram Wesley Evans, Imperial Wizard, and duly attested.

"It continues me officially in my exalted capacity as Grand Dragon of the Invisible Empire for the Realm of Indiana. It so proclaims me by Virtue of God's Unchanging Grace. So be it."

The Grand Dragon paused, inviting the cheers that thundered around him. Then he launched into a speech. He urged his audience to fight for "one hundred per cent Americanism" and to thwart "foreign elements" that he said were trying to control the country. As he finished and stepped back, a coin came spinning through the air. Someone threw another. Soon people were throwing rings, money, watch charms, anything bright and valuable. At last, when the tribute slackened, he motioned to his retainers to sweep up the treasure. Then he strode off to a near-by pavilion to consult with his attendant Kleagles, Cyclopses, and Titans.

That day, July 4, 1923, was a high-water mark in the extraordinary career of David C. Stephenson, the object of these hysterics; and it was certainly one of the greatest days in the history of that extraordinary organization the Knights of the Ku Klux Klan. The occasion was a tri-state Konklave of Klan members from Illinois, Ohio, and Indiana. The place was Melfalfa Park, the meeting place, or Klavern, of the Klan chapter of Kokomo Indiana, the host city. Actually, although planned as a tri-state convention, it turned out to be the nearest thing to a rank-and-file national convention the Klan ever had. Cars showed up from almost every part of the country. The Klan's official estimate, which probably was not far wrong in this case, was that two hundred thousand members were there. Kokomo then had a population of about thirty thousand, and naturally every facility of the town was swamped.

The Konklave was an important day in my life. I was nine years old, with a small boy's interest in masquerades and brass bands. But I was also a Catholic, the son of a Catholic who taught in the public schools and who consequently was the object of a good deal of Klan agitation. If anything worse was to come, the Konklave probably would bring it. Every week or so the papers had been reporting Klan atrocities in other parts of the country — whippings, lynchings, tar-and-feather parties — and my father and his family were logical game in our locality.

Nevertheless, in a spirit of curiosity and bravado, my father suggested after our holiday lunch that we drive out to Melfalfa Park, which lies west of the town, to see what was happening. My mother's nervous objections were overcome, and we all got into the family Chevrolet and set out for West Sycamore Road. We saw white-sheeted Klansmen everywhere. They were driving along the streets, walking about with their hoods thrown back, eating in restaurants — they had taken the town over. But it was not until we were well out toward Melfalfa Park that we could realize the size of the demonstration. The road was a creeping mass of cars. They were draped with flags and bunting, and some carried homemade signs with Klan slogans such as "America for the Americans," or "The Pope will sit in the White House when Hell freezes over." There were Klan traffic officials every few yards, on foot, on motorcycles, or on horseback, but they were having a hard time keeping the two lanes of cars untangled and moving, and the air was full of the noise of their police whistles and shouts. The traffic would congeal, grind ahead, stop again, while the Klan families sat steaming and fanning themselves in their cars. Most of them seemed to have made it a real family expedition: the cars were loaded with luggage, camping equipment, and children. Quite a few of the latter — even those too young to belong to the junior order of the Klan — were dressed in little Klan outfits, which did not save them from being smacked when their restiveness annoyed their hot and harassed parents. The less ardent or more philosophical Klansmen had given up and had established themselves, with their picnic baskets and souvenir pillows, in shady spots all along the road and far into the adjoining fields and woods. From his gilded airplane, D. C. Stephenson must have seen a landscape dappled for miles around with little knots of white.

Since there was no way of turning back we stayed with the procession, feeling increasingly conspicuous. Finally we came to the cross road whose left branch led past the entrance to Melfalfa. We turned right and started home.

So we missed seeing the Konklave close up. But the newspapers were full of it, and people who were there have been able to fill in the details for me. The program gave a good indication of what the Klan was all about, or thought it was about. The Konklave started in midmorning with an address by a minister, the Reverend Mr. Kern of Covington, Indiana. The Reverend Kern spent most of his time warning against the machinations of Catholics and foreigners in the United States. When he finished, a fifty-piece boys' band from Alliance, Ohio, played "America" and the crowd sang. Then a band from New Castle, Indiana, played the "Star-Spangled Banner" and the Reverend Everett Nixon of Kokomo gave the invocation. These preliminaries led up to a speech by Dr. Hiram

Wesley Evans, the national leader of the Klan, who had come all the way from headquarters at Atlanta, Georgia. Dr. Evans commented gracefully on the fact that the center of Klan activities seemed to have shifted from Atlanta to Kokomo, and then talked on "Back to the Constitution." In his view, the Constitution was in peril from foreigners and "foreign influences," and he urged his audience to vote for Congressmen who would legislate "to the end that the nation may be rehabilitated by letting Americans be born into the American heritage." By the time Dr. Evans finished it was lunch time, and the Klan families spread their picnic cloths through the leafy acres of Melfalfa Park. Block-long cafeteria tables lined the banks of Wildcat Creek. From these, the women's auxiliary of the Klan dispensed five thousand cases of pop and near-beer, fifty-five thousand buns, twenty-five hundred pies, six tons of beef, and supplementary refreshments on the same scale.

It was after lunch, at about 2 P.M., when the crowd was full of food and patriotic ecstasy, that D. C. Stephenson made his dramatic descent from the sky.

The rest of the day, after Stephenson's speech, was given over to sports, band concerts, and general holiday frolic. That night there was a parade down Main Street in Kokomo. And while an outside observer might have found a good deal to be amused at in the antics of the Klan during the day, no one could have seen the parade that night without feelings of solemnity. There were thirty bands; but as usual in Klan parades there was no music, only the sound of drums. They rolled the slow, heavy tempo of the march from the far north end of town to Foster Park, a low meadow bordering Wildcat Creek where the Klan had put up a twenty-five-foot "fiery cross." There were three hundred mounted Klansmen interspersed in companies among the fifty thousand hooded men, women, and children on foot. The marchers moved in good order, and the measured tread of their feet, timed to the rumbling of the drums and accented by the off-beat clatter of the horses' hoofs, filled the night with an overpowering sound. Many of the marchers carried flaming torches, whose light threw grotesque shadows up and down Main Street. Flag bearers preceded every Den, or local Klan chapter. Usually they carried two Klan flags flanking an American flag, and the word would ripple down the rows of spectators lining the curbs, "Here comes the flag! Hats off for the flag!" Near the place where I was standing with my parents one man was slow with his hat and had it knocked off his head. He started to protest, thought better of it, and held his hat in his hand during the rest of the parade.

Finally the biggest flag I have ever seen came by. It must have been at least thirty feet long, since it took a dozen or more men on each side to support it, and it stretched almost from curb to curb. It sagged in the center under a great weight of coins and bills. As it passed us the bearers called out, "Throw in! Give to the hospital!" and most of the spectators did. This was a collection for the new "Klan hospital" that was to relieve white Protestant Kokomoans of the indignity of being born, being sick, and dying under the care of nuns, a necessity then since the Catholics supported the only hospital in town. It was announced afterward that the huge flag had collected fifty thousand dollars. . . .

It may be asked, why . . . did the town take so whole-heartedly to the Klan, which made a program of misdirected hate? And the answer to that may be, paradoxically enough, that the Klan supplied artificial tensions. Though artificial, and perhaps never quite really believed in, they were satisfying. They filled a need — a need for Kokomo and all the big and little towns that resembled it during the early 1920's.

In 1923, Kokomo, like the rest of the United States, was in a state of arrested emotion. It had gone whole-hog for war in 1917–18. My own earliest memories are mostly of parading soldiers, brass bands, peach pits thrown into collection stations on Main Street to be used "for gas masks," Liberty Bonds, jam-packed troop trains, the Kaiser hung in effigy, grotesque drawings of Huns in the old *Life*. But it was mostly a make-believe war, as it turned out, and by the time it was well started it was all over.

The emotions it had whipped up, however, were not over. As Charles W. Furgeson says in *Confusion of Tongues:* "We had indulged in wild and lascivious dreams. We had imagined ourselves in the act of intercourse with the Whore of the World. Then suddenly the war was over and the Whore vanished for a time and we were in a condition of *coitus interruptus*." To pursue the imagery, consummation was necessary. With the real enemy gone, a fresh one had to be found. Find an enemy: Catholics, Jews, Negroes, foreigners — but especially Catholics.

This seemingly strange transmutation was not really strange, considering the heritage of the times. Anti-foreignism has been a lively issue in American history since before the Republic. It became a major issue from the 1830s on, as mass migrations took place from Ireland, Germany, Scandinavia, Italy, Poland, Russia, and the Far East. Before immigration was finally curbed by the quota laws, many old-stock Americans in the South and Central West had been roused to an alarmed conviction that they were in danger of being overrun. The "foreigners" with their different ways and ideas were "ruining the country"; and hence anything "foreign" was "un-American" and a menace.

Another main stream in American history was anti-Catholicism, for the good and sufficient reason that a great many of the founding fathers had come to this continent to escape Catholic persecutions. This stream ran deep; and periodically it would emerge at the surface, as in the Know Nothing Party of the 1850s and the American Protective Association of the 1890s. It was submerged but still strong as this century began, and it came to a violent confluence in the 1920s with the parallel stream of anti-foreignism. The conscious or unconscious syllogism was: (1) foreigners are a menace, as demonstrated by the war, (2) the Catholic Church is run by a foreign Pope in a foreign city, (3) therefore the Catholic Church is a menace. Here was a suitable enemy — powerful, mysterious, international, aggressive.

To some extent, of course, the violence with which the jaws of this syllogism snapped shut was a result of parallel thinking in Washington. Wilson had been repudiated, and with him the League and the World Court, and internationalism had become a bad word. The great debates accompanying these events had stirred the country as it had not been stirred since the days preceding the Civil War, and things said then by the isolationists had been enough to frighten even normally sensible people. The exact sequence is a conundrum like that of the chicken and egg: whether the isolationist politicians led the people or whether the people drove the isolationist politicians. The postwar disillusionment that swept all ranks, including the new generation of authors, would seem to indicate the latter. Great men might have controlled the tide, but they were not to be found in the administrations of Harding and Coolidge.

There were other factors too: the deadly tedium of small-town life, where any change was a relief; the nature of current Protestant theology, rooted in Fundamentalism and hot with bigotry; and, not least, a native American moralistic blood lust that is half historical determinism, and half Freud. The Puritan morality . . . gained new strength, in fact, in the revulsion against the excesses of frontier life. But Puritanism defies human nature, and human nature, repressed, emerges in disguise. The fleshly appetites of the small townsman, when confronted by the rigid moral standards of his social environment, may be transformed into a fanatic persecution of those very appetites. The Klan, which sanctified chastity and "clean living" and brought violent punishment to sinners, was a perfect outlet for these repressions. It is significant that the favored Klan method of dealing with sexual transgressors was to strip them naked and whip them, an act of sadism.

This sexual symbolism could, with not too much effort, be made to dovetail with anti-foreignism and anti-Catholicism. Foreigners were notoriously immoral, as proven by the stories the soldiers brought back from wicked Paris. The Catholic Church, the "foreign church," must condone such things; and besides, who knew *what* went on among the priests and nuns! A staple in pornographic literature for at least one hundred years had been the "revelations" of alleged ex-priests. The Klan made use of these and other fables, such as the old and ever popular one about the mummified bodies of newborn infants found under the floor when a nunnery was torn down. . . .

Thus the Catholic Church very easily assumed, in the minds of the ignorant majority, the proportions of a vast, immoral, foreign conspiracy against Protestant America, with no less a design than to put the Pope in the White House. The Knights of Columbus were in reality a secret army pledged to this aim. They kept their guns in the basements of Catholic churches — which usually had high steeples and often were located on the highest ground in town, so that guns fired from the belfries could dominate the streets. Not all Catholics were in on the plot: for example, the Catholics you knew. These were well-meaning dupes whom one might hope to save from their blindness. My parents were generally considered to be among them. . . .

Kokomo first began to hear about the Klan in 1920. In 1921 the local Nathan Hale Den was established, and within two years the town had become so Klannish as to be given the honor of being host city for the tri-state Konklave. (Of course its name helped: the Klan loved alliterative K's.) Literally half the town belonged to the Klan when I was a boy. At its peak, which was from 1923 through 1925, the Nathan Hale Den had about five thousand members, out of an able-bodied adult population of ten thousand. With this strength, the Klan was able to dominate local politics. In 1924 it elected the mayor, a dapper character named Silcott E. "Silk" Spurgeon, a former clothing salesman, and swept the lists for city councilmen. It packed the police and fire departments with its own people, with the result that on parade nights the traffic patrolmen disappeared, and traffic control was taken over by sheeted figures whose size and shape resembled those of the vanished patrolmen. It ran the town openly and insolently.

As in most of the thousands of other towns where the Klan thrived, there was a strong undercurrent of opposition. But as in most towns, few men were brave enough to state their disapproval openly. The Klan first appealed to the ignorant, the slightly unbalanced, and the venal; but by the time the enlightened elements realized the danger, it was already on top of them. Once organized in strength, the Klan had an irresistible weapon in economic boycott. The anti-Klan merchant saw his trade fade away to the Klan store across the street, where the store window carried a "TWK" (Trade with Klansmen) sign. The non-Klan insurance salesman hadn't a chance against the fraternal advantage of one who doubled in the evenings as a Kladd, Nighthawk, or Fury. It takes great courage to sacrifice a life's work for a principle.

It also takes moral conviction — and it is difficult to arrive at such conviction when the pastor of one's own church openly or tacitly takes an opposite stand. Kokomo's ministers, like her merchants and insurance men, swung with the tide. Most of them, in fact, took little or no swinging, since they saw in the Klan what it professed to be: the militant arm of evangelical Protestantism. There were a few holdouts, but they remained silent; and their silence was filled by the loud exhortations of others such as the Reverend Everett Nixon, Klan chaplain and Klan-sponsored city councilman, and the Reverend P. E. Greenwalt, of the South Main Street Methodist Church, who whipped a homemade Klan flag from his pocket as he reached the climax of his baccalaureate sermon at the high school graduation exercises. Other ministers, while less fanatic, were perhaps no less sure that the Klan was doing God's work. They found that it stimulated church attendance, with a consequent and agreeable rise in collections. They found their churches visited in rotation by a Klan "team" which would appear at the door unexpectedly, stride up the aisle with Klan and American flags flying, deposit a money offering at the foot of the pulpit, and silently depart. Generally, while this was going on, the ministers would find it in their consciences to ask the choir to sing "Onward, Christian Soldiers."

And so it went in Kokomo and in its equivalents all over the Middle West and South. The Klan made less headway in the big cities, with their strong foreign, Catholic, Negro, and Jewish populations, but from the middle-sized cities down to the country villages it soon had partial or full control of politics and commerce. Indianapolis, with a population of some two hundred thousand, was dominated almost as completely as Kokomo. D. C. Stephenson, the Grand Dragon, had his headquarters there, in a suite of offices in a downtown business building, and from there he ran the state government. "I am the law in Indiana," he said, and there was no doubt about it. He owned the legislature; he owned the Governor, a political hack named Ed Jackson; he owned most of the Representatives and both United States Senators. . . .

Stephenson in turn took his orders, after a fashion, from Atlanta, Georgia, where Dr. Evans presided over the Invisible Empire from a sumptuous Imperial Palace on fashionable Peachtree Road. Dr. Evans was a dentist by trade and an Imperial Wizard by usurpation. He had unhorsed the previous Wizard and founder, "Colonel" William Joseph Simmons, several months before the Kokomo Konklave. It was in Kokomo, incidentally, that Evans made his first Imperial appearance before a really large Klan audience, thus giving that event an extra significance for history, since it was during his Reign that the Klan was to have its greatest triumphs and sink finally almost to its nadir.

However, in understanding the place of the Klan in American life, Dr. Evans' significance is less than "Colonel" Simmons'. Evans was shrewd, aggressive, and a good administrator, but he stepped into a going concern. The concern existed because of Simmons. And it was going through the efforts not of either Evans or Simmons but those of an obscure couple named Edward Young Clark and Mrs. Elizabeth Tyler.

The tangled story of the Klan's twentieth-century rebirth opens officially in 1915, but stems back to a day in 1901 when Simmons was sitting on a bench outside his home. The future Emperor at that time was a preacher, but wasn't doing very well at it. As he sat gazing into the sky, watching the wind drive masses of cumulus clouds along, he noticed an interesting formation. As he watched, it split into two billowy lengths, and these in turn broke up into smaller clouds that followed one another in a procession across the sky. Simmons took the phenomenon as a sign from God, and fell to his knees with a prayer.

A devotee of Southern history, Simmons was even more familiar than most Southerners with the legends of the old Ku Klux Klan. Founded in 1866 in Pulaski, Tennessee, by a group of young Confederate troopers home from the war and with time heavy on their hands, it had started out simply as a social club — a device, significantly enough, to recapture some of the lost wartime excitement and comradeship. The young ex-soldiers picked their name from *Kuklos*, the Greek word for "circle," which they transformed to Ku Klux, and framed a fantastic ritual and nomenclature for their own amusement. The idea spread, and as it spread it found a serious purpose in restoring the South to home rule. Eventually the best manhood (and much of the worst) of the South took part, with General Nathan Bedford Forrest as Imperial Wizard. Finally it degenerated into mere terrorism, and General Forrest disbanded it in 1869, but not until the Carpetbaggers had been dispersed and the Klan had become immortalized in Southern memory. It was the old Klan that the convulsed mind of Reverend Simmons saw in the clouds. . . .

What Simmons called forth was not the old Klan, however, but a greatly distorted image of it. For all its excesses, the original Klan had some constructive purposes. Its prescript shows that it was devoted to restoring Constitutional rights to white Southerners, to the protection of Southern womanhood, and to the re-establishment of home rule. It operated in secrecy for the good reason that its members would have been shot or imprisoned by federal troops had they been found out.

The new Klan adopted the costume, the secrecy, and much of the ritual of the old, but very little of the substance. Its purposes are indicated in the Kloran, or book of rules and rituals:

1. Is the motive prompting your ambition to be a Klansman serious and unselfish?
2. Are you a native born, white, gentile American?
3. Are you absolutely opposed to and free of any allegiance of any nature to any cause, government, people, sect, or ruler that is foreign to the United States of America?
4. Do you believe in the tenets of the Christian religion?
5. Do you esteem the United States of America and its institutions above all other government, civil, political, or ecclesiastical, in the whole world?
6. Will you, without mental reservation, take a solemn oath to defend, preserve, and enforce same?
7. Do you believe in clannishness, and will you faithfully practice same toward Klansmen?

8. Do you believe in and will you faithfully strive for the eternal maintenance of white supremacy?
9. Will you faithfully obey our constitution and laws, and conform will-
   ingly to all our usages, requirements, and regulations?
10. Can you always be depended on?

Only in "white supremacy" did the aims of the old and new Klans co-
incide, aside from the banalities about unselfishness, patriotism, and de-
pendability. By questions 2 and 3 Simmons excluded foreigners, Jews,
and Catholics, all of whom had been accepted into the original Klan, and
thereby set his course in an altogether new direction.

While appropriating much of the ritual of the original, Simmons also
added some mumbo-jumbo of his own. The old plus the new enveloped
his converts in a weird and unintelligible system of ceremonies, sings, sig-
nals, and words. The Klan had its own calendar, so that July 4, 1923, for
example, became "The Dismal Day of the Weeping Week of the Hideous
Month of the year of the Klan LVII." The local "dens" were governed by
an "Exalted Cyclops," a "Klaliff," "Klokard," "Kludd," "Kligrapp,"
"Klabee," "Kladd," "Klagaro," "Klexter," "Klokann," and "Nighthawk,"
corresponding respectively to president, vice-president, lecturer, chaplain,
secretary, treasurer, conductor, inner guard, outer guard, investigating
committee, and proctor in charge of candidates. The Klansmen sang
"klodes," held "klonvocations," swore blood oaths, burned crosses, mut-
tered passwords ("Kotop," to which the reply was "Potok," both meaning
nothing), and carried on "klonversations." The latter were an exchange
of code words formed from the first letters of sentences.

Ayak	Are you a Klansman?
Akia	A Klansman I am.
Capowe	Countersign and password of written evidence.
Cygnar	Can you give number and realm?
No. v *Atga*	Number one Klan of Atlanta, Georgia.
Kigy	Klansman, I greet you.
Itsub	In the sacred, unfailing bond.

They would then *Klasp* left hands (Klan loyalty a Sacred Principle). If a
known non-member approached at this fraternal moment, the one who
spied him first would break off the klonversation with a warning, *"San-
bog."* (Strangers are near. Be on guard!)

Non-members were "aliens," and remained so until they were "bap-
tized" as "citizens of the Invisible Empire," whereupon they received the
"Mioak," or Mystical Insignia of a Klansman, a little red celluloid button
bearing the inscrutable words "Kotop" and "Potok." Having taken the sacred oath, the new member was reminded by the Exalted Cyclops that
"Mortal man cannot assume a more binding oath; character and courage
alone will enable you to keep it. Always remember that to keep this oath
means to you honor, happiness, and life; but to violate it means disgrace,

dishonor, and *death*. May happiness, honor, and life be yours." The member's subsequent duties included absolute obedience to the Imperial Wizard, who was described in the Kloran as "The Emperor of the Invisible Empire, a wise man, a wonder worker, having power to charm and control."

Thus equipped, the Reverend Simmons set about creating his Empire. It was uphill work, however. Five years later he had enrolled only a few thousand subjects. The times, perhaps, were not quite right, but in addition the Emperor himself lacked two mundane qualities — executive ability and calculating greed. Both of these lacks were supplied in the spring of 1920, when he met Mr. Clark and Mrs. Tyler.

This couple were professional fund raisers and publicity agents whose accounts had included the Anti-Saloon League, Near East Relief, the Roosevelt Memorial Fund, and others of similar scope. Simmons' Ku Klux Klan was almost too small to be worth their attention, but they decided that it had possibilities. As Southerners, they saw in the anti-foreign, Catholic, Jewish, Negro provisions the raw material with which to appeal to four deep prejudices among other Southerners. After they took the project on Clark became King Kleagle, or second in command, and head of the promotion department, and Mrs. Tyler became his chief assistant. Simmons was left in the misty heights as Imperial Wizard and Emperor, where he was happy. Thereafter, between them, Clark and Mrs. Tyler systematized the appeals to racial and religious hatred and organized the sale of Klan memberships on a businesslike basis.

They divided the country into eight "domains," each headed by a Grand Goblin, and subdivided it into "realms," or states, each in charge of a Grand Dragon, such as Stephenson. The initiation fee was $10 of which $4 went to the Kleagle, or local solicitor, when he signed up a recruit, $1 to the King Kleagle, the state sales manager, 50 cents to the Grand Goblin, and $4.50 to Atlanta. Robes, which were made by the affiliated Gate City Manufacturing Company at a cost of $3.28, were sold for $6.50. Newspapers, magazines, Klorans, and other Klan printed matter was turned out at a substantial profit by the Searchlight Publishing Company, another Klan enterprise, and miscellaneous real estate was handled by the Clark Realty Company. The local Klaverns were supported by dues of a dollar a month, part of which was sent to the state organization. It was somewhat like a chain letter; almost everyone seemed guaranteed to make money.

Within a year and a half, this system had netted more than a hundred thousand members. It had also, according to the New York *World*, caused four killings, one mutilation, one branding with acid, forty-one floggings, twenty-seven tar-and-feather parties, five kidnapings, and forty-three threats and warnings to leave town. The *World*'s exposé pricked Congress into an investigation in October, 1921. Emperor Simmons was called, but proved to be a slippery witness. The atrocities ascribed to the Klan were, he said, the work of imposters. The Klan did not permit violence, he assured the Congressmen, and cited instances wherein he had rebuked dens which disobeyed this rule by withdrawing their charters. The Klan was "purely a fraternal organization," dedicated to patriotism, brotherhood, and maintenance of law and order. Although circumstantial evidence was strong, the investigators could find no legal evidence that the Klan's national organization had caused the outrages or even approved of them, and the inquiry petered out.

However, the *World*'s detective work did have one notable result. Shortly before the Congressional investigation got under way, the paper printed an account of how, two years before, Clark and Mrs. Tyler had been "arrested at midnight in their sleeping garments, in a notorious underworld resort at 185 South Pryor Street, Atlanta, run by Mrs. Tyler," and hauled off to jail, to be charged with "disorderly conduct" and possession of liquor. In the resultant furor Clark submitted his resignation to Simmons, which inspired Mrs. Tyler to issue a statement calling him "a weak-kneed quitter" and repudiating him. Simmons, who was well aware of what the couple had accomplished for the Klan, refused to take action against them. Instead, the propaganda department began to grind out denials, the *World* was branded as a "cowardly and infamous instrument of murder . . . against fair woman!" and the scandal was smoothed over.

But it left a scar. As the moral custodians of their communities, the rank-and-file Klansmen were deeply shocked by the story. Some of them were not convinced by the denials. Along with the evidence presented during the Congressional hearing, it gradually fermented into a basis for an insurgent movement within the ranks. This faction grew under the loving eye of Dr. Evans, who had deserted dentistry to become Grand Dragon of the Realm of Texas, and who had ambitions to the throne. . . .

. . . By the time Dr. Evans took over, [the Klan] was adding thirty-five hundred members a day, and the national treasury was taking in forty-five thousand dollars a day. Within a year Evans could boast, probably with fair accuracy, of a membership of five million. Being in possession of that many adult voters, he and his henchmen naturally turned their thoughts to politics. Principles, they announced, were important to the Klan, not party labels; and accordingly the state and local organizations adopted whichever of the two major parties was stronger in its region. In the South, the Klan was Democratic, in the North, Republican. But since the Republicans were dominant nationally, both the arithmetic of membership and the ends of expediency dictated a stronger drive within that party. But 1924 was a poor year to interfere in Republican affairs. Calvin Coolidge was not only an extremely popular President, but represented in his person many of the parochial virtues that the Klan endorsed, and there was no point in contesting or even trying to bargain over his nomination. The Democratic convention was much more promising. The strongest candidate was Alfred E. Smith, Catholic, Tammany, wet, and a big-city product — in short, a symbol of everything the Klan was against. The Klan came out fighting for William Gibbs McAdoo and managed to split and stalemate the whole proceedings. It finally lost, but it also prevented Smith's nomination; and after many angry hours and smoke-filled meetings John W. Davis, a J. P. Morgan lawyer, was served up as a compromise. The Harding scandals were fresh in the minds of everyone, and 1924 logically should have been a Democratic year, but Davis lost. Considering later events, it is easy to speculate that the Klan's battle in the 1924 Democratic convention was a decisive event in United States and world history.

For Dr. Evans and his Goblins and Dragons it was an encouraging show of strength, despite their failure to nominate their man. They looked forward to 1928. Then, suddenly, there was a disaster. D. C. Stephenson, the Grandest Dragon of the Empire, made a mistake.

"Steve" — as he was usually known — kept a bust of Napoleon on his desk. And like Napoleon, he knew what he wanted. He wanted money and women and power, and later on he wanted to be President of the United States. . . .

Not much is known about his early life. He was born in 1891, evidently in Texas, and spent part of his youth in Oklahoma. He was a second lieutenant in World War I but saw no service overseas. He was married twice, but had divorced or abandoned both women by the time he moved to Evansville, Indiana, shortly after the war. There he began organizing veterans, and this took him into politics. In 1920 he entered the Democratic Congressional primary as a wet. Defeated by the Anti-Saloon League, he promptly became a dry Republican and at the same time joined the newly rising Ku Klux Klan. He became an organizer for the Klan. By 1922 he had succeeded so well that he was made organizer for the State of Indiana, and shortly afterward for twenty other states, mostly midwestern. After a short period in Columbus, Ohio, he moved his offices to Indianapolis, and on July 4, 1923, at Kokomo he officially added the Grand Dragonship of Indiana to his portfolio. By that time he was well on his way to his first million dollars. . . .

One of the women he knew, but not very well, was Madge Oberholzer. She had a small job at the State House in the office of the State Superintendent of Public Instruction. She was not particularly attractive. Unmarried at twenty-eight, which in Indiana means ripe spinsterhood, she was a buxom 145 pounds, had a rather long nose, and wore her hair in an exaggerated upswing that hung over her forehead. But for some reason Steve, whose taste usually ran to ripe beauties, was interested in Madge. He took her to several parties, and once, when the legislature was considering a bill that would have abolished her state job, he gallantly killed it for her.

On the night of March 15, 1925, Madge came home about ten o'clock from a date with another man. Steve had been telephoning, and when she called him back he told her he was going to Chicago and wanted her to come and see him on an important matter before he left. He would send Earl Gentry, one of his bodyguards, to escort her.

She found Steve drinking when she arrived at his home, and according to her later testimony he "forced" her to drink with him. Three drinks later he asked her to go along to Chicago. When she refused, Steve motioned to Gentry and Earl Klenck, another bodyguard, who produced guns; the three men then led her outside and into Steve's waiting car. They drove to the railroad station and boarded the midnight train to Chicago. Steve, Gentry, and Madge went into a drawing room. Gentry climbed into an upper berth and Steve shoved Madge into the lower. "After the train started," her testimony says, "Stephenson got in with me and attacked me. He held me so I could not move. I . . . do not remember all that happened. . . . He . . . mutilated me. . . . "

The next day in Hammond, Indiana, where Steve had the presence of mind to get off the train to avoid the Mann Act, Madge managed on a pretext to get hold of some bichloride-of-mercury tablets. She swallowed six of them. By the time Steve discovered what she had done she was deathly ill. Steve tried to get her to a hospital, then offered to marry her, and finally drove her back to Indianapolis. He kept her in a loft above his garage with the threat that she would stay there until she agreed to marriage. She still refused and finally he had her taken to her home, where she died several weeks later. Before her death she dictated the full story to the prosecuting attorney, William H. Remy, who was one of the few officials of Marion County that Steve did not control. . . .

Steve's crude mistake was a disaster for the Klan not only in Indiana but everywhere. His trial was a national sensation, and his conviction [of second-degree murder] was a national indictment of the organization. It became too absurd and ironic for any Goblin or Dragon to proselytize in the name of morality. The Bible Belt might dismiss the Clark-Tyler episode as malicious gossip, but it could hardly dismiss the legal conviction of one who was probably the Klan's most powerful local leader. The Klan began to break up rapidly, leaving political chaos in its wake. . . .

The Klan died hard, however. It took a new grip on life in 1927–28, with the nomination of Al Smith again in prospect, and the old cries of "Keep the Pope out of the White House!" were heard again. Although it could not prevent Smith's nomination this time, the new wave of religious prejudice it stirred up, and the backwash of intolerance it had created in the years before, were important factors in defeating Smith for the Presidency. Thereafter it subsided again, and by the end of the decade it had only a tiny fraction of its former strength. Here and there, during the next years, one heard of it: a whipping, a castration, a cross burning. The propaganda line changed with the times. During the thirties, emphasis switched from Catholics, Negroes, Jews, and foreigners to Communism and "labor agitators." It was an unrewarding strategy, for although it may have gained contributions for employers, especially in the South, it won back few members. . . .

When a new bogey appears on Main Street to take the place of the Pope, and a new organization arises to take the place of the Klan, one can only hope that the new generation will turn out to be less ignorant than the old.

STUDY GUIDE

1. Put yourself in the place of the young Catholic child living in a tiny prairie town totally dominated by people of another, and hostile, religious faith. How would you feel? Are there still pockets of old line Americanism where a non-Protestant could feel intimidated in the 1990s? If so, where? If not, why not?

2. Relate the display of Klan prejudice in the 1920s to the emotions stirred up in the "Red Scare" of 1919. How were the fears that nurtured these movements similar? How were they different?

3. What role did Protestant theology and social values play in the rise of the Klan? Were there nonreligious benefits in being a Klansman in Kokomo?

4. In considering the activities and the careers of Edward Young Clark, Elizabeth Tyler, and D. C. Stephenson, can you explain the comment of one historian, who said that many members of the Klan were privately fascinated and attracted by what they publicly condemned?

5. Compare the Klan revival of the 1920s with other nativistic movements of that decade. What might connect the Klan with (a) the movement for Prohibition; (b) the passage of the Immigration Act of 1924, which discriminated against southern and eastern Europeans; and (c) the anti-Catholic campaign conducted against Alfred E. Smith when he ran for president in 1928?

BIBLIOGRAPHY

An excellent introduction to some aspects of American nativism in the 1920s will be found in the chapter entitled "The Tribal Twenties" in John

Higham, *Strangers in the Land* (1955). There are a number of books on the Klan. David M. Chalmers, *Hooded Americanism: The First Century of the Ku Klux Klan* (1965) and Arnold S. Rice, *The Ku Klux Klan in American Politics* (1962) are both useful surveys of the origins of the Klan and the motivations and activities of its members. An interesting aspect of the operation of the Klan in the 1920s is explored in Kenneth T. Jackson, *The Ku Klux Klan in the Cities, 1915–1930* (1967).

Rumrunners and the law.

12

ALLAN EVEREST

Heyday of the Bootlegger

One of the issues of the 1920s revealing the conflict between the values and traditions of the rural America of the past and the urban America of the present was Prohibition. Originally rooted in a sincere desire to protect people, particularly working people, from the economic and physical devastation that excessive drinking could cause, the movement for Prohibition became wedded to other concerns in the early twentieth century. Some of its opponents in the 1920s believed that it derived from the American tendency toward Puritanism, which journalist H. L. Mencken defined as "the haunting fear that someone, somewhere, may be happy." Probably more important was that proponents saw in it a way of controlling potentially dangerous tendencies among workers, immigrants, and the lower classes generally. Depriving them of alcohol would render them less likely to misbehave, and eliminating the saloon, the primary center of social life for many working-class men, would facilitate their adoption of proper Anglo-Saxon Protestant middle-class American ways. (It also made it more difficult for the radicals among them to meet, hatch plots against the constituted order, and recruit followers, possibly befuddled by drink, for their nefarious schemes.) The final step in the victory of Prohibition came during World War I, when arguments were advanced that the nation needed the grain that would go into the production of alcohol and that the effective prosecution of the war effort demanded sobriety.

Once adopted, however, the Eighteenth Amendment and the Volstead Act that was passed to implement it proved to be less than smashing successes. There is little doubt that alcohol consumption declined. But it was certainly not eliminated. And many people

questioned the price being paid to achieve what seemed rather modest success. They called Prohibition an infringement of personal liberty. They pointed to the number of people who died or suffered
permanent damage to their health from drinking illegal liquor that
was literally poisonous. And, increasingly, they argued that Prohibition's most significant effect was to provide a highly profitable field
of activity for gangsters and thus to pave the way for them to exercise
great, and damaging, influence.

Most of the men whom Allan Everest talks about in the following selection were small-time operators who probably represented no
real threat to the social order. But the difficulties involved in enforc-
ing Prohibition, which Everest's account makes clear, caused concern. The Wickersham Commission was appointed by President
Hoover in 1929 to conduct an investigation; it concluded in effect
that the alternatives were either to step up the enforcement effort
substantially or to repeal the law. In 1933, with the adoption of the
Twenty-first Amendment, the nation chose the latter course.

Although Prohibition is a thing of the past, some of the issues
underlying the debate about it remain matters of current concern. In
the controversy over the legalization of marijuana, the decriminaliza-
tion of prostitution, smoking bans, laws mandating seat belt use, and
so forth, are echoes of a fundamental question in the conflict over
Prohibition: how far can society go, legitimately and effectively, in
forcing people to do what is good for them?

Twenty-year-old Billy hummed a lively tune as he drove his old Dodge
car south toward Chazy. If he did say so himself, he had just put on a
good performance at the Canadian border. The result might have been
quite different, he knew, because he was carrying ten burlap bags of beer.
At the border he was stopped and questioned, as he had known he would
be. Of course it helped to be recognized as the son of a prominent citizen
of Plattsburgh, but he thought it also helped to project a friendly, candid
personality which he had developed over the months of his new career —
bootlegging.

He knew that although the border was the most crucial part of his
journey, he still faced hazards on his way south. For example, Miner's
Woods were just ahead. Was there a trap awaiting him there? And what

Excerpts from *Rum Across the Border: The Prohibition Era in Northern New York*, by Allan S.
Everest (Syracuse, N.Y.: Syracuse University Press, 1978), are reprinted by permission of
Syracuse University Press.

about the city of Plattsburgh or Poke-o'-Moonshine? If he got through safely this time, perhaps he should vary his routine on the next trip and not appear at the same place too often. So far he had been lucky.

Men like Billy went into rumrunning for many reasons, including money and prestige. In the early years some young men had just been released from the army, with no jobs in sight. A few ex-troopers and patrolmen turned to bootlegging in protest against what they conceived as unfair treatment or against society in general. But for many of the younger bootleggers the thrill of the work was more satisfying than the money. The excitement of a successful chase was enough to make them go back to Canada again and again. Bucky Ladd, whose father was the respected head of customs at Rouses Point, had a profitable brokerage business there which he neglected in favor of the more risky profits of bootlegging. Francis "Sam" Racicot, a bootlegger in Rouses Point as a young man, puts into words what he and his friends did not then: "Most of the bootleggers considered that it was an unfair law and a law which had been foisted on us, which had no validity. We knew that it wasn't being supported by the general public, that it was disliked, and that we didn't feel we were lawbreakers."

Numerically, the largest group was the petty smugglers, who had vacationed in Canada or had visited the border night spots and wanted to return home with a bottle or two. If caught at the border, they were usually relieved to get off with a small fine and the loss of the liquor. Occasionally, a man like Thomas McBeetry of Saranac Lake refused to pay the five dollar fine even when his companions did so, and too late found himself held in $1,000 bail for a session of federal court. An unexpected by-product of this traffic was the shipping of carloads of American-made pint flasks to Canada for sale to American tourists. The United Cigar Stores in Quebec became almost too busy to sell any tobacco.

In the towns along the border, teenagers comprised another category of smugglers. Elmer Caron, later sheriff of Clinton County, recalls how the boys of Churubusco used to buy a little beer at Toissant Trombly's across the border: "An officer once stopped a group of them on their return and found one bottle. The boys were considered innocent of smuggling but they were thoroughly frightened." Howard Curtis remembers that as a schoolboy in Mooers a sixteen-year-old classmate once asked him to cut school and go to the movies in Plattsburgh in his Model T. When they reached town they drove into a garage, where some cases were unloaded from the rear seat, and then they went to the show. Howard discovered that at about the age of fifteen he had unwittingly been a party to beer-running, "my only participation that I know of at this time."

The seventeen-year-old son of a member of the Board of Education in Utica came north in search of adventure and money. Another boy of the same age arrived on foot at the Sanger home on Rand Hill, recalls Ralph Sanger. Cold and wet, he had been forced to abandon his load and run into the snow-covered woods. Ralph's mother gave him breakfast while she lectured him on the foolishness of his ways, as she did others who came to her door. . . .

It was men in their twenties and thirties, however, who accounted for most of the volume of smuggled goods. One group was the self-employed who owned their own cars. Most towns had several of them, and they were often good friends who shared their fun and information with each other. Yet on the road they were usually lone wolves, traveling by themselves and seeking their own markets.

Another group included the eager beavers who could be hired to drive a load across the border. When they did so they became a part of an enterprise organized by professionals from Saratoga, Glens Falls, or New York City. The car might be furnished for them, but more often they used their own. They were paid either fifty dollars a week and expenses, ten dollars a day, a flat rate per trip, or a case of liquor. At a time when a day's pay in other work was only $1.50–2.00, bootlegging seemed a quick way to get rich. The money enabled them to dress snappily, their wardrobes invariably including a coonskin coat, and gave them some distinction among their peers.

Sometimes the contacts between professional and driver were accidental. A Plattsburgh youth once went to a dance in Rouses Point where he was propositioned to bring a load of liquor from Canada. He attempted it, got through, and subsequently made regular trips for his employer. But there were also places like the Union Hotel in Plattsburgh, which were known as meeting places of professionals and drivers, as recalled by Darwin Keysor of Plattsburgh, who clerked there during high-school. There the drivers got their instructions, and after a successful trip they were treated to a steak dinner and given a great deal of flattering attention, "and they thought they were big shots." The professional could afford to do this because he could anticipate good profits downstate while at the same time running almost no risk himself. But the driver, if caught, could expect no help, and he would almost certainly lose his car, liquor, and perhaps his freedom.

Regional hierarchies were important in the bootlegging fraternity. The "king" of bootleggers won the title by unusually daring and successful exploits. Dick Warner of Saratoga seems to have been the first, but his eventual arrest and jailing left the field open to other hopefuls. The "queen" of bootleggers was a female counterpart. For a while Dorothy Swartout of Saratoga was the unchallenged title-holder. She and Warner shared many adventures on the northern border. While the less daring might hope to be known as "baron" or "duke," none of these terms meant much in northern New York. . . .

If nothing else, the techniques developed by bootleggers were imaginative and ingenious. The petty smugglers often risked concealment of liquor on their persons. Pockets were used, but so were less obvious places. Men had belts made especially to hold bottles, and false vests with pockets large enough for a pint bottle each. Women, who were often expected to run the risks for their male partners, concealed liquor in their bloomers as well as under their corsets. A large person could more successfully disguise odd bulges than a small one, and the loose clothing styles of the day also helped.

Border residents developed some smuggling schemes in the best rural tradition. A Mooers cow made the rounds with her owner between Hemmingford, Mooers, and Champlain. "This dutiful old cow," as Howard Curtis describes her, carried a bale of hay on each side. Finally Officer John O'Hara, who seemed to have a sixth sense in detection, became suspicious of an animal that needed to be bred so often, and upon examining the hay discovered that each bale was hollow and filled with bottles of whiskey. Horses were also put to good use. Leo Filion of Champlain, who was in the business of rumrunning himself, remembers one owner who lost three horses by gunfire. He also tells of a Champlain farmer who had horses trained as bootleggers. He could load one with liquor in Canada and turn it loose, confident that it would avoid all human contact and find its way home through the woods. A great deal of local smuggling was done on foot or snowshoes or with toboggans. Filion remembers a man who could carry four cases at a time on his back. "That would be four dozen bottles and would have weighed more than one hundred pounds," he points out.

But these homely methods hardly sufficed to smuggle goods in the quantity the market demanded, so concealment in cars was tried and found amazingly successful. Sometimes nothing mechanical had to be done to the vehicle. The Mooers undertaker found his hearse perfectly suited to a sideline in smuggling. He always had all the necessary papers for crossing the border, presumably with a body in the coffin. But Officer O'Hara began to wonder about the sudden rise in the death rate, and when he opened the casket he found no body, but plenty of liquor.

Most car owners did not have the natural advantages of the hearse. Some thought that driving without lights or plates shielded them from discovery at night, even though they created hazards for other travelers when they persisted in driving fifty miles an hour. Rumrunners learned to use cars with reinforced springs to support heavy loads. They found that they could wire liquor under the car, or conceal it behind or under seats, in tool boxes, and in spare tires or trunks. They rebuilt cars with false floors of tin through which lengthened pedals and shifting levers were devised; this created a space large enough to store twenty quarts of liquor. Another ruse was the false gas tank. The tank was divided so that one part carried a little gas, but the other part could hold many quarts of liquor. Still another was a false top. Cars of the day were made with fabric tops, and between two layers of fabric a storage space four inches deep was constructed that could carry 180 pints of liquor. Such a top seems to have been the specialty of a garage in Napierville, Quebec. . . .

Bootleggers who wanted to be prepared in case of pursuit provided themselves with a means of making smoke. Some pumped oil into the exhaust. Others used a fire extinguisher filled with a chemical; the pump was bolted to the door of the car and the nozzle connected with a tube running to the exhaust chamber. One or two charges were enough to lay a dangerous smoke screen. Still others had an air-compression machine which stirred up the dust of the road. A smoke screen was illegal, dust was not, yet it was often as effective.

In the winter, whether the roads were open or not, much smuggling was done by sleigh. This traffic was quite safe because it was conducted across the fields away from the patrolled highways. Almost all farmers had flat-bottomed sleighs which they used to haul potatoes and other produce to market. But in winter they were inclined either to do a little bootlegging themselves or rent their conveyances to others. Some boot-leggers also took their loads across the ice of Lake Champlain. They did not always remember to check the thickness of the ice, and in February 1924, two men and a sleighload of Canadian ale went into seven feet of water in Trombly's Bay. With help from ashore, horses and sleigh were saved, but the neighbors had to wait until spring to bring up the beer with hooks.

Sleighs were good only for slow, local traffic. Bootleggers kept their cars on the road except after heavy snows and high winds, and even then they tried to keep some of the back roads open for their own use. Diane Filion recalls doing some of this work for her friends with her new Ford; then, she says, customs officers planted two bottles of whiskey on the car and seized it: "I decided not to make a legal case of it because even if I won, my life would be intolerable afterwards."

Informal intelligence networks were organized by the bootleggers. One variety employed youngsters to watch the customs house, especially at night. When the officers left on patrol, the boys either signaled or tele-phoned to a loading spot across the border that the coast was clear. Youngsters were also employed to follow a patrolman by motorcycle and telephone back the direction he took. In Rouses Point the telephone op-erator helpfully relayed information concerning the whereabouts of en-forcement officers to bootleggers who called in.

Once across the border the bootlegger had a choice of roads. He also had a choice of procedures. He might decide to make a run for it on his own. If he was part of an organization he joined a caravan, which sent scouts ahead in a pilot car to make sure the road was clear. If the pilot car was stopped no harm was done because it was "clean." If it was not challenged for ten to twenty miles, the driver telephoned back that the road was clear. The run, at least as far as Elizabethtown, was often plotted in advance, with farmers' barns or garages rented for quick concealment during a pursuit or as a rest stop while the pilot car scouted the next stretch of road. Farmers even flagged down bootleggers to warn them of danger ahead and to offer sanctuary. Normally, however, the barns were rented by the month. Patrolman Philip Auer reports that bootleggers once tried unwittingly to rent a garage from his wife. . . .

Smugglers were early drawn to the possibilities of the railroad. The small-timers, like those in automobiles, discovered many hiding places. They might tie an individual bottle to a string and hang it out of the window during customs inspection at Rouses Point. If the bottle broke the owner pulled in only a jagged bottle neck; sometimes it was only the string when local boys made off with the bottle, according to Sam Racicot. Liquor was also concealed in ventilators, light fixtures, the springs of Pullman seats, upper berths, and mattresses. Panels in staterooms and washrooms were unscrewed to provide hiding places. Trunks were constructed with false sides and bottoms where many pints could be stored. The so-called "suitcase brigade" consisted of those who simply tried to smuggle liquor in their personal luggage.

Large-scale smugglers, however, were intrigued with the possibilities of the freight car, which offered many advantages over smuggling by automobile. It could be made to carry a load fifty times that of a car. Trains were not stopped by winter weather. Furthermore, it was safer for both smuggler and receiver because false bills of lading made their identities impossible to discover even if the shipment was detected and seized. Bootleggers sometimes gained access to empty freight cars in Canada and constructed false ends three feet deep that created space for almost 200 cases of beer in each end. But just as often they shipped a full car of liquor billed as fish, lumber, hay, or lime. The car was loaded at Napierville or other railroad centers in Quebec and consigned to a receiver in New York or New Jersey. The liquor was concealed under a thin covering of the legitimate cargo named in the bill of lading, and a car could easily carry 100 to 150 barrels of beer. It was then sealed for the trip across the border. There was probably some connivance by Canadian railroad officials, but this was not necessary under the normal procedures for shipping by the carload. . . .

Except in winter, Lake Champlain offered many opportunities for transporting liquor. With a rowboat or an outboard motorboat the small-time smuggler could shuttle back and forth all night. But the professionals used high-powered craft like Chrysler, Chris-Craft, and Gray, some of them elaborate twenty to forty-foot cruisers. Billy Hicks, one of the most active of the local bootleggers, owned a forty-foot boat which he painted black and used at night. When fully loaded it carried 300–400 cases of beer and was barely out of water. A favorite loading place was in the cove just north of Fort Montgomery, but boats could safely navigate the Richelieu River all the way from St. John.

There were man-made hazards on water as well as land. The swing bridge on the railroad across the lake always had to be opened for the larger craft and for almost all boats during high water in the spring. Some rumrunners went through nevertheless, but others unloaded near Rouses Point and continued their journey by land. There were also lake patrols. If a patrol boat approached, the smugglers dropped the liquor overboard so as not to be caught with the evidence.

A capacious device for smuggling by water was the "submarine," a low-lying craft without its own power. Towed behind a large boat, it was cut loose and allowed to sink during a pursuit. With luck the bootleggers could later return and recover the sunken craft; the floating rope would show them where it lay.

A similar device made use of a small wooden box of rock salt. If a pursuit became hot the bags of liquor were dropped overboard, each attached by a long rope to a box of salt. When the salt dissolved the box returned to the surface and guided smugglers to their lost goods.

There were also natural hazards on the lake. Engine failure was always a possibility. Customs officers easily seized a thirty-foot launch abandoned off Cumberland Head lighthouse when its engine stopped. Reefs and irregular shoreline were a danger to pilots unacquainted with the lake. Their threat was made worse by sudden, violent storms that sometimes ravaged the waters. Willsboro Point was such a place, and five bootleg boats came to grief there within a period of two years. The crew usually escaped, but their load and sometimes the boat went to the bottom of the lake. . . .

The market for alcoholic beverages was almost universal, but bootleggers preferred the centers of population. The speakeasies of Rouses Point and Plattsburgh tapped into the flow, although the large markets and high prices were to be found in Glens Falls, Saratoga, Albany, and New York. Profits from smuggling depended upon the kind of liquor, the place of sale, and the number of people who had to share the proceeds. The individual operator could buy beer in Canada for $4.50 or $5.00 a case and sell it in Plattsburgh for $10.00. By carrying it to New York, he could get up to $25.00. Two trips a week were feasible in summer, one in winter if the road was open. If he took a small carload of twenty-five cases, a smuggler could make as much as $600 a run, less his expenses. When smuggling was the work of an organization, the added costs included the relays of drivers, storage charges near the border (up to $3.00

a case), and the rental of barns and storage depots along the way. These expenses were trifling considering the large volume of alcohol that a professional could keep moving.

The most popular Canadian beer in the United States was probably Molson's, closely followed by Black Horse Ale, Carling's Red Label, and Labatt's. Favorites among the whiskies were... Canadian Club, and White Horse Scotch. Bootleggers in Rouses Point sometimes took telephone orders for specific champagnes or whiskies for special occasions in downstate cities.

Champagne could be bought in Canada for $4–7 a bottle and might bring up to $20 in New York. Rye was available for $4, brought $7–9 in Plattsburgh and $12 in New York, for a profit of $8. Scotch provided a $12 markup. When it was available, pure alcohol was also profitable. Canadian businessmen were allowed to buy and store it for industrial purposes at ninety-eight cents a gallon. Sam Racicot found a perfume manufacturer who was willing to sell it for $2. He and Roy Ashline would "go through this little false door and pull out the five-gallon tins and load them in the car and head directly for the border and take them down to New York." There they sold it for $15 a gallon. . . .

Bootleggers wanted a fast car and one capable of carrying 25–40 cases of liquor. Cadillacs, Packards, Pierce-Arrows, and Marmons were highly regarded, although every kind was used in the trade, and beginners had to be satisfied with smaller and older cars. Bootleggers could buy cars through the usual retail outlets that other people used. They could also bid at government auctions of seized cars, but the wary decided that these cars were too well known by the patrolmen and would easily be recognized if they were put back into the smuggling business.

The major source of bootleggers' cars was, therefore, a stolen car center in Albany. Cars were cheap, no questions were asked, and since the state had not developed registration procedures, only money and a simple bill of sale containing a fictitious name changed hands. In 1922 Sam Racicot bought a 1917 Cadillac there for $200, used it for a year, and sold it, after he had wrecked it, for his purchase price. Its top speed was fifty miles an hour, and up to sixty going downhill. The speed of the early cars has been exaggerated, and even if they had been capable of eighty miles an hour, which they were not, the condition of the roads would have made such speeds impossible. The Cadillac owner found that the hill out of Elizabethtown toward Keene was so steep that he had to go up in reverse. Gasoline was cheap, but tires were expensive. A bootlegger learned to carry spares because he could not expect much more than two months of use from the tires of the day. . . .

Rumrunners had a number of advantages that lessened the hazards of their profession. The number of officers was insufficient to form more than a token patrol along the border, and bootleggers came to know the personal weaknesses of some of the officers and to exploit them. They also knew that some of them were less dedicated than others and were apt to show indulgence to petty or youthful offenders.

The terrain fitted the needs of the rumrunners. Northern New York was mostly rural, with occasional small towns between the border and Plattsburgh, twenty miles away. Numerous roads crossed the border, but only a few of them had customs stations. The many wooded areas along the highways offered refuge to bootleggers who abandoned their cars in flight; the great majority of them made good their escape, to be back in business a few days later.

Customs stations were closed at night, and the border was unguarded except for the patrols. Serious bootleggers consequently learned to make their big runs after ten or eleven o'clock, when the stations were dark. Ralph Sanger remembers seeing a caravan of as many as fourteen cars pass his home on Rand Hill. A reporter for the *Plattsburgh Republican* conducted a series of interviews along the border in 1923 and documented the extent of this traffic. He was told in Mooers that thirty cars an hour passed through the village during the night. A caravan of fourteen cars had recently passed unchallenged through Mooers, the pilot having first stopped to ask a villager whether the road was clear ahead. Residents of Champlain and Mooers said that if they got up to look every time a car roared by, they would get no sleep. At about the time of the interviews, 132 cars passed the Rouses Point customs house in one night without stopping to report. The office was then being kept open to help conscientious people obtain proper clearance in and out of Canada. Bootleggers obviously never stopped; anyway, many used roads which avoided customs completely.

During the summer months, bootleggers had another bonus at the customs stations. Students from St. Lawrence University in Canton, New York, received temporary appointments as customs officers. Young and inexperienced, they could sometimes be fooled by the tricks of the old-timers. Bootleggers assert that they were even able to walk out of a station with a suitcase full of seized liquor, unrecognized and unchallenged. The margin of safety for the bootlegger was usually the degree of assurance and naturalness he could put into his actions.

The countryside was dotted with farmers who, if unwilling to rent their barns for storage, as many of them did, sympathized with the bootleggers, gave them tips, and provided temporary shelter. Nevertheless, according to Darwin Keysor, an occasional farmer double-crossed a bootlegger by telling him that someone had stolen his load. A well-known garage in Rouses Point, located about a block from the customs house, served the bootleggers well as a transfer point. A loaded Canadian car arriving at the edge of town was made to backfire and then crawled to the garage for help. Once inside, the liquor was transferred to an American car which was casually driven away unchallenged, while the "clean" Canadian car dutifully reported to customs down the street. . . .

For relaxation bootleggers maintained camps, at least during the summer months. The one that served the Malone area was at a remote spot in the northern Adirondacks. The one for the Mooers–Champlain–Rouses Point fraternity was located at Rochester Point on Lake Champlain south of Rouses Point. Here the men enjoyed good food prepared by local women employed for housekeeping duties. Each weekend prostitutes were brought from Montreal, and nudist bathing, plenty of liquor, and other pleasures helped to ease the tensions created by the smugglers' trade. The camp also served as a depot for liquor brought by rowboat from Canada and later reshipped in power boats.

Despite the many conditions that worked in his favor, the bootlegger knew that he was only one step from a stretch in jail, although this was a part of the fascination. He was aware of the danger to his life from gunfire and high-speed driving. If captured, he could expect the penitentiary. If he was challenged but managed to escape, he faced the loss of his car and its contents. Gaston Monette recalls that the dangers he experienced were "so close they are still almost scratching my back."

The narrow, crooked dirt roads of the day often denied the smuggler the speed of which his car was capable, although this factor worked equally against troopers and patrolmen. The sheer distances involved in the liquor traffic added to its complexities. On the map Plattsburgh looked like a short run from the border, but the routes were full of pitfalls. The trip to Glens Falls was 140 miles, to Albany 195 miles, while New York City, the most profitable market, was 350 miles away. Aside from dangers from "the law," the trip was both monotonous and fatiguing. Sam Racicot and Roy Ashline wrecked their car on a trip back from New York when Sam, who was driving, fell asleep.

Car trouble brought many smugglers to grief because all disabled cars attracted attention. Rumrunners were plagued with flat tires, but broken springs and motor failures also took their toll. Gunfire caused breakdowns as well. A patrolman's shots into a gas tank, tires, or radiator usually forced a bootlegger to abandon his car, although some managed sensational escapes on flat tires or with a drained radiator. A rumrunner with a mechanical breakdown could get help by a telephone call to his buddies, but on the party lines of the day he might be overheard and reported. So some preferred to hike to the nearest garage. Billy Colerich once walked a mile for help after the breakdown of his Model T Ford containing a load of beer. On his return he took the precaution of approaching through the woods, only to see customs officers about to seize his car. He escaped and hitchhiked back to Plattsburgh. The wary ones who had breakdowns learned to conceal their loads in the woods before they went for help. William Riley of Newark, New Jersey, lacked any opportunity of getting away. In his beer-laden truck he broke through the planks of a bridge south of Mooers. Only the steel girders prevented him from plunging into the river. . . .

For the most part northern New York was spared the gang warfare that scarred the metropolitan areas during the twenties and early thirties. The so-called Yancey gang moved into the area and although tough, was willing to live and let live with the other bootleggers. When an even tougher gang from New York moved in, however, the Yancey gang opposed them, and eventually the two groups shot it out at the Meridian Hotel. Although only whispered at the time, it was presumed that two members of the new gang were killed and the rest scattered, never to return. The bodies were supposed to have been bound in chains and dumped into Lake Champlain near the railroad bridge.

If a bootlegger could stay out of jail and avoid the other pitfalls of his profession, he might make a great deal of money. Yet the consensus of opinion among the participants is that only a few held onto their money. It seems to have been "easy come, easy go" for most of them. A few substantial businessmen remain in the county who used the profits of rumrunning to start a legitimate enterprise. Farmers who rented their facilities were sometimes able to expand their farms and improve their buildings, but the majority of bootleggers seem to have dissipated their earnings on a succession of expensive cars, necessary to their trade, and on good clothes, women, and other dazzling objects so tempting to the possessor of sudden wealth. Says Keysor, "They bought the most expensive suits and they lived high, they had a good time."

STUDY GUIDE

1. After reading the selection, what impression do you get of the degree of professionalism of the bootleggers? Are there generalizations one can easily make about them as a group or were they a diverse type? If the first, how would you categorize them; if the latter, what categories would you establish in order to subdivide them?

2. What information does this essay provide regarding the competence of the government in policing the Prohibition laws and amendment?

3. What appears to be the attitude toward Prohibition of the residents of these border communities? Did this hinder or help law enforcement? Why?

4. Was bootlegging profitable and, if so, what factors determined the extent of the profits that could be garnered?

5. Does this essay support the recommendation of the Wickersham Commission that the federal government should either support the Prohibition amendment with money and manpower or repeal it? Why?

BIBLIOGRAPHY

The literature on Prohibition is abundant and interesting. Many of the comical aspects of the era are told in Henry Walsh Lee, *How Dry We Were: Prohibition Revisited* (1963). Andrew Sinclair's study, *Prohibition: The Era of Excess* (1962), published in paperback as *Era of Excess: A Social History of the Prohibition Movement,* emphasizes the nativistic and backward-looking tendencies of the movement. A similar point of view is taken by Joseph R. Gusfield in *Symbolic Crusade: Status Politics and the American Temperance Movement* (1963) and by Norman Clark in *The Dry Years: Prohibition and Social Change in Washington* (1965). James H. Timberlake, in *Prohibition and the Progressive Movement, 1900–1920* (1963), makes a case for Prohibition as a facet of Progressive reform. In "New Perspectives on the Prohibition 'Experiment' of the 1920s" (*Journal of Social History,* Fall 1968, pp. 51–68), John C. Burnham disagrees with those who have labeled the Prohibition movement a failure. Burnham contends, and offers a number of statistical studies to prove his point, that as a consequence of Prohibition, the social and medical health of the nation — and particularly lower income groups — improved markedly.

This modern "ice man" calls once—with Frigidaire—and the ice stays always

Be Sure it *is* a Frigidaire!

THERE are now more than two hundred thousand users of Frigidaire Electric Refrigeration. And these users are telling their friends and neighbors that Frigidaire has brought to their homes and places of business a measure of convenience and economy unequaled by anything they have ever known.

You have heard of Frigidaire—of the constant, dependable and economical service it renders, of the *better* way in which it keeps all foods,

of the convenience of the ice it makes and the desserts it freezes.

You are probably thinking *now* of electric refrigeration for your own home. Be sure, when you *do* buy, that you get a genuine Frigidaire. Look for the name itself—you'll find it on every Frigidaire. It identifies the product of General Motors. It is your assurance that you will enjoy the combined advantages which only Frigidaire can give.

There is a wide range of Frigidaires built complete with metal cabinet, finished in white Duco, lined with seamless porcelain enamel. They are priced as low as $245. Frigidaire mechanical units for installation in the standard makes of iceboxes, as low as $190. All prices f. o. b. Dayton. Any Frigidaire may be purchased on the GMAC deferred payment plan.

DELCO-LIGHT COMPANY, *Subsidiary of General Motors Corporation*, Dept. V-34, DAYTON, OHIO

Frigidaire
ELECTRIC REFRIGERATION

BE SURE IT _IS_ A FRIGIDAIRE ~ PRODUCT OF GENERAL MOTORS

The 1920s saw the introduction of modern appliances into the American home.

13

RUTH SCHWARTZ COWAN

Women and Housework in the 1920s

Except for a sharp but short-lived economic downturn early in the decade, the 1920s were quite prosperous. Productivity and real wages — that is, the amount of goods and services that a person could buy with an hour's labor — both rose. New industries such as radio and aviation became prominent and profitable. Older industries such as automobile production, the movies, and advertising enjoyed rapid growth. People spoke of "The New Era" in the nation's economic life, in which mass production was linked to mass consumption in such a way as to generate uninterrupted growth and general prosperity and ensure that depressions would become relics of the past. That optimism was proved erroneous when the stock market crash of 1929 signaled the start of the worst depression the nation had ever endured.

Still, the prosperity of the 1920s, temporary as it may have been, had permanent effects on the way Americans lived, in large part because the primary driving force behind the decade's economic growth was spending on consumer goods. The introduction and widespread use of installment-plan buying, time-purchase plans, and other forms of consumer credit permitted millions of Americans to acquire the automobiles, radios, and other glittery new gadgets that a flourishing mass-production economy was turning out for their delight.

That avalanche of new consumer goods had a dramatic impact on the American home. There were significant differences between social classes in "typical" household furnishings, and the impact of the new mass-consumption society was much greater on urban than on rural America. Still, by the end of the 1920s the majority of Americans — rural and urban, and of all social classes — lived in homes that were quite different from those of their parents or grandparents. The following essay by Ruth Schwartz Cowan focuses primarily on how the definitions and the conduct of housework changed during the 1920s, but it also provides clues as to how American life in general was transformed by industrial technology and new buying habits.

In the twentieth century, the proliferation of household technology has dramatically altered women's lives but has not in the least mitigated the assignment of housework to women. When the twentieth century opened, the vast majority of American women spent most of their waking hours feeding, clothing, cleaning, and sustaining themselves and their families; eighty years later, as the century is drawing to a close, the vast majority of American women are still spending many of their waking hours feeding, clothing, cleaning, and sustaining themselves and their families, albeit with markedly different tools. . . .

While it is no doubt true that every family is unique, it is also true that, at any given time and place, families living within the range of a certain standard of living confront similar material conditions in their homes and similar public attitudes about what distinguishes a "good" or a "decent" home from one that is neither. Each of us may bring a unique combination of psychic and social factors to our work; but, in any given time or place, depending upon the class to which we belong, women tend to organize their kitchens in more or less the same way and to read the same magazines, newspapers, and books. If our work, at least part of the time, is housework, then no matter how different we may be from each other, our work processes will be fairly similar. Hence, although it is difficult for a historian to learn much about *what* individual women and men felt about the work that was (or was not) being done in their homes, it is somewhat easier to learn *how* that work was being done. Between 1900 and 1940, the differences in the work processes of housework between those who were rich and those who were poor, were striking — so striking, indeed, that they remained engraved, consciously and unconsciously, on the minds and in the behavior of later generations. . . .

The second generation of twentieth-century women came to maturity during the First World War, bore their children during the Roaring Twenties, and struggled to keep their households functioning during the dreary years of the Depression. Enormous technological and social changes occurred between their mothers' time and their own; and these changes began — but only just began — to alter not only the work processes of housework but also the fundamental differences between women of the two great social classes.

Material Conditions for Those Who Were Still Living Comfortably

During the 1920s and the 1930s, a housewife of the more prosperous classes did not regularly work for wages, despite the fact that she was better educated than her mother had been and more likely to have worked for a few years before marriage. Only one in forty of the "business class" housewives who were studied by Helen and Robert Lynd in Muncie, Indiana ("Middletown"), in 1925 had worked for wages in the previous five years. The typical comfortable housewife of this generation lived in a house that was fairly similar to the one in which she had been raised (if she were lucky enough to have been the daughter of a prosperous father); it was spacious, perhaps a bit smaller than her parents' had been, lacking a spare bedroom or an old-fashioned parlor, but not much smaller; and it was equipped with many of the same modern conveniences (telephones, hot and cold running water, indoor plumbing, gas and electricity). By the end of the 1920s, the daughter was likely to have had one or two appliances that had not been available to her mother (perhaps an electric washing machine, or a refrigerator, or an automobile); but, even more significantly, she would have acquired the conveniences and the appliances earlier in her marriage, when her children were still young and the burden of her work was heaviest, and when her household routines (which are very resistant to change) were first established. In 1926, 80 percent of all the affluent households that were studied by market researchers in thirty-six American cities had vacuum cleaners and washing machines. More than half of all the households in the United States had an automobile by 1930, and every single one of the business-class households of Muncie had one by 1925. When the Lynds returned to study Muncie again in 1935, 40 percent of all the households whose assessed value was over two thousand dollars (a sum the Lynds regarded as the dividing line between adequate and inadequate housing) had a refrigerator.

Taken together, the vacuum cleaner, the washing machine, the refrigerator, and the automobile had profound implications for the reorganization of work in the households of the prosperous. Possession of an electric washing machine meant that a "decent" housewife could do her wash at home and by herself without undue drudgery; these early washing machines did not go through their cycles automatically and did not spin the clothing semi-dry (they had electrically powered wringers), but they did eliminate a good deal of the hauling and the hand wringing that had once made laundry work inconceivable for a woman of "status." The vacuum cleaners of the day were heavy instruments; but since they could be wheeled, they eliminated not only the drudgery but also the stooping that had once been associated with heavy cleaning and thus eliminated the perceived necessity for a servant to undertake it. Vacuum cleaners also cleaned more thoroughly than brooms and thus made it possible for the young housewife to dispense not only with the horrors of spring cleaning but also with the women whom her mother had hired to help with it. The young housewife's refrigerator reinforced the tendency — which had actually commenced when either her basement or her mother's had been converted from a storage room to a furnace room — to purchase foodstuffs in small, rather than large, quantities and to dispense with delivery services provided by the retailer. The automobile served only to accelerate that trend as well as to create a host of other transportation services (such as taking children to parties and to doctors) that women of an earlier generation had not provided for their families. The average comfortable housewife of the generation before the First World War had done some of her housework herself and managed the labor of other people who did the rest of it; the average comfortable housewife of the generation that came to maturity after the war managed more appliances than people.

The availability of appliances and conveniences was one — but not the only one — of the factors that stimulated this reorganization. One study of the relationship between the acquisition of household appliances and the organization of household work in this period reported that, while most of the families of students at Mount Holyoke College had acquired four or five major appliances in the decade between 1919 and 1929, and 96 percent of the families had also decreased the amount of household help that they employed, only a small fraction of these attributed the decrease solely to the acquisition of the appliances. The other families were probably responding to a new set of demographic factors (namely, a severe contraction in the available supply of servants) and to a new set of ideological factors (namely, new attitudes articulated in women's magazines and advice books during the 1920s). . . .

The supply of servants was shrinking for many reasons. The European conflict and, after that, the immigration restrictions of the mid-1920s drastically reduced the influx of foreign-born young women, who had previously constituted the largest portion of the servant population. In addition, the expanding economy of the 1920s increased the opportunities in factories for women without skills. In Indiana, for example, the ratio of servants to households was 1 in 20 in 1920; and the business-class wives of Muncie reported that they employed approximately half as many servant-hours as their mothers had done, at roughly five times the wages (salaries for people in the middle-income ranges had roughly doubled in the same period). Only one quarter of the seven hundred urban households of college-educated women that were studied carefully by the United States Department of Agriculture in 1930 employed a domestic servant, as did only 17 percent of the three thousand middle-class families studied a year later by President Hoover's Conference on Home Building and Homeownership — percentages that would have been astounding twenty years earlier. . . .

"Really doing it yourself" had once been considered demeaning, but attitudes were changing. In the early decades of the century, women's magazines had repeatedly offered advice to housewives who were, for one unfortunate reason or another, coping with their homes singlehanded, but the emphasis in those articles had been on the word *unfortunate*. The housewife was told, for example, that if help was scarce, it was easiest to serve children the same food adults were eating, although clearly it would be better for the former's digestion and your temperament if they ate with a nursemaid in the nursery; with luck, the servant shortage would soon pass. "Decent" housewives were never depicted, in those years, as doing the heavy work of their households themselves; when instructions for proper laundry work or sanitary cleaning were proffered, a tell-tale "instruct your laundress" or "see that your maid" would always slip through. In the years after the First World War, as advertisements for refrigerators, washing machines, and vacuum cleaners replaced those for iceboxes, laundry tubs, and brooms, servants disappeared from the advertisements — to be replaced by housewives, neatly manicured and elegantly coiffured, but housewives nonetheless. In those same years, the language used in the nonfiction material in women's magazines also underwent a subtle change, coming to imply that housework was to be thought of no longer as a chore but, rather, as an expression of the housewife's personality and her affection for her family. Laundering had once been just a task to be finished as quickly as possible; now it was an expression of love. The new bride could speak her affection by washing tattle-tale gray out of her husband's shirts. Feeding the family had once been just part of a day's work; now it was a way to communicate deep-seated emotions:

> When the careful housekeeper turns from the preparation of company dinner to the routine of family meals, she will know that prime rib roast, like peach ice cream, *is a wonderful stimulant to family loyalty,* but that it is not absolutely necessary for every day.

Diapering was now a time for building a baby's sense of security, and cleaning the bathroom sink became an exercise for the maternal instincts, protecting the family from disease.

Clearly, tasks of such emotional magnitude could not be relegated to servants. The servantless household may have been an economic necessity for people in the 1920s and the 1930s; but, for the first time, that necessity was widely regarded, at least in the public press, as a potential virtue. And whether or not she regarded it as a virtue, the average comfortable housewife of this generation learned to organize the work in her household without the assistance of servants or with far fewer hours of assistance than her mother had had. Where a servant had been replaced by a vacuum cleaner, the comfortable housewife was spending more time than her mother had spent getting the floors and the rugs into shape; where a laundress had been replaced by a washing machine or a deliveryman by the household automobile, a housewife was spending time and energy on chores that, in her mother's day, had been performed by other people. No matter how a household chose to slice the cake of available resources in the interwar years, every decision to "do it myself" was a decision to increase the time that the housewife would spend at her work. In households that were prosperous, the labor saved by labor-saving devices was that not of the housewife but of her helpers. This is the most salient reason that every time-study of affluent housewives during these years (and many such studies were done, as these were the years in which home economists, like so many other Americans, were fascinated by "efficiency studies") revealed that no matter how many appliances they owned, or how many conveniences were at their command, they were still spending roughly the same number of hours per week at housework as their mothers had. The most comprehensive of those studies, covering fifteen hundred urban and rural households, in the years 1924–25 and 1930–31, found a range of hours spent in housework from a high of sixty-one (for rural farm homemakers) to a low of forty-eight (for college-educated urban women living in large cities) — figures that were not markedly different from those reported by Leeds and Woodbury twenty years earlier.

This second-generation prosperous housewife had also expanded certain aspects of her job description, which could not be mediated by technology at all — namely, those aspects having to do with the care of her children. Infant care was much more complex than it once had been, because in an effort to combat infant mortality (which had been scandalously high in the United States in the pre-war period)* — mothers were watching scrupulously over their children's diets, weighing them several

*The infant mortality rate was 100 per 1,000 live births in 1915 (one of the highest in the Western world), 71.7 in 1925, and 55.7 in 1935. By comparison, in 1978 it was 13.8.

times a day, and repeatedly carrying them to physicians' offices for check-ups. Child care no longer consisted of teaching young children to read, write, and add and in seeing to it that children were adequately clothed and regularly fed; it now also involved attending child-study meetings, becoming involved in the local schools, reading books and magazines about children, supervising them in playgrounds, and transporting them to lessons and social events.

> I accommodate my entire life to my little girl. She takes three music lessons a week and I practice with her forty minutes a day. I help her with her school work and go to dancing school with her.

> My mother never stepped inside the school building as far as I can remember, but now there are never ten days that go by without my either visiting the children's school or getting in touch with their teacher. I have given up church work and club work since the children came. I always like to be here when they get home from school so that I can keep in touch with their games and their friends. Any extra time goes into reading books on nutrition and character building.

> I put on roller skates with the boys and pass a football with them. In the evenings we play cards and on Sundays we go to ball games. My mother back East thinks it's scandalous.

Experts repeatedly suggested that a mother was the single most important person in a child's life, and that the child raised by nursemaids was a child to be pitied. The young boy raised by servants would never learn the upright, go-getting resourcefulness of the truly American child, would never become a useful member of the egalitarian republic, and would probably fail in the business world; his sister, deprived of the example of her mother, would not know how to manage the myriad appliances of the modern kitchen, would never learn how to decorate a pineapple salad or wash silk underwear in an electric machine, and might thus never be able to capture a husband. Even more worrisome was the thought that children raised by nursemaids might never reach adulthood because they would be tended by persons who were unfamiliar with the latest medical and nutritional information. Mothers were being asked to take more of a hand in the rearing of their children, and many mothers were responding to the challenge.

Thus, the comfortably situated housewife of the interwar years expended most of her time and energy, just as her mother had, in the interests of her family. Even during the worst years of the Depression, she continued to run her household "decently"; her husband was still employed, the family was not on relief; they still owned their own home, and they still kept it up; the interior was orderly, the meals arrived regularly, the children stayed in school, the family went to church, their health — whatever strain they were under — remained reasonably stable.

But something subtle had changed. Emily Post summed it up better than anyone else when she added a new chapter to the fifth edition (1937) of the famous etiquette book that had first appeared in 1915. This chapter dealt with the problems faced by "Mrs. Three-in-One" — the woman who had to be guest, waitress, and cook at her own dinner parties. Like her mother she understood the rituals of gracious entertaining, knew how to make guests comfortable in her home, knew precisely which foods should be served on which occasions, knew how to reflect the status of her household in her own behavior. But unlike her mother, either because of inclination or circumstance, she was also a manual laborer: she had to chop the onions, roll the pastries, manipulate the cooking times, arrange the platters, carry them to the table, carve the roast, remove the dirty plates, pour the coffee — all the while appearing as if she were not doing any of these tasks. As part of the process of reallocating the time she spent in household work, she had ceased managing the labor of others and had substituted her own. This transformation, which might properly be called the "proletarianization" of the work of economically comfortable housewives, did not occur overnight. Its fullest effects would not be felt until the next generation had reached maturity, but the handwriting was on the wall. In an effort to sustain the standard of living to which an earlier generation had been accustomed, the prosperous housewife of this generation started down the path of "doing it herself," the implications of which would not become entirely clear until her daughter had completed the journey.

Material Conditions for Those Who Were Still Struggling to Make Ends Meet

Meanwhile, during these decades, many Americans — in fact, still the majority of Americans — were struggling, as their parents had, to maintain their families at something over the level of mere subsistence. The fabled "prosperity" of the 1920s was more apparent than real, more intermittent than continuous, for the families of industrial workers, small farmers, day laborers, and skilled craftsmen. Industrial productivity — particularly of consumer goods — multiplied during the 1920s and then multiplied again. Automobiles were appearing in ever more front yards, radios proliferated, the number of pages devoted to advertisements in newspapers and magazines trebled and then quadrupled. In communities across the land, however, more than half of the households were still living below — and, in some cases, far below — what was then defined as the minimum standard of "health and decency". Helen and Robert Lynd calculated, for example, that in Muncie in 1924, $1,920.87 was required to achieve this standard for a family of five (the estimate included the cost of rent, food, fuel, clothing, insurance, union dues, and other such items as well, significantly enough, as one full day per week of paid household help), and that somewhere between 70 percent and 88 percent of all the households in town, in that year did not attain it. Similarly, in 1926, in Zanesville, Ohio, 70 percent of all families had incomes below $2,000. Wages for skilled and unskilled workers and prices for agricultural goods were indeed better in the 1920s than they had been in any previous decade; but the problem, for the families of men so employed, was that good wages and prices could not be depended upon to be continuous: factory workers were likely to be laid off at a day's notice when business was slow; farmers had good seasons but also bad ones; day laborers were paid only during certain seasons of the year; illness and accident could strike at any moment and, in the absence of guaranteed sick leaves and adequate workmen's compensation, could cripple a family for substantial periods. A nationwide study conducted by economists at the Brookings Institution in 1929 — when the boom had presumably been booming for close to a decade — revealed that 59 percent of the nation's families appeared to be living below a minimally decent standard; needless to say, that figure went up, rather than down, during the next decade.

There were, to put it simply, still more "uncomfortable" people than "comfortable" ones during the supposedly gay 1920s, and there were considerably more during the depressing 1930s. During the 1920s, sheer subsistence may not have been as much of a problem as it had been for an earlier generation; but families still found that, periodically, they needed two incomes in order to get by. Fifty-five out of 124 "working class" wives studied by the Lynds in Muncie had worked for wages between 1920 and 1924: "the mister was sick and I had to"; "it takes the work of two to keep a family nowadays"; "we are always needing extra money."

Admittedly, some of that extra money was being spent on goods and services that would have been totally out of reach twenty years earlier. The hard-pressed housewife of the 1920s was not investing in luxuries (although some contemporary critics accused her of doing so); but when times were good, she and her husband were trying to create for themselves the standard of living to which more prosperous families had become accustomed before the First World War. With the help of building-and-loan associations, these families were buying their own houses; in Zanesville, for example, where 70 percent of the households earned less than two thousand dollars, 79.9 percent of them were owners rather than renters of their dwellings. The houses in which the second generation of hard-pressed housewives lived were neither spacious nor elegant (a typical one would have been a four-room, one-story bungalow), but they were likely to be wired for electricity (73.7 percent of the houses in Zanesville), outfitted with running water (90 percent), perhaps a bathroom with in-door toilet and a tub (60 percent), piped gas (96 percent), a gas range (89.6 percent), and a telephone (69 percent); and if things had gone par-ticularly well for the family, or if there was more than one continuous breadwinner, there might even be a car (48 percent of the families in Zanesville had one at a time when only 30 percent of the families were living above the poverty level). Those social critics who disparaged these expenditures (because "money was being wasted on luxuries," or because "the pressure to conform and to consume is everywhere more intense," or because "people are today so willing to put themselves into debt to satisfy expanded wants") were uniformly members of the more comfortable classes. From the point of view of those who had known the discomforts of poverty in their youth, these amenities were not so much amenities as basic decencies too long withheld. To own one's home meant to be out from under the thumb of a landlord who could evict a family at a mo-ment's notice; to have electric lights meant an end to eyestrain, kerosene explosions, and the need to clean lamps; to have running water, an end to exhausting labor; to have a toilet, an end to the discomfort of a privy on a snowy night and to typhoid fever in the summer; to have a telephone, the possibility of easy communication with members of one's family; to have a gas range, the end to coal dust all over the kitchen; to have an automobile, the possibility of a Sunday in the country (is that luxury?) and also, of finding a job on the other side of town in case the plant close to home shut down (is *that* a luxury?).

In the period after the First World War, the diffusion of these ameni-ties, combined with public health measures that were becoming more prevalent (purification and inspection of milk, water treatment plants, sewers for poor neighborhoods, diphtheria inoculations, regular refuse collection, fortification of certain foods with vitamins, certification of meat and poultry supplies) meant that the standard of living for this gen-eration was considerably higher (or rather the standard of death and ill-ness considerably lower) than it had been for their parents. Nationwide, the infant mortality rate continued to fall — in part, at least, because milk and water ceased to be contaminated; and physicians learned how to control diarrhea, tuberculosis, congenital syphilis, and diphtheria (which had all been major killers of infants). Some of the dreadful epidemic dis-eases that had either killed or debilitated adults and older children in an earlier generation (cholera, typhoid fever, smallpox) were virtually eradi-cated by the 1920s; and other diseases (such as tuberculosis, rickets, syph-ilis, and dysentery) were vastly diminished in their destructive power: in Chicago the death rate from typhoid fever had gone as high as 174 per 100,000 per population in the latter years of the nineteenth century, but was down to 2 per 100,000 in the 1920s; tuberculosis, which had been the second most prevalent cause of death in the United States in 1900, had declined to tenth by 1930, and the death rate from tuberculosis dropped by an incredible one third (from 150 to 98) just in the four years between 1918 and 1922; Salversan was being widely used to control syphilis, and cod liver oil (however awful it may have tasted) and fortified flour and margarine (whatever natural food buffs today may think of them) were just as widely used to control rickets. All of this, needless to say, went a long way toward easing a poor housewife's concern about the health of her family and toward relieving her, as her mother could not have been relieved, of the difficult work of caring for those who were ill.

The trouble was that neither the amenities nor the public health measures did much to lighten the burden of her other chores. While the hard-pressed housewife may have entered the twentieth century in terms of electricity, running water, and pasteurized milk, she had not entered it in terms of birth control. In 1924, for example, the Lynds found that in Muncie all of the business-class housewives approved of the use of contraceptives, but that only half of the working-class housewives did. Thus, not surprisingly, only one business-class home among those the Lynds studied had six or more children, but there were seven such working-class homes. In the 1920s, although the birth rate was dropping nationwide, the poor continued to have markedly more children than the "comfortable." In the 1930s, although the birth rate in urban areas dropped off markedly for all classes of the population, that in rural areas — where many such housewives lived — was as high as it had ever been. Nothing is, of course, better calculated to increase the burden of housework than the presence of children, especially small ones. When there are eight or nine mouths to feed (or even five or six), cooking is a difficult enterprise, even if it can be done at a gas range; and the drudgery of laundry (especially if there are diapers) is not greatly eased by having the hot water come out of a tap instead of a pot. The electric appliances that would have made some aspects of housework markedly easier simply remained too expensive for those who were still struggling to make ends meet. Even when electric service was available, an electric washing machine cost between sixty and two hundred dollars (a month's wage for a workingman), and only the more expensive models would have been truly labor saving, since the less expensive ones had small tubs, which had to be emptied and filled manually, and hand-cranked wringers. Small wonder, then, that in 1926 only 28 percent of the homes in Zanesville had electric washers, and that the vast majority of them were in affluent homes. What was true for the washer was true also for the vacuum cleaner (only 52.6 percent of homes, of whom slightly more than half were affluent homes) and mechanical refrigeration (.4 percent).

In any event, in both the 1920s and the 1930s, a substantial number of poor housewives were either rural or black or both and thus lacked access to amenities, public health measures, and appliances. Among the tenant farmers that Martha Hagood studied in 1934 in Tennessee, only eight out of two hundred households could afford electric service (although the area in which they lived was considered progressive in rural electrification), and not a single one had running water — at a time when 83 percent of all urban and rural non-farm residences were electrified. In "Plainville," a rural town studied by James West in 1940, only three homes had bathrooms, and they belonged, respectively, to the funeral director, the veterinarian, and the mayor. The Farm Housing Survey, undertaken by the United States Department of Agriculture in 1934, revealed that, for example, only 20 percent of the farmhouses in Missouri had a kitchen sink with a drain, that only 7 percent of those in Kentucky had a bathroom, that only 25 percent of those in the state of Washington (which was considered a particularly prosperous agricultural state) had flush toilets, and that only 17 percent of those in Ohio (which was also fairly prosperous) had electricity. On farms across the land, the birthrate was still high, the average length of life still low, the "old-fashioned" diseases still appallingly prevalent, and various discomforts, both of body and of mind, were part and parcel of daily experience.

Even the hard-pressed housewife who had access to amenities, and had invested in appliances, could not be certain that they would be there when most needed. The washing machine, the car, and the living-room furniture were all likely to have been bought on installment plans, the house carried a mortgage, and the utility companies presented their bills monthly. Thus, in bad times, when her husband was out of work or disabled, and she was forced into the labor market — precisely the time when she dearly needed her washing machine to do the laundry or her car to reduce her trips to market — the family was more than likely to have fallen behind in its payments; and, as a result, the electricity might be turned off or the car repossessed. The Lynds described the technological condition of working-class homes, under the best of conditions, as a "crazy quilt":

> A single home may be operated in the twentieth century when it comes to ownership of an automobile and vacuum cleaner, while its lack of a bathtub may throw it back into another era and its lack of sewer connection and custom of pumping drinking water from a well in the same backyard with the family "privy" put it on par with life in the Middle Ages.

• • •

To make matters even worse, the hard-pressed housewife of this generation had begun to read — as her mother probably had not — many of the magazines that were addressed to her more affluent contemporaries; and the daughters of both classes were taking the same home economics courses in school. Through these various sources of information, such a housewife learned about ways to feed her family, furnish her home, do her laundry, and otherwise conduct her daily life — ways that were approved of by "experts," and that would have been totally foreign to her mother: nutritionally balanced meals, carefully structured family budgets, four-hour intervals between infant feedings, cabinets and extensive work surfaces in kitchens, completely tiled bathrooms, percale sheets, and many, many more. Unfortunately many of these products were very expensive; and if the price was not beyond the hard-pressed housewife's means at a particular moment, it may well have been beyond her ability to plan for. How do you make out a budget when you cannot predict what your income will be next month? How do you feed an infant on a four-hour schedule when you have a toddler who eats all the time, a husband who gets his breakfast at six in the morning and returns home hungry at seven at night, and a school child who eats at seven, at noon, and at five o'clock?

If inability to rearrange her life in the "recommended" fashion were not enough to make the struggling housewife feel inferior, the women's magazines were delivering yet another message deliberately calculated to make her feel even worse: to wit, that if her family were not socially accepted, if her children and her husband were not healthy, if her home were a breeding ground for germs, if she herself looked old and tired before her time, or if her babies failed to gain weight — or, worse yet, if they died — she was entirely to blame, since remedies for those conditions were easily at hand and easy to apply. If such a notion had ever crossed her mother's mind, it was at least not confirmed, over and over again, on almost every printed page. In her mother's day, when copywriters composed advertisements for soap or sheets or sealing wax, they thought in terms of the ingredients in the product, or the cleanliness of the factory where it was made, or the various ways in which a clever housewife could use it. In the years between the wars, they thought about "guilt" and did so intentionally, because psychologists were telling them that "guilt," "embarrassment," and "insecurity" would sell goods faster than any other pitch. Thus, the hard-pressed housewife was being told that if she failed to feed her babies special foods, to scrub behind the sink with special cleaners, to reduce the spread of infection by using paper tissues, to control mouth odor by urging everyone to gargle and body odor by urging everyone to bathe, to improve her children's schoolwork by sending them off with a good breakfast, or her daughter's "social rating" by sending her off to parties with polished white shoes — then any number of woeful events would ensue, and they would all be entirely her fault: not God's will, and certainly not a result of the greed of capitalists or the cupidity of public officials. This message was reiterated so frequently, and the visual material accompanying it was so blatant, that it could not have failed to make an impression on such a housewife and, at the very least, to undermine her self-confidence. Small wonder, then, that some of these housewives went out to work even when their husbands had steady jobs: with the additional cash, these wives could at least purchase the clothing, the cosmetics, the appliances, and the sundries that the magazines were suggesting would so markedly improve a family's way of life and a mother's own peace of mind.* "I began to work during the war," one housewife in Muncie reported,

> when everyone else did; we had to meet payments on our house and everything else was getting so high. The mister objected at first, but now he don't mind. I'd rather keep on working so my boys can play football and basketball and have spending money their father can't give them. I have felt better since I worked than ever before in my life. . . . We have an electric washing machine, electric iron, and vacuum sweeper. I don't even have to ask my husband anymore because I buy these things with my own money.

Older cultural values may have suggested that a working wife was a sign of economic distress and social disorganization in a family (which no doubt is why many "misters" didn't approve of their wives going out to work, and why many wives avoided such work), but newer cultural values suggested that it was the responsibility of both parents to improve the standard of living of their children; and some women no doubt concluded, as had the mother just quoted, that they could achieve this aim faster and more surely with cash in their pockets then with bread dough on their hands.

Thus while the comfortably situated housewives of this generation were slowly marching down the road to proletarianization, their less comfortably situated contemporaries were heading toward greater productivity. Improvements in technological systems were having the same effect on the households of people with small incomes as they have in giant factories and offices: an increase in the goods or services that can be produced for the person-hours that are being expended. Low-income housewives worked very hard in the interwar years. None of the working-class wives of Muncie reported spending less than four hours a day on cooking, cleaning, and laundering (marketing and child care were not even inquired after), and most reported seven or more hours a day, seven days a

---

*Whether women of the lower economic classes worked for "pin money" or out of real economic necessity is a question that has been endlessly debated, one commentator's pin money invariably turning out to be another commentator's "real necessity." The most recent analyses of working women in the interwar years are no exception: Winifred Wandersee sees married women's workforce participation as a result of the "pursuit of luxury"; while Alice Kessler-Harris sees it as an effort to maintain or to improve a family's standard of living. Kessler-Harris seems to me to be right; the "rising expectations" of this period were the expectations of working-class people that they had a right to the same conveniences and amenities that had long been associated with the standards of the more comfortable classes. What Wandersee seems to regard as luxuries were washing machines, automobiles, additional changes of clothing, a four-room apartment, and a chance for children to stay in school longer that their parents had.

week. Yet for some of those housewives, some of that hard work was paying off, some of the time. If a hard-pressed mother of this generation had more cash than her mother had had, then her children ate better than she had as a child; since more fruits and vegetables were available, fresh and cheap, at more seasons of the year, their diet was more varied and more healthful. If she and her husband had managed to buy a house, then it was, like as not, more spacious than the one in which she had been raised, and it was better ventilated, warmer in the winter and cooler in the summer, and more likely to have running water and a toilet. With the running water and a hot-water heater and a sewing machine, she could keep her children cleaner, better dressed, more comfortable, and possibly even healthier than she had been as a child, without spending much more time than her mother had spent in the doing of it. She certainly could not afford to pay the wages of human servants; but when times were good, she was beginning to invest in electrical appliances and she knew that they, too, could increase her productivity: that a washing machine meant the ability to change the sheets every week or underwear every day, and a vacuum cleaner meant that dust could be kept from accumulating in the house.

Conclusion

In the years between the two world wars, there were still many differences between the two great segments of the population — not the least of which was that, for those who were poor, any gain in their standard of living in one year was likely to be lost in the next. In some communities, at some times, the gap between the standard of living of the two classes was as great as it had ever been: the poor still begot many children and took them out of school early, still lived with filth and ate in their kitchens, still suffered ill health, lost their teeth and smelled bad, still handed down their clothes and took their shoes from the ragpile. But in other communities, at other times, the ability to live at a minimum standard of health and decency was no longer the privilege only of those who were affluent. Public health was improving, housing conditions were better than they had been, various amenities and conveniences were becoming more widely diffused; and even those who were poor in relative terms could profit from some of these changes. All of them worked together to make hard-pressed housewives more productive and less uncomfortable than their mothers had been and to make their housework bear fruit in improving the health and the prospects of their families. The gap between those who could afford to live "decently" and those who could not may have been as wide as ever; but in the years between the wars, the average housewife of less than modest means was living, at least some of the time, at a higher standard than her mother had been able to attain.

Looking back, we can readily understand why she, and her daughter in the next generation, believed that gas ranges, pasteurized milk, electricity, washing machines, fortified margarine, and vacuum cleaners had played a significant role in this accomplishment. We can also understand why these women continued to believe not just that their place was in their homes but that the work that they did there had enormous value. Small wonder then that these women, and their descendants, accepted the yoke of women's work in the home and viewed the modern tools with which they did it as liberating, rather than as oppressive, agents.

STUDY GUIDE

1. According to Cowan, what were the main differences between the households of the relatively prosperous and those of the people who were "struggling to make ends meet"?

2. What were the main differences between living conditions in homes in rural America and those in urban America?

3. How did the definition of the housewife's proper role change during this period for both groups Cowan discusses? What factors are responsible for these changes?

4. One of the traditional ideas about the 1920s is that there was a "revolution in manners and morals" during the decade that involved, among other things, changes in women's roles and in notions about what constituted proper feminine behavior. From the evidence in this selection, does it seem to you that such a "revolution" occurred? Why or why not?

5. What major changes in the lives of Americans were brought about by the growth of a mass-consumption society in the 1920s?

6. Cowan points out that even when they had jobs outside the home, women remained primarily responsible for doing the housework. How do you explain this? Today, with a much larger percentage of women holding jobs outside the home, they are still primarily responsible for it. How do you explain that?

BIBLIOGRAPHY

Frederick Lewis Allen's nearly contemporary account of the 1920s, *Only Yesterday* (1931), remains lively and informative more than fifty years after its publication. William E. Leuchtenberg's *The Perils of Prosperity, 1914–1931* (1958) and Ellis W. Hawley's *The Great War and the Search for a Modern Order, A History of the American People and Their Institutions, 1917–1933* (1979) are more scholarly. George Soule's *Prosperity Decade: From War to Depression,*

1917–1929 (1947) is the standard economic history of the decade. For how ordinary Americans were living, see two books by Robert S. Lynd and Helen Merrill Lynd, *Middletown* (1929) and *Middletown in Transition* (1937), detailed studies of life in Muncie, Indiana. The lives of women in the 1920s are discussed in Dorothy M. Brown, *Setting a Course: American Women in the 1920s* (1987).

V DEPRESSION AND WAR

The prosperity of the 1920s came to an abrupt end in 1929. The causes of the Great Depression that lasted from 1929 to 1941 can be found in the unbalanced economy — both domestic and international — of the twenties: the tendency to use profits for speculation rather than for productivity, an unregulated banking system and unsupervised stock market, a declining income for the farmer, inadequate wages and a reduction in the number of jobs (through automation) for the industrial worker, a lack of balance in international trade patterns, and a political philosophy that limited the role of government in reacting to the economic and social needs of many Americans.

The Depression of the 1930s touched almost every facet of American life. Unemployment was the most serious problem: for almost a decade the number of unemployed Americans ranged from ten to fifteen million. Industrial productivity declined sharply, crop prices tumbled, foreclosures on houses and farms became everyday occurrences, and the entire nation found itself in the grip of an economic paralysis to which no ready solution could be found. The first selection in this section describes the impact of the Great Depression on the lives of ordinary citizens; the second focuses on the various relief programs funded by the New Deal to alleviate the suffering of the unemployed population of the country. Both essays provide us with a perspective on the 1930s: the first gives a description of the socioeconomic impact of the Great Depression and the second details the response of the New Deal to these conditions.

The Depression came to an end when Congress voted huge appropriations for fighting World War II — expenditures that both Congress and the nation had been reluctant to vote for peacetime needs. War brought a swift end to unemployment and to the grim texture of American economic life, and brought both prosperity to the economy and a greater sense of purpose to our national existence. Some of the social consequences of World War II for the nation as a whole are described in the last selection, taken from *Don't You Know There's a War On?* Together these three selections survey the many moods of a nation making its way — within a decade and a half — from the depths of the Great Depression to participation in a global war and a prosperous economy.

Carrying a sandwich sign in the hope of putting food on the family table, 1934.

14

CAROLINE BIRD

The Nation Confronts the Great Depression

Karl Mannheim, one of Europe's greatest sociologists, has stressed the importance of trying to understand human behavior as a response to an experience shared by members of a particular generation. Several historical examples of an experience that served to influence the outlook of an entire generation can be cited: the bitterness and anger experienced by southern whites as a consequence of their defeat at the hands of the North in the Civil War and the humiliation of the Radical Reconstruction that followed; the disillusionment of the generation that went to war in Europe trying to fulfill Woodrow Wilson's promise to "make the world safe for democracy"; and the susceptibility of the German people to the glorious future offered them by Adolf Hitler and his Nazi regime after their defeat in World War I and their postwar social and economic agonies. The Great Depression of the 1930s was a similarly traumatic experience for millions of Americans left without jobs and, in some instances, without food or shelter. These Americans shared a common generational experience: hunger and want, an unemployed father, no money for recreation or schooling and a constant fear of what their economic future might be.

The pervasiveness and the duration of the Great Depression are unparalleled in the history of the American people. The stock market crash of 1929 — which wiped out the hopes and the savings of all but a few — only served as the first act of a drama that was to last for more than a decade. By the early thirties, hundreds of banks were failing, tens of thousands of businesses were going bankrupt, and millions of Americans were being added to the unemployment rolls each month. Industrial production by 1933 fell to pre–World War I levels, farm prices plummeted to unprecedented lows, and foreclosures were common as the farmer lost his land and the city dweller his home.

While the pursuit of material wealth has always been central to the American ethos, one may find a causal relationship between the deprivations suffered by the generation of Americans who grew up in the 1930s and their frenzied postwar pursuit of material comforts — new suburban homes, annual editions of chrome-decorated automobiles, and credit cards for every occasion. The Great Depression, as this selection by Caroline Bird makes amply clear, created an "invisible scar" — and a lasting one.

You could feel the Depression deepen, but you could not look out of the window and see it. Men who lost their jobs dropped out of sight. They were quiet, and you had to know just when and where to find them: at night, for instance, on the edge of town huddling for warmth around a bonfire, or even the municipal incinerator; at dawn, picking over the garbage dump for scraps of food or salvageable clothing.

In Oakland, California, they lived in sewer pipes the manufacturer could not sell. In Connellsville, Pennsylvania, unemployed steelworkers kept warm in the big ovens they had formerly coked. Outside Washington, D.C., one Bonus Marcher slept in a barrel filled with grass, another in a piano box, a third in a coffin set on trestles. Every big city had a "Hooverville" camp of dispossessed men living like this.

It took a knowing eye — or the eye of poverty itself — to understand or even to observe some of the action. When oranges fell off a truck, it wasn't always an accident; sometimes they were the truck driver's contribution to slum kids. A woman burning newspapers in a vacant lot might be trying to warm a baby's bottle. The ragged men standing silent as cattle, in a flatrack truck parked on a lonely public road, might be getting the bum's rush out of town. In the Southwest, freight trains were black with human bodies headed for warm weather. Railroad dicks shooed them off at stations. Deming, New Mexico, hired a special constable to keep them out of town. When the Southern Pacific police ordered the men off the train, the special constable ordered them back on again.

From *The Invisible Scar* by Caroline Bird. Copyright © 1966 by Caroline Bird. Reprinted with permission of Longman, Inc., White Plains, New York.

Everyone knew of someone engaged in a desperate struggle, although most of the agony went on behind closed doors. The stories were whispered. There was something indecent about them. A well-to-do man living on the income from rental property could not collect his rents. His mortgages were foreclosed, and his houses sold for less than the debt. To make up the difference, he sold his own home. He moved himself and his wife into a nearby basement and did odd jobs for the people upstairs in exchange for a room for some of his six children. He mowed lawns, graded yards, and did whatever common labor he could find in order to pay for groceries, until his health broke down under the unaccustomed work. The doctor told him that he needed an operation and would have to rest for a year afterward.

A 72-year-old factory worker was told that he could no longer be employed because he was too old. He went home and turned on the gas. His 56-year-old widow, who had worked as a proofreader before developing heart trouble, sat alone staring at their few sticks of furniture for three days after her husband's death. Then she too turned on the gas. The neighbors smelled it in time and saved her life.

Neither the property owner nor the widow was an uncommon case. They merely were lucky enough to be among the Hundred Neediest Cases chosen by *The New York Times* for 1932. Unlike the hardship cases of the 1960s, who are often urgently in need of psychiatric help, these people were in trouble only because they were physically sick and had no money. By the charitable standards of the rich at that time, they were regarded as the "deserving poor," as distinguished from the undeserving poor, who were thought to be unwilling to work or to save.

If the "deserving poor" had been few, charitable help might have sufficed. But there were too many, and more all the time. In December 1929, three million people were out of work. The next winter, four to five million. The winter of 1931–1932, eight million. The following year, no one knew exactly how many, but all authorities agreed that additional millions were unemployed. In 1965, unemployment is a "problem" when one in twenty is idle. In the fall of 1932, *Fortune* thought that 34 million men, women, and children — better than a fourth of the nation — were members of families that had no regular full-time breadwinner. Estimates differed, but none included farmers unable to make both ends meet, in spite of the blessing of seven-day, sunup-to-sundown employment, or factory hands who were making out on two or three days' work a week.

There were too many in want to hide. There were too many in want to blame. And even if the poor were shiftless, a Christian country would not let them starve. "Everyone is getting along somehow," people said to each other. "After all, no one has starved." But they worried even as they spoke.

A few were ashamed to eat. The Elks in Mt. Kisco, New York, and Princeton University eating clubs were among the organizations that sent leftovers from their tables to the unemployed. A reporter on *The Brooklyn Eagle* suggested a central warehouse where families could send their left-overs for distribution to the needy. John B. Nichlos, of the Oklahoma Gas Utilities Company, worked out a leftover system in detail and urged it on Hoover's Cabinet. It provided:

> Sanitary containers of five (5) gallons each should be secured in a large number so that four (4) will always be left in large kitchens where the res-taurants are serving a volume business. The containers should be labeled "MEAT, BEANS, POTATOES, BREAD, AND OTHER ITEMS." Someone from the Salvation Army with a truck should pick up the loaded containers every morning and leave empty ones. The civic clubs, restaurants, the pro-prietors and the workers should be asked to cooperate in order to take care of all surplus food in as sanitary a way as possible. In other words, when a man finishes his meal he should not (after lighting his cigarette or cigar) leave the ashes on the food which he was unable to consume.

Many more fortunate people turned away from the unemployed, but some tried to help in the traditional neighborly way. A Brooklyn convent put sandwiches outside its door where the needy could get them without knocking. St. Louis society women distributed unsold food from restau-rants. Someone put baskets in New York City railroad stations so that commuters could donate vegetables from their gardens. In New York, Bernarr Macfadden served six-cent lunches to the unemployed and claimed he was making money. In San Francisco, the hotel and restaurant workers' union arranged for unemployed chefs and waiters to serve ele-gant if simple meals to the unemployed.

But there was more talk than help. A great many people spent a great deal of energy urging each other to give, to share, to hire. President Hoover led a national publicity campaign to urge people to give locally and to make jobs. At the suggestion of public-relations counsel Edward L. Bernays, the first President's Emergency Committee was named "for Employment" (PECE) to accentuate the positive. In 1931 it was reorga-nized more realistically as the President's Organization for Unemploy-ment Relief (POUR). Both undertook to inspire confidence by the issuing of optimistic statements; POUR chairman Walter Gifford told a Senate committee offhandedly that he did not know how many were unem-ployed and did not think it was the committee's job to find out.

Local groups responded by pressing campaigns of their own to "Give-A-Job" or "Share-A-Meal" until people grew deaf to them. Carl Byoir, founder of one of the country's biggest public-relations firms, declared a "War against Depression" that proposed to wipe it out in six months by getting one million employers to make one new job each.

Results of such appeals were disappointing. Corporation executives answered the pleas of PECE and POUR by saying they had no right to spend stockholders' money hiring men they did not need. Even in New York City, where the able and well-supported Community Service Society pioneered work relief, there were enough hungry men without money to keep 82 badly managed breadlines going, and men were selling apples on every street corner. Newspapers discovered and photographed an apple seller who was formerly a near-millionaire.

The well of private charity ran dry. A Westchester woman is said to have fired all her servants in order to have money to contribute to the unemployed. "Voluntary conscription" of wages helped steelworkers weather the first round of layoffs in little Conshohocken, Pennsylvania, but the plan broke down as there were more mouths to feed and fewer pay envelopes to conscript. Local charities everywhere were overwhelmed by 1931, and the worst was yet to come.

Kentucky coal miners suffered perhaps the most. In Harlan County there were whole towns whose people had not a cent of income. They lived on dandelions and blackberries. The women washed clothes in soapweed suds. Dysentery bloated the stomachs of starving babies. Children were reported so famished they were chewing up their own hands. Miners tried to plant vegetables, but they were often so hungry that they ate them before they were ripe. On her first trip to the mountains, Eleanor Roosevelt saw a little boy trying to hide his pet rabbit. "He thinks we are not going to eat it," his sister told her, "but we are." In West Virginia, miners mobbed company stores demanding food. Mountain people, with no means to leave their homes, sometimes had to burn their last chairs and tables to keep warm. Local charity could not help in a place where everyone was destitute. . . .

A Quaker himself, Hoover went to the American Friends Service Committee. The Philadelphia Meeting developed a "concern" for the miners. Swarthmore and Haverford students ventured into the hollows, winning the confidence of suspicious miners. They systematically weighed the children, so they could feed those in greatest need first. Hoover gave them $2,500 out of his own pocket, but most of the contributions seem to have come from the Rockefellers.

"No one has starved," Hoover boasted. To prove it, he announced a decline in the death rate. It was heartening, but puzzling, too. Even the social workers could not see how the unemployed kept body and soul together, and the more they studied, the more the wonder grew. Savings, if any, went first. Then insurance was cashed. Then people borrowed from family and friends. They stopped paying rent. When evicted, they moved in with relatives. They ran up bills. It was surprising how much credit could be wangled. In 1932, about 400 families on relief in Philadelphia had managed to contract an average debt of $160, a tribute to the hearts if not the business heads of landlords and merchants. But in the end they had to eat "tight."

Every serious dieter knows how little food it takes to keep alive. One woman borrowed 50¢, bought stale bread at 3½¢ a loaf, and kept her family alive on it for 11 days. Every serious dieter knows how hunger induces total concentration on food. When eating tight, the poor thought of nothing but food, just food. They hunted food like alley cats, and in some of the same places. They haunted docks where spoiled vegetables might be thrown out and brought them home to cook up in a stew from which every member of the family would eat as little as possible, and only when very hungry. Neighbors would ask a child in for a meal or give him scraps — stale bread, bones with a bit of good meat still on them, raw potato peelings. Children would hang around grocery stores, begging a little food, running errands, or watching carts in exchange for a piece of fruit. Sometimes a member of the family would go to another part of town and beg. Anyone on the block who got hold of something big might call the neighbors in to share it. Then everyone would gorge like savages at a killing, to make up for the lean days. Enough people discovered that a five-cent candy bar can make a lunch to boom sales during the generally slow year of 1931. You get used to hunger. After the first few days it doesn't even hurt; you just get weak. When work opened up, at one point, in the Pittsburgh steel mills, men who were called back were not strong enough to do it.

Those who were still prosperous hated to think of such things and frequently succeeded in avoiding them. But professional people could not always escape. A doctor would order medicine for a charity case and then realize there was no money to pay for it. A school doctor in Philadelphia gave a listless child a tonic to stimulate her appetite and later found that her family did not have enough to eat at home.

A reporter on *The Detroit Free Press* helped the police bring a missing boy back to a bare home on Christmas Day, 1934. He and his friends on the paper got a drugstore to open up so they could bring the boy some toys. *The Detroit Free Press* has supplied Christmas gifts for needy children every year since.

A teacher in a mountain school told a little girl who looked sick but said she was hungry to go home and eat something. "I can't," the youngster said. "It's my sister's turn to eat." In Chicago, teachers were ordered to ask what a child had had to eat before punishing him. Many of them were getting nothing but potatoes, a diet that kept their weight up, but left them listless, crotchety, and sleepy.

The police saw more than anyone else. They had to cope with the homeless men sleeping in doorways or breaking into empty buildings. They had to find help for people who fell sick in the streets or tried to commit suicide. And it was to a cop that city people went when they were at the end of their rope and did not know what else to do. In New York City, the police kept a list of the charities to which they could direct the helpless. In 1930 they took a census of needy families, and city employees started contributing one percent of their salaries to a fund for the police to use to buy food for people they found actually starving. It was the first public confession of official responsibility for plain poverty, and it came not from the top, but from the lowest-paid civil servants, who worked down where the poor people were.

Teachers worried about the children who came to school to get warm. They organized help for youngsters who needed food and clothing before they could learn. Sometimes Boards of Education diverted school funds to feed them. Often the teachers did it on their own. In 1932, New York City schoolteachers contributed $260,000 out of their salaries in one month. Chicago teachers fed 11,000 pupils out of their own pockets in 1931, although they had not themselves been paid for months. "For God's sake, help us feed these children during the summer," Chicago's superintendent of schools begged the governor in June. . . .

Men of old-fashioned principles really believed that the less said about the unemployed, the faster they would get jobs. They really believed that public relief was bad for the poor because it discouraged them from looking for work or from taking it at wages that would tempt business to start up again. According to their theory, permanent mass unemployment was impossible, because there was work at some wage for every able-bodied man, if he would only find and do it. Charity was necessary, of course, for those who were really disabled through no fault of their own, but there could never be very many of these, and they should be screened carefully and given help of a kind and in a way that would keep them from asking for it as long as possible. . . .

The view persists. In 1961, the mayor of Newburgh, New York, cut off relief to make the unemployed find jobs. In 1965, it was thought that raising the minimum wage would hurt the poor by pricing them out of jobs.

Thirty years earlier, respectable folk worried about the idea of public relief, even though accepting the need for it. On opinion polls they agreed with the general proposition that public relief should be temporary, hard to get, and less than the lowest wage offered by any employer. In the North as well as in the South, relief stations were closed at harvesttime to force the unemployed to work at getting in the crops, for whatever wages farmers offered.

It was a scandal when a relief client drove an old jalopy up to the commissary to lug his groceries home. In some places, a client had to surrender his license plates in order to get relief, even if the old car meant a chance to earn small sums to pay for necessities not covered by relief.

Phones went, too, even when they were a relief client's only lifeline to odd jobs. It was considered an outrage if a woman on relief had a smart-looking winter coat, or a ring, or a burial-insurance policy, or a piano. She was made to sell them for groceries before relief would help her. The search for hidden assets was thorough. One thrifty family in New York was denied relief "because it does not seem possible for this family to have managed without some other kind of assistance."

When a woman on relief had triplets, newspapers pointed out that for every 100 children born to self-supporting parents, relief parents produced 160. It was hard even for the social workers to see that big families were more apt to need relief. Almost everybody thought relief caused the poor to become irresponsible and to have children they could not support — if, in fact, they did not have babies deliberately in order to qualify. . . . During the Depression, if some way could have been found to prevent married couples on relief from indulging in sexual intercourse, there would have been those who would have demanded it.

People who took public relief were denied civil rights. Some state constitutions disqualified relief clients from voting, and as late as 1938 an opinion poll showed that one out of every three Republicans thought this was right. In some places, village taxpayers' organizations tried to keep the children of tax delinquents out of the local schools. People suspected of taking public relief were even turned away from churches.

During the first and worst years of the Depression, the only public relief was improvised by cities. Appropriations were deliberately low. If funds ran out every few months, so much the better. The poor would have to make another effort to find work. Every program was "temporary." In most cases, this was sheer necessity. Cities could not afford otherwise. Their tax bases were too narrow. Some of them had lost tax money when banks folded. Detroit could not collect property taxes because landlords could not collect the rent from their unemployed tenants. Bankrupt Chicago was living on tax anticipation warrants doled out by bankers. Some well-heeled citizens refused to pay their taxes at all. Cities cut their own employees, stopped buying library books, and shot zoo animals to divert money to relief. . . .

Cities had to ration relief. In 1932, family allowances in New York City fell to $2.39 a week, and only half of the families who could qualify were getting it. Things were worse elsewhere. In little Hamtramck, Michigan, welfare officials had to cut off all families with fewer than three children. In Detroit, allowances fell to 15¢ a day per person before running out entirely. Across the country, only about one fourth of the unemployed were able to get help, and fewer than that in many cities. Almost everywhere, aid was confined to food and fuel. Relief workers connived with clients to put off landlords. Medical care, clothing, shoes, chairs, beds, safety pins — everything else had to be scrounged or bought by doing without food. Those on relief were little better off than those who couldn't get it. Private help dwindled to six percent of the money spent on the unemployed.

Still, Hoover kept insisting, no one starved. In May 1932, Hoover's Secretary of the Interior, Dr. Ray Lyman Wilbur, reassured the National Conference of Social Workers meeting in Philadelphia. "We must set up the neglect of prosperity against the care of adversity," he philosophized. "With prosperity many parents unload the responsibilities for their children onto others. With adversity the home takes its normal place. The interest of thousands of keen and well-trained people throughout the whole country in seeing that our children are properly fed and cared for has given many of them better and more suitable food than in past good times."

Social workers were indignant. "Have you ever seen the uncontrolled trembling of parents who have starved themselves for weeks so that their children might not go hungry?" social worker Lillian Wald demanded. Others told how fathers and even older brothers and sisters hung around the street corners while the younger children were being fed, for fear they would be tempted to eat more than their share. The social workers knew the facts. They also knew the newspaper reporters. In 1932, the public began to listen.

"Mrs. Green left her five small children alone one morning while she went to have her grocery order filled," one social worker reported. "While she was away the constable arrived and padlocked her house with the children inside. When she came back she heard the six-weeks-old baby crying. She did not dare touch the padlock for fear of being arrested, but she found a window open and climbed in and nursed the baby and then climbed out and appealed to the police to let her children out."

Eviction was so common that children in a Philadelphia day-care center made a game of it. They would pile all the doll furniture up first in one corner and then in another. "We ain't got no money for the rent, so we's moved into a new house," a tot explained to the teacher. "Then we got the constable on us, so we's movin' again." Philadelphia relief paid an evicted family's rent for one month in the new house. Then they were on their own. Public opinion favored the tenant. An eviction could bring on a neighborhood riot.

Landlords often let the rent go. Some of them needed relief as much as their tenants, and had a harder time qualifying for it. In Philadelphia a little girl whose father was on relief could not get milk at school, under a program for needy children, because her father "owned property." Investigators found some unemployed tenants sharing food orders with their landlords. In the country, where poor farmers had been accustomed to paying their taxes in work on the roads, tenants who could not pay their rent sometimes did the landlord's road work for him.

It was not true that "no one starved." People starved to death, and not only in Harlan County, Kentucky. The New York City Welfare Council counted 29 deaths from starvation in 1933. More than fifty other people were treated for starvation in hospitals. An additional 110, most of them children, died of malnutrition.

A father who had been turned away by a New York City welfare agency was afraid to apply for help after public relief had been set up. Social workers found one of his children dead; another, too weak to move, lay in bed with the mother; the rest huddled, shivering and hungry, around the desperate father.

A New York dentist and his wife died rather than accept charity. They left a note, and then took gas together. "The entire blame for this tragedy rests with the City of New York or whoever it is that allows free dental work in the hospital," the note read. "We want to get out of the way before we are forced to accept relief money. The City of New York is not to touch our bodies. We have a horror of charity burial. We have put the last of our money in the hands of a friend who will turn it over to my brother."

Health surveys were made to pound home the fact that poor people are sicker than the well-to-do. Doctors, nurses, teachers, and social workers warned that privation was ruining the nation's health. In 1933, the Children's Bureau reported that one in five American children was not getting enough of the right things to eat. Lower vitality, greater susceptibility to infections, slower recovery, stunting, more organic disease, a reversal of gains against tuberculosis — all were freely predicted. Medical care for the poor was sketchy. Doctors were hard hit financially, and they did not always live up to the Oath of Hippocrates. Frequently, the poor were afraid to call a doctor because they did not have the money. New York City surgeons sometimes demanded cash in advance or delayed operations until the family could get money together.

Middle-class people put off the doctor and the dentist. "Illness frightens us," John Dos Passos writes of his Depression days at Pacific Grove, California. "You have to have money to be sick — or did then. Any dentistry also was out of the question, with the result that my teeth went badly to pieces. Without dough you couldn't have a tooth filled." Hospitals could never fill the private rooms that helped to pay for their charity cases, with the result that they had fewer patients than they do now, but sicker ones. They learned to be tough in admitting people who could not pay.

The harder the middle class looked, the more critical poverty seemed. It did not seem possible that people could stand lack of regular food, unstable homes, medical neglect. The Depression would leave its mark in the future. "If we put the children in these families under a period of malnutrition such as they are going through today, what sort of people are we going to have twenty years from now?" Karl de Schweinitz of the Philadelphia Community Council asked a Senate committee in 1932. "What will we say at that time about them?". . .

. . . The Depression did not depress the conditions of the poor. It merely publicized them. The poor had been poor all along. It was just that nobody had looked at them. The children of Depression grew up to be bigger and healthier than their parents, who had enjoyed the advantages of a prosperous childhood. World War II recruits were more fit in every way than doughboys drafted in World War I. The death rate did not rise in the Depression. It kept going down. The health record of the Depression parallels that of rapidly industrializing societies everywhere: infectious diseases dropped, but mental illness, suicide, and the degenerative diseases of an aging population rose. . . .

. . . The poor survived because they knew how to be poor. The Milbank Foundation found more sickness among the poor than among the well off, but they also found that the newly poor were sicker more often than those who had always been poor. In the 1960s, social work provided steady jobs for people who often were close to poverty themselves. In the 1930s, charity was work for middle- and upper-class volunteers, who were charmed and awed by the techniques for survival that they discovered.

A family eating tight would stay in bed a lot. That way they would save fuel, as well as the extra food calories needed in cold weather. The experienced poor, particularly the Negroes, knew about eating the parts of the animal normally rejected. And the poor generally did not spend as much money on food as their middle-class advisers thought they should be spending.

The poor worked at keeping warm. A family with no money for the gas company would economize by cooking once a week. When it was cut off, they would cook in the furnace. They gathered scrap wood to keep the furnace going. They saved by heating only the kitchen. When fuel was low, the experienced poor would sneak into a movie house. Even if they had to spend ten cents to get in, they could sometimes keep out of the cold for two double features. When the electricity was turned off, some men found ways to steal current by tapping a neighbor's wire.

Shoes were a problem. The poor took them off when they got home, to save them. Do-it-yourself shoe-repair kits were popular with the middle class, but if you could not afford the dimestore item you could resole a pair of shoes with rubber cut from an old tire, or wear rubbers over a wornout sole. Clothes were swapped among the family. One mother and daughter managed to get together an outfit both could wear. They took turns going to church.

The poor whose lives were laid bare by the Depression lived in the same world of poverty that Michael Harrington has recently described in *The Other America,* and Oscar Lewis in his studies of the working classes in

Mexico. They lived for the present without much thought for their own past or future. They ate literally from hand to mouth. Even when they had a little money, they did not lay in stocks of food. They paid high interest rates on what they bought or borrowed, and seldom got their money's worth. Their world was small, limited to the people they saw every day, and they did not venture out of it. A trip to the relief office was a daring undertaking. They had few friends. They did not read. Without outside contacts, they could not organize or revolt or escape.

A year after his defeat by Roosevelt, Hoover — who had repeated so many times that no one was starving — went on a fishing trip with cartoonist "Ding" Darling in the Rocky Mountains. One morning a local man came into their camp, found Hoover awake, and led him to a shack where one child lay dead and seven others were in the last stages of starvation. Hoover took the children to a hospital, made a few phone calls, and raised a fund of $3,030 for them. . . .

The Depression gave the middle classes a double vision of the poor. They did not give up the notions that the poor should have saved or that they did not want to work, or that their poverty was their own fault. These were concepts hard to change. While firmly holding to these ideas, however, they saw contradictory facts before their eyes. When the Depression forced them to scrutinize the condition of the working people, they could see that wages were too low and employment too intermittent for most wageworkers to save enough money to see them through emergencies, or old age, even if banks had not failed. A favorite cartoon of the times pictured a squirrel asking an old man sitting on a park bench why he had not saved for a rainy day.

"I did," said the old man.

STUDY GUIDE

1. What would you consider the major socioeconomic differences (for example, in employment) between the 1930s as described by Caroline Bird and the 1990s? Are there segments of American society today experiencing the conditions described by Bird? Who? Where?

2. What services, institutions, and agencies has our nation established — during and since the Depression — to prevent the kind of suffering described by the author? Could this nation enter another depression similar to the one of the 1930s? Why or why not?

3. What impression do you get of the frame of mind of the millions of poor and the unemployed? How does the author account for the divergent responses to the Depression by various socioeconomic segments of American society?

4. Explain how each of the following institutions and groups responded to the plight of the American people during the Depression: (a) newspapers; (b) industrialists; (c) social agencies; (d) landlords; and (e) political leaders.

5. Some historians have suggested that many Americans may have accepted the sufferings of the Depression out of a feeling of guilt — an acceptance of the notion that their unemployment and their inability to provide the basic necessities for their family were consequences of their own deficiencies rather than the results of defects in the economic system of the nation. Does this idea — the passivity of the nation in the face of joblessness and hunger — seem to be borne out by this essay? Or do the American people appear to have been hostile or angry or rebellious during the Depression? If so, at whom? If not, why not?

BIBLIOGRAPHY

There is a great deal of historical literature — and journalistic material as well — on the 1930s. No serious student of the decade can afford to overlook the most concise and scholarly introduction to the decade, William E. Leuchtenburg, *Franklin D. Roosevelt and the New Deal* (1963). More discursive is Arthur M. Schlesinger, Jr., *The Age of Roosevelt* (1957, 1959, and 1960). Older, yet valuable, surveys of the social problems of the American people in the 1930s will be found in Dixon Wecter, *The Age of the Great Depression, 1929–1941* (1948) and Frederick Lewis Allen, *Since Yesterday* (1940). The poor farmers and their lot are described in David E. Conrad, *The Forgotten Farmers* (1966); the plight of the worker is definitively treated in Irving Bernstein, *Turbulent Years: A History of the American Worker, 1933–1941* (1970). Also worth reading are Milton Meltzer, *Brother Can You Spare a Dime?* (1969); Charles A. Jellison, *Tomatoes Were Cheaper: Tales from the Thirties* (1977); and those selections dealing with the 1930s in Isabel Leighton's edited volume, *The Aspirin Age: 1919–1941* (1949). And, finally, a short but vivid anthology of recollections of the Depression is Don Conger, ed., *The Thirties: A Time to Remember* (1962).

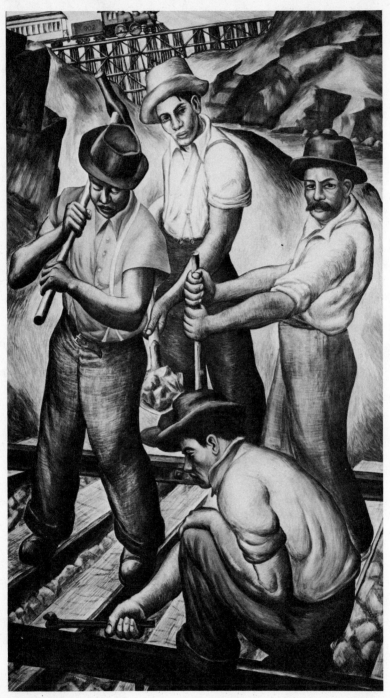

One of hundreds of murals painted by artists working for the WPA. Its focus on how ordinary working people built America is characteristic of American art in the 1930s.

15

EDWARD ROBB ELLIS

Work Relief in the Great Depression

The social and economic crisis that gripped the American nation in 1933, the year Franklin D. Roosevelt came into office, was, in many ways, more serious than any other crisis since 1861, when Abraham Lincoln came into the White House on the eve of the Civil War. By 1933, the stock market crash had turned into a full-fledged depression: World War I veterans marched on Washington and were dispersed by federal troops; one-quarter of the work force was unemployed; farmers were halting foreclosures on their land by threats of armed violence; and in the cities, a rising tide of radical protest appeared to be equally imminent. Only within this context of economic deprivation and social tension can one understand the depth and breadth of the legislation of the New Deal — and the contribution made by that singular figure in the history of the American nation in the twentieth century, Franklin Delano Roosevelt.

The New Deal program of social and economic reform, launched by Roosevelt in 1933, endured until 1939, when World War II broke out in Europe. This program massively reformed our country's institutions and way of life to a far greater degree than had the unrealized reforms demanded by the Greenbackers and Populists in the late nineteenth century or those enacted into law by the Progressives in the early twentieth. In addition to New Deal efforts to promote recovery and reform of the nation's economic institutions, the reformers of the 1930s launched an unprecedented program of relief for the poor and the unemployed. In contrast to the sociopolitical philosophy of Herbert Hoover, whose "rugged individualism" consigned relief programs to private philanthropy, Franklin Roosevelt accepted the notion that ultimately — if all else proved inadequate — clothing, housing, and feeding the nation's poor was the responsibility of the federal government.

The relief programs funded by the federal government can be divided into two basic categories: *direct relief,* funded by the federal government and administered by the states and the cities, and *work relief,* funded by the federal government and administered out of Washington. As the selection by Edward Robb Ellis makes clear, work relief was both a controversial and significant element of the New Deal. By the end of the decade, however, millions of Americans had found succor through one of the relief programs sponsored by the New Deal: the multifaceted Works Progress Administration (WPA), the conservation-oriented Civilian Conservation Corps (CCC), and the National Youth Administration (NYA), a program for high school and college students.

Harry Hopkins loped into the federal security building in Washington, D.C., twisting his scrawny neck from side to side and barking orders at the assistants trying to keep up with him.

The previous day, May 22, 1933, President Roosevelt had named him the administrator of the Federal Emergency Relief Administration. His lips taut, his movements jerky, Hopkins scurried down a hall, saw a desk that had not yet been moved into the room that was to become his office, flopped down into the chair behind it. Oblivious to the confusion swirling about him and raising his voice to be heard over the clatter of heels in the corridor, the former social worker began dictating telegrams to the governors of all forty-eight states. . . .

Harry Lloyd Hopkins was born in Sioux City, Iowa, on August 17, 1890, the fourth of David and Anna Hopkins' five children. His father was a harness maker; his mother taught school. After Harry became the most influential man in the United States government, next to Roosevelt himself, he continued to boast about his humble origins — sometimes to the annoyance of his friends. Frances Perkins thought this a sign of insecurity — that he always felt inferior to others despite what she considered to be his superior mind and character.

Reprinted by permission of the Putnam Publishing Group from *A Nation in Torment* by Edward Robb Ellis. Copyright © 1970 by Edward Robb Ellis.

When Harry was two years old, his family moved to Nebraska. By the time he was eleven the Hopkins had settled in Grinnell, Iowa, a folksy town with a strong Methodist flavor. From his mother, a zealous Methodist, he got his strong sense of righteousness, while from his father he inherited geniality and wit. As a boy Harry scrubbed floors, beat carpets, milked cows and toiled on nearby farms like other underprivileged young people. In 1908 he entered Grinnell College, a small institution with a high reputation for scholarship. He made only average grades, seldom revealing the probing intelligence which later caused Winston Churchill to dub him Lord Root of the Matter. . . .

In 1912, after graduation, he headed for the East Coast. One of his professors, who was connected with a Manhattan settlement house named Christodora House, had won his appointment as head of a summer camp for boys across the Hudson River in New Jersey. When camp was over, he began working in Christodora House itself, located on Manhattan's Lower East Side, and there the naïve youth from the Corn Belt met Jewish boys for the first time in his life. He was amazed to see gangsters stroll into settlement dances and street bullies fighting with broken bottles.

Over the next few years Hopkins developed into a social worker and an executive of social agencies, slaving sixteen hours a day, organizing boys' clubs, plodding up tenement stairs, listening to the laments of the underprivileged, making pioneer surveys of unemployment. Humble and sincere, he was able to get along with all kinds of people. With the stench of the slums constantly in his nostrils, he made a slight turn to the political left and seemingly was registered for a while as a Socialist — a matter of some concern after he entered the federal government. And after his divorce he suffered so much personal strain that he had himself psychoanalyzed. . . .

"Dole" had become an emotionally charged word ever since the advent of the Depression. Throughout the Thirties people criticized the dole or praised the dole, often in a slipshod way since they did not bother to define the term and applied it to a variety of conditions and plans. Their arguments frequently ended in semantics — a debate over the meaning of meaning. . . .

Franklin D. Roosevelt, for his part, tried to balance idealism with practicality. As governor of New York he had said that "to these unfortunate citizens aid must be extended by government, not as a matter of charity, but as a matter of social duty." Nonetheless, while still governor, he had also said: "The dole method of relief for unemployment is not only repugnant to all sound principles of social economics, but is contrary to every principle of American citizenship and of sound government. American labor seeks no charity, but only a chance to work for its living."

Harry Hopkins agreed with Roosevelt. He detested direct relief. Work relief, said Hopkins, "preserves a man's morale. It saves his skill. It gives him a chance to do something socially useful." Both the President and his key relief administrator were keenly aware that the Federal Emergency Relief Administration was a quick thrust at a massive problem calling for greater leverage. On November 27, 1934, Roosevelt wrote to a friend: "What I am seeking is the abolition of relief altogether. I cannot say so out loud yet but I hope to substitute work for relief. . . ."

. . . The heavily Democratic Seventy-fourth Congress opened its first session on January 3, 1935, and one day later the President delivered his annual message. After reporting that more than $2 billion had been spent in direct relief, he went on to say: "The federal government must and shall quit this business of relief. I am not willing that the vitality of our people be further sapped by the giving of cash, of market baskets. . . . "

Roosevelt then announced that he intended to establish a new relief system. . . . This new program, the President added, would be guided by the following principles:

1. All work to be as useful and permanent as possible.

2. Relief wages to be higher than those paid under the FERA and CWA, but not so high as to discourage men from taking jobs in private industry.

3. More money to be spent on wages than on materials. . . .

On April 5, 1935, the Senate and House passed a joint resolution giving the President the relief money he had sought — $4 billion in new funds and $880,000,000 unused from previous appropriations. This $4.8 billion was the largest peacetime appropriation in American history. One day later the bill was signed by the Vice President and the Speaker of the House and put on a plane bound for Jacksonville, Florida. Roosevelt, who had been fishing off the coast, came back to port, boarded a northbound train and on April 8 signed the measure to the contrapuntal clickety clack of train wheels. . . .

On May 6, 1935, the President issued an executive order establishing the Works Progress Administration. As of that date no one could foretell that, with one change of name, it would continue in existence until June 30, 1943 — eight years and two months.

The WPA was designed as the key agency in the government's entire works program, which came to include a total of forty federal agencies. It withdrew the federal government from the field of direct relief, leaving that responsibility to the various states and cities. Roosevelt flatly said that the principal purpose of the WPA was to provide work.

Hopkins began this new job with his usual demonic energy. At one of the first WPA staff meetings he raised the question of whether women should be paid the same wages as men. Everyone said no. Everyone, that is, except Hopkins' assistant administrator, Aubrey Williams, who said he thought women should be paid equal wages with men.

"Oh, you do?" Hopkins barked. "What makes you think you could get away with it?"

Williams said he did not care whether he could get away with it or not.

"Do you know who disagrees with you?" Hopkins persisted. "The secretary of labor — a woman!"

"Pay 'em the same!" Williams said doggedly.

Hopkins, who was testing his assistant, baited him further until Williams became silent and glum.

Then Hopkins ended the session with the words: "Well, fellows, thank you very much. Aubrey's right about this, and that's what we'll do."

As the others walked out, Hopkins turned to Williams, smiled a lopsided smile and asked: "What's wrong with those other fellows?"

The WPA paid wages slightly higher than the grants for direct relief but lower than wages prevailing in private industry. There were exceptions, however, for the WPA refused to lower its rates to meet the substandard ones prevailing in certain districts, notably in the South. For wage-fixing purposes the country was divided into four regions. Monthly rates of pay in each region varied according to the character of the work and to the population. Unskilled work paid as little as $19 a month while professional and technical jobs paid up to $94 a month — and sometimes slightly higher.

The nerve center of the WPA — and thus of the nation's entire works program — was located in the Walker-Johnson Building in Washington at 1734 New York Avenue, NW, a few blocks from the White House. It was a dirty, shabby old place with a blind newsdealer on its front steps. Upon entering it one smelled antiseptic odors and then rode in an elevator so rickety it was frightening. But Hopkins, who detested elegance, felt this was what a relief office should be like. . . .

In the aggregate the WPA did spend a great deal of money, but, as has been indicated, individual wages were hardly lavish. In December, 1935, WPA workers averaged $41.57 a month. Between 60 and 70 percent of those on the rolls were unskilled workers.

But among the skilled workers were accountants, architects, bricklayers, biologists, carpenters, chemists, dentists, draftsmen, dieticians, electricians, engravers, foresters, firemen, geologists, gardeners, hoisting engineers, housekeepers, instrument men, ironworkers, jackhammer operators, janitors, kettlemen, kitchen maids, librarians, linotypers, locksmiths, lumbermen, millwrights, machinists, musicians, nurses, nutritionists, oilers, painters, plasterers, plumbers, patternmakers, photographers, printers, physicians, quarry men, quilters, riveters, roofers, roadmakers, riggers, sculptors, seamstresses, stonemasons, stenographers, statisticians, teamsters, truck drivers, teachers, tabulators, upholsterers, veterinarians, welders, woodchoppers, waiters, watchmen, X-ray technicians — and others.

During its more than eight years of existence, the WPA employed 8,500,000 different people in more than 3,000 counties and spent in excess of $11 billion on a total of 1,410,000 projects. It was by far the biggest employer and spender of all the New Deal agencies. WPA workers built 651,087 miles of highways, roads and streets; constructed, repaired or improved 124,031 bridges; erected 125,110 public buildings; created 8,192 public parks; built or improved 853 airports. Besides its immediate importance to the people who worked on this massive program, Americans were using and enjoying some of these facilities one-third of a century later. More than anything else, however, the WPA was an escape hatch from the trap of the Depression.

Early in the program Roosevelt had warned: "It must be recognized that when an enterprise of this character is extended over more than three thousand counties throughout the nation, there may be occasional instances of inefficiency, bad management, or misuse of funds." Cases of this kind did, of course, occur. A few Senators, Congressmen, governors, state WPA directors and small-time politicians tried to enrich themselves and enhance their power by means of the WPA.

Harry Hopkins was incorruptible and, for a man who liked to spend money, strangely economy-minded in some ways. Loathing organizational charts and fossilized bureaucratic procedures, he ran the national organization with the smallest possible staff and the smallest possible overhead. He got help to the people as directly and quickly as possible. "Hunger is not debatable," he liked to say. "People don't eat in the long run — they eat every day."....

The New Deal did more to promote culture than any previous administration in the history of this nation....

The WPA's arts division consisted of four separate programs. As overall supervisor of them Harry Hopkins chose Jacob Baker, liberal in his tastes and a believer in experimentation. The music program was headed by Nikolai Sokoloff, conductor of the Cleveland Orchestra and a frequent guest conductor of many other symphony orchestras throughout the nation. The art program was directed by Holger Cahill, an art critic, authority on folk art and an outstanding museum technician. The theater project was headed by Hallie Flanagan. The writers' program was headed by Henry Alsberg, an editorial writer for the New York *Evening Post* and a foreign correspondent for liberal magazines.

Alsberg told Hopkins that the WPA could make a lasting cultural contribution to the nation if the men and women employed by the writers' project were put to work preparing a series of guidebooks about the states, one for each state. He pointed out that the latest issue of Baedeker's guide to America had been issued in 1909 — so outdated that it advised Europeans planning to visit this land to bring along matches, buttons, and dress gloves. Agreeing, Hopkins gave Alsberg the word to launch the American Guide Series. . . .

Alsberg began hiring unemployed writers and editors, librarians and photographers, until at last he had 7,500 people at work. A director was named for each of the forty-eight states, and they, in turn, received the help of local reporters, historians, genealogists, librarians and businessmen. Each did his part in the massive chore of researching, writing, editing and publishing the state guidebooks, and soon copy was pouring into the Washington headquarters at the rate of 50,000 words a day. . . .

One of the greatest accomplishments of the writers' project was its historical records survey, instituted in 1936. Relief workers took inventories of local public records stored in city hall cellars, library lofts and courthouse garrets. They indexed old newspaper files. They made abstracts of court cases containing nuggets of local history. They examined business archives, looked through church records, studied tombstones to verify vital statistics. The perfection of microfilm had made it possible for them to photograph, and thus to preserve, millions of pages crumbling into decay. They measured, sketched, diagrammed and photographed 2,300 historic buildings.

In 1937 the American Guide Series became a reality with publication of the first of the set, a book about Idaho. By the end of its life the project produced 378 books and pamphlets — a volume for each of the forty-eight states, 30 about our major cities, others about historic waterways and highways, such as *The Oregon Trail*. Various commercial and university publishers issued these works, with royalties either paying for everything except labor costs or going into the federal treasury.

In a *New Republic* article Robert Cantwell said of the writers' project: "The least publicized of the art projects, it may emerge as the most influential and valuable of them all." Nearly one-third of a century later the American Guide Series continued to be a prime source of information for every serious writer of American history.

Musicians were suffering even before the beginning of the Depression. The popularity of radio, the advent of talking movies and the death of vaudeville had thrown 50,000 musical performers out of work. After the Crash there were few Americans who could afford music lessons for their children, so music teachers lost their pupils or had to cut their fees for the few who remained. Music publishers, recording companies and manufacturers of musical instruments earned less or suffered heavy losses. To most of these people the federal music project, under Nikolai Sokoloff, came as salvation.

Established in July, 1935, the music program put musicians to work in orchestras and bands, in chamber music and choral and operatic groups throughout the nation. Forty-five cities obtained their own WPA symphony orchestra, while 110 other cities got orchestras with more than thirty-five players. Just before the start of a concert by a WPA orchestra in Florida, a violinist apologized to the audience on behalf of his colleagues and himself for the quality of their concert. He explained that their fingers were stiff because of their previous relief job — working on a road gang.

When the music project was at its peak it supported 15,000 people. They gave a total of 150,000 programs heard by more than 100,000,000 people, many whom had been unfamiliar with anything but popular songs. Each month more than 500,000 pupils attended free music classes. WPA musical groups relieved the boredom of hospital patients. Project workers dug out and recorded American folk music — the Cajun songs of Louisiana, the Indian-flavored songs of early Oklahoma, the British-born ballads of Kentucky mountaineers, the African-inspired songs of Mississippi bayous.

Although the program was designed to help performers more than composers, since the former outnumbered the latter, it established a composers' forum-laboratory. Before the project was terminated, 1,400 native composers produced 4,915 original compositions — some bad, many mediocre, a few hailed by music critics as "distinguished." One prominent critic, Deems Taylor, wrote in 1935: "It is safe to say that during the past two years the WPA orchestras alone have probably performed more American music than our other symphony orchestras, combined, during the past ten."

Thanks to this project, music became democratized in this country. In about the year 1915 there had been only 17 symphony orchestras in the United States; by 1939 there were more than 270. Europe's leadership in the musical world, together with its snobbish aloofness, had been shattered.

The WPA art project was set up by Holger Cahill on "the principle that it is not the solitary genius but a sound general movement which maintains art as a vital, functioning part of any cultural scheme."

All a person had to do to get on the art project was to obtain proof from local authorities that he needed relief and that he had once had some connection, however tenuous, with the world of art. As a result, of the more than 5,000 people ultimately hired, fewer than half ever painted a picture, sculpted a statue or decorated a building with a mural.

This does not mean that the art program was a boondoggle. While creativity flowered among the great artists — Jackson Pollock, Aaron Bohrod, Ben Shahn, Willem de Kooning, Concetta Scaravaglione, Anna Walinska and the like — those with limited talent taught free art classes, photographed historic houses, painted posters and designed stage sets for the federal theater project. Others maintained sixty-six art centers which attracted a total of 6,000,000 visitors.

In addition to the invaluable and enduring artworks produced by the most gifted relief workers, the art project left all of us a monumental *Index of American Design.* This part of the program was directed by Constance Rourke and gave employment to about 1,000 artists. Wishing to find and preserve specimens of early American arts and crafts, they ransacked New England farmhouses, museums, antique shops, historical societies, Shaker barns and California missions. They photographed or painted every treasure they discovered — embroidered seat covers, oil paintings, watercolors, carved figureheads, antique quilts and samplers, weather vanes and such. Collectively, these artists produced 7,000 illustrations of every variety of native American art.

On May 16, 1935, the phone rang in the Poughkeepsie, New York, home of a small, red-headed middle-aged woman named Hallie Flanagan. When she answered it, she heard Jacob Baker, the head of the WPA's four arts program, saying that he was calling from Washington. "Mr. Hopkins wants you to come to Washington to talk about unemployed actors," Baker said. Miss Flanagan was in charge of Vassar College's Experimental Theatre. She knew Hopkins, for they had grown up together in Grinnell, Iowa, and attended the same college. . . .

Actors, as Miss Flanagan knew, were suffering severe hardships. Like musicians, many had lost their jobs with the death of vaudeville and the birth of the talkies. No one knew for sure just how many performers were out of work. Actors Equity said there were 5,000 unemployed actors in New York City alone, while WPA officials put the nationwide total at 20,000 to 30,000 people. In Harlem black entertainers were kissing the Tree of Hope, a local talisman, for luck.

In 1931 two-thirds of Manhattan's playhouses were shut. During the 1932–33 season eight out of every ten new plays failed. The Shuberts had plunged into receivership. In 1932 no less than 22,000 people registered with Hollywood casting bureaus. *Variety* had reduced its price from 25 to 15 cents. . . .

On July 27, 1935, Miss Flanagan was sworn in as administrator of the new federal theater project. The ceremony was held in a Washington playhouse called the old Auditorium, a vast hulk of a building now abuzz with rushing people, whirring electric fans, riveting machines and cement-slapping plasterers. She sat down in a new cubicle and conferred with her staff of four about the possibility of getting at least 10,000 theater people back to work within a short time.

Since Broadway was the heart of the American theater, Miss Flanagan wanted an especially able man to direct the New York City unit of her project, and her choice was Elmer Rice. The forty-three-year-old Rice had proved himself as a playwright, stage director and novelist. With the deepening of the Depression, his plays had shifted from realistic reporting to social and political themes. Rice already had sent Hopkins a letter outlining a plan for the establishment of a national theater, but he hesitated about accepting Miss Flanagan's offer because he was about to begin writing another novel.

"What could we do with all the actors?" he asked her. "Even if we had twenty plays in rehearsal at once, with thirty in a cast, that would keep only a fraction of them busy."

Badly wanting Rice, she grabbed at a straw and impulsively said: "We wouldn't use them all in plays. We could do *Living Newspapers*. We could dramatize the news with living actors, light, music, movement."

This idea appealed to Rice, who cried: "Yes. And I can get the Newspaper Guild to back it!". . .

Elmer Rice was paid $260 a month on the theory that he worked thirteen days at $20 a day, but actually he worked from early morning until late at night every day of the month, including Sundays. It amused him to get nasty letters accusing him of making a fortune on a soft government job. Sometimes he opened press conferences by saying to reporters: "Well, what do you vultures want to swoop down on now?"

At first jobs were limited to entertainers on home relief rolls, but this excluded many who had been too proud to ask for help. Miss Flanagan and Rice managed to get this rule modified. She watched in horror as a man applying for work went mad and beat his head against a wall. A famous clown was taken on the WPA rolls, became so excited at the chance to work again that on the opening night of the show he suffered a stroke from which he never recovered. . . .

Into the project flocked young men and women who later became celebrated actors — Joseph Cotton, Orson Welles, Arthur Kennedy, Burt Lancaster, Arlene Francis, Ed Gardner, Rex Ingram, Canada Lee, Howard da Silva, William Bendix, Bil Baird. Another employed by the WPA, but not on the theater project, was Robert Ryan, who worked as a paving supervisor.

At its peak the program gave work to 12,700 theater people in twenty-nine states. Besides the actors themselves, there were producers, directors, playwrights, stagehands, electricians, propmen — all the crafts found in stage work. Hopkins told Miss Flanagan: "We're for labor — first, last and all the time. WPA is labor — don't forget that." He insisted that $9 of every $10 be spent on wages, leaving only about $1 to meet operating costs. Nine out of every 10 people hired had to come from relief rolls. Wages averaged $83 a month, although some actors were paid up to $103.40 a month for performing in New York City. According to the place and circumstance, admission to WPA shows was free, or cost 10 cents, 25 cents, 50 cents, and in rare instances as much as $1.

The federal theater project presented many different kinds of shows — Negro drama, dance drama, children's theater, puppet and marionette shows, a documentary about syphilis, classical drama, modern drama, foreign language drama, musicals, Living Newspapers, pageants, vaudeville, circus, religious drama, spectacles, opera and radio programs. . . .

George Bernard Shaw let the WPA stage his plays at $50 a week, writing to Miss Flanagan: "As long as you stick to your fifty-cents maximum for admission . . . you can play anything of mine you like unless you hear from me to the contrary. . . . Any author of serious plays who does not follow my example does not know what is good for him. I am not making a public-spirited sacrifice; I am jumping at an unprecedentedly good offer."

Eugene O'Neill released his own plays on similar terms, telling reporters: "The WPA units can present important plays before audiences that never before have seen an actual stage production. The possibilities in this respect are thrilling. . . . These units are translating into action the fact that the government has an obligation to give a reasonable amount of encouragement and assistance to cultural undertakings."

Sinclair Lewis had been offered a lot of money by commercial theater producers to make a play out of his novel *It Can't Happen Here*. Instead, he offered it to WPA. The red-headed writer told reporters: "I prefer to give it to the federal theater for two reasons: first, because of my tremendous enthusiasm for its work and, second, because I know I can depend on the federal theater for a non-partisan point of view."

Lewis and his collaborators began their rewrite work in the Essex House on Manhattan's Central Park South — but not at government expense. Much newspaper space was given to the fact that this famous author was working on a play for the WPA. Some editorial writers and readers felt that his study of the rise of an American dictator was Communist-inspired, or the result of Fascism, or a plot to reelect Roosevelt, or a scheme to defeat him. Huey Long had been dead only about a year, so New Orleans officials would not book this show into a city where the late dictator still had many friends. *It Can't Happen Here* became so controversial that before it premiered, the nation's newspapers printed 78,000 lines of pro and con comment about the production.

On October 27, 1936, the play opened simultaneously in twenty-one theaters in seventeen states — the most multiple and extensive first night in the history of the American theater. From Bridgeport and Cleveland, Miami and Birmingham, Detroit and Indianapolis — from each of the several cities came reports that audiences had received the play with wild enthusiasm. In its first few weeks it drew more than a quarter million spectators.

In the New York *Times* Brooks Atkinson wrote: "Mr. Lewis has a story to tell that is calculated to make the blood of a liberal run pretty cold. . . . *It Can't Happen Here* ought to scare the daylights out of the heedless Americans who believe, as this column does, that it can't happen here as long as Mr. Lewis keeps his health."

A smash hit, the play was presented here and there across the country for a total of 260 weeks. . . .

The federal theater project was sponsored and patronized by unions and schools, colleges and universities, Catholics and Jews, Protestants and civic groups, industrial and philanthropic organizations. It brought the living theater to youths who never before had seen flesh-and-blood actors. In the *Federal Theater Magazine* a writer described this huge audience in these words: "We're a hundred thousand kids who never saw a play before. We're students in colleges, housewives in the Bronx, lumberjacks in Oregon, sharecroppers in Georgia. We're rich and poor, old and young, sick and well. We're America and this is our theatre.". . .

Earlier, while the government was setting up the Civilian Conservation Corps, Eleanor Roosevelt lamented that it did nothing for girls. She wanted single, jobless women brought together in urban clubs somewhat similar to CCC camps, but got nowhere. Trying to go it alone, she held a series of meetings in her Manhattan home with a group of about thirty underprivileged young people.

Ensnared in the Depression, few young men and women could afford to attend college, while at the same time they found it increasingly difficult to get jobs. Between 1920 and 1930 college attendance had more than doubled, but from 1932 to 1934 college enrollment fell by 10 percent. High schools, colleges and universities slashed their budgets and cut the salaries of teachers, many of whom went for months without getting a paycheck. By the spring of 1935 a total of 3,000,000 people between the ages of sixteen and twenty-five were on relief — an average of 1 in 7. Even more distressing was the fact that many youths became transients; on a single day in May, 1935, the WPA's transient service counted 54,000 of them registered at its camps and shelters.

Besides the intrinsic misery of this situation, it was also politically dangerous. One confused young man said: "If someone came along with a line of stuff in which I could really believe, I'd follow him pretty nearly anywhere." In Germany and Italy millions of youths had harkened to the evil music of those corrupt pipers, Hitler and Mussolini.

Here in America the President's wife felt it would be wise to create a kind of junior CCC or WPA to help young people and give them a sense of direction. Perhaps such a program could be set up as a subdivision of the WPA. She explained her plan to Harry Hopkins and his assistant, Aubrey Williams, who liked it so much that they expanded on it and outlined what became the National Youth Administration. However, they hesitated about presenting the idea to the President. Hopkins told Mrs. Roosevelt: "There may be many people against the establishment of such an agency in the government, and there may be bad political repercussions. We do not know that the country will accept it. We do not even like to ask the President, because we do not think he should be put in a position where he has to say officially 'yes', or 'no' now."

One night Eleanor Roosevelt entered her husband's bedroom as he was about to go to sleep. When he saw the expression on her face, he smiled: "Well, well — what new program is hanging fire?"

She described the idea for the National Youth Administration, frankly adding that Hopkins was unsure of the wisdom of pushing it.

The President asked: "Do you think it is right to do this?"

"It will be a great help to the young people, Franklin. But I don't want you to forget that Harry Hopkins thinks it may be unwise politically. Some people might say it's like the way Hitler is regimenting German youths."

This, as Mrs. Roosevelt may have intended, was a challenge to the President.

"If it is the right thing to do for the young people," he said, looking up at her, "then it should be done. I guess we can stand the criticism, and I doubt if our youth can be regimented in this way or in any other way."

On June 26, 1935, President Roosevelt issued an executive order creating the National Youth Administration. Its purpose was to administer a relief and unemployment program for young women between the ages of sixteen and twenty-five, for young men of this age who were physically unsuited for CCC labor, for the children of rural families, for those no longer attending school regularly and for needy students who wanted to finish their educations but lacked the means. The NYA was set up as a part of the WPA. As executive director of the new agency the President appointed Aubrey Williams. . . .

Now he [Williams] faced an enormous task. The first fiscal year Williams had $41.2 million to spend, and in 1936 he got $68 million more. Because the President wanted the NYA to be as decentralized as possible, separate administrations were set up in each of the forty-eight states and a special one in New York City, owing to its size. These forty-nine administrations were supplemented by district and local directors, together with advisory committees throughout the nation.

Just about the time of the creation of the NYA, a twenty-six-year-old Texan by the name of Lyndon B. Johnson suffered a shock. For nearly three years he had worked in Washington as secretary to Representative Richard M. Kleberg of Texas. Johnson, an aggressive young man, pretty much dominated his boss, and when Mrs. Kleberg told her husband that the boy was planning to run against him in the next election, the enraged Congressman fired his secretary. Johnson scurried to Representative Maury Maverick of Texas with the sad news that he was just out of a job. Maverick, who liked Johnson, knew that President Roosevelt was about to name forty-eight state NYA directors.

On easy terms with Roosevelt, Maverick went to him to say he knew just the man to direct the Texas NYA — Lyndon Johnson. The President was agreeable until he learned that Johnson was only twenty-six years old. He scoffed that he would not give such an important position to a child, but the Texas Congressman persisted. "After all," said Maverick, "you need someone who's honestly interested in helping his own generation work their way through high school and college and improve themselves, rather than sit around unemployed." In July, 1935, President Roosevelt named Lyndon Baines Johnson the head of the NYA in Texas.

Johnson, who hero-worshiped Roosevelt then and thereafter, flew from Washington to Texas and opened state headquarters of the NYA on the sixth floor of the shabby Littlefield Building in Austin. Then he flew back to the national capital to attend the first nationwide meeting of state NYA directors, called into session by Aubrey Williams on August 20, 1935. Johnson was not shy about telling reporters that he was the youngest of all the state directors and was delighted when this news item was published in newspapers from coast to coast. Also making a good impression on Williams, he obtained more funds for Texas than had originally been allocated to it. . . .

During the twenty months that Lyndon B. Johnson served as state director of the NYA in Texas, he helped 18,000 students by giving them money to go to school and by arranging part-time work in colleges at 35 cents an hour. He also aided 12,000 out-of-school youngsters, seeing that they learned trades and did useful work on public projects. Since Texas was the biggest state in the union, Johnson spent much of his time traveling, and the contacts he made were of use to him in furthering his political career.

In the spring of 1937 he decided to run for Congress. When the news reached Aubrey Williams in the national capital, Williams called the White House and spoke on the phone with Presidential aide Tommy Corcoran.

"Tommy," said Williams, "you've got to get the President to make this guy Johnson lay off running for the Congressional seat down in Austin. He's my whole youth program in Texas, and if he quits, I have no program down there."

Corcoran spoke to Roosevelt, who gave him orders to make sure that Johnson stuck to his NYA job and forgot about running for Congress. But before Corcoran could locate Johnson to relay this word from on high, LBJ had quit his NYA post and filed for Congress.

Richard M. Nixon, who succeeded Johnson as President in 1969, also benefited from the New Deal. In September, 1934, Nixon arrived in Durham, North Carolina, to enter Duke University's new law school. Having been graduated second in his class from Whittier College in California, the twenty-one-year-old student had been given a $200 tuition grant; to keep it he had to maintain a B average at Duke. Because of the Depression, his family was able to send him only $35 a month. To supplement this grant and allowance, Nixon accepted aid from the National Youth Administration, earning thirty-five cents an hour for doing research in the law library. . . .

With three other students he rented a room in a ramshackle farmhouse a mile from the campus and set in the midst of tall pines. They shared two double beds in a big room heated by an old iron potbellied stove. Their quarters lacked any lights, so Nixon studied in the law library. It was also without water, so he showered in the university gym. He used his trunk for a closet, could afford only secondhand books and paid twenty-five cents a meal in a boardinghouse.

Helen Gahagan Douglas, with whom Nixon later feuded politically, was a member of the California state committee of the NYA. Eric F. Goldman, who developed into a noted historian and educator, got through Johns Hopkins University at Baltimore with NYA help. Raymond Clapper was another who had reason to be grateful to the NYA. After Clapper became a famous columnist, he wrote that "some of our leading citizens who are so violently opposed to institutions like the National Youth Administration are not so opposed to subsidizing college students for football teams."

Arthur Miller, who subsequently won renown as a dramatist, got NYA aid while attending the University of Michigan. Of those days he later wrote:

> I loved the idea of being separated from the nation, because the spirit of the nation, like its soil, was being blown by crazy winds. Friends of mine in New York, one of them a *cum laude* from Columbia, were aspiring to the city firemen's exam; but in Ann Arbor I saw that if it came to the worst a man could live on nothing for a long time.

I earned $15 a month for feeding a building full of mice — the National Youth Administration footing the bill — and out of it I paid $1.75 a week for my room and squeezed the rest for my Granger tobacco (two packs for thirteen cents), my books, laundry and movies. For my meals I washed dishes in the co-op cafeteria. My eyeglasses were supplied by the Health Service, and my teeth were fixed for the cost of the materials. The girls paid for themselves including the one I married.

While still in college, Miller wrote several plays. In the spring of 1938 he was graduated, and two months later he was on relief. Then he returned to his hometown, New York City, where he joined the federal theater project. Before the project could present his first play, though, its activities were ended.

A sampling of 150 NYA work projects for out-of-school youths showed that the young men and women employed on them engaged in 169 types of work. Among other things, they installed floodlights in airports, built athletic courts, beautified parks, made brooms, canned vegetables and fruits, took care of infants, cleaned bricks for reuse, cleaned lagoons, cleared land, clipped newspapers in libraries, cooked for lunchrooms, excavated for artifacts, made furniture, worked as nurses, laid pipes, planted grass and so on.

In Fort Morgan, Colorado, fifty-two NYA boys converted a dump into a public recreation ground with 40 acres of grass, shrubs, trees and a new 5-acre swimming pool. At Gloucester, Massachusetts, rubber-booted NYA youths took eggs from lobsters to restock a federal fish hatchery. On the Onondaga Indian reservation in New York State some Indian boys working for the NYA chopped down trees, shaped logs and built a summer camp for children. At the Fort Valley Normal and Industrial School in Georgia a group of Negro boys and girls, few of whom had finished grade school, were paid by the NYA as they were trained in farming, homemaking and various trades. In the Flint-Goodridge Hospital in New Orleans black NYA girls helped regular staff members in every department of the hospital.

Under NYA rules the youths were to work no more than eight hours a day, forty hours a week or seventy hours a month. They earned from $10 to $25 a month, depending on prevailing local wage standards. What did they do with these meager earnings? First they helped their families. Then they bought themselves new clothes, since they had worn nothing but hand-me-down clothing for years. Telling what the NYA meant to him, one boy said: "Maybe you don't know what it's like to come home and have everyone looking at you, and you know they're thinking, even if they don't say it, 'He didn't find a job.' It gets terrible. You just don't want to come home. . . . But a guy's gotta eat some place and you gotta sleep some place. . . . I tell you, the first time I walked in the front door with my paycheck, I was somebody!". . .

However, to some Americans who ate three square meals a day without the help of the government, the overall program of the Works Progress Administration seemed less than noble. One of the popular pastimes was telling WPA jokes like the following:

"A farmer asked a druggist for 'some of that WPA poison. It won't kill squirrels, but it will make them so lazy I can just stomp them to death.' "

"A WPA worker sued the government because he hurt himself when the shovel he was leaning on broke."

"Why is a WPA worker like King Solomon? . . . Because he takes his pick and goes to bed."

"I hear Harry Hopkins is planning to equip all of his WPA workers with rubber-handled shovels."

"Don't shoot our still life — it may be a WPA worker at work."

"There's a new cure for cancer, but they can't get any of it. It's sweat from a WPA worker."

Some of these jokes were thought up by professional comedians, but at last the American Federation of Actors ordered all its members to stop poking fun at the WPA. . . .

As has been said, the WPA employed 8,500,000 people in 1,410,000 projects in more than 3,000 counties at a cost of more than $11 billion. Naturally, in a program of such magnitude there were bound to be inequities and injustice, scandals and corruption. Campaigning by WPA staff members in Pennsylvania, Kentucky and Tennessee in the 1938 Congressional elections led to adverse comment and passage of the Hatch Act of July, 1939, curbing "pernicious political activities" by federal appointees. President Roosevelt discharged at least one state WPA director and began keeping a closer eye on the others.

Harry Hopkins was loved and hated by relief workers and politicians according to how well the WPA treated them. While he certainly had personal preferences in which he indulged, he was totally honest and therefore beyond the reach of provable scandal. Except for betting on the horses and lifting a glass of champagne with rich friends, he maintained his modest way of life. None of that $11 billion ever found its way into his pockets. . . .

In 1939 the Works Progress Administration had its name changed to the Works Projects Administration, and it continued in existence until June 30, 1943.

This vast, long-lived agency created enduring public works, helped the United States prepare for the approaching war, increased purchasing power and left grateful memories among millions of Americans who, without it, might have lost their lives, their hope of salvation, their faith in their country.

STUDY GUIDE

1. What impression do you get of Franklin Delano Roosevelt in the following areas as a result of reading this essay: his temperament, his social outlook, and his accomplishments?

2. What was the reasoning behind the establishment of these cultural programs by the New Deal? On what grounds were these programs criticized — and which ones came in for the greatest criticism? Do you feel these criticisms were justified? If so, why; if not, why not?

3. What was the total cost of the WPA program, and how many Americans benefited from it? Do you consider this cost excessive? If so, why; if not, why not?

4. Given a depression similar to that of the 1930s, would there be a controversy *today* over the need for work relief for the unemployed? If so, why; if not, why not?

BIBLIOGRAPHY

The most intensive study of the New Deal and the leadership provided for it by Franklin Delano Roosevelt — both of which receive a favorable evaluation from the author — is Arthur M. Schlesinger, Jr., *The Age of Roosevelt*, in three volumes: *The Crisis of the Old Order* (1957), *The Coming of the New Deal* (1959), and *The Politics of Upheaval* (1960). Two one-volume studies are also excellent: Basil Rauch's older, yet useful, *History of the New Deal, 1933–1938* (1944) and William E. Leuchtenburg's judicious *Franklin Delano Roosevelt and the New Deal, 1932–1940* (1963). A revealing portrait of the decade in social terms is found in Dixon Wecter, *The Age of the Great Depression, 1929–1941* (1948). Two critical views of the New Deal, from an ultra-liberal point of view, are *The New Deal* (1967), by Paul Conkin, and "The New Deal," an essay by Barton J. Bernstein, Jr., in his edition of *Towards a New Past* (1968).

The plight of the unemployed and their families in the 1930s is treated in Mirra Komarovsky, *The Unemployed Man and His Family* (1940); in E. Wight Bakke, *Citizens Without Work* (1940); and, from an economic point of view, in Eli Ginzberg, *The Unemployed* (1943). The assistance the New Deal provided to the youth of the nation is covered in Kenneth Holland and Frank Ernest Hill, *Youth in the CCC* (1942) and Betty and Ernest K. Lindley, *A New Deal for Youth* (1938). For discussions of social welfare, see Grace Abbott, *From Relief to Social Security* (1941); Edith Abbott, *Public Assistance* (1940); Grace Adams, *Workers on Relief* (1939); Josephine Chapin Brown, *Public Relief* (1940); and Donald Howard, *The WPA and Federal Relief Policy* (1943). A recent publication entitled *Wall-to-Wall America: A Cultural History of Post-Office Murals in the Great Depression* (1982), by Karal A Marling, sheds much light on the socioartistic aspects of the New Deal era.

Culver Pictures

A military wedding, 1944. Family allotments and full employment made early marriage possible for millions.

16

RICHARD R. LINGEMAN

The Home Front
During World War II

On a number of counts, World War II was an ideal war for the American people. American casualties — compared to the death and destruction brought on by the Civil War or the millions of Russians, Germans, Chinese, and Japanese killed during World War II — were relatively light. Dissent among the American people over the righteousness of the war or its justification was minimal. In addition to an exhilarating sense of national solidarity, the war brought full employment and a high level of affluence to a large proportion of the population. As the federal government pumped billions of dollars into the economy, millions of Americans were once more steadily employed — in some instances for the first time in more than a decade. Although women's hosiery and cigarettes were in short supply and it was necessary, at one point, to place price controls on or ration consumer goods, the consequences for the American people were not enormously painful. Much of World War II was taken in good humor; the threats to the home front were few, and the attitude of the civilian population enthusiastic — and, in some respects, euphoric.

World War II marked more than a military victory over Nazi Germany and Imperial Japan; the war brought profound and permanent changes in the socioeconomic policies of the American nation. World War II ended our commitment to a laissez-faire economy; the Full Employment Act and other legislation reflected the general agreement among the nation's political leaders that the federal government is responsible for maintaining the economic prosperity and the social well-being of the American people. World War II was also

253

a turning point in other ways: the postwar civil rights movement for American blacks had its origins in developments that took place during the war; the war also brought millions of women out of the home into the offices and factories of the nation. Demographically, the war brought marriage to millions at a younger age, and an increase in the number of children per family.

Perhaps the most important consequence of the war in terms of the quality of postwar American life came in the field of education. Through an unprecedented piece of legislation — and a generously wise one — millions of Americans were sent to college under the GI Bill of Rights (the Serviceman's Readjustment Act); on the campuses of the nation ex-servicemen acquired the skills and the university degrees that made the United States the leader of the world in research and technology. And finally, World War II left a legacy of ominous proportions — atomic energy. How this legacy of World War II research is ultimately employed will determine the very existence of the human race.

In *Don't You Know There's a War On?: The American Home Front, 1941–1945*, Richard R. Lingeman has captured much of the mood of the American people during this crucial period in our history. From this book, we have selected a chapter that portrays the changes on the home front — the social consequences of an overseas war that nonetheless altered many aspects of life on this side of the Atlantic.

The end of Hard Times was a motley caravan observed on Route 66, near Albuquerque, New Mexico, a road that was both *via doloroso* and passage of hope in John Steinbeck's *Grapes of Wrath*. Now, by the same route, in early 1942 the Okies were returning home. They came in old battered sedans and wheezing trucks and Model T's, sometimes twelve in a car, with all their possessions strapped on the tops and sides — rockers, buckets, shovels, stoves, bedding and springs. A few of the migrants were fleeing what they regarded as the imminent invasion of California by the Japanese, but the attitude of most was summed up by the man who said: "We ain't war-scared or anything like that, but a lot of others were pulling up and clearing out — not all of 'em understand — and Ma and I figured that if we was going back, now was the time. And, besides, Ed Lou is pretty big now and there ought to be a job for him in the oil fields and maybe for me too."

There were still more than 3,600,000 men unemployed. So the migration had momentum to gain as hillbillies from Appalachia, po' whites and Negroes from the South, farmers from the Midwest, garment workers from New York City picked up stakes and swarmed to the centers of war production.

The factories were rising up out of the raw, graded earth. The year 1942 was a year of frantic construction — more than $12 billion worth of it financed by the federal government, most of that on military camps, factories and installation of heavy machinery.

Near the little town of Starke, Florida, Camp Blanding had been erected in six months of feverish building. The workers turned the little town upside down. "Why, people were sleeping in the streets, in the churches, in the trees," one resident recalled. The local grocer reminisced: "I had two stores and I sold groceries to the construction gangs. Two stores and I couldn't get any help. I worked 18 to 20 hours a day. My weekend profits were unbelievable, but I wouldn't want to go through it again. These fellows from the construction jobs — these carpenters and plumbers — were getting more money than they'd ever had in their lives and they had no place to spend it except in Starke. They were always hungry and they were always buying. It went for five or six months. We all got rich." . . .

To millions who had suffered the Depression years on relief, with occasional spells of odd jobs, this meant a time of opportunity, a time to pick up stakes and head to the war production centers, where there were steady jobs and good money to be had. In times of depression people tend to crawl into their holes and lick their wounds; in good times they head for the money. Estimates of the number of Americans who left their homes to seek work elsewhere — in a different county, a different state or even a different region — ranged as high as 20,000,000. Probably the true number will never be known, but the Census Bureau attempted to capture the figures as best it could, before the time was irretrievably gone. Based on a sample of 30,000 persons, the bureau took a demographic snapshot of the nation in March, 1945, and compared it with the prewar period. The Bureau estimated that by 1945, 15,300,000 persons were living in counties different from those in which they lived at Pearl Harbor; 7,700,000 of these migrants were living in a different state and 3,600,000 in a different part of the country. . . .

A major source of this migration was the farm, where, most agrarian economists agreed, there were about 2,000,000 too many people in 1940. Between Pearl Harbor and March, 1945, nearly 5,500,000 people left the farms to live and work in the city (another 1,500,000 went into the armed forces). So effectively did the war siphon off the surplus that there were severe labor shortages on the farms, and in 1943–44, farm deferments were drastically increased by Selective Service. Women, city teen-agers, Axis war prisoners, interned Japanese-Americans and even GI's were pressed into service to help out with the harvest (a time when an additional 3,000,000 laborers are needed). The grip of the agriculture depression, which had held since the early twenties, was at last broken, and farmers' profits soared to record highs. With all this farm prosperity, a reverse migration trend was also operative, for some 2,500,000 people moved from nonfarm to farm areas, presumably to take up farmwork. Still, the farm population suffered a net loss of nearly 17 percent, not counting those in the armed forces. . . .

The greatest percentage of the immigrants settled in the immediate environs of the city or cities, rather than inside the cities. This was reflected in the mushrooming growth of war worker towns and federal housing projects laid out where there were only rural fields before or, even worse, the ubiquitous "New Hoovervilles" — trailer camps, tent settlements, shanty towns, "foxhole houses" and all the other temporary conglomerations of people which sprang up over the countryside, often as satellites of the new war plants which had been erected on unused land. What this further meant was that these settlements were often located outside the service ambit of city and township governments. They were in a jurisdictional limbo, and there was no local government unit to take responsibility for them; further, many of the small towns to which they were often closest, hence most directly affected, lacked the resources with which to help them, even if they had wished to. Most of the migrants were nonvoting, nontaxpaying, nonhomeowning — in effect, political pariahs.

The geographical flow of the migration was strikingly skewed. Between April, 1940, and November, 1943, thirty-five states showed a net *loss* in total civilian population. The thirteen states that gained did so in numbers varying from California's 1,020,000 to Delaware's 7,240, but the geographical pattern was clear: By far the largest gainer was the Far West — the three coast states of California, Washington and Oregon, in that order, and to a much smaller degree, Arizona, Utah and Nevada. Next to the Pacific coast states, were three South Atlantic states: Maryland, Florida and Virginia. (In a class by itself was the District of Columbia, which gained 162,469 people; the federal government was also a booming war industry.)

The people went to the Far West because the opportunity was there, and the opportunity was there because the war money went West: California alone, with 6.2 percent of the population had by 1944 received war contracts totaling $15.8 billion, or 9.7 percent of the total for the nation. More than half the wartime shipbuilding took place in the three Pacific coast states, and nearly half the airplane manufacture. Because of its location on the sea and the existence of a prewar aircraft industry, California logically helped itself to a large chunk of this production. When the war ended, an estimated 1,000,000 war workers would be out of work, but till then California was truly the Golden State. All told its population increased by almost 2,000,000 between 1940 and 1945. Per capita income rose apace, reaching $1,740 annually, the highest in the nation. Here was the real gold rush in California's colorful history.

In sum the general pattern of the great national migration seemed to be this: Deep South po' whites to the shipyards around the Gulf crescent and in the Hampton Roads–Newport News–Norfolk complex and, farther North, to the Michigan manufacturing complexes.

Southern Negro sharecroppers and tenant farmers to the shipyards and factories of the West Coast; up the East Coast and to the factories of the Middle West.

Arkies, Okies, Tennessee, Kentucky and West-by-God-Virginia hillbillies to Illinois and Indiana and Michigan or to the southern oilfields and shipyards.

Kansas, Nebraska, Iowa, North and South Dakota plowboys to the great aircraft factories of the West Coast.

New York and other urban small-manufacturing workers to the Mid and Far West.

They came in cars, driving their rubber down to the rims and then paying exorbitant prices for used tires or retreads en route; or, more likely, they sat up or stood in the aisles for days and nights on crowded trains; or they packed their few working clothes into cardboard suitcases, made dust down the red dirt roads of the backwoods South to the crossroads store, and there waited for the bus to take them on the long trip to Pascagoula or Mobile or New Orleans. . . .

Everyone, on the move. Young wives with colicky babies, making the long journey to join their husbands at this new war job. Lone men, creased and weathered by work, and pink-cheeked young farm boys, migrating West because they heard there was plenty of work out there, sitting in the dark loneliness of the bus at night, only the glow of the orange spark of their cigarettes for company, their thoughts set free to range back and forth in time and space from regret to hope, over the vast American landscape of shadowy, empty hills and somber forests and little towns, their dark windows staring like empty-skulled eye sockets. In the next seat might be another man, he too sitting staring out at the landscape at night, he too coming from somewhere but off to somewhere else. The low voices hummed in talk of "where-are-you-going?" and "what's-it-like down there?" . . .

Men were picking up stakes and moving on. Some left signs on the doors of closed businesses, letting their customers and friends and the whole world (and maybe even God) know that they had vamoosed, flown the coop, skedaddled, made tracks, hit the road, up and went. Signs that read like the one on the door of Joe's Country Lunch in Alabama:

Maybe you don't know there's a war on. Have gone to see what it's all about. Meanwhile good luck and best wishes until we all come home. (Signed) Joe.

Or that of Lem Ah Toy, Chinese laundryman of Seattle:

Go to war. Closed duration. Will clean shirts after clean Axis. Thank you....

Signs, signs. Cocky, patriotic signs. The whole country, it seemed, was bursting out in a springtime of patriotism.... On bar mirrors in small dusty roadside taverns were soap-scrawled fighting slogans, like:

SLAP THE JAPS OFF THE MAP!
TO HELL WITH THE JAPS!
REMEMBER PEARL HARBOR!!! . . .

Young girls sitting in soda fountains adorned themselves with the unit patches of their boyfriends, sergeant's stripes or lieutenant's bars; the soda fountain they were lounging in purveyed such patriotic combinations as: Blackout Sundae, Commando Sundae (War Workers, Get Your Vitamins the Delicious Way), Flying Fortress Sundae, Morale Builder and Paratroops Sundae (Goes Down Easy). In more and more windows hung service flags: red border, surrounding a white rectangle in which were one or more blue stars. Gold ones were making their appearance too. ("THE WAR DEPARTMENT REGRETS TO INFORM YOU THAT YOUR SON.... " The papers printed names on casualty lists, but never gave total killed and wounded until mid-1942.) Along with the service flags in homes and places of business, small towns had erected Honor Roll signs, with lengthening lists of names and branches of service of their local boys....

At last the journey would near its end, and the migrant would catch a glimpse of the city of his destination: "snowy plains where great manufacturing plants jut up among their parking lots like mesas in the desert ... mills that smear the sky with brown smoke out of tall cylindrical chimneys. . . . "

In green, gently rolling farmland, long, low dull-red brick factories rose up where bulldozers had scraped the land bare. Walter Wiard owned a farm and orchard in an area near Ypsilanti, Michigan, known as Willow Run after a stream that meandered through it on its way to the Huron River. In early 1941, Walter Wiard's land lay next to the site the Ford people had chosen for their new bomber plant, and the Ford people came to him and offered him a nice price for the land. Then Wiard watched as the giant groundbreaking machines went to work. Later he remarked: "It took me twenty-nine years to plant, cultivate and make that fine orchard. It took those tractors and bulldozers just twenty-nine minutes to tear it all down." . . .

So the workers arrived at the towns and cities where the war plants had risen and got off their crowded buses and walked the streets looking for a job, which was easy to find, and a bed, which was not. They might have landed in LA or San Francisco or Detroit or Pascagoula or Buffalo or Mobile. . . .

San Diego, once a quiet coastal town, was inundated with a lusty gang of workers and servicemen. For a new dry dock the Navy dug a hole that seemed as deep as the Grand Canyon, and one old resident described it as "a hole that you could have dumped most of this town [into] when I first saw it 70 years ago." Another graybeard, shaking his head in wonderment, recalled, "We used to go to bed by ten, or anyway, by eleven. Now some theaters and cafes never close! I remember it was like that in the Klondike. Now when boatloads of sailors hurry ashore, and all those soldiers from Fort Rosecrans and Camp Callan swarm in on payday, this town goes crazy. In one day they eat 50,000 hot dogs! Even shoe shine boys get the jitters. Sherman's Cafe has ten bars, and a dance floor so big that 5,000 of 'em can dance at once." Ten years before, exactly 6 men worked in San Diego's one aircraft factory; now there were 50,000. Any innocent tourist who decided to sit for a moment on a park bench would find himself approached by a series of people wanting to hire him to do some kind of job. . . .

Consider the town of Beaumont, Texas, which needed an incinerator. Next door to the Pennsylvania Shipyards stood a giant garbage dump which exhaled a miasma that could be smelled miles away when the wind was right. With the nauseating smells came flies. An official of the shipyards described what the flies were like: "The flies we get from the dump in the executive offices are so thick that it is almost impossible to concentrate on our duties. Twice a day the rooms are sprayed and the dead swept out with a broom. As soon as it gets warm we have to send people around the yard to spray the men on the job, or they would be eaten up by mosquitoes and flies."

The incinerator had been approved by the Federal Works Administration, and work had been begun. Then the WPB [War Production Board] refused the town a priority on a needed bit of equipment worth about $14,000. And so work stopped, and a half-finished incinerator stood in the midst of the stench and rotting garbage, a monument to government shortsightedness, while the stink grew and the danger of typhoid increased apace. . . .

Housing was an immediate and frequently insoluble problem for the migrant war workers. The government and private builders, largely with federally insured mortgage money, built a total of $7 billion of new housing, much of it temporary — barracks, trailers, demountable homes, dormitories, and the like. The NHA [National Housing Agency] calculated that it had to provide new or existing housing for 9,000,000 migratory workers and their families. To do this, it built and it scoured up existing vacant rooms and houses with the assistance of local community groups. Existing housing took care of 600,000 workers and their families. Over and above this, private companies built something more than 1,000,000 new units and the federal government 832,000 for a total of 1,800,000 units or housing for about 5,000,000 people: housing for at best 7,000,000 out of 9,000,000 migrants was provided; the remaining 2,000,000 presumably had to scour up their own shelter.

These bare statistics do not of course reflect the flesh and blood of the housing situation — the thousands who had to live in trailers, converted garages, tents, shacks, overpriced rooms, "hot beds," even their own cars during the early part of the war; the rent gouging that went on, even though rents were regulated by the Office of Price Administration; and the difficulties people with children had, especially the wives of service-men who followed them to their training camps.

Landlord hostility to the newcomers was endemic in this sellers' market. An ad in a Fort Worth, Texas, newspaper revealed it: "Fur. Apt., no street-walkers, home wreckers, drunks wanted; couple must present marriage certificate." On the West Coast, which had had an influx of more than 2,000,000 newcomers, it was chaotic. In San Francisco people lived in tents, basements, refrigerator lockers and automobiles. A city official reported in 1943: "Families are sleeping in garages, with mattresses right on cement floors and three, four, five to one bed." In Richmond, where the Kaiser shipyards were located, people were living under conditions that were worse than the Hoovervilles of the Depression. A trailer camp in San Pablo was crowded with people in trailers, tents and shacks; there was no sewage, and children waded about in a stagnant pond. A family of four adults and seven children lived in an 8-by-10-foot shack with two cots and one full-sized bed. A war housing project at Sausalito offered good living conditions for 4,500 people with self-government, low rentals and health insurance; but when a 90-mile-an-hour gale hit the area in January, 1943, all the tarpaper roofs of the temporary housing blew off. . . .

The philosophy underlying the governmental housing program was that "the government doesn't belong in the housing business," which meant that private housing interests were deferred to. In San Francisco, for example, which had a population increase of 200,000, local realtors had initially opposed war housing, saying there were 10,000 vacancies in the area. They were fearful of the competition, of course, but then, when the housing situation reached crisis proportions, they did a turnabout and blamed the federal government for not building enough war hous-ing. And though they had relented on allowing government housing, they were adamant in their demands that only temporary housing, which could be torn down after the war, be built, lest property values suffer. This insistence that war workers be given only temporary or demountable housing was widespread and reflected not only the real estate man's pocketbook talking but also fear that the outsiders would stay after the war. As a result (and also because of the shortage of building materials), much government housing was jerry-built — instant slums, they might be called. . . .

One of the better federal housing projects was that erected near the Willow Run bomber plant. Because of opposition on the part of the townspeople in nearby Ypsilanti and the Ford Motor Company to a planned permanent residential area known as Bomber City . . . and material shortages, construction of alternate, temporary units was proposed and finally got under way in 1943. The first units — a dormitory for single workers called Willow Lodge — were open for occupancy by February, 1943. There followed trailer homes and prefabricated units for families, which were completed in August, 1943. In all there was housing for about 14,000 workers — or one-third the number working at Willow Run plant at peak production.

By wartime housing standards these units were luxury housing, although they were not much to look at, being row upon row of gray, monotonous, flat-roofed buildings. The residents often had difficulty locating their own quarters. One lady always marked her house by a bedspring leaning against the adjoining unit. So much did she come to rely on the bedspring that she forgot the number of her own dwelling, and so one day, when inevitably, the bedspring was removed, she spent hours searching for her place. . . .

Most of the married workers with families overcame these minor hardships at Willow Run and turned it into a stable community. Still there were problems that could have been predicted among such a large and fluid population, many of them unmarried immigrants from the South. One reporter was critical of the "lack of wholesome recreational facilities and the generally drab social environment of Willow Run" which "stimulated private-party types of entertainment, featured by heavy drinking and promiscuous sex relations among fun-starved workers."

The center of the "promiscuous sex" was, not surprisingly, the Willow Lodge dormitory, which the FPHA [Federal Public Housing Agency] had opened to unmarried workers of both sexes. The result: "Professional gamblers and fast women quickly moved in for a clean-up." The co-ed policy was quickly dropped, however, and tenant policing, in cooperation with the FPHA, cleaned up the budding Gomorrah. . . .

Roving youngsters with nowhere to go were widespread. In Mobile, there were more than 2,000 children who didn't go to school at all, and one high school with an enrollment of 3,650 had a total of 8,217 absences during a single month. One movie theater owner joked with the local lady truant officer: "Miss Bessie, why don't you bring your teachers down here? My place is always full of children." . . .

Some towns, even without federal assistance, made an effort to set up day-care centers and nursery schools in a variety of ways, and the unions and war industries made an even greater contribution, the latter prodded by the labor shortage and the need to attract women workers, the former by a doctrine of demanding work rights. On the other hand, there was a distinct strain of prejudice against working mothers, who were regarded as selfishly materialistic; forgotten was the desperate need for them in the plants, the fact that many were servicemen's wives who needed to supplement their allotments, and the desire of others to take advantage of an opportunity to save up some money for the future. One of the leaders in the opposition to women working was the Catholic Church, which in many areas opposed nursery schools and day-care centers. . . .

Not unrelated to the shortage of day care, the overcrowded schools, the entry of youngsters into industry, and the lack of parental supervision was an increase in the incidence of crimes committed by teenagers (a term that came into wide currency during the war, along with juvenile delinquency). Juvenile arrests increased 20 percent in 1943; in some cities it was even higher — San Diego, for example, reported an increase of 55 percent among boys and 355 percent among girls. This was not a reflection of a nationwide crime wave, for crime on the whole — at least according to FBI figures — dropped during the war, with the exception of assault and rape. This was because the young men, who committed the largest percentage of crimes, were off in service. One of the heaviest areas of increase was among girls under seventeen who were arrested not only for various forms of "sex delinquency" such as prostitution, but also for violent crimes. In 1943 alone, the number of girls arrested for prostitution increased by 68 percent over the previous year.

Among the boys, it was largely theft and a striking incidence of acts of vandalism, destruction and violence. Some of these acts seemed a kind of acting-out of war fantasies — such as the thirteen-year-old "thrill saboteur" who put a stick of dynamite under a railroad track, lit the fuse and ran. The dynamite did not go off because he had attached no cap. He explained his action by saying he was attempting to close off all roads into the town and set himself up as "dictator."

With the girls, delinquency took the form of an aggressive promiscuity, and the lure was the glamor of a uniform. These "khaki-whacky" teenagers — some barely thirteen — were known as V-(for Victory) girls. They hung around bus depots, train stations, drugstores or wherever soldiers and sailors on leave might congregate, flirted with the boys, and propositioned them for dates. They were amateurs for the most part, the price of their favors being a movie, a dance, a Coke or some stronger drink. (A joke of the time ran: Sailor: "I'm going to Walgreen's to meet a girl." "What's her name?" "How should I know?")

The V-girls were easily recognizable in their Sloppy Joe sweaters, hair ribbons, anklets or bobby sox and saddle shoes, trying to look older with heavily made-up faces and blood-red lipstick. In Detroit the Navy had to build a fence around its armory, located in the city, to keep out not the enemy, but the bobby-soxers. In Chicago, sailors said it was worth one's life to try to walk from the Navy Pier to State Street, where the V-girls swarmed like flies. In Mobile, the girls themselves bought contraceptives for their dates, and when one druggist refused to sell them to a group of girls, he was jeered at and called an old fuddy-duddy.

The V-girls had their similarities all over the country. Some of them followed their lovers when they were transferred to another post, but many were left stranded when the boyfriend left. These often ended up working as waitresses or barmaids in servicemen's hangouts, passing from one uniform to another.

There had always been teen-age girls who "did it," of course; war made them more visible, more independent, more mobile. One estimate had it that the V-girls represented at most only one in 1,700 out of their age group. More conservative girls, caught up in the transitoriness of war-time meetings and the glamor of a uniform, might also "do it," but they were more discreet and less promiscuous and conducted their assignations in more privacy.

The V-girl was next door to being a prostitute, yet there was about her at least a certain refreshing lack of cold professionalism. She offered a lonely GI transitory fun and excitement, devoid of the professional's matter-of-fact indifference. She could also, of course, offer him VD, for there was a higher incidence among the amateurs than among the professionals. In 1941, Congress, worried about the mother's vote, had passed the May Act, which forbade houses of prostitution near military bases. The result was that a lot of establishments were closed down and their inmates put out to walk the streets. These and their amateur competitors were found to inflict VD at a much higher rate than the house-based girls. . . .

The guardians of morality — whose view on the subject had been expressed in a 1942 *Reader's Digest* article by Gene Tunney entitled "The Bright Shield of Continence" — of course were against any kind of sex by soldiers with women other than their wives (if that) and would be shocked at the idea of brothels near Army camps where innocent young selectees would be exposed to unholy, irresistible temptation leading to inevitable corruption. (There was a similar logic running through the efforts of temperance groups to ban the distribution of beer to combat troops or its sale at PX's.)

As for the servicemen themselves, the Army traditionally liked to say that 15 percent "won't," 15 percent "will" and the remainder occasionally would succumb to temptation if the serpent insinuated itself (these figures derived from World War I). For that wavering 70 percent, the problems of finding "nice girls" in the camp towns, whether their intent was to deflower them or take them to the Sunday night meeting of the Epworth League, were often insuperable. . . .

Still, if the number of marriages and families formed is any sort of index to the degree of adherence to the American fundamental belief in marriage, the war period could be looked upon as fostering a salubrious moral climate. Beginning in 1940, as prosperity began to take hold and the Depression receded, the marriage rate began to rise abruptly — one is tempted to say alarmingly. . . .

The rush to wed was impelled as much by prosperity as it was by the war. A justice of the peace in Yuma, Arizona, a marriage town just over the California border, explained the sudden upswing in business in 1941. Not love but "aircraft did it for us," he said. "The figures began going up as soon as those boys were given employment in those plants at San Diego and Los Angeles and were taken off W.P.A. [Works Progress Administration]." Aircraft workers had been issued 90 percent of the licenses since the summer of 1941. "You see, when they were on the dole they had girls but no money. Once off the dole and once getting good money they began sending for the girls back home — girls in the Middle Western states, a great many of them. The girls wouldn't waste any time in coming in and then on weekends — we get the great rush on weekends — they'd all come hustling to Yuma." It was the same story in Cincinnati, where weddings involving defense workers increased 51 percent; in Baltimore, where they were up 47 percent; and in Youngstown and Akron (up 17 percent) and Detroit (up 12 percent).

Of course, at that time a wife would also qualify as a dependent and men with dependents were deferred, until Congress discouraged this by establishing an allotment system in 1942. Under it, a man's wife would receive a minimum of $50 a month, $22 of which was deducted from his pay and $28 contributed by the government. To preserve family life and also perhaps to encourage a population increase to offset anticipated manpower losses in the war, the Selective Service Act deferred fathers until 1943, when manpower needs were so pressing that so-called pre–Pearl Harbor fathers were drafted.

Whether the Selective Service Act's policy was responsible or not (and we must give the parents some credit for initiative), the birthrate did go up during the war in a preview of the postwar baby boom when returning GI's set about forming families as fast as they could. Since the 1920s the birthrate, like the marriage rate, had been declining, but in 1943, it rose to 22 per 1,000 — the highest in two decades. Most of the babies were "good-bye babies," conceived before the husband shipped out. Since the wife's allotment check would be increased upon the child's arrival, finances were no longer a major worry. In addition, there were compelling emotional reasons: The father, faced with the possibility of being killed in battle, was depositing a small guarantor to posterity, an assurance that someone would carry on his name, while the wife was given something to hold onto, a living, breathing symbol of their marriage. . . .

So they were married, this courageous young couple; perhaps they did know each other well and were in love, or perhaps they had met on a weekend pass and married in haste. Or perhaps the woman had eyed covetously the allotment check and looked forward to a life of some ease (and if he was killed, there was always the $10,000 to the widow from his life insurance). A $50-a-month allotment was of course not princely, but a GI overseas, with nothing else to spend it on, would usually send part of his regular pay home.

With the going rate only $50 per month per husband, a really ambitious girl might decide she needed four, five, six or more husbands to support her in any kind of style. Inevitably there developed the wartime racket of bigamous marriage for allotment checks. The girls who engaged in it came to be known as Allotment Annies. They posted themselves in bars around military bases and struck up acquaintances with lonely servicemen, otherwise known as shooting fish in a barrel. The men, desirous of the certainty that when they went off to battle, there would be a girl back home waiting for them, writing them V-mail letters, could often be had. So they married, the hero went off to war, and Annie stayed home and collected a lot of those pale blue-green checks from the U.S. Treasury Department.

A representative Allotment Annie was a hustling seventeen-year-old named Elvira Tayloe, who operated out of Norfolk, Virginia, and specialized in sailors shipping out from the large naval base there. Working as a hostess in a nightclub, she managed to snare six live ones and was working on her seventh when caught. This came about because a couple of sailors on liberty had met in an English pub, and as servicemen are wont, as the warm beer flowed, took out wallets and exchanged pictures of their gorgeous wives. Both were surprised, to put it mildly, when their pictures turned out to be identical, both of Elvira. A fight ensued over whose wife was being adulterous with whom. After the shore patrol had cooled them off, the boys joined forces, Elvira was traced and her career of cupidity brought to an end. . . .

Wartime marriage was hard, and the real miracle was that so many survived it. What the husband did overseas during off-duty hours is beyond our scope, but the girls back here were, largely, brave — and true. Not heroic; but they got by. Some, it is true, cracked up, or fell into dalliance with a representative of the local supply of 4-F's and joyriding war workers.

Life gave another portrait of the typical Army wife. Her husband is a lieutenant in India and her $180-a-month allotment makes her atypical right there, yet she adds some less dramatic hues to the portrait. She lives in a 3½-room apartment, rent $65 a month; she spends $45 a month on food for herself and the baby; she doesn't go out on dates, goes to parties unescorted and doesn't have a great deal of fun ("There's always some woman who thinks you're trying to take their man away"); sometimes at night she gets the blues and cries, but her baby son cheers her up a lot; she writes her husband a letter every day; she spends her evenings listening to the radio a lot (Guy Lombardo's is her favorite orchestra); when she hears "Soon" — "their song" in 1935, when they were married — she becomes sad. . . .

Dr. Jacob Sergi Kasanin, chief psychiatrist at Mount Zion Hospital in San Francisco, went so far as to identify a neurotic syndrome characteristic of servicemen's wives in 1945. Like many men who went overseas and cracked up before they reached combat (there were estimates that as high as one-half of the combat-trained troops avoided battle by "psyching out," getting a dishonorable discharge and the like), the wives had their own form of crackup. The physical symptoms included depression, colitis, heart palpitations, diarrhea, frequent headaches. Hardest hit were the recently married who had no children. They often developed "pathological reactions" in the form of resentment against their husband or even inability to recall what he looked like. (This was true even among fairly normal wives. One such wife decided to knit a sweater for her husband. As the months of separation drew on, her idea of her tall husband grew accordingly. He sent a picture of himself in the new sweater: it reached halfway down to his knees.) These women often had followed their husbands to his embarkation point; then in symbolic identity with him, they stayed there, and some couldn't take the loneliness, away from home, and began going to the bars, meeting other servicemen in transit. (The ratio of female alcoholics — defined as those who got into trouble with the police — to male alcoholics in Chicago was one to two, compared to one in five in 1931.)

For the more mature marriages, the ones in which the couple would pick up the pieces of their life and put them back together after long separation, there were still changes to be faced. A Navy doctor took a look at himself in the mirror one day and saw that he had grown bald and fat. He wrote about this to his wife, and she wrote back, sadly, "You will find that three years have done quite a bit to me, too."

The war, then, upset the social topography as it did the physical landscape; people met new places, new situations, new jobs, new living conditions, new ways of life, new temptations, new opportunities. There were social ills aplenty, but for all their novelty, they were perhaps the familiar ones; war simply exaggerated them and made them more visible. A sociologist writing on juvenile delinquency in *Federal Probation Officer* expressed a view that most diagnosticians of society would share:

> . . . many mothers of school-age boys and girls work in normal times; families are "broken" either physically or psychologically in normal times; children are exploited in normal times; some young people have always earned good wages and spent them unwisely; families always have moved from one neighborhood or community to another; some recreational facilities of an

undesirable nature can be found in most communities in normal times. . . .
Actually war does not create new problems with which we are unfamiliar. It
accentuates old problems and in so doing the number of boys and girls
affected is increased greatly.

One can only add that, in view of the familiarity of the problems and
their increased magnitude, the governmental agencies might have done
more to alleviate them. But of course, to Congress, stepped-up programs
of social welfare would have smacked of "New Deal social experiments,"
and besides — don't you know there's a war on?

The citizenry out in the provinces who thought they had problems
could take a measure of malicious satisfaction, if they wanted to, over the
fact that their nation's capital was perhaps the most mixed-up, down-at-
the-heels war town of them all. Its traditional industry was mainly
government, of course, but everybody in the provinces knew that Washington's "bit" was doing the war's desk work — paper shuffling, tabu-
lating, enumerating, filing. What people in Washington did was concoct
complicated forms and schedules, issue directives, create agencies and,
when they had some spare time, which was often, sit around and lobby,
trade favors, peddle influence, gossip, boondoggle and, above all, take
part in colorful feuds for the delectation of newspaper readers everywhere.

An exaggeration of course, but Washington was easy to poke fun at. It
was a sort of sitting lame duck for conservative writers who gleefully
pointed to whopping inefficiencies, pullulating paper work, labyrinthine
bureaucracies, overlapping jurisdictions and a steady stream of executive
directives. (FDR issued more executive orders during his Presidency than
all previous Presidents combined.) "Washington Wonderland," they called
it; "A red-tape-snarled, swarming, sweating metropolis"; "an insane asylum run by the inmates"; or in the words of a taxi driver: "the greatest
goddamn insane asylum of the universe."

Overcrowding was Washington's most obvious physical symptom. Since
1940, more than 280,000 government job seekers had poured into town
to hold down jobs as clerks and typists in the burgeoning wartime
bureaucracy. Most of them were girls; most came from small towns all
across the nation. They were drawn by the lure of higher wages — a girl
could make $1,600 a year as a typist — and though they reveled in their
newfound affluence, they could never get over the high prices, at which
they clucked and shook their heads like tourists.

They were set down into a sort of Dogpatch with monuments, plagued
by an acute housing shortage, overburdened and capricious public transportation, a cost of living that gobbled up their salaries (that government
typist making $1,600 was lucky if she saved $25 in a year) and temporary
office buildings that were as homey to work in as a railroad station.

Washington's housing shortage became an overused comic premise in
movies and plays about the city, but to the people who lived there it was

not always so funny. People paid $24 or $35 or more a month for glorified cubicles or jammed into shabby boardinghouses. They jostled for bathroom access with a herd of fellow boarders and were lucky if they could get a bath once every ten days. Landladies discouraged women tenants because they were wont to do their own laundry, request kitchen privileges and entertain gentlemen callers in the parlor. "Men, on the other hand," observed one concierge, "don't wash anything but themselves and eat all their meals out."

Hotels limited guests to a three-day stay. Hospitals had reverted to something out of Dickens; it was the practice to induce childbirth, for otherwise a room might not be available at the right time. . . .

For a family — especially a family with children — it was nearly impossible to find a place. Pathetic want ads appeared in the newspapers: "Won't someone help a refined enlisted Navy man and wife, employed, no children, to obtain an unfurnished room or two with kitchen?" Houses for sale were flagrantly overpriced, and people in Georgetown bought up old, run-down houses for $3,000, renovated them and sold them for five times what they had paid. Renting a house was dearer yet: tiny Georgetown houses rented for a minimum of $250 a month, and some larger houses in other neighborhoods that were by no means mansions were going for $1,000 a month. After President Roosevelt's death, the thought quickly occurred to a lot of people at the same time that the new President would soon be moving out of his two-bedroom, $120-a-month, rent-controlled apartment. The switchboard at Mr. Truman's building was jammed with calls; the operator told each caller that the President had already promised the apartment to at least three people. . . .

Uniforms were everywhere, representing a rainbow of international military pageantry. At night American soldiers and sailors crowded into the little nightclubs, and Washington night life boomed as it never had before or since. As part of its hospitality to servicemen, Washington offered, in addition to man-starved G-girls ("Washington is the loneliest town," one of them said), the highest VD-contraction rate among servicemen of any city in the country. . . .

Like housing, office space was in short supply, even with the ugly new temporary buildings. The government resorted to pressuring businesses and private residents to move out, and the President spoke darkly of "parasites" — useless people occupying vitally needed space. About the only solution to the office shortage was for the government to move out of town. This it did, in part, setting up branch offices in Richmond, New York, Chicago, St. Louis, Cincinnati, Kansas City, Philadelphia and Baltimore. More than 35,000 government employees moved out, too. . . .

In 1942 the world's largest office building was completed across the Potomac near Arlington. Called the Pentagon, its labyrinthine corridors and offices housed 35,000 office workers. When people wondered what in the world the War Department would do with such an enormous building in peacetime, the President explained that it would be used to store government records and quartermaster supplies, which seemed to satisfy everybody.

STUDY GUIDE

1. World War II brought an end to the widespread unemployment of the Great Depression. Is there any hint in the author's narrative of a regret on the part of the nation that it took a war — and a massive one at that — to pull the country out of the Depression?

2. What impression do you get of the spirit of the nation in its newly found prosperity and employment: a sense of dedication to the war effort; gratitude to the government for a job and a weekly income; sadness that a war was going on?

3. How did the federal government respond to the *social* needs of war workers? Was housing for workers planned as well or as extensively by the government as, for example, munitions plants or airplane factories? Support your answer with evidence from the essay.

4. What similarities and what differences do you find between the behavior of teenagers during the war and their attitudes and activities today? Do you feel, on the basis of this essay, that there was more or less juvenile delinquency during World War II than there is in our contemporary society?

5. On the basis of this essay, would you conclude that marital relationships during World War II were better or worse than marriages are today?

6. The title of Richard Lingeman's book is *Don't You Know There's a War On?* What is the author trying to suggest by this title?

BIBLIOGRAPHY

The volume from which this selection was taken — Richard R. Lingeman, *Don't You Know There's a War On?: The American Home Front, 1941–1945* (1970) — provides an entertaining account of the American people during World War II. Contemporary accounts of social developments during World War II include the following: Francis E. Merrill, *Social Problems on the Home Front* (1948); William F. Ogburn, ed., *American Society in Wartime* (1943); and Jack Goodman, ed., *While You Were Gone* (1946), a series of essays on American life during the war. A recent and more comprehensive and scholarly description of the war's impact on the nation is Richard Polenberg, *War and Society: The United States, 1941–1945* (1972). Informative and interesting recent publications are Geoffrey Perret, *Days of Sadness, Years of Triumph* (1973); William Manchester, *The Glory and the Dream: A Narrative History of America, 1932–1972* (1974); and Lisle A. Rose, *The Long Shadow: Reflections on the Second World War Era* (1978).

VI AFFLUENCE AND ITS DISCONTENTS

The material well-being of the American people during the decades since the end of World War II contrasts sharply with their poverty during the Great Depression of the 1930s. While not all Americans shared equally in the postwar prosperity, most enjoyed a standard of living far higher than that of previous generations. Furthermore, American influence abroad also reached its zenith following the end of World War II.

But the decades following the end of World War II were also marked by internal insecurities and divisions and external wars that belied the façade of confidence and contentment. In the Truman-Eisenhower years, from 1945 to 1960, the second Red Scare and the Korean War disturbed and divided the nation. Three assassinations in the 1960s, of John F. Kennedy, Robert Kennedy, and Martin Luther King, Jr., provided further proof that social and political stability do not necessarily go hand in hand with material prosperity and national power. Despite Lyndon B. Johnson's announcement of the "Great Society" and Richard Nixon's promise "to bring the American people together," developments from the mid-1960s to the late 1970s showed clearly that neither vision was being fulfilled. Instead, conflict and crisis seemed to rule. The sixties saw protest movements and bitter disagreements over the Vietnam War; the seventies, Watergate, the energy crisis, and the Iranian hostage crisis. Public opinion polls showed that Americans were increasingly disillusioned with their society, particularly their political institutions and leaders.

The essays in this section reflect the widely varying experiences of our nation since the end of World War II. In the first, Landon Y. Jones looks at the baby boom and the move to suburbia that postwar affluence made possible. The next two deal with two of the significant attacks on the status quo in the 1960s, the civil rights movement and the counterculture. The fourth examines the experiences of the soldiers who fought the Vietnam War. The last describes recent changes in Americans' sexual behavior and attitudes.

Suburbia — the home of the baby boom.

17

LANDON Y. JONES

The Baby Boom

A popular television program of not too long ago was set in the 1950s. The title, "Happy Days," reflects not only nostalgia for a previous, presumably happier era, but also the feelings of many Americans at the time. To be sure, the Cold War was an ever-present fact of life, and the prospect of nuclear destruction was terrifyingly real. There were unresolved racial tensions in the nation, McCarthyism revealed the excesses that a fear of political dissent might lead to, and many social commentators were disturbed by what they saw as a trend toward an all-encompassing and deadening conformity in American life. Yet, life for most Americans was quite pleasant. They had endured the worst depression and the largest foreign war that the nation had ever experienced, and felt, understandably, that they were due for a little enjoyment. And they were able to afford it. During World War II, there had been an unintentional and unforeseen redistribution of income which significantly improved the economic condition of the middle class. This, in turn, became the foundation for an extended period of virtually uninterrupted prosperity. More Americans had more disposable income than ever before in the nation's history, and this affluence affected all other aspects of American society during the 1950s.

One important result was the move to suburbia. With large numbers now able to buy their own homes, Americans streamed out from the center cities in search of the traditional good life to be found in one's own house on one's own plot of land. They usually conducted the search in a ranch-style house with a picture window instead of in the rose-covered cottage with white picket fence of folklore. But while the architecture was new, the values and aspirations of those living inside were comfortably old-fashioned.

The resurgence of traditional values in the 1950s can be seen in the centrality of family life. Seldom, if ever before, had the family received as much attention or praise as it did at this time. Popular magazines praised the virtues of "Togetherness"; a family room to serve as the home's social center was almost a necessity in all new houses. Popular novels such as *The Man in the Gray Flannel Suit* by Sloan Wilson showed heroes who chose family solidarity over wealth, power and success, and women were told in all sorts of ways by all sorts of cultural authorities that they truly belonged in the home and that their proper role was to ensure that their husbands and children were healthy, happy, and well-adjusted.

And, finally, there was the baby boom, an unprecedented increase in the birthrate that flabbergasted demographers who had been serenely confident that Americans would have fewer babies than before. Instead, they proceeded to have more than ever, faster than ever. In retrospect, we can see that the baby boom was closely tied to many of the social trends of the 1950s. The following selection by Landon Y. Jones examines some of the connections.

In the early 1950s, the huge Census Clock in Washington was clicking like a runaway taxi meter. Every seven seconds the Birth Light blinked off a new baby. Boys were arriving with familiar names like Robert, John, James, Michael, William, Richard, Joseph, Thomas, Steven, and David, making a Top Ten of favorite names that was proudly all-American. Girls were named Linda, Mary, Barbara, Patricia, Susan, Kathleen, Carol, Nancy, Margaret, and Diane. And perhaps thanks to Debbie Reynolds, "Deborah" would have a run all of her own later in the decade.

Like the steel industry, mothering was running at close to 100 percent capacity, and it was harder and harder to keep up. In January of 1952, General Electric decided to celebrate its seventy-fifth anniversary by awarding five shares of common stock to any employee who had a baby on October 15. Some public-relations whiz tried to predict the eventual number of winners by dividing the total of 226,000 G.E. employees by the U.S. crude birthrate. Unfortunately, he forgot that G.E. workers as a population were considerably more fertile than the United States as a whole, since they contained no one under 17 nor over 65. In the end, the

Reprinted by permission of The Putnam Publishing Group from *Great Expectations: America and the Baby Boom Generation* by Landon Y. Jones. Copyright © 1980 by Landon Y. Jones.

company's guess that thirteen G.E. babies would be born amounted to underestimation on a grand scale. The workers, true to the thriving surplus economy of the era, came through with no less than 189 new G.E. babies that day.

But General Electric was not about to complain. It was investing $650 million in new plants and assembly lines over seven postwar years to prepare for the boom in babies. As early as 1948, *Time* noted that the U.S. population had just increased by "2,800,000 more consumers" (*not* babies) the year before. Economists happily predicted that the new babies would set off a demand explosion for commodities such as homes, foodstuffs, clothing, furniture, appliances, and schools, to name only a few examples. *Fortune* pronounced the baby boom "exhilarating" and with an almost-audible sigh of relief concluded that the low birthrates of the 1930s were a "freakish interlude, rather than a trend." "We need not stew too much about a post-armament depression," the magazine wrote. "A civilian market growing by the size of Iowa every year ought to be able to absorb whatever production the military will eventually turn loose."

As the economic and baby booms surged on together, the cheerleading became almost feverish. Public-service signs went up in New York City subways reading, "Your future is great in a growing America. Every day 11,000 babies are born in America. This means new business, new jobs, new opportunities." After-dinner speakers began to talk about "Prosperity by Population" and lofted tantalizing guesses of up to five million new babies a year by 1975. Financial magazines editorialized about the joys of "this remarkable boom." "Gone, for the first time in history," announced *Time* in 1955, "is the worry over whether a society can produce enough goods to take care of its people. The lingering worry is whether it will have enough people to consume the goods."

The most euphoric article of all, perhaps, was a story *Life* printed in 1958, at the height of the boom. Three dozen children were crowded onto the cover along with the banner headline: KIDS: BUILT-IN RECESSION CURE — HOW 4,000,000 A YEAR MAKE MILLIONS IN BUSINESS. Inside, the article began with another headline — ROCKETING BIRTHS: BUSINESS BONANZA — and continued chockablock with statistics and photographs about new citizens who were "a brand-new market for food, clothing, and shelter." In its first year, *Life* calculated, a baby is not just a child but already a prodigious consumer, "a potential market for $800 worth of products." Even before returning from the hospital, an infant had "already rung up $450 in medical expenses." Four-year-olds are not just sugar and spice or puppy-dog tails but rather represent a "a backlog of business orders that will take two decades to fulfill." A rhapsodic *Life* then clinched its case by visiting Joe Powers, a thirty-five-year-old salesman from Port Washington, New York. He and his wife, Carol, had produced ten children and were buying

77 quarts of milk and 28 loaves of bread a week, just for starters. Faced with examples like that of meritorious devotion to the Procreation Ethic, little wonder that some American mothers felt as if it were their *duty* to have children. Either they were pregnant or, if not, wondered whether they should be.

The baby-boom kids had kicked off in America a buccaneering orgy of buying and selling that carried all things before it. The only thing like it earlier was the Gilded Age of the post–Civil War 1870s, which the historian Vernon Louis Parrington so aptly dubbed "the Great Barbecue." Here was a feast spread out for an entire nation, and everyone scrambling for it. More food was spoiled than eaten, perhaps, and the revelry was a bit unseemly, but no one minded. Everywhere people were getting rich in a demographic debauch.

The spending boom started, literally, at the bottom. Diapers went from a $32-million industry in 1947 to $50 million in 1957. The diaper services (disposables had not yet arrived) also prospered. Mothers and fathers were paying $5 million annually (twice the preboom business) to have baby's shoes bronze-plated at L.E. Mason, Inc., in Boston. The under-5 appetite, which had grown from 13 million mouths to 20 million by 1960, more than one out of every ten Americans, was consuming baby food at a rate of 1.5 billion cans a year in 1953 (up from 270 million cans in 1940).

As the kids grew up, so did the markets. Throughout the 1950s, the 5–13 age group grew by an additional one million baby boomers every year. The toy industry set sales records annually after 1940, growing from an $84-million-a-year stripling to a $1.25-billion giant. Sales of bicycles doubled to two million a year; cowboy outfits became a $75-million sub-industry; space-science toys claimed another $60 million. Children's clothes became a boom market, and packaging researchers suddenly discovered the troika of "family" sizes — Giant, Economy, and Supereconomy. At its peak, the juvenile market was ringing up a staggering $33 billion annually.

The rain of spending did not fall evenly on society. Rather, it was both a cause and an effect of what amounted to the opening of a new American frontier: the suburbs. Historians had already suggested that America's expansiveness during the nineteenth century was built on the common goal of settling the West. Now there was a new impetus behind the conquering of the suburban frontier: babies. The suburbs were conceived for the baby boom — and vice versa. Here in green garlands around the cities, Americans were creating new child-oriented societies, "babyvilles" teeming with new appetites, new institutions, and new values. Families who were asked why they moved to the suburbs first mentioned better housing and leisure, as if they were conforming to the old goal of a country place that began with the French aristocracy. But then, invariably, they added that they thought suburbia was "a better place to bring up the kids." The common acceptance of this goal united the suburbs. "Instead of the wagon train, where people leaned on one another as they moved across the continent," historian Daniel Boorstin remarked, "Americans in suburbs leaned on one another as they moved rapidly about the country and up the ladder of consumption." Author William H. Whyte found the same communal spirit in his examination of the mythical suburb of Park Forest. Families shared baby-sitters, cribs, lawn mowers, tea services, and baseball equipment. "We laughed at first at how the Marxist society had finally arrived," one suburban executive told Whyte. "But I think the real analogy is to the pioneers."

As an internal migration, the settling of the suburbs was phenomenal. In the twenty years from 1950 to 1970, the population of the suburbs doubled from 36 million to 72 million. No less than 83 percent of the total population growth in the United States during the 1950s was in the suburbs, which were growing fifteen times faster than any other segment of the country. As people packed and moved, the national mobility rate leaped by 50 percent. The only other comparable influx was the wave of European immigrants to the United States around the turn of the century. But, as *Fortune* pointed out, more people moved to the suburbs every year than had ever arrived on Ellis Island.

By now, bulldozers were churning up dust storms as they cleared the land for housing developments. More than a million acres of farmland were plowed under every year during the 1950s. Millions of apartment-dwelling parents with two children were suddenly realizing that two children could be doubled up in a spare bedroom, but a third child cried loudly for something more. The proportion of new houses with three or more bedrooms, in fact, rose from one-third in 1947 to three-quarters by 1954. The necessary *Lebensraum* could only be found in the suburbs. There was a housing shortage, but young couples armed with VA and FHA loans built their dream homes with easy credit and free spending habits that were unthinkable to the baby-boom grandparents, who shook their heads with the Depression still fresh in their memories. Of the 13 million homes built in the decade before 1958, 11 million of them — or 85 percent — were built in the suburbs. Home ownership rose 50 percent between 1940 and 1950, and another 50 percent by 1960. By then, one-fourth of *all* housing in the United States had been built in the fifties. For the first time, more Americans owned homes than rented them.

We were becoming a land of gigantic nurseries. The biggest were built by Abraham Levitt, the son of poor Russian-Jewish immigrants, who had originally built houses for the Navy during the war. The first of three East Coast Levittowns went up on the potato fields of Long Island. Exactly $7900 — or $60 a month and no money down — bought you a Monopoly-board bungalow with four rooms, attic, washing machine, outdoor barbecue, and a television set built into the wall. The 17,447 units eventually became home to 82,000 people, many of whom were pregnant or wanted to be. In a typical story on the suburban explosion, one magazine breathlessly described a volleyball game of nine couples in which no less than five of the women were expecting.

Marketers were quick to spot what amounted to capitalism's Klondike Lode. "Anybody who wants to sell anything to Americans should take a long look at the New Suburbia," marveled *Fortune* in 1953. "It is big and lush and uniform — a combination made to order for the comprehending marketer." It went far beyond toys and diapers. In suburbia's servantless society, laborsaving devices were necessary adjuncts to having children. The number of washing machines sold in America went from 1.7 million in 1950 to 2.6 million in 1960. Sales of electric clothes dryers doubled during one two-year stretch. With a then-astonishing average family income of $6500 (compared to $3800 for everyone else), the suburbanites were creating an American way of spending organized around children and the needs they created. Retailers eagerly followed them to the suburbs, opening branch stores by the dozen and clearing the way for the later age of shopping malls.

The settlers of suburbia also brought with them beasts of burden. They had Fords in their future — and Chevys and De Sotos and Hudsons and Studebakers. The car, especially the second car, was the one indispensable suburban accessory. Car registrations soared along with the birthrate: from 26 million in 1945 to 40 million in 1950 to 60 million by the end of the decade. The number of two-car families rose 750,000 a year and doubled from 1951 to 1958. Station wagons, the housewife's version of the Willys Jeep, began crisscrossing the suburbs like water bugs, dropping off husbands, picking up children, stopping by the supermarket. "A suburban mother's role is to deliver children obstetrically once," said Peter De Vries, "and by car forever after." *Time* joked that "if the theory of evolution is still working, it may well one day transform the suburban housewife's right foot into a flared paddle, grooved for easy traction on the gas pedal and brake."

Even in those days, the automobile had seized its central place in the emotional life of the baby boom. It was the first entire generation to be driven before it walked. It was the first generation to grow up in cars, even to seek its entertainment in cars. Back in 1933 a chemicals manufacturer named Richard Hollinshead had turned a parking lot in Camden, New Jersey, into the World's First Automobile Movie Theatre. Fifteen years later, there were only 480 drive-ins in the country. But between 1948 and 1958 the number zoomed to 4000, equipped with everything from playgrounds for the kids to Laundromats for Mom. For millions of baby-boom parents, a night at the drive-in neatly solved the suburban dilemma of what to do if you couldn't get a baby-sitter. Much later, the adolescent baby boomers would find their own use for the passion pits. Here is Lisa Alther in *Kinflicks:*

> Mixed with the dialogue were the various sighs and gasps and sucking sounds from the front seats and blasts from car horns throughout the parking area as, in keeping with Hullsport High tradition, couples signalled that they'd gone all the way.

Nowhere was the postwar baby-suburb-car symbiosis more symbolically apparent than during the gasoline shortage of July 1979 in the Philadelphia suburb of Levittown, Pennsylvania. There some 75,000 people live on 7000 acres of suburb. But, for a city of such density, it is served by little mass transportation. Threatened by the loss of their cars, angry young Levittowners staged the nation's first gas riot, burning cars, stoning ambulances, and battling police. Ironically, many of the 195 who were arrested belonged to the same families who had originally settled there during the baby-boom years and who, in 1960, won the Little League World Series for Levittown.

Meanwhile, the suburbs continued to grow and prosper and create a whole new sequence of bench marks for American Studies teachers. In 1956, white-collar workers outnumbered blue-collar workers for the first time. In 1970, the suburbs became the largest single sector of the nation's population, exceeding both central cities and the farms. By 1972, the suburbs were even offering more jobs than the central cities. Everyone was enthusiastically buying "on time" (as it was called then), and the number of Americans who thought installment financing was a good thing increased from 50 percent to 60 percent in ten years.

Sociologists began to pursue the suburbanites like doctors after a new virus. The baby-boom parents were poked and prodded and examined with the kind of fascination hitherto reserved for South Sea Islanders. They were, to be sure, pioneering a life-style (the dread word first came into currency then) that would be predominant in America. Often living in small houses filled with children, they moved outside to their patios and barbecue pits and created a new, rigorously informal style. Lawn and porch furniture sales went from $53 million in 1950 to $145 million in 1960. Hot dog production likewise zoomed from 750 million pounds to more than 2 billion pounds in the decade. Everyone first-named everyone and no one criticized the neighbor's kids (at least in front of a neighbor). Books of the time began to portray a strange netherworld of rathskellers and dens, of cheese dips and cocktails (the required icebreakers in a highly mobile society), of Kaffeeklatsches and card parties, and of outer-directed husbands and neurotic corporate wives.

Some of these studies no doubt revealed more of the anxieties of the examiners than the examined. (Did ordinary citizens really have "identity crises"?) But, if there was a common message, it was of the *sameness* of suburbia. It was as if the same forces that produced prosperity and fertility also produced homogeneity. Parents had rediscovered the old verities — home, hearth, children, church. But they had also made a faith out of brand names, modular housing, and gray flannel suits. Everywhere were the same drugstores, the same franchises, the same music on the radio. The children, too, were being shaped by a world of repeatable experience. But they were not being molded by their parents or their teachers. Instead, there was another dominant presence in the early lives of the baby boomers. It was one that would forge their unity as a generation. It would mobilize them as a consumer force. It was television. In 1938, E. B. White prophesied that "television is going to be the test of the modern world and . . . in this new opportunity to see beyond the range of our vision we shall discover either a new and unbearable disturbance of the general peace or a saving radiance in the sky. We shall stand or fall by television — of that I am quite sure." In the year White wrote that, barely 2 percent of American families owned the small, flickering Philcos and DuMonts dwarfed in their elephantine cabinets. But in less than a decade, the age of television swept over us. From fewer than 6000 sets manufactured at the baby boom's outset in 1946, production leaped, almost impossibly, to 7 million a year by 1953. Eighty-six percent of American homes had television sets at the end of the decade and, by 1967, 98 percent of all homes had sets, effectively saturating the market. The exponential growth curve of television was steeper than that of any other technological innovation of the century — including the telephone, radio, and automobile.

It was also the most important new child-care development of the century, one that would redefine the environment in which Americans grew up. Some of the oldest baby-boomers remember when the first sets were lugged into their homes. But, for most, television was not an intruder in the home but what Buckminster Fuller called "the third parent," practically a family member itself. These children treated the glowing box not with the awe due a mysterious and wonderful invention but with the unquestioned familiarity of an old armchair or the kitchen sink.

Families wanted to stay home in the 1950s, and television made it easier. Aside from the growth in drive-ins, movies almost withered away during the baby-boom years. In 1946, the first year of the boom, Hollywood had recorded its biggest year ever: 400 features were released and 90 million went to the movies every week. Then in 1947, movie attendance dropped 10 percent as parents stayed home with their babies. By January 1953, when a record 50 million of them watched another baby-boom mother, Lucy Ricardo, have her baby on *I Love Lucy,* movie attendance had been cut to one-half the 1946 level, despite such lures as 3-D movies. (The first was *Bwana Devil* in 1952.) With most of its screens located in emptying downtowns instead of expanding suburbs — in New York City alone, 55 theaters closed in 1951 — Hollywood lost an audience it would not even begin to reclaim until it squeezed theaters into suburban malls twenty years later.

Television, meanwhile, was giving the baby-boom children a series of vivid images that would color their memories forever. They all sang "M-I-C-K-E-Y M-O-U-S-E" with Karen and Doreen. (In those days, no one noticed that there were no black or Asian or Hispanic Mouseketeers.) They grew up glued to *Howdy Doody*, part of a vast Peanut Gallery in a national Doodyville. Mr. Bluster was a faintly disguised Ike, and as author Jeff Greenfield has observed, Clarabell was the original Yippie. Two decades later, in the aftermath of the Vietnam antiwar strife, Buffalo Bob and Howdy put together a road show that offered a burned-out student generation a return to a childhood myth that somehow seemed more real, or at least comforting, than the 1960s had been.

The baby-boom parents themselves were mirrored in nuclear-family dramas like *The Adventures of Ozzie and Harriet, Father Knows Best*, and *The Life of Riley*. Yet, on TV at least, the birthrate remained surprisingly low — evidently the bumbling Ozzie Nelsons and Chester A. Rileys were a lot more savvy about some family matters than their children ever could have suspected. (*The Brady Bunch*, with its amalgam of six children by two different marriages, was more of a postboom family that arrived ahead of its time.) Perhaps the prototypical baby-boom family was the Cleavers in *Leave It to Beaver*. Beaver Cleaver could have been penned by Norman Rockwell as a sort of Tom Sawyer relocated in Pasadena. The rumor that the actor who played Beaver, Jerry Mathers, had been killed later in Vietnam seemed cruelly symbolic of the death of the generation's own innocence. (The reality was, if anything, even more appropriate: Mathers had actually gone from selling insurance to real estate, while his klutzy buddy, Eddie Haskell, had really become a cop with the Los Angeles Police Department.)

At the same time, the television series the baby boomers watched were relentlessly programming a vision of the American family that was either unrealistic or unattainable. No one, as Jeff Greenfield has pointed out, is ever alone in Televisionland. There is little real despair. Problems can be worked out and almost always are. More TV parents are widowed than divorced. Anger is cute, rarely ugly. A child who would believe television would believe that most problems are soluble, usually within the half hour, and that sacrifices and compromises rarely involve human pain. Beaver Cleaver never had to worry that his parents would announce a trial separation. And if Ozzie Nelson had a drinking problem or was otherwise unemployable — why else was he always hanging around the house? — no one worried about it. . . .

Television also gave the baby boom its first lessons in the little dishonesties of adult life. The numbing repetition of Saturday-morning ads for candied cereals and electric toys did not turn every child into a drooling consumer. Many of them simply developed built-in truth detectors. They assumed that the commercials were less than truthful, that grown-ups lied, and made judgments accordingly. (Was Watergate really a surprise to the TV generation?) Television comedies further presented an image of domestic life based largely on trickeries. How would Lucy Ricardo hide from Ricky the awful truth of her shopping spree? Would Ralph Cramden lure Norton into his latest get-rich-quick scheme? Adult life had lost its mystery. "We grew up old," said Joyce Maynard. "We are the cynics who see the trap door in the magic show, the pillow stuffing in Salvation Army Santa Clauses, the camera tricks in TV commercials." . . .

We will now be led for the rest of this century and into the next one by the first generation born and bred on television. It would be foolish to think that television is the sole decisive factor in their lives. We still know relatively little about the way television has altered our sensibilities and our capacity to think and act. But no product of technology is more intimately involved with the people of the boom generation than television. From *Howdy Doody* to the streets of Chicago in 1968, the baby boomers sought to validate and legitimatize their life on television. Television has molded their style and controlled their daily habits. It has helped bind them to their peers while driving wedges between them and their parents. It has given them economic power and a spurious sense of omnipotence. It has given them sophistication without understanding. It has taught that self-gratification is no farther away than the off-on switch.

Now the first young generation raised on television is becoming the first generation of parents who have spent their lives with television. If we know little about how television affected them as children, we know even less about its long-term effects on adults. The baby boom is the first generation of adults whose attitudes about marriage, family, and consumption were formed during a lifetime of television use. It will eventually become the first generation of elderly people to have grown up with television. How will that life stage be altered? The worrisome question that remains is whether we will become the masters of this powerful medium — or vice versa.

STUDY GUIDE

1. What social conditions existed in the late 1940s and early 1950s that might explain the origins of the baby boom? Why, contrary to all expectations, did Americans have so many children during this period?

2. What were some of the consequences of the affluence of the postwar period besides paving the road to suburbia and making the baby boom possible?

3. Like the 1950s, the current period is one in which there is a greater than usual expression of reverence for the family and the traditional values the family supposedly represents. Is this rooted in something similar to the social conditions that existed in the 1950s? In what other ways does the current period resemble that decade?

4. Several of the television shows mentioned in the article are being rerun in syndication. Watch some of them to see what they seem to indicate about the period when they were first made. What strikes you about them? How does the life they depict resemble or differ from what you are familiar with? If there are differences, are they due to differences between the 1950s and the present day or to the differences between the real world and the world as it exists on television?

BIBLIOGRAPHY

Eric Goldman, *The Crucial Decade — and After: America, 1945–1960* (1960) gives an overall view of America during the postwar period. Charles C. Alexander, *Holding the Line: The Eisenhower Era, 1952–1959* (1975) focuses primarily on political matters but also deals with American society. John Kenneth Galbraith, *The Affluent Society* (1959) shows how American life has been affected by the nation's wealth. Herbert J. Gans, *The Levittowners: Ways of Life and Politics in a New Suburban Community* (1967) and William Whyte, *The Organization Man* (1956) both deal with life in suburbia. David Riesman, et al., *The Lonely Crowd* (1950) was one of the most widely read non-fiction books of the 1950s. An important cultural document in its own right, it also offers stimulating interpretations of American society. Erik Barnouw, *Tube of Plenty: The Evolution of American Television* (1975) is a good general view of the development of the medium. Horace Newcomb, *TV: The Most Popular Art* (1974) analyzes the content and meaning of several television programs, including most of those mentioned in this selection. The book from which the selection is taken, Landon Y. Jones, *Great Expectations: America and the Baby Boom Generation* (1980) repays reading in its entirety. It not only deals in great detail with the social factors that produced the baby boom, but also takes the story of the baby boom generation forward into the 1960s and 1970s, providing interesting insights into these decades.

Charles Moore/Black Star

Those working for civil rights, like these demonstrators in Birmingham, Alabama, were often victims of violence.

18

DOUG McADAM

The Struggle for Civil Rights

One can make a good argument that for most of the period since World War II the single most important domestic issue in the United States has been the struggle to achieve equality for black Americans. Slavery was destroyed after the Civil War, but it was quickly replaced by a system of "second-class citizenship" for blacks, which included segregation, denial of equal access to education, jobs, and political power, and the general assumption by the majority of white Americans that blacks were inherently and unalterably inferior. While challenges to this system were never entirely absent, it remained remarkably intact until well into the twentieth century, particularly in the South, where "Jim Crow," a system of laws requiring racial segregation and including the nearly universal deprivation of blacks' right to vote, was an inescapable fact of life.

Attacks on the system began to accelerate, however, during and after World War II. Two particularly important events occurred in the mid-1950s. In 1954 the Supreme Court struck a major blow against one of the most important bastions of the whole system of Jim Crow when it held that racial segregation in public education was unconstitutional. In 1955 blacks took another significant "stride toward freedom" with their boycott of city buses in Montgomery, Alabama. This marked a turning point in the struggle for black equality in several ways. First, it was the occasion for the rise to national prominence and leadership of Dr. Martin Luther King, Jr., who was to remain until his assassination in 1968 the most important spokesman for the idea of the civil rights movement as a moral crusade. Second, it marked the first widespread use of direct mass action by blacks themselves, a tactic that was to be used over and over again in the

285

civil rights struggles of the 1960s (and in the other protest movements of that decade as well). Third, it was a direct challenge to Jim Crow in the very heart of Jim Crow country.

For the next ten years, from 1955, when the Montgomery bus boycott was begun, to 1965, when President Lyndon Johnson signed the Voting Rights Act into law, the South was the major focus of civil rights activity in the United States, direct mass action was the preferred method of attack, and the primary target was Jim Crow, that massive system of racial segregation and subordination written into the laws of the southern states. While many individuals and organizations were involved in the struggle, the spearhead of the movement in the early 1960s was SNCC (pronounced "Snick"), the Student Nonviolent Coordinating Committee. Early in its existence, it turned to the attempt to build permanent political power for southern blacks as the shortest path to the ultimate goal of racial equality. In the summer of 1964, the leaders of SNCC conceived the idea of "Freedom Summer," during which hundreds of volunteers, mostly white college students from the North, were to conduct a massive voter registration drive in Mississippi, the poorest state in the nation and the one in which the racial situation was universally regarded as the most oppressive. The following selection by Doug McAdam tells part of the story of that summer's effort, giving an insight into the kind of opposition the civil rights movement encountered and the type of courage it took to challenge the racial status quo.

For most of the volunteers, Freedom Summer began not in Mississippi, but at the Western College for Women in Oxford, Ohio. There, in mid-June, the National Council of Churches sponsored two, week-long orientation sessions for volunteers accepted for work in Mississippi. The first session was held June 14–20 and was tailored to those who were to work in voter registration. A second session, for Freedom School teachers, was held the following week.

If the volunteers had expected a languid, leisurely week in the early summer freshness of rural Ohio, they were to be disappointed. The intensity that was to mark the entire summer was very much in evidence at Oxford. It is interesting that the volunteers interviewed have retained so few specific memories of orientation or of the summer itself. They seem to attribute this to the fact that the events in question occurred nearly twenty-five years ago. In contrast, they usually have very detailed memories of events *prior* to the summer, such as when and how they heard about the project in the first place. Possibly the reason for the lack of specific memories is simply the pace of events that summer. Things happened too quickly to allow time for the reflection required to commit specific events to long-term memory. The volunteers were feeling, seeing, experiencing too much.

Some of the intensity of the experience owed to the specific activities planned for the week. The volunteers were subjected to a daunting schedule of general assemblies, section meetings, and work groups. The general assemblies brought all the volunteers together to hear what amounted to broad orientation sessions on Mississippi or some aspect of the movement. Sometimes staff members spoke at these assemblies; more often, it was invited speakers from outside the project. Established civil right leaders, such as Bayard Rustin, Vincent Harding, and James Lawson, spoke. So too did native Mississippians, trying to give the volunteers a better understanding of their state. Jess Brown, one of only three civil rights lawyers in the state, apprised the volunteers of the "unique" quality of Mississippi justice. Long-time state civil rights leader, Aaron Henry, gave a short history of the movement in Mississippi. Even the Justice Department dispatched a representative to the orientation. In a sobering and, for many, radicalizing session, John Doar warned the volunteers not to expect federal protection while in Mississippi. "Maintaining law and order," he argued, "is a state responsibility." In the weeks to come, the volunteers would have ample opportunity to see just how Mississippi exercised that responsibility.

Section meetings were more focused planning groups involving twenty to thirty people who were expected to be engaged in the same type of work during the summer. Work groups were smaller still, consisting of between five and ten people who would actually be working with one another in Mississippi. What these smaller groups lacked in drama and emotional intensity, they made up for in relevance. It was here that the volunteers met and got to know their fellow project members and were trained in the basics of their work assignments.

The power of orientation, however, derived less from this mix of planned sessions as from the informal aspects of the experience. For many of the volunteers it was the beginning of an intensely stressful, yet exhilarating, confrontation with traditional conceptions of America, community, politics, morality, sexuality, and, above all else, themselves. What the volunteers were beginning to experience at Oxford was, to use Peter Berger's term, "ecstasy," that giddy, disorienting sense of liberation that comes from "stepping outside . . . the taken-for-granted routines of society." It was not so much a case of the volunteers *choosing* to take this step, as being compelled to do so by virtue of their contact with a project staff that had itself become more radical and alienated as a result of three long years of struggle in Mississippi. If ever a group embodied the risks and rewards of an "ecstatic" way of life, it was the SNCC veterans. The volunteers were clearly fascinated by them and drawn to the way of life they represented. One volunteer interviewed by Sarah Evans "claimed that the first night of the orientation session in Oxford changed her life 'because I met those SNCC people and my mouth fell open'." In a letter home, another volunteer, Margaret Aley, described the SNCC staff in equally glowing terms:

> I've never known people like them before; they are so full of heart and life. They are not afraid to show their emotions, they cry when they are sad; they laugh and dance when they are happy. And they sing; they sing from their hearts and in their songs they tell of life, struggle, sadness and beauty. They have a freeness of spirit that I've rarely seen. But I think that's because they don't worry about maintaining the status quo. When we arrived here Saturday, I had a feeling that I didn't belong. . . . [Now] somehow I feel like I've found something I've been looking for for a long time. I feel like I've finally come home. I now have no doubt that I belong here.

Ruth Steward put the matter a bit more succinctly. In a letter to her parents, she explained that "you can always tell a CORE or SNCC worker — they're beautiful." What these statements betray is a growing identification with the activist community and with a way of life that would later be dubbed the "counterculture."

Other aspects of the orientation sessions also reinforced this sense of identification. For many, the legions of reporters and television cameramen swarming over the campus had that effect. Their presence communicated a sense of "history-making" significance that was intoxicating. Not that the hypocrisy and sensationalism of the media was lost on the volunteers. This too was a part of the radicalizing process they were undergoing. In her beautiful book describing the Freedom Summer experience, another volunteer, Sally Belfrage, wrote of how the media

> followed us into the classrooms and dormitories, around the lounges, out along the paths. They asked people to sing that song again for the American public. There was footage, yardage, mileage of every face in the place. "At the beginning it made me feel important," a boy from Utah said at lunch. "But they have a way of degrading everything they touch." "It's because we need them more than they need us," his neighbor returned, "and they know it." "It's just their job," commented a third. "Well, I feel unclean," the boy from Utah said.

Degrading or not, the volunteers' letters home are filled with entreaties to parents to "save the *Life* magazine picture for me," or to "watch CBS tonight; I may be on." Degrading or not, the media attention clearly reinforced the volunteers' sense of their own and the project's importance.

More than anything else, however, it was the volunteers' growing appreciation of the dangers inherent in the project that had the greatest impact on them. If they had not realized the extent of these dangers before orientation, they certainly did by the time they left Ohio. This was no accident. In planning the sessions, one of the overriding goals had been to overwhelm the volunteers with the savagery and violence of life in Mississippi. It was hoped that by doing so, the staff might be able to persuade the naive or those with lingering doubts to stay home. So in session after session, staff members recounted the litany of horror they had seen in Mississippi. In turn, the volunteers duly recorded these sessions in their journals or letters home. Margaret Rose wrote:

> Last night's objective narration of facts is shot to hell by a breakdown in my defensives against fear and intimidation. The straw to break the back was the narration of a white leader here (a face mangled by scars) about a near death experience on the road coming up here. Fifteen guys in 3 cars ran them off the road (normal) and all in the car experienced the intent of the group: murder. It was somehow absolutely clear. A car full of leaders. Too good to pass over. One man, an exchange professor from Pakistan in a Mississippi university, happened to say he was a foreigner and had a passport. Some small doubt cross [sic] the minds of one of the 15. Somehow the mood shifted. They did not murder. He said we could expect this kind of encounter. He means it.

Another volunteer wrote:

> There is a quiet Negro fellow on the staff who has an ugly scar on his neck and another on his shoulder where he stopped 45 slugs. . . . Another fellow told this morning how his father and later his brother had been shot to death. . . . I'd venture to say that every member of the Mississippi staff has been beaten at least once and he who has not been shot at is rare. It is impossible for you to imagine what we are going in to, as it is for me now, but I'm beginning to see.

Role playing sessions and lessons in how to protect oneself if attacked only underscored the growing fear the volunteers were feeling. A volunteer described the general response to one such session: "John Strickland [a volunteer] stood ashen, staring at the lad curled up on the ground. Like the rest of the crowd, he was silent. Their eyes stayed riveted to the frozen tableau of a violence that till that moment had existed for them only in grade-B movies and tabloid spreads."

But no planned simulation could ever have dramatized the dangers of Mississippi life more forcefully than the real life event that took place in Neshoba County, Mississippi, on June 21, just as the second group of volunteers were arriving at Oxford, Ohio. Less than twenty-four hours after arriving in Mississippi, one in the first group of volunteers, Andrew Goodman, climbed into a station wagon with staff members James

Chaney and Michael Schwerner, and drove off to investigate a church bombing near Philadelphia, Mississippi. They never returned. Arrested in the afternoon on traffic charges, the three were held until the evening, and then released into the Mississippi night. It was the last time they were seen alive. Their burned-out station wagon was found near Bogue Chitto Swamp the next day. But it was not until August that the bodies were discovered beneath an earthen dam near Philadelphia: Chaney's showed signs of a savage beating, and Goodman's and Schwerner's, single gunshot wounds to the chest.

Back at Oxford, news of the disappearance reached the volunteers during a general assembly. Sally Belfrage describes the scene:

> There was an interruption then at a side entrance: three or four staff members had come in and were whispering agitatedly. One of them walked over to the stage and sprang up to whisper to Moses, who bent on his knees to hear. In a moment he was alone again. Still crouched, he gazed at the floor at his feet, unconscious of us. Time passed. When he stood and spoke, he was something else; it was simply that he was obliged to say something, but his voice was automatic. "Yesterday morning, three of our people left Meridian, Mississippi, to investigate a church-burning in Neshoba County. They haven't come back, and we haven't had any word from them. . . . "
> Then a thin girl in shorts was talking to us from the stage: Rita Schwerner, the wife of one of the three. She paced as she spoke, her eyes distraught and her face quite white, but in a voice that was even and disciplined . . . Rita asked us to form in groups by home areas and wire our congressmen. . . . We composed telegrams, collected money and sent them, and tried to rub out the reality of the situation with action. No one was willing to believe that the event involved more than a disappearance. It was hard to believe even that. Somehow it seemed only a climactic object lesson, part of the morning's lecture, an anecdote to give life to the words of Bob Moses. To think of it in other terms was to be forced to identify with the three, to be prepared, irrevocably, to give one's life.

Word of the disappearance did, in fact, force the volunteers to confront the possibility of their own deaths. Some, like Stuart Rawlings, did so dispassionately:

> What are my personal chances? There are 200 COFO volunteers who have been working in the state a week, and three of them have already been killed. I shall be working in Forrest County, which is reputedly less violent than Neshoba County. But I shall be working on voter registration, which is more dangerous than work in Freedom Schools or Community Centers. There are other factors which must be considered too — age, sex, experience and common sense. All considered, I think my chances of being killed are 2%, or one in fifty.

Others expressed their fears more emotionally. "The reality of Mississippi gets closer to us everyday. We know the blood is going to flow this summer and it's going to be our blood. And I'm scared — I'm very scared.". . .

Voter Registration

Voter registration was the cornerstone of the Summer Project. This is not to say that it was necessarily the most important part of Freedom Summer. However, it did supply the strategic impetus to the project. It was the success of the Freedom Vote campaign in the fall of 1963 that led SNCC and COFO to approve Bob Moses' plan for an even more ambitious political project the following summer. Originally, the plan was simply to use large numbers of white students — à la the Freedom Vote — to register as many black voters as possible. However, as long as the state Democratic party was effectively closed to blacks, it was unclear how beneficial the simple registration of voters would be. To address the problem, SNCC spearheaded the establishment of the Mississippi Freedom Democratic Party (MFDP) at a meeting held in Jackson on April 26, 1964. The MFDP then selected and ran a slate of candidates in the June 2 Democratic Primaries for Senator and three House seats. Not surprisingly, all four of the MFDP candidates (Fannie Lou Hamer, Victoria Gray, John Houston, and the Rev. John Cameron) were soundly beaten. So, following the primary, they obtained and filed the necessary number of signatures to be placed on the November ballot as independents. The Mississippi State Board of Elections rejected these petitions. Thus stymied, the SNCC/MFDP leadership returned to the strategy that had served them so well the previous fall. If they were to be shut out of regular electoral politics in the state, they would conduct a mock election to challenge the Mississippi Delegation to the August Democratic National Convention to be held in Atlantic City.

For the volunteers, this meant they would be involved in two parallel tasks: persuading blacks to attempt to register as official voters and "freedom registering" voters on behalf of the MFDP. Freedom registration forms could be filled out in the applicant's home; official registration meant a trip to the courthouse. That made the latter process the much more difficult of the two. Neither, however, was easy.

> Canvassing is very trying, you walk a little dusty street, with incredibly broken down shacks. The people sitting on porches staring away into nowhere — the sweat running down your face! Little kids half-naked in ragged clothes *all* over the place — this is what you face with your little packet of "Freedom Forms". . . . Unfortunateley [*sic*], Freedom registration is terribly [*sic*] remote to these people. I almost feel guilty — like I'm playing for numbers only; . . . you walk up to a porch, knock on a door and enter into another world. . . . The walls are inevitably covered with a funeral hall calendar, a portrait calendar of President Kennedy, old graduation pic-

tures. Maybe a new cheap lamp from Fred's dollar store.

You meet an afraid, but sometimes eager, curious face — one which is used to . . . saying "Yes Sir" to everything a white man says. . . . You see their pain, the incredible years of suffering etched in their worn faces; and then if you convince them to sign you leave. You walk down the deteriorating steps to the dirt, to the next house — the next world and start in on your sales pitch again, leaving behind something which has broken you a little more. Poverty in the abstract does nothing to you. When you wake up to it every morning, and come down through the streets of it, and see the same old man on the ground playing the accordian [sic], the same man selling peaches out of [a] basket to [sic] heavy for his twisted body, the same children, a day older — a day closer to those men — after this everyday, poverty is a reality that is so outrageous you have to learn to . . . become jaded for the moment — or else be unable to function.

I work in voter registration. . . . On a normal day we roll out of bed early in the morning. We may have slept in the Freedom House, or in the home of some generous and brave farmer. . . . We study the map of the county, decide where we will work for the day. We scramble for breakfast and hit the road.

The work is long and hot. We drive from farmhouse to farmhouse. I have averaged almost 200 miles a day in the car. The roads are in despicable condition . . . where the pavement stops the Negro sections are likely to begin. And if there is not even gravel on the roads, we can be reasonably sure that we are in a "safe" neighborhood. Such is not always the case, though, and more than once we have been cursed and threatened by someone for knocking on a white man's door.

When we walk up to a house there are always children out front. They look up and see white men in the car, and fear and caution cover their expressions. Those terrified eyes are never quite out of my mind; they drive me as little else could. Children who have hardly learned to talk are well-taught in the arts of avoiding whites. They learn "yassah" as almost their first words. If they did not, they could not survive. The children run to their parents, hide behind them. We walk up, smile, say howdy, and hold out our hands. As we shake hands I tell them my name. They tell me their names and I say Mr. ———, how do you do. It is likely the first time in the life of this farmer or housewife a white man has ever shaken hands with them, or even called them "with a handle to their names." This does not necessarily bode well with them; they are suspicious. Chances are they have heard about the "freedom riders" passing through. The news is usually greeted with mingled fear, excitement, enthusiasm and gratitude. But the confrontation is more serious and more threatening. They think, if Mr. Charlie knew . . . , and they are afraid. They have good reason to be. . . . Many . . . are sharecroppers, who must turn over a third to a half of the year's harvest to a man who does not work at all, but who owns the land they till. They may be evicted, and have often been for far less serious offenses. Nearly everyone black in Mississippi is at least a year in debt. The threat of suspended credit and foreclosure is a tremendous burden. . . .

Freedom Schools

In planning for the Summer Project, the SNCC staff was smart enough to realize that the oppression of Mississippi's black population depended on more than restricting access to the political system. An elaborate array of caste restrictions and institutional inequities also contributed to the maintenance of the racial status quo. Among these was Mississippi's separate but clearly unequal school system. . . . State educational expenditures in 1964 averaged $81.66 per white student and $21.77 for each black student. The fact that Mississippi was one of only two states without a mandatory education law merely underscored the lack of importance accorded public education. So too did other bits of evidence. At the time of the fall cotton harvest, many of the black schools in the delta were routinely closed to take advantage of the cheap source of labor the students provided. Within the classroom, curriculum content was carefully controlled. State-selected textbooks glorified the "Southern way of life" and made no mention of significant achievements by black Americans. In some districts, school superintendents even forbade the history of the Reconstruction period from being taught in the black schools. The Freedom Schools were an effort to counter the obvious inequities and insidious political messages inherent in this system.

The chief architect of the Freedom Schools was veteran SNCC field secretary Charlie Cobb. Drafted in the fall of 1963, Cobb's proposal called for the establishment of Freedom Schools "to provide an educational experience for students which will make it possible for them to challenge the myths of our society, to perceive more clearly its realities, and to find alternatives, and ultimately new directions for action." To put the necessary curricular flesh on the bones of Cobb's proposal, the National Council of Churches sponsored a March, 1964 meeting in New York City. There, educators, clergy, and SNCC staff members hammered out a basic curriculum for the schools emphasizing four principal topic areas: (1) remedial education, (2) leadership development, (3) contemporary issues, and (4) nonacademic curriculum. This basic framework was modified again following the appointment of Staughton Lynd, a history professor at Spelman, as director of the Freedom School program. In a mimeographed packet sent out just before the start of the Summer Project, the prospective teachers were informed that "the kind of activities you will be developing will fall into three general areas: (1) academic work, (2) recreation and cultural activities, (3) leadership development." In effect, the second and third topic areas designated in the original proposal had been lumped together under the single heading of "leadership development." Judging from the letters and journals written by the teachers, most projects adhered to this modified framework in organizing their Freedom School programs. Most offered a variety of basic courses in

"leadership development," or what came to be known as the core curriculum. This consisted of courses in the history and philosophy of the
movement, current events, and black history. "Academic work" was represented by nearly as many courses as there were students interested in
taking them. Offerings ranged from basic remedial courses in reading
and math to a variety of specialized classes in such topics as French, science, dance, and debate. Finally, a variety of "recreation and cultural activities" served to round out the Freedom School program. Among the
most notable of these activities were the establishment of student-run
newspapers on several projects and the writing and performing of an
original play by the students in the Holly Springs project.

By any standard, the Freedom Schools were a success. Where project
staff had hoped to attract 1,000 or so students, between 3,000 and 3,500
showed up. This in the face of a lack of facilities, the fears of black parents, and considerable violence directed at the schools. In McComb,
seventy-five students showed up for classes the morning after a bomb lev-
eled the church that had been serving as their school. Classes were held
on the lawn in front of the smoldering church while younger children
played in the ruins. In the small town of Harmony, the volunteers and
townspeople set to cleaning up and repairing four abandoned school
buildings to be used as classrooms.

> Then the sheriff came with about six white men, who were introduced as
> the "Board of Education." If they weren't Klan men, then they were at least
> Citizen Council [a more moderate segregationist group] people. God, they
> hated us ... they told us we should not use it [the school building]; it is
> county property. We told them it was private property. We are getting a
> lawyer and will fight in court. Meanwhile ... we will teach in a nearby
> church and outside.

Predictably, the court ruled in favor of the "Board of Education." Un-
daunted, the community erected its own school/community center.

> Everyday this week ... the men of the community hammered and poured
> cement. At noon, about 7 or 8 women all gathered at the center with fried
> chicken, fish, salad, gallons of Kool-Aid, and apple turnovers, and served
> them to the men, we teachers, and each other. It is a thing of beauty to see
> us all work together.... We are a living repudiation of the "too many
> cooks" theory. It should be up by Saturday, or at latest Tuesday.

Eventually construction was finished and classes were held in the new
building, if only for the final week of the summer.

In the classroom, the volunteers discovered most of the frustrations
teachers have always faced. Overcrowding was frequently a problem:

> It became evident quite early that we were going to have many more than
> the expected 75 students. We called Jackson and got a promise of more

teachers — at full strength we will have 23. This was when we expected 150 students. On registration day, however, we had a totally unexpected deluge: 600 students! . . . After a while, as they were coming in, it changed from a celebration to a crisis. This is 26 students per teacher — much better than the local or usual ratios, but still not enough . . . to do all we want to in six weeks.

Complaints about a lack of "educational standards" or "academic discipline" were common as well:

The . . . class tends to degenerate into discussion of anything from standards of Negro beauty to the Marxist view of private property. . . . They are eager to argue, in some ways less eager to learn; some days ago I was attempting to give some minimal account of certain facts, when one of the more brilliant and remarkable pupils, but somewhat headstrong, declared that no offense, but, all this was rather boring, and it would be better if other people got a chance to speak, and if we could have discussions. I often think of the difficulties which . . . we will (for these schools will be continued all year) have in making the transition from this school to one where solid academic discipline must be imposed.

Add to this list the problems of absenteeism, staff dissension, and teacher "burn out," and one might well be describing the generic teaching experience. But there was a difference. The volunteers also experienced the emotional rewards reserved for those teaching students who are there voluntarily and who are being taken seriously for perhaps the first time in their lives.

I can see the change. The 16 year-old's discovery of poetry, of Whitman and Cummings and above all else, the struggle to express thoughts in words, to translate ideas into concrete written words. After two weeks a child finally looks me in the eye, unafraid, acknowledging a bond of trust which 300 years of Mississippians said should never, could never exist — I can feel the growth of self-confidence.

The atmosphere in the class is unbelievable. It is what every teacher dreams about — real, honest enthusiasm and desire to learn anything and everything. The girls come to class of their own free will. They respond to everything that is said. They are excited about learning. They drain me of everything that I have to offer so that I go home at night completely exhausted but very happy in spirit because I know that I have given to people. . . . Every class is beautiful. The girls respond, respond, respond. And they disagree among themselves. I have no doubt that soon they will be disagreeing with me. At least this is one thing that I am working towards. They know that they have been cheated and they want anything and everything that we can given them. I feel inadequate to the task of teaching them but I keep saying to myself that as long as I continue to feel humble there is a chance that we might all learn a whole lot together.

In talking to the volunteers today it is clear that they *did* learn a lot from their experience as teachers. Some became more politically radical as a result of the courses they taught or the discussions they had with other teachers. Others altered their career plans because of the satisfaction they had derived from teaching. The schools, then, had an impact beyond the students; the teachers, too, were taught.

Life in the Black Community

While not discounting the time and energy the volunteers expended on their jobs, it may well be that work was the least demanding part of their summer experience. After all there was a certain familiarity about their work assignments. Many of those who taught either were studying to become teachers or had taught before. Those with no teaching experience had at least spent years going to school as students, so the classroom was hardly a foreign place to them. As for the voter registration workers, 76 percent had participated in some form of civil rights organizing prior to the summer.

Very few of the volunteers, however, had had experiences that prepared them for life in the black community. For one thing, few had ever lived in rural areas. Their letters capture a kind of bemused appreciation of the new experiences this afforded them.

> Man, like I don't even believe what I just did. You really had to be there to appreciate it. I took a bath. But no ordinary bath 'cause there's no running water. No, we take this bucket out in the back yard and fill it with water warmed over a fire. It's pitch black so we shine Mr. Clark's truck lights on the bucket. Then I strip down naked and stand in the bucket to wash. That is the way you take a bath around here.

> [T]here are several [chickens] and several roosters. Roosters have this habit — one sits by the window and at dawn melancholically crows in a refrain reminiscent of a man falling off a cliff. The dog outside is just thrilled by this and barks his approval. The rooster thinks about this for a while — then to show he's no party-pooper he lets go again. This sends the dog in to sheer ecstasy. A little while later they pal it up and do a duet. By this time I usually wake up for the third time convinced that someone is being murdered at the foot of my bed.

More significant and more sobering than the volunteers' introduction to rural life was their exposure to "the other America." The publicity accorded Michael Harrington's 1962 book of the same name may have made the volunteers intellectually aware of poverty, but their class advantages had insulated them from any real experiential understanding of the problem. No such comfortable distance was possible in Mississippi. The volunteers' generally optimistic, idealistic upbringing had not prepared them for the underside of the American dream.

> This was the most appalling example of deprivation ever seen by any of us who were canvassing. Upon approaching the house, we were invited on the porch which was strewn with bean shellings, rotten cotton sacks, pieces of a broken stove, and other assorted bits of scrap. . . . On a drooping cot to our right as we came in the door lay a small child (six months old). The child's eyes, nose, and mouth were covered with flies. Not being able to stand such a sight, I tried to chase them away only to be met with the reply of the mother of the child. "They will only come back again."
>
> The whole house seemed diseased, rotten, and splitting at the seams with infection. Nevertheless, the people knew what we were coming for, and the forms were filled out without our asking. . . . This is a scene that was burned into all of our minds and which will make quiet sleep impossible.

> One day has passed in Shaw and the other America is opening itself before my naive, middle-class eyes. The cockroaches draw patterns across the floor and table and make a live patchwork on the bed. Sweat covers my skin and cakes brown in my joints — wrist, elbow, knee, neck. Mosquito bites, red specks on white background.
>
> The four-year-old grandson is standing by my side. I wonder how our presence now will affect him when he is a man?
>
> I saw other children today who bore the marks of the Negro in rural Mississippi. One had a protruding navel the size of the stone he held in his hand. Several had distended stomachs.
>
> Is America really the land that greets its visitors with "Send me your tired, your poor, your helpless masses to breathe free"?
>
> There is no Golden Door in Shaw.

These images had a powerful impact on the volunteers, especially those whose upbringing had failed to provide them with even an ideological awareness of the problem. One especially sheltered volunteer, raised in an upper-middle-class suburb of Chicago, remembers "crying myself to bed at night [in Mississippi]. . . . I was just seeing too much, feeling too much. Things weren't supposed to be like this. I was just a mess. I just remember feeling sad, guilty and angry all at the same time."

In the face of these feelings — especially the guilt — the warmth, openness, and acceptance the volunteers felt from the black community was both confirming and confusing at the same time. Confirming because it communicated a kind of redemptive forgiveness that assuaged the guilt many of the volunteers were feeling; confusing because they didn't feel they deserved the special attention they were receiving. It all added up to a rich welter of feelings that left a good many of the volunteers overwhelmed. In a letter to her parents, Pam Parker struggled to communicate all she was feeling:

> I am starting to ramble because there is so much in my head and heart that I want to say but cannot. It has been a big week filled with so much enth-

siasm and love that I feel overwhelmed. The girls I work with . . . have accepted me completely. They have told me this in a way they have responded in class, and some have told me this directly in their essays they have written me or in actual conversations. . . . This abundance of love and gratitude and acceptance makes me feel so humble and so happy.

Even today this jumble of emotions is evident in the former volunteers' recollections of the summer. Elinor Tideman Aurthur movingly recalled the daily lunchtime ritual at the Freedom School where she taught.

[T]he women from the church everyday would bring food for all the teachers. . . . I used to look forward to it so much, and the fact that they would give this to us everyday, you know, was just wonderful . . . they had fried chicken and deviled eggs and potato salad. . . . They would spread it out on the table and they would, it was so nice [starts to cry] . . . it was so touching . . . to be cared for . . . that [way] . . . I felt like I belonged; I felt like they liked me and they wanted me to be there and I, it was so healing, you know, knowing what the divisions were . . . and yet somehow you can heal . . . I don't mean to say that they idealized us . . . because I don't think they did, but I think there was a kind of love . . . and a kind of compassion for us that they showed. It was a daily demonstration of love and acceptance . . . they were feeding us; they were giving us nourishment.

For many of the volunteers, the most immediate purveyors of this love and acceptance were the families that housed them. Sally Belfrage describes her introduction to her summer hostess: "[Mrs. Amos] hadn't planned to house summer volunteers, but Cora Lou's guest immediately became to her another child . . . she hugged me, fed me fried chicken and cornbread and installed me in the back bedroom."

Midway through the summer another volunteer described her "home life" to her mother:

I have become so close to the family I am staying with — eleven people — that Mrs. H. finally paid me a great compliment. She was introducing me to one of her Negro women friends and said, "This is Nancy, my adopted daughter!" I baby-sat for her one night and in general we have become very close friends. She is a beautiful mother. My favorite picture of her is sitting peacefully in a summer chair with her 2-year old baby girl in her lap; the baby, sucking her bottle, with one hand inside her mother's dress resting on her bosom. It is such a human sight; such love oozes from this house I can't begin to explain.

The hospitality of the local families was all the more touching for the risks they ran in housing the volunteers. Sheltering the "invaders" was grounds for harassment, dismissal from a job, or worse. David Gelfand relates an incident that took place while he was living with a prosperous black family in Meridian:

[D]uring the five or six days I was there, there had been numerous . . . threatening phone calls and his [the black homeowner's] wife was quite upset about it. And one morning he came and woke me up. I was sleeping on the couch in the living room. And we had put a single piece of hair on Scotch Magic Tape across the hood, so you always checked before you got in the car. And the tape was broken. He had checked it. And the carport was right next to the kids bedroom — ages four to twelve . . . And so he said, "okay, let's not do anything but release the emergency break and roll it out to the road." And we did that and then opened the hood. And there were four sticks of dynamite tied [to] . . . the ignition coil.

On occasion the volunteers were reluctantly asked to leave following incidents such as this. More often than not their hosts responded with a resiliency and toughness that impressed the volunteers. In his journal, Gren Whitman recounted the following early-morning encounter with the woman in whose house he was living:

I am writing this at 6 A.M. Just now coming down the hall from the bathroom, I met Mrs. Fairley coming down the hall from the front porch carrying a rifle in one hand [and] a pistol in the other. I do not know what is going on . . . [All she said was] "You go to sleep; let me fight for you."

Nor was this volunteer's experience unique. In their journals, letters, or interviews, many of the volunteers recounted similar incidents. For a group not raised around guns, it was yet another eye-opening aspect of the summer, and one that would lead a number of the volunteers to re-think strongly held pacifist convictions. . . .

Confrontation with White Mississippi

During the course of the summer, COFO compiled a running chronology of "hostile incidents". . . . The list is twenty-six mimeographed pages long and covers everything from threatening phone calls to the disappearance of the three workers. Oddly, instead of being viscerally powerful, the list is curiously unaffecting. The sheer number of incidents simply overwhelms the reader, leaving one emotionally numb to the specifics of any given incident. A summary of violence during the summer has much the same effect. So that the following statistics:

4	project workers killed
4	persons critically wounded
80	workers beaten
1000	arrests
37	churches bombed or burned
30	black homes or businesses bombed or burned

fail to inform in an emotional sense. To gain some empathetic understanding of these events, one really has to read the volunteers' own accounts of them. Only then does one begin to appreciate the combination of shock, anger, disillusionment, and fear the volunteers felt in the face of the violence and terror they were witnessing.

I really cannot describe how sick I think this state is. I really cannot describe the feeling in my stomach when I hear a typical story of injustice. . . . I cannot describe the real courage it takes to stay down here. I cannot describe the fears, the tensions and the uncertainties of living here. When I walk I am always looking at cars and people: if Negro, they are my friends; if white, I am frightened and walk faster. When driving, I am always asking: black? white? It is the fear and uncertainty that is maddening. I must always be on guard. . . . When confronted with a crisis, then the action is clearly defined. But when I do not know what to expect, but always know to expect something, then the tensions mount and I think of courage and of how deep my commitment has to be, and I think of getting the hell out of this sick state. I live day to day. I wake up in the morning sighing with relief that I was not bombed, because I know that "they" know where I live. And I think, well, I got through that night, now I have to get through this day, and it goes on and on. Even as I write this letter we are told that our office might be bombed by an anonymous voice, "to get rid of it once and for all."

Yesterday while the Mississippi River was being dragged looking for the three missing civil rights workers, two bodies of Negroes were found — one cut in half and one without a head. Mississippi is the only state where you can drag a river any time and find bodies you were not expecting . . . Negroes disappear down here every week and are never heard about. Things are really much better for rabbits here. There is a closed season on rabbits when they may not be killed. Negroes are killed all year round. So are rabbits. The difference is that arrests are made for killing rabbits out of season . . . Jesus Christ, this is supposed to be America in 1964.

Tonight the sickness struck. At our mass meeting, as we were singing "We Shall Overcome," a girl was shot in the side and in the chest. We fell to the floor in deathly fear; but soon we recovered and began moving out of the hall to see what had happened. . . . When I went out I saw a woman lying on the ground clutching her stomach. She was so still and looked like a statue with a tranquil smile on her face. I ran to call an ambulance.

While the presence of so many reporters in the state muted the violence to a degree, there was still no shortage of celebrated atrocities. In Greenwood a local activist, Silas McGhee, was shot in the head while he sat in his car out in front of a local club. Three volunteers raced him to the hospital only to be told they couldn't bring him in because they didn't have shirts on. They had taken their shirts off to bandage McGhee's head. On the evening of July 8, the front wall of the McComb Freedom House was destroyed by eight sticks of dynamite. Miraculously, the workers sleeping inside sustained only minor injuries. In Hattiesburg, two days later, five voter registration workers (including a rabbi visiting from Ohio) were attacked and severely beaten by two local men armed with lead pipes. And so it went, day in and day out, an endless string of incidents that lent a brutal and frightening texture to the volunteers' lives.

Had the volunteers been in their home states, they would invariably have turned to the police for protection from such incidents. Obviously, this was not practical in Mississippi. Often the police were implicated in the very incidents they were called to investigate. For instance, it turned out that Neshoba County Deputy Sheriff Cecil Price had coordinated the kidnapping and murders of Chaney, Goodman, and Schwerner. Even acting in their official capacity as law enforcement officers, the police spared few opportunities to harass or terrorize the volunteers. The following two affidavits filed by project volunteers recount typical incidents:

On July 9, 1964 Mary Lane, George Johnson and I accompanied Phillip Moore to the Greenwood Police Station. His purpose was to swear out a warrant against one of the local whites who had beaten him on the street. While Moore was thus occupied in another room, Miss Lane (Negro), Johnson (white) and I waited in the station room. There were three officers present — Desk Sergeant Simpson, Officer Logan and another unidentified officer. Logan was not in uniform — evidently off duty.

Logan took a long knife out of his pocket and started to sharpen it, [directing] a running stream of threats at the three of us. He asked Johnson how he liked "screwing that nigger" (indicating Miss Lane). Then he said, while sharpening the knife: "sounds like rubbing up against nigger pussy." He poked the knife against my ribs a few times; then he held it out toward me, told me to put my hand on it and asked: "Think it's sharp enough to cut your cock off?" Then he looked at Officer Simpson and said "You'd better get me out of here before I do what I'd like to do." At no time did Simpson or the other officer make any move to restrain him or protect us.

Shortly thereafter, he walked over behind the desk and took out a pistol from his trousers pocket. He brandished it in our direction and spun the chamber, then tucked it in his shirt front. He walked over to the door. Miss Lane was standing about eight feet from the door in front of him with her back turned to him. He took out his gun again, pointed it at Miss Lane for a few seconds and put it in his pants pocket. Then he opened the door with his left hand and simultaneously reached out and gave Miss Lane a shove with his right fist, knocking her several feet across the room. He swore at her; then Officer Simpson joined in and told Miss Lane: "Nigger, you get your ass away from that door." Miss Lane refused to move, explaining that she wasn't in the doorway, especially since Logan had knocked her practically across the room. Both the officers shouted threats at her, threatening to throw her in jail if she didn't move.

We went out about 15 minutes later and found that the tires of my car had been slashed. We went back in and reported the vandalism to the police but to no avail.

I pulled over and stopped, even though I heard no siren and had no definite knowledge that the following car contained police . . . and waited until the man in the car arrived. He came up to the truck and told me to get out. I asked for identification. He didn't show me anything, but told me to get out of the truck. I got out . . . and he and I walked to his car. Eric also got out and we received a . . . lecture while he was writing a ticket for speeding. . . . A highway patrol car arrived. . . . A third car then pulled up, which was unmarked and contained one man not in uniform. We would tell he had been drinking because of his actions and because we could smell the liquor.

After a short interchange between him and the first man, the first man left and the third man took me back to the car of the highway patrolman. He opened the car and told me to get inside. I got inside and sat on the back seat. He told me to move over and got in. All the doors and windows were shut. He said, "I can't kill you, but you know what I'm going to do to you." I answered, "No, sir." At this time he pulled his gun out of his holster and started to hit me on the head with the gun butt. I put my hands up to protect my head and rolled into a ball on the seat. Over a period of about a minute he hit me about four times on the head and about eight to ten times on the left hand. He also hit me about three times on the left leg, twice on my right hand, and once on my left shoulder. All of this was with the gun butt. . . . Three of them then went up to Eric. They had a conversation with Eric which I could not hear and one of the men raised a gun and struck Eric, knocking him down. He got up and was knocked down again. I had been sitting in the car through all of this. I felt the blood on my face and on my arm. The man who had beaten me then came back to the car and sat down in the back seat. He picked up a flashlight and hit me across the mouth with it. I then rolled into a ball again and he put the gun to my temple and cocked it. He said, "If you move, I'll blow your brains out."

Arrest often held a special kind of terror for the volunteers. As generations of Mississippi blacks had learned, there was virtually no end to the physical and psychological brutality Southern jailers could inflict upon a prisoner. In this the volunteers achieved equality. The police accorded them the same treatment.

Upon entering [the] cell block we were taken to "nigger bull pen." Then [we] were shoved inside and officers said, "Here they are, get' em boys." This is very unusual practice for whites to be put into the Negro section. The Negroes expressed confusion and fear. They were moved to beat us. Five minutes later, two officers took us into a white cellblock. This was about 12:30 A.M. Wednesday. At the white cell, the officers tried to incite white prisoners to take out their aggressions on the volunteers. ("It's wooping [sic] time.") The officers left and white prisoners gathered about. R——— opened a conversation with one, and eased some of the tension. At this point, a Mexican spoke up and R——— spoke to him in Spanish to help develop a rapport. After several minutes, a Mississippian announced that he hated all niggers and nigger-lovers and that COFOers were there to be beaten by the whites. However he was going to let us go.

We lay down and listened to the argument, that lasted about three hours, on whether or not to beat us up. Sporadically, police officers and trustees would enter argument, attempting to incite white prisoners to "do justice." Morning arrived without real incident.

About 10 A.M. officers took us out of the cell into fingerprinting rooms. As they were fingerprinting and [taking mug shots of] me, the officers told ———— sordid stories about brutality that had been imposed upon fellow COFOers since the day before . . . and that a fellow white girl worker had been brutally raped and was on her death bed. At this point R———— fainted. Upon awakening, the back of his head bleeding, we both were escorted to the lobby where attorneys from COFO in Jackson were waiting. . . . Local police refused to return personal papers, mainly handwritten notes, and denied they had even taken them. . . . In a subsequent interview, FBI agents expressed no interest in the mental harassment which occurred during the 12 hours spent in jail. . . . When taken to jail, R———— had been told he was being arrested on a vagrancy charge. The following morning the sheriff said there were no charges.

Even when nothing happened, the possibility that something might could turn an evening alone in jail into an exhausting experience. In a letter home, William Hodes described his feelings during just such an evening.

So there I was: alone in a Southern jail. First thing I did was check the layout of the cell in case I had to protect myself. I pulled the mattresses halfway off the beds so that I wouldn't hit any sharp corners as I went down. I planned to stay on one of the beds in the corner, so that I could get between two beds and a wall, and make myself hard to get at, except maybe by kicking. I was very jumpy, and was terrified at every door slam, phone call, and particularly key ring jingle jangle. My pulse was . . . over a hundred the whole three hours or so that I was in jail. . . . Then I was sure they would suddenly decide to drop charges and put me out into the hostile night. That would be really bad, because I knew that trouble was brewing all over the city. I could see the big police wagon outside my cell window, all ready to go. Cops with gas masks and sheriffs with rifles jump into cars and zoom off. I heard dogs barking, police dogs. I figured that I would refuse to leave the station until they gave me a phone call: "You didn't let me have one when I came in, so you might as well give it to me now," I imagined myself saying. Could I hit a cop to get rearrested, or would that beating be worse than the possibility of getting caught by a mob? You can see why my pulse wasn't normal. . . .

I went home to bed, absolutely exhausted. The mental strain of being in there alone was just too much. While I slept, the office was shot into.

The cumulative effect of these confrontations with the enemy was to wear the volunteers down. As the summer wore on, the physical and emotional strain grew progressively worse. "Fear *can't* become a habit," wrote one volunteer to a friend. But in fact it had. The quality of Mississippi violence — random, savage — necessitated the habit. It was a means of survival. But it was achieved at the cost of physical and psychological exhaustion. Writing late in the summer, Sally Belfrage acknowledged that

"there are incipient nervous breakdowns walking all over Greenwood."
Tensions within the projects only added to the strain. . . .

All things considered, it had been a remarkable summer for a remarkable group of people. As it drew to a close, the volunteers found themselves exhausted and exhilarated in equal measure. There simply had
been no letup in intensity from the time they had arrived at Oxford. For
the better part of two months they had been subjected to one emotionally
draining experience after another. They had confronted their own mortality, experimented with new lifestyles, reveled in transcendent community, known terror, lived in poverty, felt the sting of racial hostility, and
experienced the development of a radical new political consciousness.
Theirs was an interesting dilemma. As much as they wanted the psychic
barrage to stop, so too did they want the "high" to continue. In letters
home the volunteers acknowledged the strong and conflicting feelings
they were having:

> All I have to do is sit and the world piles in on me. I would like something
> simple, to go swimming once, or see a movie, or walk in a field, or go for a
> drive without having to look out the back window or just to sit somewhere
> cool and quiet with a friend. Only once might work. . . . I'm simply ex-
> hausted. I yell at everybody. No, I don't yell at anyone at all, I only think I
> do, but I can't. Madness, a constant agitation, unrest. It could all be ex-
> plained by fatigue. . . . But there's a strange mechanism at work on us at
> night . . . when the children are gone, the chicken eaten, the mass meeting
> over, then there are still all of us left to egg each other on, everyone full
> and fed up with it but somehow longing for the next disaster. . . . All I've
> got is a fabulous depression, split in two — I can't bear another moment of
> it but it's impossible to believe that it can end in three weeks. How can I
> leave? How can I leave people I love so much? What made me think I could
> accomplish anything in this length of time? There's nowhere else I want
> to be.

The volunteers resolved this conflict in very different ways. At least
eighty decided to stay in Mississippi indefinitely. While there had been
little encouragement from SNCC to do so and no official mechanism set
up to retain people, these volunteers were not ready to leave in August.
Their letters home reflected both their resolve and the anguish they were
causing their families.

> I have been here nearly two months. I know the drudgery, the dangers,
> and the disappointments. I know what it's like to eat meatless dinners, to be
> so exhausted you feel as though you will drop, to have five people show up
> at a meeting to which 20 should have come. Yet I also know what it's like to
> sing, "We Shall Overcome" with 200 others till you think the roof will ex-
> plode off the church. I know what it's like to see the organization which you
> have nurtured come to life and begin to function and create. I know what
> it's like to have a choir of little girls sing out, "Hi, Ellen," as I walk down the
> road and envelop me in their hugs.

Only now that I know these things can the decision to stay be mature and meaningful.

Furthermore, maturity does not develop from facing a familiar routine from year to year. Maturity comes from having to face new situations, from making new decisions, from coming to terms with a new world. . . .

This summer is only the briefest beginning of this experience — both for myself and for the Negroes of Mississippi. So much of it will seem pointless if it ends now, or if it is taken up again in two years. A war cannot be fought and won if the soldiers take twelve-month leaves after every skirmish. . . . I have considered your parental qualms; really I have. But I'm afraid they cannot counterbalance the feelings of my duty here.

Many people, including those who supported my going to Mississippi as part of the Summer Project, and those who believe that the Summer Project has been an important thing, have expressed shock and disapproval at my decision to go back to Mississippi, and have attempted to dissuade me from returning. I have been amazed at this response.

There is a certainty, when you are working in Mississippi, that it is important for you to be alive and to be alive doing just what you are doing. And whatever small bit we did for Mississippi this summer, Mississippi did ten times as much for us.

I guess the thing that pulls me back most are the people who made us a part of their community. People I knew in Mississippi could honestly and unselfconsciously express affection in a way that few people I know in the North are able to do. They did not have to be "cool" or "one up" or "careful." . . . In Mississippi I have felt more love, more sympathy and warmth, more community than I have known in my life. And especially the children pull me back.

The majority of the volunteers *did* go home. However, for many the decision to do so was just as wrenching as it had been for those who remained behind.

August 6

I had a very hard time . . . convincing myself that I should leave Mississippi. . . . It is so necessary that people stay, especially northern white students. Holly Springs has so much potential and could really develop into something much greater than it already is if there are the right leaders here. I would love to be a part of making the Freedom School into a real ongoing concern with the adults and kids of the community doing most of the teaching and leading themselves. However, I have come to realize that there is still a great deal that I need to learn. I feel that I still have a lot of growing up to do. But most of all I see what this kind of life can do to you and I think that I need a rest and a change of environment to prepare myself for a life-long commitment wherever I might be needed.

Even harder than the decision to leave was the painful sense of dislocation many of the volunteers felt once they were out of Mississippi. They had arrived in the state in groups, buoyed by the exhilarating sense of community they had felt at Oxford. Now they trickled out of Mississippi one by one, alone and exhausted, without ever having an opportunity to process or come to grips with all they had seen and felt. If Oxford had oriented them to life in Mississippi, nothing prepared them for life after Mississippi. For many the transition was rough. Barely three weeks after writing the previous letter, Pam Parker struggled to express how she was feeling:

> I have been putting off writing my concluding thoughts on my experiences in Mississippi because I have been unable to sort out my thoughts and feelings since leaving. I will try to at least give you a picture of the reactions of one girl on entering the free, white world of her past once again. No one can go through an experience such as Mississippi without coming out changed. I do not believe that many of those who spent their summer in Mississippi will be able to go back to their old way of living.
>
> I am out of Mississippi and glad to be out for a while. I have always loved to take walks at night but never have I felt so grateful for the opportunity to take peaceful walks as these last few days. I could sit for hours on the porch of our friends' place in New Hampshire, soaking in the peacefulness and the quiet of the countryside. I feel so relaxed . . . but I am not relaxed, not completely. I wonder if I will ever relax fully again. . . .
>
> I have found that instead of Mississippi seeming distant from my life, it and all that it exemplifies in a magnified form of our society has become unbearably real to me.

She was not alone in what she was feeling. On the very same day, another volunteer in another state echoed her sentiments: "I've felt depressed since I've returned. I don't know how much is personal, and how much it is a reaction to that place and the people I've left behind, and a heightened awareness of so much that is wrong up here." Contrast the underlying tone of these two letters with that expressed in a third letter written the same day by a volunteer who had stayed on in Mississippi:

> We were sitting on the steps at dusk, watching the landscape and the sun folding into the flat country, with the backboard of the basketball net that is now netless sticking up into the sunset at a crazy angle. Cotton harvesters went by — and the sheriff — and then a 6-year-old Negro girl with a stick and a dog, kicking up as much dust as she could with her bare feet. As she went by, we could hear her humming to herself, "We shall overcome."

The psychic and geographic distance from Mississippi was great indeed. Even greater was the gulf between the volunteer's summer experiences and their previous lives. Bridging that gap would prove difficult for many, impossible for some. For many the old adage, "you can always go home," would prove a lie. For some of the volunteers there would be no "going home" except in a geographical sense. They had simply seen and felt too much to ever experience their world in the same way again. They had been changed in some very fundamental ways. The extent and significance of these changes would become apparent over the next few months.

STUDY GUIDE

1. What were the specific obstacles that the summer volunteers faced in Mississippi in getting blacks registered to vote?

2. Why was it thought necessary or desirable to establish Freedom Schools? What were the schools intended to do?

3. In 1964, Mississippi ranked at or near the bottom of all the states in various measures of economic health and prosperity. In addition to being among the poorest states, if not absolutely the poorest, Mississippi also probably had the worst record in regard to racial oppression and violence. What evidence do you find in the selection that these two conditions may have been connected? What other connections may there have been between poverty and racial oppression?

4. What were the effects on the volunteers, positive and negative, of their experiences in Mississippi?

5. The selection clearly shows that those involved in Freedom Summer felt a curious mixture of hope and fear about what they were doing. To what extent was this mixture of feelings prevalent in the rest of the civil rights movement of the 1950s and 1960s? To what extent were the violence and threat of violence that marked Freedom Summer characteristic of the rest of the movement?

BIBLIOGRAPHY

John Hope Franklin's *From Slavery to Freedom* (1978) is a general history of African-Americans. C. Vann Woodward, *The Strange Career of Jim Crow* (1974) is a relatively brief but very rich account of race relations in the South from the end of the Civil War to the recent past. Harvard Sitkoff, *The Struggle for Black Equality: 1954–1980* (1981) is a very good short history of the civil rights movement. Taylor Branch's *Parting the Waters: America in the King Years, 1954–1963* (1988) tells a part of that story in much greater detail. Martin Luther King, Jr., expressed his own views in *Stride Toward Freedom: The Montgomery Story* (1958) and *Why We Can't Wait* (1964). For another perspective on racial issues in the United States, *The Autobiography of Malcolm X* (1965) is essential reading. The history of SNCC is related by Clayborne Carson in *In Struggle: SNCC and the Black Awakening of the 1960's* (1981). Cleveland Sellers with Robert Terrell, *The River of No Return: The Autobiography of a Black Militant and the Life and Death of SNCC* (1973) and Mary King, *Freedom Song: A Personal History of the 1960's Civil Rights Movement* (1987) are memoirs of a black and a white member of SNCC, respectively, who were directly involved in the events of Freedom Summer and most of the other significant actions the organization undertook.

The Haight-Ashbury section of San Francisco was the headquarters of the counterculture.

19

JAY STEVENS

The Counterculture

The 1960s were many things, most certainly a decade of tumult and upheaval, marked by the emergence of a number of protest movements — the civil rights movement, the student movement, the women's rights movement, the antiwar movement, the environmental movement. Those who enlisted in these causes were, of course, demonstrating their unhappiness with the existing state of affairs and their desire to change it in some way. We may distinguish two broad types of protest or rebellion: One type — the civil rights movement and the protests against the Vietnam War for example — was directed toward social change through political action. The other type — for example the "consciousness raising" efforts of the women's movement, trying to make women aware of the disadvantages they faced solely because of their gender — might be called cultural rebellion, in that the action was not directed so much against particular laws, policies, or institutions, but against the values and ways of thinking out of which those laws, policies, and institutions grew. The goal was not to get laws repealed or policies revised but to change the way people thought.

Another example of cultural rebellion is the counterculture. In the 1950s, a small group of artists and intellectuals known as the Beats, including such people as the poet Allen Ginsberg and the novelists Jack Kerouac and William Burroughs, had begun to argue that American society and culture were intellectually and spiritually sterile. Throughout the 1950s the Beats were little more than a curiosity to most Americans, more ridiculed for their strange appearance or reviled for their use of drugs than listened to for their ideas. By the 1960s, increasing numbers came to share the Beats' notion that

America was deeply flawed in fundamental ways and that drastic revisions were necessary. The counterculture was born out of the resulting search for alternatives to the dominant culture.

The term "counterculture" is difficult to define with precision, for the people who comprised it were a diffuse group with divergent ideas and goals. In general, however, one can say that they were united by a common belief that modern America was materialistic, overcentralized, competitive, conformity-ridden, and riddled with conflict and anxiety. In its place, they hoped to construct a new culture based on individual freedom and love. Frequently, perhaps even usually, these ideas were so vague as to be nearly meaningless, and many of those who eventually became involved in the counterculture were self-indulgent sensation-seekers. This was true in large part because of the central place drugs held in the counterculture experience. Initially regarded as a means by which individuals could "expand their consciousness," achieve important insights about themselves, the universe, and their place in it, the drug experience soon degenerated for many into a quest for nothing more profound than a good time, immediate gratification, "kicks." In the following selection Jay Stevens tells the story of the counterculture, where it came from, what it was all about, and what happened to it.

There is no simple way to explain what went on in the Sixties, no easily identifiable event, like the assassination at Sarajevo, which one can point to and say, "there, tensions might have been growing for decades, but that's the spark that touched off the explosion." Indeed, the more thoroughly you study the Sixties, the more comforting becomes a concept like the *zeitgeist*. Strip away the decade's thick impasto of sex, drugs, rebellion, politics, music, and art, and what you find is a restless imperative to change, a "will to change," if you will, and one that could be as explanatory for the latter half of this century as Nietzsche's "will to power" was for the first.

Change jobs, spouses, hairstyles, clothes; change religion, politics, values, even the personality; try everything, experiment constantly, accept nothing as given. It was as though the country as a whole was undergoing a late adolescence, and not just the 20 million Baby Boomers whose leading edge began turning eighteen in 1964. Either that or the Boomers, the

From the book *Storming Heaven: LSD and the American Dream*, copyright © 1987 by Jay Stevens. Used by permission of the Atlantic Monthly Press.

largest generation ever, possessed enough mass of their own to alter the normal spin of things.

But alter it in what direction? Somehow the satire of *Mad* magazine and the kinetic electricity of Elvis, the surreal dailyness of Beaver Cleaver and the fear of the Bomb; somehow the awful drabness of Dad in his official corporate uniform, the gray flannel suit, and the awful sameness of the suburbs, those theme parks of the good safe life; somehow all these had combined into a combustible outrage. It was an almost obscene irony, but the kids who had enjoyed the richest, most pampered adolescence in the history of the world had now decided that it was all crap. "We've got so many things we could puke," they said. "We live in the most manipulated society ever created by man."

Since infancy (or so it seemed to the Boomers) their minds had been measured, their psyches sculpted, their emotions straitjacketed, and for what? Why, to preserve the good old Corporate American Way of Life!

The corporations, so omnipotent during the Fifties, were vilified as the source of most of what was wrong with America, whether it was the imperialism that had brought on the Vietnam War or the subtler neurosis that caused people to measure their self-worth in terms of the number and quality of the consumer items they were able to surround themselves with. The same throwaway culture that the parents found convenient and liberating was dismissed by the children as ugly, trashy, and stupid when measured against the ecological cost of living in such a manner.

But the kids also realized that the corporations were only the visible tip of the iceberg, that the real menace was less tangible, although by the late Fifties it already had a number of provocative names: *the military-industrial complex, the power elite, the Garrison Society,* and — the ultimate winner in terms of usage — *the Establishment.*

What these terms attempted to describe was a conspiracy of money and power whose tentacles stretched into every nook and cranny of daily life. Corporations were members of the Establishment. But so were labor unions. Politicians were valued players, of course, but so were teachers, reporters and generals. Republicans and Democrats were merely different frequencies in the Establishment spectrum, while liberalism was nothing more than a clever way of allowing the illusion of change while maintaining the perquisites of power. Uniting these disparate elements was an overt commitment to anticommunism and American hegemony abroad, together with a domestic brand of democracy that sounded more like a well-run corporation than the noble experiment of the Founding Fathers. Instead of "the people," Establishmentarians talked about the managed and the managers, a formula that was not too dissimilar to the one followed in the Establishment's archenemy, the USSR.

Reflecting upon this woeful state of affairs, the Baby Boomers decided that not only didn't they want to be managed, but they could do without the occupation of manager as well. Norman Mailer caught their mood exactly when he wrote that "the authority had operated on their brain with commercials, and washed their brain with packaged education, packaged politics. The authority had presented itself as honorable, and it was corrupt, corrupt as payola on television, and scandals concerning the leasing of aviation contracts—the real scandals as everyone was beginning to sense were more intimate and could be found in all the products in all the suburban homes which did not work so well as they should have worked, and broke down too soon for mysterious reasons. The shoddiness was buried deep. . . . "

Of course not every Sixties kid accepted this critique. For each one who wanted to seize power, dismantle the Establishment, and redistribute the wealth, there were at least ten others who just wanted to get through school, get laid, get a job, and get out of going to Vietnam; for every kid who grew his hair long, smoked dope, listened to rock music, and proclaimed an urgent longing to make a clean break with American society, there was a corresponding kid who drank beer, worshiped the local football team, and measured his personal worth by the car he drove. The differential between silent majority and noisy minority probably varied little for the kids of the Sixties from that of their parents. But it didn't seem that way, if only because the silent majority is never news. And they are even less so when the *zeitgeist* is changing rapidly.

Compared to the quiescent teens of the Fifties, the Baby Boomers seemed a generation of Jacobins, a rude, unwashed, overeducated mob who, if not precisely endangering the State, certainly threatened one's peace of mind.

One of the difficulties in writing about the Sixties is deciding when the story began. Was it the day President Kennedy was assassinated in Dallas, a day imprinted on every Baby Boomer the way Pearl Harbor was for their parents? Kennedy was the Establishment's best salesman; with programs like the Peace Corps he almost managed to sell liberalism to the Baby Boom. But his death left a vacuum that was soon filled with anger and cynicism.

Or was it during the first freedom marches in Mississippi, when the kids learned just how loath the Establishment was to extend basic rights to the Blacks? Reflecting on what had happened to the consciousness of those kids who went South in the summer of 1964, Michael Novak later wrote: "Enough young people have been beaten, jailed and even killed while trying to bring about simple constitutional rights to American Negroes to have altered the inner life of a generation. The young do not think of law enforcement as the enforcement of justice; they have experienced it as the enforcement of injustice."

Or did it begin in the fall of 1964, when a group of Berkeley students staged a spontaneous sit-in that quickly grew into the Free Speech Movement?

The seeds of the FSM were sown in early September, when Berkeley Chancellor Clark Kerr, perhaps acting upon the liberal assumption that politics in the old sense was dead, banned all politicking outside Berkeley's main gate on Bancroft Way. For years Bancroft Way had been an ideological flea market, with groups of every persuasion soliciting funds and dispersing literature. Although Kerr's decision drew protests from nearly every student group, from the fledgling Students for a Democratic Society to Youth for Goldwater, Kerr refused to relent and in late September suspended eight students for political activities.

Then, on October 1, a young mathematics graduate student named Jack Weinberg was arrested for refusing to abandon the table he was manning for CORE — the Committee on Racial Equality. A campus squad car was dispatched and when it arrived Weinberg went limp, a technique he had acquired the previous summer during the freedom marches in Mississippi. As the security guards dragged him to the car, an outraged crowd began to form, effectively blocking the exit. For the next thirty-two hours, speaker after speaker climbed atop the car's hood, exhorting the students to seize the moment and strike. It was as though somebody had touched a match to a mood that had been building for years, not just a few weeks.

I felt "torn open, everything boiling in me," wrote Michael Rossman in *The Wedding Within the War,* his memoir of the Sixties. A colleague of Weinberg's in the Berkeley mathematics department, and a fellow radical, Rossman described the aftermath of the cop car siege as "the Tearing Loose — the active beginning of the end of my life within the old institutions."

On December 2, 1964, four hundred members of the Free Speech Movement seized Sproul Hall and held it until they were dragged out singing by hundreds of helmeted riot police. Five days later, an audience of eighteen thousand gathered at Berkeley's Greek Theatre to listen as Clark Kerr poured forth his vision of the true academic community as a "knowledge factory" whose purpose lay in creating socially productive individuals. Now this was the wrong tack to take with students who increasingly resented the factory analogy, but the real mistake came after the speech. As the meeting ended, Mario Savio, a young philosophy major who had become one of the leaders of the FSM, stepped to the rostrum. He intended to invite everyone to a mass rally where Kerr's speech could be debated, but before he could open his mouth to speak he was grabbed by two policemen and wrestled to the floor. A wave of anger swept the crowd. As Godfrey Hodgson later wrote, "one minute Clark Kerr, the champion of liberalism, had been talking about the powers of persuasion against the use of force, and the next moment armed agents of the University were choking his opponent, the symbolic representative of free speech."

The next afternoon the faculty voted 824–115 to accede to the FSM's demands. The Baby Boom had received its first taste of political power.

Not surprisingly, the facts attending the birth of the FSM were drowned in an ocean of learned speculation, as journalists and political scientists rushed to explain this momentary aberration. Although few of the commentators could see beyond their own ideological categories — Lewis Feuer, a reputed expert in left-wing political phenomena, dismissed the FSM as "intellectual lumpen-proletariats, lumpen beatniks, and lumpen agitators" who espoused a "melange of narcotics, sexual perversion, collegiate Castroism and campus Maoism" — most divined the central theme of the protest, which was a hearty dislike of the liberal ideal of a rationally managed society. It was a revolt against the depersonalization implied by the factory analogy that Kerr was so fond of, which was why the IBM card, with its ubiquitous warning "do not fold, spindle or mutilate," became the symbol of all they despised. Rossman described the target of the FSM as the Big Daddy Complex, which was his name for the species of liberal paternalism that had banished political diversity not only from Bancroft Way, but from the University curriculum as well. The motto of the Big Daddy Complex, he wrote, was the phrase "for your own good," and its "effect is to inhibit autonomous adulthood."

This last was a crucial point: instead of adopting the definition of psychological maturity that the mental health movement had proposed in the Fifties, with its emphasis on conformity and responsibility to the larger ideals of society, the Baby Boomers were moving in the opposite direction. The ability to let go, to explore the depths of one's own psyche, to conform to individual rather than social imperatives — these were the new benchmarks of psychological maturity.

Another element that the commentators completely ignored was the exhilaration that came from collective action. During the fifteen-hour occupation of Sproul Hall, life had been lived in a wholly new key. It was, to bend Maslow's term, a collective peak experience whose import lay not so much in the demands that had brought them together, as in the fact that they *were* together. The protesters had turned Sproul Hall into a carnival, with Chaplin movies on the walls and folksingers in the stairwells. "We ate terrible baloney sandwiches and then established the first Free University, conducting some dozen classes cross-legged atop the Civil Defense disaster drums stored in the basement," remembered Rossman. "People smoked grass in the corners . . . and at least two women had their first full sexual experiences under blankets on the roof, where walkie-talkies were broadcasting news to the outside.". . .

The word *hippie,* indeed the whole phenomenon of the Haight-Ashbury, first came to light in September 1965, in the course of a San Francisco *Examiner* article about a coffeehouse called the Blue Unicorn.

The Unicorn, which advertised the cheapest food in the city, was a little hole in the wall on Hayes Street, near Golden Gate Park, in the midst of a twenty-five-block district that derived its name from two intersecting streets — Haight Street, which ran in a flat line toward the Pacific Ocean; and Ashbury, a much shorter thoroughfare which climbed up Mt. Sutro and stopped. Like the Unicorn, the Haight-Ashbury was something of a hole-in-the-wall district, full of ornate but shabby Victorian houses dating back to the Teens, when so many politicians had built themselves mansions above Haight Street that the area had been nicknamed "politicians' row."

But in the intervening years the Haight-Ashbury had tumbled so far down the socioeconomic ladder that during World War II it had been considered an appropriate spot for worker housing. After the war refugees from Eastern Europe and a small population of Orientals had tried to resuscitate its former splendor, but when Blacks began moving into the district — encouraged by urban renewal, which was razing their traditional ghetto to the west — these homesteaders had packed up, leaving the Haight in the curious position of offering lavish living for dirt cheap prices. For a few hundred dollars it was possible to rent a whole house, complete with leaded windows and ballroom.

Now it happened that this abandonment coincided with the disintegration of the North Beach Beat scene, due to a combination of rising rents, police harassment, and obnoxious tourists who flocked to see the beatnik in his native habitat. The Haight was an obvious solution, and by the time the *Examiner* tumbled to what was happening, it supported a thriving bohemian community, of which the Unicorn was the heart and soul.

This, then, was the gist of what journalist Michael Fallon had to report to his readers: the Beat movement, far from being dead, was alive and flourishing in what had once been one of San Francisco's tonier neighborhoods. But if the Haight was where the Beat movement had fled to, then something had happened in the passage. Compared to the moody, nihilistic beatniks of old, those clichéd cave creatures in their black turtlenecks, the patrons of the Unicorn were like vivid butterflies in their pink striped pants and Edwardian greatcoats. They were sunny and cheery, and the word *love* punctuated their conversation with alarming frequency: all kinds of love, elevated ethereal love and plain old physical love. And on nights when LEMAR — the acronym for the legalize marijuana movement — wasn't meeting at the Unicorn, the Sexual Freedom League was.

Like any scientist fortunate enough to discover a new class of fauna, Fallon's first instinct was to give it a name, which he did by borrowing Norman Mailer's hipster and contracting it into hippie, a word that caught some of the Unicorn's buoyancy, but one the hippies themselves were never fond of. From their perspective, hippie was just another example of the subtle derogation practiced by the mainstream media whenever it was confronted by something outside its usual ken. Hadn't Fallon's fellow journalist, Herb Caen, done something similar when he tagged Ginsberg & Co. with the diminutive beatnik?

But whether they liked it or not, hippie it was and would be.

Oddly, Fallon's inventiveness later served to obscure the fact that in many respects the hippies were second-generation Beats. This was clearer in the early days, when it was still easy to trace the connection between the old Beat fantasy of creating an alternative culture — the word "counterculture" was still years off — and what was aborning in the Haight. "We have a private revolution going on," wrote Bob Stubbs, the owner of the Unicorn, in one of the policy statements he used to distribute to his customers. "A revolution of individuality and diversity that can only be private. Upon becoming a group movement, such a revolution ends up with imitators rather than participants."

A very private revolution: at the time of Fallon's article, there were probably only a dozen houses scattered throughout the Haight that could have been characterized as hippie. And yet the district pulsed with energy. "Even if you lived elsewhere, your forays to the neighborhood were always important," wrote one frequent visitor. "The Haight-Ashbury had four or five grapevines cooking at all times . . . and the two words that went down the wire most often in those days were *dope* and *revolution*. Our secret formula was grass, LSD, meditation, hot music, consolidation, and a joyous sexuality."

Had you lived in any of those houses in the autumn of 1965, it would have been immediately clear that the key ingredient in that formula, the reason why the Haight was not the North Beach six years later, was LSD. LSD was the Haight's secret weapon, with emphasis on secret. "Taking it was like being in a secret society," remembers one pioneer. "Hardly anything was being said about it publicly . . . [although] not an illegal drug, people acted as if it were; it seemed illegal."

It also seemed intensely serious. In the compelling phrase of one hippie, LSD was hard kicks: "hard kicks is a way of looking at your existence, not like mistreating your body or throwing your mind to the crows. It's a way of extending yourself [so that] something spectacular and beautiful can be available to you."

It was axiomatic, in the beginning, that hard kicks were dangerous. They were not a game for the timid or insecure. But insofar as they offered a way out of the white suburban world that so many of the early hippies had been born into, they were worth the risk. . . .

According to the hippies, LSD was "one of the best and healthiest tools available" for the examination of consciousness. "Acid opens your door, opens the windows, opens your senses. Opens your beam to the vast possibilities of life, to the glorious indescribable beauty of life." You could "drop down into your unconscious to see the pillars and the roots of the tree which is your personality. . . . You see what your hangups are; you might not even overcome them but you cope with them, and that's an amazing advance."

The Haight then, in its earliest incarnation, was a kind of sanitarium, an indigenous Baden Baden that offered a therapeutic regime of good vibes and drugs, rather than mountain air and mineral springs. . . .

By June 1966, an estimated fifteen thousand hippies were living in the Haight, an increase that baffled the hippies about as much as it did everyone else. "God has fingered that little block system between Baker and Stanyon Street," they told the curious. "And we spend all our time, verbally and nonverbally, trying to discover why." Helen Perry, one of the first of the social scientists to arrive on the scene, likened the Haight to "the delta of a river," where all the unrooted sediment of America was washing ashore. But even Perry was unclear as to why the undercurrents of American life should be sweeping so many into this odd backwater . . . asked why they had chosen the Haight, the hippies murmured vague things like, "I fell in with some vibrational energies and ended up here." . . .

Although the Summer of Love officially began on June 21, the summer solstice, its actual beginning occurred the previous fall, specifically on October 6, 1966, the day the California law making possession of LSD a misdemeanor went into effect.

Declaring that the long arm of the State was reaching into their psyches, the hippies welcomed the new law with a sort of Boston tea party — plenty of drugs, free food, and music — which took place in a narrow strip of park paralleling Haight Street known as the Panhandle. The get-together had a name, the Love Pageant Rally, and to everyone's surprise and delight, several thousand extravagantly garbed hippies turned out, prompting one middle-aged tourist to remark to a local journalist: "Why, you don't see anything like this in Philadelphia."

Nor, discounting the Trips Festival, which already seemed ancient history, had anything like it been seen in San Francisco before. For the first time, surrounded by fellow freaks, it dawned on the hippies that their ruling fantasy might really be correct, that the evolutionary tides might really be flowing in their direction. Perhaps it was a consequence of all the LSD, but from the Love Pageant on, a naive optimism permeated the Haight, combined with a mystical faith that whatever was needed would be provided. Almost overnight the Haight found itself with its own newspaper, the San Francisco *Oracle*, its own police force, the Hells Angels, and its own radio station, KMPX, whose lobby usually included a hippie or two in full lotus; its own Chamber of Commerce in the HIP [Haight Independent Proprietors] merchants and its own social workers in the Diggers. And there was talk of a hip employment agency, a hip hotel, and a hip cafeteria that would serve food grown on communal farms run by hippies tired of the urban grind. . . .

The first Diggers — the name originally belonged to a group of seventeenth-century religious communists who made the mistake of demanding access to the uncultivated land in Cromwellian England, and were exterminated — were actors. They belonged to a theatrical enterprise known as the San Francisco Mime Troupe, which performed a kind of political *commedia dell'arte* wherever there was space for stage and audience. The Mime Troupe specialized in street theater, which was perhaps why a few of the company began to see the Haight as a wonderful context for a perpetual theater of the absurd.

The Diggers announced their presence in a series of anonymous broadsides that mocked the smell-the-flower fatuousness of so many of the hippies. Cosmic was fine, LSD was fine, they said, but when you came back down you still had to cope with outrageous rents and bad food and all the temptations of the established culture, particularly money. "Money lust is sickness," the broadsides said. "It kills perception . . . almost all of us were exposed to this disease in childhood, but dope and love are curing us." Not surprisingly, the HIP merchants were a frequent target of Digger critiques. "How long will you tolerate people [straight or hip] transforming your trip into cash?" And they even went so far as to picket one festival, the First Annual Love Circus, because admission was a steep $3.50.

From broadsides the Diggers progressed to street theater: the Birth and Death ritual, the New Year's Wail, the Invisible Circus, the Death of Money parade. This last, consisting of six pallbearers wearing enormous papier-mâché animal heads and carrying a black-draped coffin down Haight Street, was a spectacle worthy of the surrealists. Gradually, however, the Diggers began talking less and doing more. They set up shop in an old garage known as the Free Frame of Reference, which was a reference to the huge yellow frame that they lugged around, largely so they could make the pointed joke of inviting onlookers to "step into our frame of reference now." They opened a Free Store that was full of cast-off clothes and housewares scrounged in daily forays around San Francisco. And the goods really were free. More than one Samaritan watched in astonishment as the Diggers, after ceremoniously accepting a contribution, proceeded to light their cigarettes with it. And if anyone demanded to see the person in charge, the Diggers always replied, "You are!"

The Diggers made their most substantial contribution, however, with the food feeds. Every afternoon at 4 P.M. their Dodge truck arrived in the

Panhandle loaded with big aluminum garbage cans of soup, the fruits of the sort of artful hustling that the Beats had perfected back in the Fifties. . . .

One reason this was happening was because the Haight-Ashbury was about to undergo an ambiguous fifteen minutes of fame as the most notorious streetcorner in the world. Every national magazine and major newspaper in the country would send a reporter to do a standard "I Was a Hippie for a Day" story. Some, like the *Chronicle's* man, stayed undercover for a couple of weeks, and Washington *Post* reporter Nicholas Von Hoffman took in the whole three-act play that summer. But most donned blue jeans and a paisley shirt and spent a day or two standing around outside the Drugstore, trying not to sound like a narcotics agent, asking things like. "Why do you wear your hair so long?" *Because I think I'm beautiful.* "Why are your clothes so colorful?" *Because I have self-respect. Say, have you ever stopped to think that writing STOP on a sign is a pretty silly way to communicate that concept? It'd be much better if stop signs had God's eyes on them, don't you think. People would stop for God's eyes.* And so on, until you asked how he knew what God's eyes looked like, and he'd wink and say, "cause I looked into them, baby."

There was something about the psychedelic temperament that couldn't resist baiting the straights. They were so nervous about life; all you had to do was walk up to them on the street and hand them a flower and they'd freak, as though you'd just given them a joke flower that was about to spray them with *eau de deviant.* Perhaps the best put-on, the grandest, was the Great Banana Conspiracy, which first broke in the Berkeley *Barb* that March. A new psychedelic had been discovered, the *Barb* reported, one anyone could obtain, since the only ingredient was dried banana peel. Dry the peel, scrape off the inner portion, and smoke it. The high, according to cognoscenti quoted in the *Barb*, was comparable to opium, with some nice psilocybin shadings.

From the *Barb* the banana hoax bounced to the wire services and thence across the country. Students held banana smoke-ins and grocery stores experienced a repeat of the run on morning glory seeds a few years earlier, as scraggly young kids began appearing at the checkout counters with carts full of bananas. Was America going to have to ban the banana? Or require licenses before people could buy them? A congressman from New Jersey jokingly introduced two new acts to Congress: the Banana Labeling Act of 1967 and the Banana and Other Odd Fruit Disclosure and Reporting Act of 1967. But not everyone was laughing. United Fruit was more than a little alarmed. They asked Sidney Cohen to find out whether bananas really were hallucinogenic, a question that the FDA also was taking very seriously. And after a lengthy and sober evaluation, it was announced that bananas were good sources of potassium and fiber, and definitely not hallucinogenic.

When it came to the hippies, the country alternated between "we are amused" and "we are not amused." A hippie is someone who "dresses like Tarzan, has hair like Jane, and smells like Cheetah," quipped the newly elected governor of California, Ronald Reagan, while in another speech he described the Bay Area as a hotbed of evil that he intended to stamp out. *Look* described the archetypical hippie pad as "a filthy litter strewn swarming dope fortress that was a great deal less savory and sanitary than a sewer," while *Time* praised its occupants as leading "considerably more virtuous lives than the great majority of their fellow citizens. This, despite their blatant disregard for most of society's accepted mores and many of its laws — most notably those prohibiting the use of drugs." But others detected, in their talk of pushing evolution and creating a new Man, the aroma of fascism. The hippies are a "fascistic reservoir" because "they are a rootless community that makes a fetish of having no leaders [and thus] may easily be mobilized by an unscrupulous leader." . . . Would they be rejected, or would the hippies, their internal compasses skewed by the drugs, follow like a slavish mob? Writing in the *Nation*, poet Karl Shapiro described the hippies as the "perfect cultural broth for fascism. The Beat people had a marginal politick and a sense of community; their drug was weed. The new generation has no need of politick or community or poetry. They have acid." . . .

There were the usual fulminations against LSD as a dry rot in the American soul and the usual symposiums of experts asking themselves why the kids of America were rejecting the time-honored stimulants of their parents. Sociologist Kenneth Keniston attributed it to "psychological numbing." Part of the price of living in an advanced industrial society, he explained, was a deadening of the senses. "Our experiences lack vividness, three dimensionality and intensity. Above all, we feel trapped or shut in our own subjectivity." The hippies were using LSD as "a chemical sledgehammer for breaking out of [their] shell," Keniston wrote, and while he deplored the means, he couldn't help but acknowledge the legitimacy of the search.

But that didn't console the San Francisco city fathers. Drug abuse was costing the city an estimated thirty-five thousand dollars a month; since the beginning of the year San Francisco General had been seeing an average of four bad LSD trips a day, many of them runaway adolescents barely out of puberty; and in two years the city-wide venereal disease rate had risen by a factor of six. The Haight was an open sore, and now these misguided deviants had the chutzpah to invite the youth of America to join them in a summer-long orgy of drugtaking and loitering. Mayor Shelley, in March, issued a statement that said, in effect, not in my city, you don't. "I am strongly opposed to any encouragement of a summer influx of indigent young people who are apparently being led to believe by a certain element of society that their vagrant presence will be tolerated in this city," said the mayor.

A few days later a platoon of health inspectors descended on the Haight, accompanied by a full complement of reporters. No doubt they were expecting a confirmation of filth and degradation thesis, since the adjective *dirty* had attached itself to the hippies like a birthmark. However, as public health director, Dr. Ellis D. ("LSD") Sox was forced to admit, "The situation is not as bad as we had thought." Of the fourteen hundred buildings examined, only sixty-four had violations, and only sixteen of those housed hippies.

But the raid presaged an increasingly active policy of official harassment. Police began daily raids in the Haight, sweeping the streets, demanding proof of age, arresting runaways, busting careless hippies for possession of pot and LSD, and in general wreaking havoc with the private revolution.

Paranoia, which was the shadow side of the kind of ecstatic energy that seemed to accompany prolonged LSD experimentation, began to build. A fascist putsch was being planned, went the whispers, every hippie in prison by July. "All spring the Haight shook with premonition," remembers Michael Rossman, "the airways of gossip were incessant with flashes of apocalypse . . . deep fear throbbed in the Haight."

As the Summer of Love approached, the Haight quivered in a contagion of first-night jitters.

Charles Perry, in his history of the Haight-Ashbury, describes the Haight in the summer of 1967 as "part old Calcutta with beggars squatting on the sidewalk, part football stadium crush, with people selling programs — the *Oracle*, the *Barb* and two new papers, the Haight-Ashbury *Tribune* and the Haight-Ashbury *Maverick*." The street scene was a visual equivalent to the posters Bill Graham was commissioning to advertise the Fillmore, a swirling, colorful anarchy whose bizarre calligraphy, indecipherable at first, soon became second nature. So it was with the Haight. What to outsiders appeared demented madness was perfectly clear to anyone who was *attuned*.

Take clothes. An astute observer could date the various hippie fauna just by the cut of their clothes. The earliest residents were dandies, partial to cowboy outfits and Edwardian rigs, complete with bowlers and canes. Then came the Day-Glo superhero collages that the Pranksters had pioneered, followed by the ethnic borrowings, the serapes and desert robes, the peasant blouses, the Tibetan prayer costumes. Standing on Haight Street during the Summer of Love, an astute observer could pick out the older hippies, moving like peacocks through a monotonous sea of gray sludge: faded denim was the dominant hue that summer, blending into the fog that came rolling up Haight Street, mingling with

the garbage smell and the dirt, accentuating the loneliness and despair —
by midsummer it was clear that the yin had arrived to balance out the
yang of the Be-In glow.

Haight Street, said the *Oracle,* had become the "abstract vortex for an
indefinable pilgrimage . . . walking barefoot with hair askew, hand-made
robes over torn blue jeans, the young people wander from noon until
nearly two. Wandering aimlessly up Haight St., over to the free store at
Carl and Cole, then back to Masonic for a cream pie and coke or to the
Panhandle for Digger stew." And these wanderers weren't the true brothers of the post Be-In visions; rather they were the imitators that Bob
Stubbs had warned about. They weren't beautiful, they had bad teeth
and acne scars and it was easy to see they hadn't been voted homecoming
king or queen back in Oshkosh or Biloxi, or wherever they'd come from.
These kids were rejects; they'd come here because they were losers, and
while that had a certain Christian appropriateness, it was not what the
Council for the Summer of Love had expected. And along with the sheep
came the usual complement of wolves, the hustlers and petty criminals.
For the first time crimes other than shoplifting became a problem. One
day Jerry Garcia was strolling down Haight Street when he came across a
chilling bulletin:

> Pretty little 16-year-old-middle-class chick comes to the Haight to see what
> it's all about & gets picked up by a 17-year-old street dealer who spends all
> day shooting her full of speed again & again, then feeds her 3000 mikes &
> raffles off her temporarily unemployed body for the biggest Haight Street
> gang bang since the night before last.

Garcia was amazed. Why would anyone print such a depressing piece of
news? "That was the point," he recalls, "where I thought, this scene cannot survive with that in there. It just goes all wrong."

Complicating the problem were the tourists, who crawled down Haight
Street, bumper to bumper, windows shut, doors locked, as though passing
through one of those zoos where the animals roam free and it is the hu-
mans who're encaged. In March the Gray Line, a bus company that had
operated a similar tour during the heyday of the beatniks, began advertising the Hippie Hop: for six dollars it would take ordinary Americans
beyond the "bearded curtain," on the "only foreign tour within the continental limits of the United States. . . . Among the favorite pasttimes of
the hippies, besides taking drugs, are parading and demonstrating, semi-
nars and group discussions about what's wrong with the status quo; ma-
lingering; plus the ever-present preoccupation with the soul. . . . "

The hippies devised various strategies to deflect this boorish scrutiny.
At first they loped into the traffic and distributed mocking handbills
which read, "Middle Class Brothers! Loosen Up, let God flow through
you. Remember we are with you as you drive through the valley of the

shadow of death." Then they discovered the mirror game. In one of their scrounges the Diggers came across a bin of broken mirrors. The next time the Gray Line buses arrived, the hippies ran alongside holding up mirrors to the windows so the tourists could take a good look at themselves. But then the Diggers thought up the walk-ins, which involved hundreds of people walking across the street in geometric patterns, snarling traffic for miles, and generally ending with the arrival of a vanload of police.

Then in early July a small riot broke out, as a group of frustrated hippies began jumping up and down on car bumpers, banging on hoods, terrifying the tourists. The police arrived, twenty carloads of them, and a fight broke out amid cries of "fascist bastards" and "police brutality." Although numerous bones were broken, the only fatality was a dog, clubbed to death by an overexcited policeman.

Malnutrition, overcrowding, a few bad apples, paranoia, bad drugs, big egos, the absence of any leaders who were willing to call themselves leaders, the constant police harassment — there were dozens of reasons why it was going bad. Meetings were called to try to puzzle out a strategy. . . . There was no dearth of suggestions, things like: "We have to say the Ommm sound. Every day there should be a procession down Haight Street to bring the good vibes back." Or: "I think it would be a good idea to open a cathouse because there's lots of straight guys on the street who're always asking where they can get laid. And when they can't get laid their energy gets very negative." Everyone knew the vibes were turning sour, could sense it with that awakened third eye. Whenever they took LSD it was all black apocalypse and visions of the bloody crucified Christ flying across the immense nothingness of the universe.

Bad trips became the most frequent trips (San Francisco General was treating an average of 750 panic reactions a month), and for the first time the LSD psychotic became something more than a media favorite. William Irwin Thompson, a historian who was teaching at MIT, ran into the dark side of the hippie dream one night at Esalen: "His hair was very short, and it was clear from his looks that he had not been with the movement very long. Zen and the *I Ching* meant nothing to him, but the weeks of grass, speed and acid seemed to be taking him into a hell that increased his contempt and resentment for the hippies who surrounded him with talk of love." As Thompson watched, appalled, the kid began to chant to himself, "Blood, Blood, Blood, Hate, Hate, Hate." It was one thing, Thompson realized, to celebrate, à la Leary, the death of the mind. But it was something quite different "to stare unperturbed into the violent eyes of a person who has gone out of his mind."

Ralph Metzner, who had moved to California and was working up the coast from San Francisco at Mendocino State Hospital, had some equally grim visitations, as casualties from the Haight-Ashbury began arriving at the hospital. One told him, "It's coming so fast I can't function at that speed." Another said, "You, Leary and Alpert started this whole mess. That's why I took acid. Now I'm going straight to hell. I can't stop it."

Three days later he slit his wrists and bled to death.

Instead of coming together as one beautiful tribe, the Haight was getting zooier. Those who could, got out of town, like hosts abandoning their own party; others, like the Diggers, began carrying guns.

A miscalculation had been made, perhaps as far back as the gray November day when Leary, over hot milk, had rejected Huxley's elitist perspective in favor of Ginsberg's *pro bono publico* perspective. And this, with a generous nod to Kesey and the Pranksters, was the result: kids gobbling LSD wherever and whenever they could, completely ignorant of set and setting, without the least bit of interest in the Unspoken Thing. As Nicholas Von Hoffman, who was perhaps the most astute journalist to visit the Haight that summer, observed, "Their own genius for manipulating the mass media and dominating the youth culture undid them. The taste and demand for acid increased exponentially; the programming diminished. People didn't prepare themselves for dropping it; they didn't take it within the bounds of the little millennarian communities of the Haight . . . they just swallowed pills anywhere because they wanted to get stoned and see colors."

LSD wasn't a trip to the Other World for these kids: it was mind-blowing fun, better than a fast car or a quick orgasm. When there wasn't any acid around, they were equally willing to shoot up methedrine (which had the added byproduct of decreasing hunger) or heroin. The cliché that nobody who grokked the meaning of LSD could poison their body with speed or heroin turned out to be just that, a cliché. The older hippies ran around putting up signs saying "Speed Kills" but it didn't do any good. Instead of creating a taste for enlightenment, LSD was promoting a love of sensation, the more intense the better, and it began to dawn on the hippie leadership that there were a lot of kids in the Haight that summer who were going to keep sledgehammering at their shells until there was nothing left but the ubiquitous dust. . . .

It was rumored that the Mafia was moving in on the psychedelic trade, circulating bad acid so that the hippies would turn to more lucrative habits, like heroin and speed. Signs appeared saying "Boycott Syndicate Acid," but how could you tell?

It was a classic case of projection. The problems were not out there — they were at the heart of the Haight itself, and perhaps even at the heart of the psychedelic experience. There was a point, during every LSD user's career, when the trips to the Other World became negative. In a therapeutic sense, this was good. It meant that the subject was finally confronting the various repressions and neurotic clusters that were inhibiting the smooth evolution of the self. And provided the therapist or guide was skilled, the subject could usually pass through this personal Dark Wood and continue the journey. But what happened with individuals also happened with groups. There was a period when the group mind also passed through the shadow, as it were, and it was here, as the Pranksters learned during the Watts Acid Test, when the urge to erase all limits, to annihilate everything was overwhelming.

The Haight had reached this point in its collective journey, and one of the reasons it was unable to summon the wisdom to guide itself past this darkness was STP.

People took STP and went on three-day trips, many of them terrifying. "I saw myself on fire and then I began to feel the pain of fire . . . I was in hell." It was the ultimate macho trip and descriptions of it sounded like war stories, people exploding through the envelope and burning, or filled with a cold wind that wouldn't stop blowing through the hollows of their mind. STP didn't stay a secret for long. The authorities knew about the new superpsychedelic ("the next step," enthused the chemists, the first of many new combinations) almost immediately because as soon as STP hit the street the emergency rooms filled with nervous, flipped-out kids who quickly became screaming, sobbing kids when the thorazine (the traditional antidote for a bad LSD trip) took effect. Apparently thorazine acted as a booster to the STP, pushing the horror up a few more notches.

That wasn't the whole story, by any means, although it was the one that the average citizen received. What happened to most STP users was subtler, and perhaps even more profound. When Dick Alpert took it, he generally liked it and predicted a useful future. But he also made a curious remark: "I felt I had lost something human. I felt that I had lost my humanity." Alpert wasn't particularly bothered by this (for reasons that will become clear) but it really worried Ken Kesey. Kesey took STP and "forgot something. I lost a thing we take for granted, something that's been forged over I don't know how many thousands of years of human effort, and it's now in us. All I knew when this high was over was that I'd forgotten it, and it was the most important thing I'd ever known and I'd known it since I was a kid." Kesey had a hard time articulating exactly what this was ("a way of relating that, when it's gone, leaves you mighty bleak") but finally he settled for "the tiller." STP had burned away his tiller.

For the first time people were examining the fine print of the psychedelic contract, and one of the clauses they found most troubling was the possibility that besides burning away their "tillers," psychedelics were also altering their chromosomes. In March *Science* had reported that LSD, introduced to a test tube of chromosomes, caused significant breaks. And follow-up studies seemed to confirm that the white blood cells of people who had used LSD frequently showed a high percentage of breaks. The *New England Journal of Medicine* suggested that the effects of psychedelics might be similar to those of radiation, which was a sobering thought to the hippies, particularly since they were so fond of saying that God had given them LSD to counteract the Bomb. Although most scientists were quick to question the validity of the chromosome research (aspirin, thorazine, and the common cold affected chromosomes) and the underground newspapers published long (and ultimately valid) critiques of the work, it didn't diminish the anxiety that clutched at every hippie's heart: hadn't Leary always talked about LSD releasing cellular energies? What if it did? What if they really were becoming mutants? Or was it just another fusillade in the propaganda battle, an ingenious reply to Leary's thousand-orgasm gambit?

These were subtle psychological currents whose movements became clear only months later. At the time it was much simpler and much more satisfying to blame the government (the fascist putsch rumors had yet to abate) and the press. "This wasn't a Summer of Love" the hippie called Teddybear told one reporter. "This was a summer of bull and you, the press, did it. The so-called flower children came here to find something because you told 'em to, and there was nothing to find."

For the first time the next step was obvious. The Haight-Ashbury should die, so the rest of the country could be reborn. "I think it might be a good idea for us to get a pocketful of acid and go to Topeka, Kansas, and begin the work of turning people on," said Allen Cohen at one of the final strategy meetings. "There's a lot of turned-on people in New York and here, but in between is a tribal wasteland."

In a few days it would be a year since the California law criminalizing LSD had taken effect; a year since the Love Pageant Rally. It was a good time to say goodbye, so thousands of black-bordered notices were printed up:

> Hippie in the Haight-Ashbury District of this city
> Hippie, devoted son of Mass Media
> Friends are invited to attend services beginning
> at sunrise, October 6, 1967, at Buena Vista Park.

At noon on the sixth, a fifteen-foot coffin was solemnly paraded down Haight Street followed by some two hundred mourners in elaborate costumes shaking tambourines. Ten sweating pallbearers carried the giant box once around the entire Haight-Ashbury, ending in the Panhandle, where it was ceremoniously set alight. But someone had called the fire department and within minutes a couple of engines came screaming up. "The remains," someone yelled. "Don't let them put it out."

But they did, their giant hoses turning the coffin into a charred soggy mass. All that was left of hippie was a hissing cloud of steam that drifted off toward the center of the country. . . .

STUDY GUIDE

1. Stevens says that the sixties were characterized by a widespread "will to change." How was this desire for change manifested? Where did it come from? Since most aspects of American life in the sixties seemed pleasant on the surface, how do you explain the apparent discontent of so many people?

2. Many Americans deplored the hippies and what they stood for. What exactly did they find deplorable? Do you think their opinions were justified?

3. Describe the relationship between the hippies and the media. What was the impact of the media on the counterculture?

4. What role did drugs play in the counterculture? Why were they as important as they were? What effects did drugs have on the nature and development of the counterculture? How, if at all, was the use of drugs among the hippies different from the ways drugs are used today?

5. Most of those involved in the counterculture (and the other protest movements of the 1960s, too, for that matter) were relatively young, in their teens and twenties. Why do you suppose this was the case? What effects did the relative youth of its participants have on the counterculture?

BIBLIOGRAPHY

William O'Neill's *Coming Apart: An Informal History of America in the 1960s* (1971) is a very good place to start looking for understanding of that tumultuous decade. Morris Dickstein concentrates on its cultural history, including its popular culture, in *Gates of Eden: American Culture in the Sixties* (1977). Young people played a large role in giving the sixties a distinctive character. Landon Y. Jones, *Great Expectations: America and the Baby Boom Generation* (1980) details the impact they had. W. J. Rorabaugh, *Berkeley at War, the 1960s* (1989) tells the story of the Free Speech Movement. On the Beats, Bruce Cook, *The Beat Generation* (1971) gives a general treatment, but the writings of the Beats themselves are indispensable to understanding them. Jack Kerouac's novel *On the Road* (1957) is an autobiographical account of Beat life in which most of the prominent Beats appear as thinly disguised characters. Allen Ginsberg's poem *Howl* (1956) shows what the Beats found repellent about American civilization. On the counterculture itself, Theodore Roszak, *The Making of a Counter Culture* (1970), is a generally sympathetic scholarly account; Charles Perry, *The Haight-Ashbury* (1984), is a readable treatment of hippie life in its chief capital; and Tom Wolfe, *The Electric Kool-Aid Acid Test* (1969), paints a very vivid picture of one particular group, the Merry Pranksters, which gathered around the novelist Ken Kesey, and provides many insights into the nature of and the reasons behind the counterculture.

Many of the American troops in Vietnam were not happy about what they were doing there and made no attempt to hide their feelings.

20

LOREN BARITZ

Vietnam — and After

There is still widespread disagreement about the Vietnam War: what we might have done to achieve better results, what lessons we should learn from it, and what its long-term effects are likely to be. What seems abundantly clear is that the war traumatized the nation. We got into it without knowing precisely how, fought it for goals that were never clearly defined, argued among ourselves about it while it was in progress, and got out of it telling ourselves that we had won — knowing we really had not. As a consequence, when the war ended, most Americans seemed to want to forget the whole unpleasant experience as quickly as possible. And that included, although no one said so in so many words, forgetting the men who had actually fought — the "grunts" as they called themselves.

However much the nation as a whole may have suffered from the war, certainly the ordinary soldiers suffered most. They risked, and 58,000 of them lost, their lives. Even more were wounded, and some of the wounds meant a lifetime in a wheelchair. Thousands suffered serious psychological wounds, and psychologists began to speak about a new kind of mental disturbance that some vets exhibited: Post-Traumatic Stress Disorder. In addition, we are still investigating the long-term damage some veterans may have received as a consequence of exposure to Agent Orange, a chemical compound used in defoliants in Vietnam. And all of the veterans suffered from what seemed to them, and others, to be the indifference, ingratitude, or outright hostility of the general public. When they were remembered at all, it was frequently as social misfits who had been completely unhinged by their war experience and now constituted a threat both to themselves and to society. It certainly did not help their readjustment to civilian life.

Recently, however, evidence has appeared that things may be changing. The dedication of the Vietnam Veterans' Memorial in Washington, D.C., in November, 1982, slightly less than ten years after the withdrawal of American troops from Vietnam, was the occasion for a genuine, if somewhat belated, outpouring of support. "Coming Home," a popular film, dealt sympathetically with the problems of the veterans. Even many former antiwar activists publicly expressed their realization that the troops in Vietnam were among the war's greatest victims.

In the following selection, Loren Baritz describes the conditions that the ordinary "grunts" faced in Vietnam, how their experiences were rendered especially painful by the peculiar conditions surrounding the Vietnam War, and the problems they had to contend with once they returned to the United States. It is still too early to determine what the long-term effects of the Vietnam War may be, both on America and on the veterans, but we may be sure that they will be profound.

The drafted grunts who humped the boonies came from all over America. Street-smart ghetto kids, raised in the basketball wars, became battlefield buddies with dewy farm kids from Minnesota, patriotic, wide-eyed innocents who choked up a little when they sang "God Bless America." Hispanics, passionately ambivalent about Anglo culture, fought and drank alongside their closest war pals, the steelworkers, gas station attendants, and high school dropouts who never had a steady job. The entire nation went or was sent to war, except for the rich, the middle class, the vast majority of college students, and individuals who objected to war, or who objected to that war.

After LBJ decided to send combat troops, and after the draftees were moved into combat, the Vietnam War was fought by working-class teenagers. The draft was designed to produce that result. The average age of the American soldiers in Vietnam was just over nineteen. In World War II, the average age of the GIs who were in for the duration was about twenty-six. It was said that the military brass understood that Vietnam was a teenage war, that the kids were unruly, and that there was not much that could be done about actually imposing discipline on these postadolescents, strong boymen who were juicers and drank too much, or were smokers on skag or pot, and were too irreverent to obey by instinct or tradition. . . .

As in Korea, the army, navy, and air force rotated individuals out in twelve months, and, until 1969, the marines in thirteen. They were almost always replaced one by one by new meat, or twinks, or cherries, or FNGs (fuckin' new guys) who were twelve or thirteen months younger than they were on their DEROS (date eligible for return from overseas).

When these kids enlisted or were drafted, at least after the American invasion in 1965, they knew that the so-called crazies were protesting the war, running away to Canada, hiding in colleges. Many of these soldiers had not thought much about the war, disliked the long hair of the hippies, and were offended by TV pictures of braless young women. Like most of the rest of the nation, they rejected the war protesters without thinking much about the war. Some men enlisted to get a better deal than the draft offered, or to get a new start in their young lives, or because a close friend signed up, or to escape the family, or to see the world, or to combat Communism. Some did not know why they enlisted. For some, it was an article of faith that the President knows best, and when he calls, you go.

George Ryan enlisted after he graduated from high school in Virginia. He had only read girlie magazines, sports magazines, and racing-car magazines. "If Vietnam was such a mistake," he asked, "how come the leaders of our country, the wisest men we have . . . how come they sent us in? None of the doves I ever met had any answers to *that*."

A student of the army collected more of these reactions:

> I know one thing. Before I went in, my brother could kick my ass, but now he can't. . . . He ain't nothing no more.

> The only thing I used to read was sports. . . . So I didn't have any feelings one way or the other. I figured it was more or less right, because why would I be going if it wasn't right?

> I knew almost nothing about it. The war, I thought was like they taught us in high school, you know, you're fighting communism, you know, it was just the good guys against the bad guys.

A majority of the kids who were drafted thought of the draft as an event like measles, a graduation, the weather, something that happened to people. Young men got drafted as their fathers had in earlier wars. Sometimes brothers were already in. You had to do it because it had been done before, and probably would always be done, and you had to take your turn. It was usually more intimate and domestic than patriotism, although occasionally that too played a role. More often it was an unwillingness to let someone down, to hold up your end, and to do the right thing, as that was defined in the family and in the small circle of good friends. There is not much soul-searching required to honor so simple an obligation. Someday you have to earn a living, probably marry and have children, pay taxes, but first you get drafted.

There were more enlistees than conscripts, but the draftees were especially vulnerable. They were more likely than the enlistees to find themselves in the shooting war. The draftees made up 16 percent of the battle deaths in 1965; in 1969, they were 62 percent. Draftees represented 88 percent of infantry riflemen in 1970. The army apparently considered the draftees disposable — throw-away, nonreturnable men.

The Vietnam draft was an ideal model of discriminatory social policy. It kept the middle class from creating political pressure on the war administrations. So the draft was biased by level of income. The higher the income, the less chance of being drafted, importantly but not exclusively because of educational deferments. Poor young Americans, white as well as black and Hispanic, were twice as likely to be drafted and twice as likely to be assigned to combat as wealthier draft-aged youth. The draft rejected many blacks, but it was more likely to accept poor men than richer men with the same qualifications, or the same lack of qualifications. As a result, poor black Americans were swept into the fighting war in disproportionate numbers. Economic class, even more than race, except that people of color were more likely to be poor, was what determined who fought and who died. . . .

Education in this country is a badge of class. One study of Chicago neighborhoods found that kid from areas with low educational levels were four times as likely to be killed in Vietnam than those from more schooled neighborhoods. It was as if the war had been designed to digest America's victims, the men President Eisenhower called the "sitting ducks" for the draft. Class and education also shaped the experience of the young men who enlisted. Two staff officials of President Ford's clemency board showed that a college graduate who enlisted had about a 40 percent chance of being sent to Vietnam, while a high school graduate's chance was about 65 percent, and that of a high-school dropout was 70 percent. . . .

Survival was the strategy of the American GI, not different from soldiers in earlier wars. But, for the great majority of Vietnam grunts, there was no external purpose to the war — not defending national goals, not resisting an evil enemy, not defending motherhood and apple pie. As a result, there was no animating justification for combat or for risk. The best way to survive was to keep away from danger. This absence of external purpose made it difficult for some to develop a sense of shared enterprise with other GIs outside their own unit. Because the replacements were inserted into the war as individuals, not as members of a unit, these

GIs were in fact movable parts, separate cogs in the war's machinery. Such separateness induced a sense of fragility, probably more intense and widespread than in other wars. The separate arrivals and departures, along with the absence of shared purpose, emphasized the individuality of the grunt, even while they formed the life-saving bonds of brotherhood in their small squads or platoons. It is touching and painful to hear how often the veterans felt alone.

The grunt was the instrument of General Westmoreland's "strategy" of attrition. For entirely different reasons, the grunts' war plan became identical with the general's. There was no real estate that had to be taken and held, there were no objectives to be seized. The plan was to kill the enemy, wherever and whoever he or she was. Because the body count was the scorecard, killing supposedly proved progress. This made war sense from the grunt's perspective because it was simply based on the desire to live, not necessarily callousness or moral collapse, but war through the eyes of the walking conscripts.

That is why the "other war," the ideological war, meant nothing to most of them. It did not seem, at least in the short run, the time that really mattered, to protect their lives. So they mocked the entire effort to "win the hearts and minds" of the Vietnamese by referring to it as WHAM and embroidering it even further: "Grab 'em by the balls and their heart and minds will follow."

Luis Martinez, a Puerto Rican marine, decided he would learn something about the Vietnamese and treat them with respect because "if the Viet Cong is going to do something, he remembers you and you have a better chance of surviving." In this sense, winning hearts and minds might help him to return home in one piece. It was like money in the bank that could produce interest in the future. But in the war's twists, respect and friendship for the Vietnamese could backfire. For example, a sergeant became friends with a Vietnamese woman and her daughter. They were both killed by the NLF because they had associated with him. He decided that from then on he would leave them all alone. For most, the "other war" would take too long, was out of focus, and was therefore not a good shield for the vital or fatal 365 days they would be targets.

The grunts hated bloody fighting to take a fire base, perhaps losing buddies in the process, and then being ordered to abandon the base to fight or patrol somewhere else, and then having to endure another fire fight to recapture the first base. Some bases were retaken three or four or more times. one GI put it this way: "We don't take any land. We don't give it back. We just mutilate bodies. What the fuck are we doing here?" It seemed senseless to risk everything over and over for the same piece of turf. There was no achievement to show for the mutilations and deaths. Except the numbers. They had to train themselves to think of achievement by the numbers. Many, probably most, could not do it. They could not think of what they were doing only in terms of the body count. Even in war, death was supposed to be for something, not a thing in itself.

They recognized that the body counts were being hyped to satisfy, or shut up, corrupt officers who kept demanding higher numbers. The men could deliver any number any REMF, "rear echelon mother fucker," wanted. Of course that made the killing even more pointless. If the brass would accept fake numbers, and if the whole point of the war was numbers, why risk your life to get real kills? The war could have been fought over the radio, with a squad or company reporting whatever number was wanted. That is what sometimes happened. The grunts knew it was fraudulent and they became contemptuous of their officers. For example, after one fire fight, Herb Mock, a rifle-squad leader, said: "General Westmoreland flew in. All the news outfits and everything. It was the most hilarious thing. As these son of a bitches came out there, the GIs started lying. The newsmen would walk up to just anybody and say, 'What did you do?' 'I singlehandedly killed three hundred thousand with my bowie knife.'" Lieutenant Robert Santos spoke for many when he said, "You come home with the high body count, high kill ratios. What a fucking way to live your life." . . .

Some grunts were stunned by the open hostility of some South Vietnamese, the people they had come to defend. When they had to run up chicken wire to block the objects, including grenades, that some South Vietnamese threw at them, there was no way they could avoid wondering what they were doing there. It was maddening to discover that the food or medicine they gave to friendlies would be handed to the guerrillas after dark. It was a shock to march past an aged mama-san selling Coca-Cola on the road and notice her head nodding as each grunt passed; she was counting them. What for? What could you make of the fact that the friendlies who washed your clothes or cut your hair were found dead in your ambush of the NLF during the night? And what about the mama-san who brought you things right into your fire base and hung around a little while so she could memorize where your bunkers were so the guerrillas that night could zero in with their mortars? What about the local whores telling you where you were going next, before your own officers had announced it? This war was not like others. You could never identify the enemy. That created constant danger, not merely at the front — there was no front — but everywhere, and not merely during a battle, but anytime. Any Vietnamese could be the one. A T-shirt worn by the grunts displayed the message: KILL THEM ALL! LET GOD SORT THEM OUT!

Having no larger external purpose, there were also often no external constraints. The line beyond which an action would become a transgression was a matter of individual conscience, a Protestant formula. This was as true for the officers as for the troops. The moral formlessness of the bureaucratic war necessarily emphasized technique and means, not goals or purpose. Bureaucracies typically do not do as well at expressing where they wish to go as they do at expressing how to get there. "If you're lost, drive faster; that way you'll get it over with sooner." This left the teenage warriors to their own moral devices, such as they were. Group pressures formed one code of conduct; a watchful officer might sometimes form another. Unlike earlier wars, the Vietnam rule was the moral independence of the foot soldier and his officers.

The rapid turnover of their immediate officers — usually every six months, often less — led to the conviction that the grunts knew better than anyone else, especially better than the six-month wonders, the shake-'n'-bake lieutenants, how to stay alive. These teenage warriors were therefore thrown back into themselves in a way unusual in war. They had to take care of each other if they were to make it. After a while they could wear earrings, write almost anything they liked on their helmets and flak jackets, shoot up on drugs, get drunk, and more often than not get away with it, especially when they were in the field, which everyone called Indian country. They enjoyed getting away with it, and hated "chicken shit officers" who worried about shined shoes; but getting away with it also taught some of them that the brass did not care, and that they were on their own both as a unit and as individuals. . . .

The grunts understood that they were endangered by the guerrillas, the regular army of North Vietnam, and their own temporary, rotating officers, in no particular order of threat. They knew that the home front did not support what they were doing. If no one cared about them, they could not care about the rules or established authority. Occasionally, around 1970, grunts would scribble UUUU on their helmets: the unwilling, led by the unqualified, doing the unnecessary, for the ungrateful. Other helmets proclaimed POWER TO THE PEOPLE, KILL A NON-COM FOR CHRIST, or NO GOOK EVER CALLED ME NIGGER. It was finally as if all they could believe and remember were pain and death. One young man from the Bronx, for example, was cited for heroism:

> They gave me a Bronze Star and they put me up for a Silver Star. But I said you can shove it up your ass. I threw all of the others away. The only thing I kept was the Purple Heart, because I still think I was wounded.

A wound is the most intimate souvenir.

It cannot be surprising that the grunts found ways to resist corrupt officers in a war that could not be understood. Desertions, excluding AWOLs, in the army alone rose from 27,000 in 1967 to 76,634 in 1970, a rate increase of 21 per thousand to 52 per thousand. The marines were even worse with 60 desertions per thousand. According to the Department of Defense, the rate of desertion in Vietnam was higher than in

either Korea or World War II, and the rate increased as the intensity of
the fighting declined and absurdity increased. As President Nixon began
withdrawing troops, many of the grunts remaining on the ground lost
even more conviction about why they should stay and fight. The desertion rate from 1965 to 1971 increased by 468 percent.

Fragging, defined as an attempt to murder by using a grenade, reached
astonishing levels in Vietman. It was usually a result of the fear and hatred felt by the workers toward their bosses. For example, marine Private
Reginald Smith testified in a court-martial that his lieutenant was so slow
in setting up a listening post that by the time he sent three marines out,
the NLF was waiting and killed two of them. The troops were discussing
the incompetence of this lieutenant just before he was killed by a frag-
mentation grenade. It was frequently said that combat squads raised a
bounty to be awarded to anyone who would "waste" a particularly hated
officer. The Criminal Investigating Department of the Third Marine Am-
phibious Force said there were more than 20 fraggings in eight months
of 1969, according to the transcript of a court-martial. The Defense Department admits to 788 fraggings from 1969 to 1972. This figure does
not include attempts to kill officers with weapons other than "explosive
devises," such as rifles. Richard Gabriel calculated that "as many as 1,016
officers and NCOs may have been killed by their own men," but he points
out that this figure includes only men who were caught and tried. There
is no precedent in American military history for violence against officers
on anything like this scale.

Another response of the "workers" was to "strike," that is, to disobey a
combat order, that is, to commit mutiny. The Pentagon kept no records of
mutinies, but Senator Stennis of the Senate Armed Forces Committee
said that there were 68 mutinies in 1968 alone.

Yet another form of resistance by grunts was the pandemic use of hard
drugs. In the spring of 1970, 96 percent pure white heroin appeared in
Saigon; by the end of the year it was everywhere, sold in drugstores and
by Vietnamese children on street corners. This junk was so pure and
cheap that the troops smoked or sniffed, with only a minority reduced to
injection. Its use was not remarkable in Vietnam because smoking was
usually a group activity, accepted by almost everyone, and common for
clean-cut midwestern boys as well as for city kids. Nothing in all of military history even nearly resembled this plague. About 28 percent of the
troops used hard drugs, with more than half a million becoming addicted. This was approximately the same percentage of high school students in the States who were using drugs, but they were using softer
stuff. In Vietnam, grass was smoked so much it is a wonder that a south-
erly wind did not levitate Hanoi's politburo.

The failure of senior officers is partly reflected in the fact that they
knew what was going on and did nothing to stop it, and did not protest.

Richard Gabriel and Paul Savage concluded that "the higher officer corps was so committed to expedience that the organized distribution of drugs was accepted as necessary to the support of the South Vietnamese government, which often purveyed the drugs that destroyed the Army that defended it." The CIA and the diplomatic corps in Vietnam prevented other governmental agencies from getting at the truth, while individuals with the CIA, if not the Agency itself, helped to fly drugs into Vietnam from Laos.

Despite an occasional attempt to do something — usually punishing the troops — about the blizzard of skag, neither the U.S. government nor the military ever accomplished anything worth mentioning. The much advertised urine testing (to be conducted in what the GIs called The Pee House of the August Moon) was ineffective because the tests were unreliable, the troops who were not hooked could flush their bodies before the tests, and no one was prepared actually to help the soldiers who were addicts. One scholar concluded that "in not rooting out the sources of heroin in Laos and Thailand, the government had simply made a calculation that the continued political and military support of those groups profiting from the drug traffic was worth the risk of hooking U.S. soldiers." General Westmoreland, as usual, blamed everyone but his own senior officers: "The misuse of drugs . . . had spread from civilian society into the Army and became a major problem. . . . A serious dilution over the war years in the caliber of junior leaders contributed to this. . . . "

Racial conflict was suffused throughout the war, from 1968 until the end. Every service, including the previously calm air force, had race riots of varying magnitude. As some of America's cities burned, or rather as the ghettos in some cities burned, the domestic rage found its counterpart in the military. Fraggings were sometimes racially motivated. One battalion commander said, "What defeats me is the attitude among the blacks that 'black is right' no matter who is right or wrong." One black soldier said, "I'd just as soon shoot whitey as the VC." In one incident that is what actually happened: Two white majors were shot trying to get some black GIs to turn down their tape recorder.

White officers were sometimes offended by expressions of black solidarity, including ritual handshakes, the closed fist, swearing, black jargon, and, especially, blacks arguing that they were being forced to fight "a white man's war." (The North Vietnamese and the NLF often tried to exploit that theme through various forms of psychological warfare.) The weight of the military justice system was lowered on black GIs far out of proportion to their numbers. The congressional Black Caucus did a study in 1971 that showed that half of all soldiers in jail were black. The next year, the Defense Department learned that blacks were treated more harshly than whites for identical offenses. The occasional race riots were invariably triggered by the increasing militance of American blacks in general, the peculiarly obtuse social attitudes of many older military officers, the frustrated hopes of the Great Society, the sense of an unfair draft, and an unfair shake in Vietnam.

Trying to make it to DEROS, that miraculous day one year after they had stepped foot onto Vietnam's red soil, the foot soldiers did what they could to survive the guerrillas or North Vietnam's army or their officers. For most of them, the point of the war was the clock ticking toward the shortening of their time, and, finally, the last day, the wake up call, and home. Others, in a daze of battle, tried to put home out of mind. Many others, probably most, became increasingly cautious as their "sentence" wore down, and the ingenuity expended by the short-timers in avoiding combat, occasionally simply by threatening a hard-driving officer, was inspirational, almost enough to revive the American dream of self-reliant citizens. No one wanted to die with only hours, or days, or weeks, or months, left to serve. No one wanted to die in any case, but it was even more unbearable to think about with only a short time to go. The idea of home, the idea of making it, became increasingly real as the war became increasingly surreal.

They left Vietnam as they came, suddenly, by air, usually alone, and engulfed by impressions and anxieties that were too cascading to sort out. "We went to Vietnam as frightened, lonely young men. We came back, alone again, as immigrants to a new world," William Jayne, a marine rifleman, wrote. "For the culture we had known dissolved while we were in Vietnam, and the culture of combat we lived in so intensely for a year made us aliens when we returned." They were aliens for a great variety of reasons, some because they had grown up while their former buddies who had not gone to Nam seemed as if they had been frozen in time; they were still late adolescents whose lives revolved around six-packs, cars, and chasing girls. Others because they were stunned by the nation's refusal to welcome them home as returning warriors. Others because of the continuing pain of flesh and memory. Yet others because the war had destroyed their earlier faith in "the World," in American institutions . . . .

. . . Thomas K. Bowen thought when he got home that the entire war had been a "mistake," and said, "I mean I have no — absolutely no — respect for my government." Still others could not get jobs, and some resented the women and the nonvets who were working. Joe Boxx finally decided that "bein' a Vietnam vet didn't mean shit." Skip Sommer had re-upped to survive, but finally could not endure the army and deserted; he eventually gave himself up and was later dishonorably discharged. He was a haunted, enraged man even twelve years later. But, he said, "I don't remember anything I really am ashamed of, besides the fact that I survived." Alberto Martinez was losing his mind and in despair killed himself. Edmund Lee became an expatriate in Australia. Frank Goins, back home in south Georgia, remembered the democracy of races in the foxholes, but discovered, "When we got home, they still didn't want us to go to Mr. Charlie's cafe by the front door. . . . " David Brown was not even given the usual four or five days off the line at the end of his tour; one day he was in combat and the next night the freedom bird landed him in San Francisco. He drank too much for a year or two. Charles Rupert said: "I risked my life for my country, and now nobody gives a shit. If I have a son, I won't let him go. I'll send him to Canada first." J. C. Wilson: "We were fools."

On the other side, Lieutenant Robert Kennish, a commander of Charlie Company: "I did pretty well. No problems at all, really, that are going to afflict me for the rest of my life. I think I gained more from my experience in the military and in Vietnam than I lost." What mattered to him most was that he grew in his own self-esteem as a man. An anonymous veteran grunt said that he simply grew up in the war. David Rioux, a devout Catholic who was blinded in the war, understood and approved the war as a struggle against Communism, one that he was proud to have fought. Michel, David's brother, fought in David's company and feels that David's faith prevented him from committing suicide. David said about himself and his brother: "We both knew why we were in Vietnam, and the men around us didn't, for the most part, or saw it only confusedly, but we saw why we were there and we were proud to be there, defending a people who were being oppressed by Marxist Communism. We were doing something that was commendable, in the eyes of God, our country and our family."

The stereotypes at loose in the nation when the troops began returning were largely shaped by the reports of My Lai as well as television reports of the heroin nightmare. Many Americans assumed the returning vets were junkies. Some vets were persistently asked how it felt to kill a human being. All the vets were subjected to an embarrassed national attitude about the war, and about their role in it. It got worse when the North overran Saigon, and television showed the pictures of the scramble to evacuate the remaining Americans. Then the question became even more insistent: What did we accomplish by fighting? For the veterans who had believed in the cause, Saigon's surrender was a terrible blow. Both the Rioux brothers, along with other traditionalists, believed that "giving up" was the mistake, not intervening in the first place. For the others, those who had decided the war was not worth fighting while they were fighting it, the fall of Saigon confirmed their opinion. In any case, the veterans faced an unprecedented social and political fact when they finally made it back: The nation did not know what to do with them, and would just as soon forget, or try to forget, the entire sorry "episode." None of the vets could forget.

They were not only not welcomed home, some of them were abused for their uniforms, their decorations, and their short hair. There was a revealing false rumor that antiwar critics were shooting vets as they climbed out of their planes. It is a mass delusion, of course, but thousands of vets claim that they were spat upon when they first arrived home. . . .

Most of the veterans returned home reasonably whole, as whole as returning veterans from earlier wars. The majority were not dopers, did not beat their wives or children, did not commit suicide, did not haunt the unemployment offices, and did not boozily sink into despair and futility. Yet, some prisons are still populated with black vets; the VA hospitals still do their bureaucratic thing too often and fail to help. Some vets, more than a decade later, have not yet recovered, and some never will. The government has done less for these veterans than for those of other wars. The vets had to build their own monument. Now they are struggling to force the reluctant government to face up to the hideous question of the degree to which our war technology had poisoned our own men with Agent Orange. More than a decade after most of them had come home, the government in 1984 began to make small progress in admitting its responsibility in this issue.

Nonetheless, the majority returned home and found there was life after Vietnam. Tim O'Brien, a former grunt and prize-winning novelist, thought the adjustment was too good. He feared that the vets' experience was becoming too mellow, too nostalgic. He had hoped their recoil from war would have been more of a brake on national saber-rattling. He wished they could have retained the passion and convictions that sustained them while they were boonie-rats. He wrote, "We've all adjusted. The whole country. And I fear that we are back where we started. I wish we were more troubled."

When some grunts in Vietnam heard the news that the war was over, everyone began shouting. "They were ecstatic." One of them finally asked, "Who won?" They were told the NLF won. "They didn't care."

STUDY GUIDE

1. How did the conditions the grunts faced in Vietnam differ from what American soldiers had to deal with in previous wars? How did the reception they got at home differ?

2. Baritz's account implies that many in the Army itself, particularly those on the higher levels of command, were not as concerned as they should have been with the welfare of the troops under their command. Do you think this implication is correct? If so, how do you explain it?

3. It has been suggested that the problems within the armed forces in Vietnam, drug use, racial tension, lack of respect for authority, and so forth, were simply reflections of these problems within American society. Oth-

ers argue, on the contrary, that these problems originated in the conditions in Vietnam itself. Which explanation makes more sense to you? Why?

4. How are the conditions Baritz describes, both in Vietnam and the United States, related to the psychological problems some Vietnam veterans have experienced?

5. For some time, many Americans, especially those in the antiwar movement, saw Vietnam veterans as racist, drug-crazed murderers. How do you explain this? And how do you explain the change in attitudes toward veterans that seems to have taken place in recent years?

BIBLIOGRAPHY

The literature on the war in Vietnam is enormous and still growing. The following items represent only a tiny sample of it. One might begin by reading *The Pentagon Papers* published in many editions, including one in paperback, edited by Neil Sheehan et al. of *The New York Times* (1971). Volumes dealing with the war within the larger context of social and political developments within the United States include: Alexander Kendrick, *The Wound Within: America in the Vietnam Years, 1945–1974* (1974); David Halberstam, *The Best and the Brightest* (1972), a study of the false pride that Halberstam feels led to this and other national tragedies; William J. Lederer, *Our Own Worst Enemy* (1968), a look at the self-deception and ignorance of the American people regarding the war in Vietnam; and Frances FitzGerald, *Fire in the Lake* (1972), an account of how cultural differences divided Americans from Vietnamese and led to mutual misunderstandings that contributed to the debacle. Stanley Karnow, *Vietnam, a History* (1983) is a general history of the war derived from a television series made for the Public Broadcasting System. Accounts of the war by those who experienced it first-hand are numerous. They include Alan Dawson, *55 Days: The Fall of South Vietnam* (1977) and Michael Herr, *Dispatches* (1977) — both by journalists — and Ron Kovic, *Born on the Fourth of July* (1976) and Tim O'Brien, *If I Die in a Combat Zone, Box Me Up and Ship Me Home* (1973) — which tell the story of the war from the soldiers' points of view. Al Santoli has collected soldiers' reminiscences in *Everything We Had: An Oral History of the Vietnam War by Thirty-Three American Soldiers Who Fought It* (1981). The commanding general in Vietnam, William C. Westmoreland, gives his view of the war in *A Soldier Reports* (1976). Robert Jay Lifton, *Home from the War* (1973), discusses the impact of the war on the veterans. Harrison E. Salisbury, ed., *Vietnam Reconsidered: Lessons from a War* (1984), contains the conflicting opinions of several people on the meaning and impact of the war and the lessons that we should draw from it.

Single-parent families and changing ideas about proper gender roles are two features of modern American life.

21

JOHN D'EMILIO AND ESTELLE B. FREEDMAN

Sexuality in
Contemporary America

The sixties saw many challenges to prevailing notions concerning the way things should be and pleas — or demands — for change, often backed up by behavior that deliberately broke established rules. One of these challenges was the "sexual revolution." It was connected to the open flouting of conventions of all sorts that one found in the counterculture and to the search for alternative ways of living that members of the counterculture were conducting. It was connected to the questioning of gender roles and gender stereotypes that was a prominent feature of the women's liberation movement. It was also connected, although less obviously, to the political radicalism of the decade; to some, engaging in sexual activities that violated existing taboos was a revolutionary act, a way of affirming one's opposition to society and its norms. Perhaps most of all it was connected to the movement of the bulk of the baby-boom generation into late adolescence and early adulthood, the period during which sexual interest is certainly at its peak and sexual activity probably at its highest level. The impact on the nation of the vast numbers of the baby boomers may well have been enough, all by itself, to have resulted in a challenge to prevailing sexual attitudes and modes of behavior.

Like the other movements for social and cultural change in the sixties and early seventies, the sexual revolution caused concern, consternation, fear, outrage, or some combination of those feelings, in those who did not share the desire for change. Despite this, again like the other movements for social change, the sexual revolution does seem to have left its mark. The furor, the tumult of that earlier period has died down, but some changes have endured, among them changes in the whole system of ideas and values regarding such matters as marriage, the family, gender, and sexual conduct. The following selection by John D'Emilio and Estelle B. Freedman details a few of those changes (and some of the things that have not changed). We may be too close to the recent past to assess the scope or significance of what has occurred with complete accuracy, but we can be sure that a great many people in the United States today have ideas that are different from those of their parents or grandparents and behave in ways that previous generations would find shocking.

As entrepreneurs were weaving sexuality into the fabric of public life, Americans were simultaneously experiencing dramatic demographic changes. Between the 1960s and the 1980s, the life cycle of many Americans became considerably more complex and unpredictable. The timing of marriage and childbearing, control over fertility, the instability of the traditional nuclear family, and innovations in living arrangements all encouraged a reorganization of sexual standards.

The unusual demographic patterns of the baby-boom era reversed themselves with startling rapidity in the 1970s. Between 1960 and 1980, the marriage rate declined by a quarter. By 1985, the median age of marriage for men had risen to 25.5 years, while for women it jumped to 23.2. Along with later marriage came an overall decline in fertility. Beginning in the mid-1970s, the fertility of American women hovered at the replacement level, far below the peaks reached in the late 1950s. The accessibility of legal abortions, the accelerating trend toward sterilization, and the availability of reliable contraceptives put absolute control of fertility within reach for the married. Especially within the middle class, childlessness emerged as a serious option to consider. As one couple noted, "we are the only people we know who have a child, or at least the only people we know well. . . . Some [of our friends] are married, a few might as well be, others aren't totally opposed to the idea — and they have all either ruled out families entirely or postponed them until the very distant future." By the end of the 1970s more than a quarter of married women in their late twenties remained childless.

Not only were Americans marrying later and having fewer children, but families were much less likely to remain intact. Aided by the liberal-

Excerpt from *Intimate Matters* by John D'Emilio and Estelle B. Freedman. Copyright © 1988 by the authors. Reprinted by permission of Harper & Row, Publishers, Inc. References have been omitted.

ization of state laws, the divorce rate began a steep climb in the mid-1960s. Between 1960 and 1980, the number of divorced men and women rose by almost two hundred percent; the divorce rate itself jumped ninety percent. For blacks, the impact of divorce was even more widely felt. In 1980, over a quarter of black men and women between the ages of twenty-five and fifty-four were divorced, in comparison to less than ten percent of whites. Many of the divorced remarried eventually, yet second marriages had even less chance of surviving. Although the rush to divorce had slowed somewhat by 1980, marriages of the late seventies had only a one-in-two chance of surviving.

All of these shifts affected the size and structure of American households, which tended to grow smaller and become more diversified in composition. During the 1970s, over half of the new households created were nonfamily ones. The traditional two-parent family with children accounted for only three-fifths of all living arrangements by 1980. Even that figure tended to overstate its predominance, since many of those families would experience dissolution, and most Americans could expect to spend a portion of their childhood and adult years in "nontraditional" situations.

One widely touted demographic innovation of the 1970s was the rise of cohabitation among men and women. Hardly noted by 1960 census-takers, it became a highly visible phenomenon in the 1970s, tripling in frequency. Although cohabiting couples constituted only three percent of American households, the chances of an individual participating in such an arrangement were much higher. One study found that almost one in five American men had lived for at least six months with a woman other than their spouse. The phenomenon was more common among blacks than whites, and a majority of the men had been previously married. Surveying the changing nature of American lifestyles, the sociologists Philip Blumstein and Pepper Schwartz confidently predicted that cohabitation "will probably become more visible and more common."

In the midst of this reorganization of household and family structure, one element of change elicited special comment — the rise of the working mother. White married women had been steadily entering the labor force since World War II, and for black wives work outside the home had always been a common experience. But the rapid movement of mothers into paid employment surprised most observers. By the early 1980s a majority of mothers, including those with children of preschool age, were working for wages. Some of this change owed its origin to feminism, which validated the choices of mothers who sought employment. Some of it was due to financial necessity. As inflation escalated in the 1970s, and the changing structure of economic and social life raised the consumption needs of many families, the pressure for mothers to work mounted. Among married couples in 1980, wives with family incomes between twenty-five thousand and fifty thousand dollars were most likely to be employed. The absence of female employment consigned many families to subsistence living. Moreover, as the divorce rate mounted and more women found themselves heading households, many mothers had no choice but to work.

Whatever the motives, the high proportion of women in the work force promised upheavals in the realm of personal life and heterosexual relations. Working women were both cause and effect of many demographic changes — the rising age of marriage, later childbearing, the decline in fertility, the spread of single-person households, and cohabitation. Unhappy marriages, in which spouses felt compelled out of duty or desperation to remain together, might more readily dissolve. As Paul Glick, a Census Bureau demographer who had studied marriage and divorce for a generation, commented, "women who enter the marketplace gain greater confidence, expand their social circles independent of their husbands' friends, taste independence and are less easy to satisfy, and more likely to divorce." Or, as one Indiana wife put it, "women don't have to put up with [men's] crap — they can support themselves." Working women brought greater confidence and more power to their relationships with men. Although conflict might ensue as couples readjusted their expectations, surveys indicated nevertheless that younger males in particular preferred the more egalitarian results that came with the modification of traditional sex roles.

These demographic shifts hit the black community with special force. Although black-white differentials in family structure actually narrowed in the 1970s, nontraditional living arrangements still appeared with much greater frequency among blacks. Overall incidence rates of divorce, female-headed households, and out-of-wedlock births remained higher. By 1980 almost half of black households were female-headed, a majority of black infants were born to unmarried women, and only a minority of black children were being raised in two-parent households. Approximately half of black adults were not married and living with their spouse. In assessing these statistics, one sociologist was moved to comment that "all is not well between black men and women." In contrast to the mid-1960s, when the Moynihan report provoked so much controversy within the civil rights movement, black leaders in the eighties felt freer to air their own concerns. By the early 1980s, many were rating the issue of family life equally with jobs and education as a critical concern of the community. Eleanor Holmes Norton, who served in the Carter administration, called it "the most serious long-term crisis in the black community."

When combined with the invasion of sexuality into so much of the public realm, these new demographic patterns among Americans presaged a major shift in sexual behavior and attitudes. The later age of marriage increased the likelihood that women as well as men would enter the institution sexually experienced. The rise in divorce meant that more and more Americans would be searching for new sexual partners as mature adults. Children and adolescents would know that their parents were having sex outside of marriage; the openness with which heterosexual cohabitation, lesbianism, and male homosexuality were discussed provided visible alternatives to marriage. Postponed childbearing and low fertility made obvious the distinction between sex for procreation and for pleasure. Women who worked and had more sexual experience were better placed to negotiate the terms of a sexual relationship with a partner. The new explicitness of so much popular literature about the erotic almost guaranteed that many Americans would have their sexual repertoires greatly enhanced. Perhaps most significantly, the growing complexity of the American life cycle substantially weakened the hegemony of marriage as the privileged site for sexual expression. As one longitudinal study of families in Detroit concluded, "the decision to marry or remain single is now considered a real and legitimate choice between acceptable alternatives, marking a distinct shift in attitude from that held by Americans in the past."

Survey data from a variety of sources confirm a striking shift in sexual values toward approval of nonmarital sexuality. As late as the 1950s, for instance, polls suggested that fewer than a quarter of Americans endorsed premarital sex for men and women. By the 1970s, these figures had been reversed. Especially among the young, substantial majorities registered their approval. Although males, blacks, the college-educated and higher-income families were more likely to accept premarital sexuality, the differences between groups were disappearing. Only older Americans and religiously devout whites tended to maintain a stance of moral disapproval. The generation gap was especially pronounced over some of the more radical departures from past orthodoxy. One study found that three-quarters of Americans over sixty-five opposed the practice of cohabitation, while the figures were reversed for the under-thirty population. Similarly, when confronted with the contemporary openness of the gay community, younger Americans proved more than three times as likely as their seniors to display tolerance for homosexuality. In their study of American couples, Blumstein and Schwartz found that among married couples, cohabiting heterosexuals, gay men, and lesbians, majorities of everyone except wives expressed approval for sexual relationships devoid of love.

One important ideological source for the revamping of sexual beliefs was feminism. Particularly among younger heterosexuals, traditional notions of male and female differences weakened in the 1970s. Most looked forward to marriages in which roles blurred. Many younger males abandoned the allegiance to a double standard of behavior for their female peers. For both men and women, expectations about sexuality and intimacy changed. As Sophie Freud Loewenstein, a Boston social worker, explained it,

> Women who have taken it for granted that their sexual satisfaction was unimportant are now reading about women having multiple orgasms. Many men realize that they've been ripped off by being programmed to deny their expressive aspects. It becomes a possibility to throw out some of the old sex roles and change drastically. That change can be very frightening, but the atmosphere makes it more permissible.

As its critique of sex-role conditioning spread throughout the culture, feminism altered the attitudes of Americans about the proper behavior of men and women.

Demographic change, shifts in attitudes, and the eroticism that so much of the public realm displayed contributed to a major alteration in the sexual life of many Americans. Unmarried youth as well as conjugal pairs, urban male homosexuals as well as heterosexual couples, experienced important modifications in their patterns of sexual behavior. Among other things, sexual experience was beginning at a younger age, acts once considered deviant were more widely incorporated into heterosexual relations, and the gap between the sex lives of men and women was narrowing.

The behavior of the young and the unmarried dramatically illustrates the extent of change. From the mid-1960s onward the incidence of premarital intercourse among white females zoomed upward, narrowing substantially the disparity in experience between them and their male peers. Survey after survey of white college students in every part of the country confirmed this shift. By 1980 large majorities of female students were engaging in coitus, often in relationships that held no expectation of marriage. Among black women, too, there was evidence of change, though primarily in the age at which coitus began. Between 1971 and 1976, fifteen- and sixteen-year-olds were half again as likely to have engaged in intercourse. In the early 1970s, a much broader survey that included men and women of varying educational levels also documented the rise in premarital coitus among women. By then young women were as likely to have sex as were the men in Kinsey's study a generation earlier. Morton Hunt, the author, also confirmed a greater variety in practices. Where Kinsey had found few heterosexuals who had tried fellatio or cunnilingus, by the 1970s it was a commonplace experience among those in their twenties. The frequency of intercourse for young men and women was also substantially higher, while masturbation, especially among women, was starting earlier and had become more widespread.

Evidence of other sorts substantiates these survey findings. On college campuses, health services routinely distributed contraceptive information and devices to students. For those who began having intercourse earlier, or who did not attend college, Planned Parenthood clinics offered an alternative source of assistance. In Muncie, Indiana, for example, a third of teenage girls used the services of Planned Parenthood in 1979. The rise in births to unmarried teenagers, as well as the large number who sought abortions, also suggest that a growing proportion of the young were sexually active.

These changes in patterns of behavior took place in a social context different from that which had shaped the behavior of youth between the 1920s and the 1960s. For one, formal dating evinced a sharp decline. Teenage youth socialized casually in groups without pairing off; friendships between males and females were more common. As one high school boy described it, in drawing a contrast between himself and his father:

> Once he told me that he wasn't brought up to think about women the way guys like me do, and it was vice versa back then. 'We were scared of each other; we didn't really have *friends* of the opposite sex' is the way he said it to me. Now that's changed! I can talk with girls I'm not dating — I mean, be real friendly with them. There's one girl at school who's the person I feel easiest with there. We're pals, but I've never wanted to make out with her!

This ease of interaction had implications for the progress of sexual experience. When the young did pair off, it tended to signal an already serious relationship. They were less likely to move gradually through the stages of kissing, necking, and petting before deciding to have intercourse. In fact, one observer of the young concluded that petting, so important in the sexual initiation of midcentury adolescents, "seems destined to take its place as a historical curiosity."

The demographic patterns of the late 1960s and 1970s, as well as the less measurable effects of feminist ideology, also contributed to the shape of change. As women became sexually active earlier in life, as the age of marriage rose, and their participation in the labor force promised greater autonomy, more of them could approach sexual experience with different expectations. One twenty-eight-year-old blue-collar female, cohabiting with a male partner, firmly expressed her right to an erotic life. "I may have had an unusual upbringing, but it never occurred to me that a man wouldn't let me be sexy," she said. "I have the same needs and moods as a man, and I am not going to let some chauvinist pig stifle them." Another single woman, also in her twenties, justified nonmonogamy on the basis of her strong sexual desires. "I have a roving eye and sometimes I give in to it. . . . I consider myself a very sexual person and I need an adventure from time to time. And I think [my cohabiting partner] does too. But that's all it is — fun and a little bit of an ego thrill." Their comments suggest that at least some women had moved a long distance from the 1950s, when sexual intercourse had to be justified as a sign of an abiding romantic attachment. . . .

One reason, undoubtedly, for the shifts in heterosexual relationships was the availability of birth control. The dramatic move in the 1960s toward effective contraception continued into the 1970s. By mid-decade three out of four married couples relied on the pill, the IUD, or sterilization. Then, too, the legalization of first-trimester abortions provided a measure of last resort for wives whose contraceptive efforts failed. Though it is difficult to know how great an increase in the incidence of abortion took place in the seventies, the fact that it was medically safe and legal at least removed the dangers that formerly attached to it. The near universality of birth control practices had virtually eliminated the constraints that fears about pregnancy had imposed on the sex life of married women. It also highlighted the degree to which the erotic had been divorced from procreation.

The separation of sex from reproduction also emerged from another quarter. Not only could couples safely have sex without the expectation of conception, but technological innovations were making it possible to have babies without sex. Science was upsetting age-old certainties about the natural connection between sex and procreation. "Remember when there was only one way to make a baby?" an advertisement for a 1979 CBS special report asked. "That was yesterday. Today, nature's role is being challenged by science. Conception without sex. Egg fertilization outside the womb. 'Surrogate' mothers who can bear other couples' children. Frozen embryos stored in 'supermarkets' for future implantation." Among other things, scientific change was allowing lesbian couples to have children, without choosing marriage, through the cooperation of male sperm donors. Public policy added another dimension to technological change, as welfare agencies allowed single women and single men to adopt children, thus emphasizing the distinction between biological and social parenting. Though the new technology would raise some vexing problems of its own, as the controversy over Baby M revealed, people were nonetheless making choices that seemed to confirm that making love and making babies were not the same.

The new visibility that gay life achieved in the 1970s also emphasized the weakened link between procreation and the erotic. Although it is difficult to measure change in this area with any degree of precision, certainly the social life of gay men and lesbians had altered considerably. The many organizations that existed throughout the country allowed greater ease in making friends and acquaintances, and in embarking upon relationships. Less police harassment made it safer for bars to open and stay in operation. Regional music festivals brought thousands of lesbians together for several days of companionship; annual rituals such as the gay pride marches each June became celebrations of community cohesiveness even as they made a political statement. Church attendance, political club membership, and professional caucuses all contributed to a broadening of an identity in which the erotic played a prominent role. But the historic invisibility of gay male and lesbian life makes it impossible to compare the erotic dimension of gay experience from one generation to another. Even in the 1970s there were few studies that moved beyond the impressionism of journalistic observations.

A study that did, the work of Philip Blumstein and Pepper Schwartz, is interesting in part because of the comparison it allows between men and women, and between heterosexuals and homosexuals. The researchers found that a good sexual adjustment was as important to a successful relationship among gay male and lesbian respondents as among heterosexuals, and that the higher the frequency of sex the greater the sense of satisfaction. But lesbians seemed content to have sex less often, and after two years in a relationship, the lesbian couples tended to see a significant decline in the frequency of sex. Young lesbians were more likely to engage in oral sex than were older women, and among all the couples, gay men placed the greatest stock in variety in sexual technique. Lesbians proved very similar to heterosexual men and women in the extent of non-monogamy — twenty-eight percent of lesbians, twenty-five percent of husbands, and twenty-one percent of wives — whereas for gay men, non-monogamy was a way of life. Furthermore, among couples that did not practice monogamy male homosexuals tended to have sex with a far larger number of partners. One percent of the lesbians, seven percent of the husbands, but more than two-fifths of the gay men, had sex with more than twenty partners while living with a mate.

Even in the era that witnessed an expansion of erotic opportunities, the experience of some urban gay men appeared to stand outside the norm. When Kinsey undertook his study in the 1940s he found that although male homosexuals on average had sex less frequently than heterosexual men, some of them had far more partners in the course of a lifetime. In the 1970s, as the urban gay subculture became larger and more accessible, the chances for sexual encounters multiplied. Heterosexuals may have had their singles bars where they could meet a partner for an evening of sex, but in large cities, gay bathhouses, bars with back rooms, and stores showing pornographic films allowed gay male patrons to have sex with a series of men in rapid succession. For many, sexual promiscuity became part of the fabric of gay life, an essential element holding the community together. Yet the fact that such sex businesses could operate in the 1970s relatively free of police harassment and that the media could spotlight them in discussions of gay life says as much about heterosexual norms as about those of gay men. In the larger metropolitan areas, male homosexuals were no longer serving as symbols of sexual deviance; their eroticism no longer divided the good from the bad. Heterosexuals sustained a vigorous singles nightlife, and advertised in magazines for partners; suburban couples engaged in mate-swapping; sex clubs were featuring male strippers, with women in the role of voyeur. By the end of the decade, some "straight" men and women were even patronizing a heterosexual equivalent of the gay bathhouse, as the success of places like Plato's Retreat in New York demonstrated. The experience of the urban gay subculture stood as one point along a widened spectrum of sexual possibilities that modern America now offered.

Although it would be foolhardy to deny the depth and breadth of the changes that had occurred by the end of the 1970s, one must also acknowledge the continuities with the past. Blumstein and Schwartz, for instance, found that "there *are* new men and women, among both heterosexual and homosexual couples, who are dealing with sexual responsibilities in new ways and trying to modify the traditions that their maleness and femaleness bring to their relationships." But they were fewer in number than the pair of sociologists expected to find, and the persistence of tradition was particularly hard for some heterosexual women whose partners proved "less 'liberated' than she — or he — thought he was." Marriages were happier and more intimate than a generation earlier, but partly because so many unhappy ones ended in divorce. In a culture that was coming to identify frequent, pleasurable, varied, and ecstatically satisfying sex as a preeminent sign of personal happiness, the high rate of marital dissolution could easily mean that large numbers of Americans were failing to reach these standards. The differences in the patterns of behavior of gay men and lesbians also pointed to the continuing salience of gender in shaping sexual meanings. Moreover, while lesbians and male homosexuals had carved out some space for themselves in society, the frequency of physical assaults upon visibly gay men and women suggested that their form of nonprocreative sex still provoked outrage. Feminism, too, may have opened new realms of sexual expressiveness for women, but the extent of rape and other forms of male sexual violence still made sex an arena of danger for them. The much-vaunted "sexual revolution," though real in many ways, was hardly complete.

Two issues, in particular, were emerging by the end of the 1970s to suggest the contradictory emotions that still enshrouded sex. Since the advent of penicillin in the 1940s, the threat of venereal disease had, to a significant degree, faded as an inhibitor of nonmonogamous sexual expression. But, in the midst of Americans' recently acquired sexual "freedom," the media spotlighted a new venereal scourge. Herpes, which *Time* magazine labeled "today's scarlet letter" and the "new leprosy," was reaching epidemic proportions among young urban heterosexuals. Though the condition posed far less physical danger than syphilis, it provoked guilt and panic as well as a pulling back from erotic encounters for some. A medical professional reported that "we hear it over and over: I won't have sex again." Among victims, the disease elicited feelings of self-pollution —

"you never think you're clean enough," said one. The *Soho Weekly News*, a New York paper popular among young professionals in the city, was moved to proclaim "current sexual practice" as "the real epidemic." For many, the spread of herpes came to symbolize the inherent flaws in an ethic of sexual permissiveness. Pleasure brought retribution; disease became a marker of weak moral character.

Another "epidemic," that of teenage pregnancy, also highlighted ambivalence about the erotic. Although most Americans tended to look benignly upon sex between unmarried adults, the spread of sexual experience among teenagers troubled them. To a large extent, adolescents were pursuing the erotic without the approval or the guidance of their elders. Despite the visibility of sex in the culture, the acquisition of knowledge by the young remained sporadic and haphazard, largely "a private, individually motivated and covert affair," in the opinion of one sex researcher. Some parents felt it was simply wrong, despite their own experience. As one middle-class mother in Muncie had phrased it, "just because it was right for me doesn't make it okay for my kids." A survey of high school youth in the early 1980s found that almost half had learned nothing about sex from their parents. Nor were schools rushing to fill the gap. By the late 1970s only half a dozen states mandated sex education; in most places, curriculum remained up to the local school districts, which generally displayed the same caution or disregard that occurred in the home. In one New York City suburb, a high school principal refused to let the editor of the school paper print an article about birth control methods. A California school district provided sex instruction in conjunction with drivers education, indicating how marginal it was to the academic curriculum. "In order to avoid controversy," according to the authors of *Sex and the American Teenager*, "schools embrace boredom."

The result of this abdication of responsibility by schools and parents was that the young were often left to drift into sexual activity without guidance and with little knowledge. Teenagers whose parents were unwilling to talk with them about sex, or who did not receive sex education in school, were more prone to engage in intercourse. Yet they were also likely to be ignorant of how conception occurred or how to prevent it. Even when schools did provide instruction, they often acted too late. One North Carolina fifteen-year-old learned about condoms in a junior high school class, after he had been having intercourse for two years. "And then I realized, man, I've been taking a lot of chances. Thirteen, fourteen, fifteen . . . Lord's been good to me," he said. Others were not so lucky, as the incidence of teenage pregnancy revealed. In 1976, among the premaritally sexually active, twenty-seven percent of white girls and forty-five percent of blacks had become pregnant by the age of eighteen. Ironically, in view of the laissez-faire stance that adults seemed to take, the young were looking for advice. As Robert Coles and Geoffrey Stokes concluded on the basis of their work with high school students,

> it seems clear from our interviews that some kids who are planning to enter sexual relationships *want* to be told to wait. But those who can't talk to their parents hear either nothing or a ritualized naysaying that has no bearing on their *immediate* situation — and those who can may find their parents unwilling to take the responsibility for saying anything more than "Be careful."

Meanwhile, for those who had made their choice to have sex, accurate information about reproduction, conception, and birth control might at least save them from the tragedy of unwanted pregnancies.

That so many teenage girls were becoming pregnant in an age when reliable contraception was available says much about the contradictions within the sexually permissive culture of the 1960s and 1970s. From everywhere sex beckoned, inciting desire, yet rarely did one find reasoned presentations of the most elementary consequences and responsibilities that sexual activity entailed. Youth had more autonomy from adult supervision than ever before, allowing them to explore the erotic at a time of profound physiological changes, but adults seemed to respond by implicitly drawing a boundary at sexual activity during adolescence. Perhaps one could not stop the young from experimenting, but neither would society endorse their behavior. The result was a social problem of tragic dimensions, one that placed in bold relief the ambivalence of American society toward sex. And, the fact that young girls were left to pay a higher price for sexual activity served as a poignant commentary on the persistence of gender in the structuring of sexuality in the postliberal era.

The reshaping of sexuality in the 1960s and 1970s was of major proportions. The marketing of sex, new demographic patterns, and the movements of women and homosexuals for equality all fostered a substantial revision in attitudes and behavior. In some ways, the process of sexualization represented pushing the logic of sexual liberalism to its extreme: once sex had been identified as a critical aspect of happiness, how could one justify containing it in marriage? Even before the 1960s, the behavior of youth and the commercial manipulation of the erotic had suggested the vulnerability of the liberal consensus. By the end of the 1970s, it was obvious that the consensus had dissolved. As Americans married later, postponed childbearing, and divorced more often, and as feminists and gay liberationists questioned heterosexual orthodoxy, nonmarital sexuality became commonplace and open. And, all of this took place in a social environment in which erotic imagery was ubiquitous.

The collapse of sexual liberalism did not, however, lead to a new, stable consensus. By the end of the 1970s, conservative proponents of an older sexual order had appeared. Their efforts to stem the tide of change and, indeed, to restore sexuality to a reproductive marital context would demonstrate the continuing power of sex to generate controversy.

STUDY GUIDE

1. The authors describe many things that have changed in Americans' sexual behavior and their attitudes toward it, but they also point out that some things have not changed. What are the most important changes? Are there any that the authors have not mentioned? What are the most important things that have remained more or less the same? Again, are there any you can think of that the authors have not mentioned?

2. Why have sexual behavior and attitudes about it changed as they have?

3. This selection describes conditions before people became fully aware of the extent and seriousness of AIDS. How has AIDS affected sexual behavior? What is its long-term impact likely to be, assuming no cure is found?

4. What is, what has been, what will be the impact on the subjects discussed in this selection of the recent upsurge of religious fundamentalism?

5. How, if at all, is the current controversy about abortion related to the changes the authors describe?

6. Does it seem likely to you that changes in traditional ideas about sex, marriage, and so forth are going to continue? Are they going to speed up? Slow down? Will there be a movement back toward traditional ideas? What makes you think so?

BIBLIOGRAPHY

Sidney Ditzion, *Marriage, Morals and Sex in America: A History of Ideas* (1953), Carl N. Degler, *At Odds: Women and Family in America from the Revolution to the Present* (1980), and Christopher Lasch, *Haven in a Heartless World: The Family Besieged* (1977) provide historical background on some of the subjects covered in this selection. Beth L. Bailey, *From Front Porch to Back Seat: Courtship in Twentieth-Century America* (1988), is informative about changing sexual behavior and attitudes. Alfred Kinsey, et al., *Sexual Behavior in the Human Male* (1948) and *Sexual Behavior in the Human Female* (1953) are massive surveys of the subject, limited because of their nearly exclusive focus on middle-class men and women, but valuable nevertheless. Randy Shilts, *And the Band Played On: Politics, People, and the AIDS Epidemic* (1987), is not only the best single treatment of the whole issue of AIDS, it also has a great deal to say, directly and indirectly, about current attitudes concerning sex.

To the student:

We, as publishers, realize that one way to improve education is to improve textbooks. We also realize that you, the student, have a large role in the success or failure of textbooks. Although teachers choose books to be used in the classroom, if the students do not buy and use books, those books are failures.

Usually only teachers are asked about the quality of texts; their opinions alone are considered as revisions are written or as new books are planned. Now, HarperCollins would like to ask you about this book: how you liked or disliked it; why it was successful or dull; if it taught you anything. Would you fill in this form and return it to us at: HarperCollins Publishers Inc., 10 East 53rd Street, New York, NY 10022. It is your chance to affect directly the publication of future textbooks.

Book title: _____ School: _____

Course title: _____ Course enrollment:_____

Instructor's name: _____

1. Did you like the book? _____

2. Was it too easy? _____

   Did you read all the selections?_____

   Which did you like most?_____

   Which did you like least?_____

3. Did you like the cover?_____

   Did you like the size?_____

   Did you like the illustrations?_____

   Did you like the type size?_____

(over)

4. Were the study questions and bibliographies useful? _____

   How should they be changed? _____

   _____

5. Are the introductions useful? _____

   How might they be improved? _____

   _____

6. Do you feel the instructor should continue to assign this book next year? _____

7. Will you keep this book for your library? _____

8. Please add any comments or suggestions on how we might improve this book, either in content or in format.

   _____

   _____

   _____

   _____

   _____

9. May we quote you, either in promotion for this book or in future publishing ventures? ____ yes ____ no

_____   _____

Date   Signature